Pedestrian Accidents

Pedestrian Accidents

Edited by

ANTONY J. CHAPMAN
FRANCES M. WADE
and
HUGH C. FOOT

Department of Applied Psychology
University of Wales Institute of Science and Technology
Cardiff U.K.

1807 1982

175 YEARS OF PUBLISHING

JOHN WILEY & SONS

Chichester · New York · Brisbane · Toronto · Singapore

British Library Cataloguing in Publication Data:

Pedestrian accidents.
  1. Traffic accidents
  2. Pedestrians
  1. Chapman, A. J.
  II. Wade, F. M.   II. Foot, H. C.
  363.1'251   HE5614

ISBN 0 471 10057 9

Photosetting by Thomson Press (India) Ltd., New Delhi
and printed at Page Brothers (Norwich) Ltd.

List of Contributors

S. J. ASHTON   Department of Transportation and Environmental Planning, University of Birmingham, P.O. Box 363, Birmingham B15 2TT, UK

I. D. BROWN   Medical Research Council, Applied Psychology Unit, 15 Chaucer Road, Cambridge CB2 2EF, UK

A. J. CHAPMAN   Department of Applied Psychology, University of Wales Institute of Science and Technology, Llwyn-y-Grant, Cardiff CF3 7UX, UK

D. E. FIRTH   Behavioural Research Consultants, West Wind Manor, Maidenhead Road, Windsor, Berkshire, UK

H. C. FOOT   Department of Applied Psychology, University of Wales Institute of Science and Technology, Llwyn-y-Grant, Cardiff CF3 7UX, UK

G. B. GRAYSON   Road User Characteristics Division, Transport and Road Research Laboratory, Old Wokingham Road, Crowthorne RG11 6AU, Berkshire, UK

M. J. GUNN   Department of Law, University of Nottingham, University Park, Nottingham NG7 2RD, UK

C. I. HOWARTH   Department of Psychology, University of Nottingham, University Park, Nottingham NG7 2RD, UK

N. P. SHEEHY   School of Communication Studies, National Institute for Higher Education, Dublin 9, Ireland.

A. SINGH   School of Education, University of Reading, London Road, Reading RG1 5AQ, UK

F. M. WADE   Department of Applied Psychology, University of Wales Institute of Science and Technology, Llwyn-y-Grant, Cardiff CF3 7UX, UK

Contents

PART II: THE DRIVER AND THE VEHICLE

PART III: THE ENVIRONMENT

PART IV: PEDESTRIAN ACCIDENTS: AN
ANNOTATED BIBLIOGRAPHY

Preface

Despite a steady growth in research on road safety in recent years this volume is the first to review psychological aspects of road accidents involving pedestrians. This is all the more remarkable in view of the world-wide interest in pedestrian behaviour and the extensive commitment of research funds. The book offers a broad coverage and is intended for a wide international readership—from members of police forces, road safety officers, teachers and parents to research workers in the social sciences, engineering, planning and medicine. Although most of the contributors come from psychological backgrounds, the book will interest those concerned with multi-disciplinary approaches to understanding and alleviating social problems. After an introduction to empirical methods and theoretical orientations, three sections focus respectively on issues relating to pedestrian behaviour and education, on driver behaviour and vehicle design, and on physical, social and legal aspects of the environment. There then follows an annotated bibliography of some 700 reports relating to pedestrian accidents.

The introduction (Chapter 1) maps out the nature and extent of pedestrian accidents and in so doing paves the way for the eight specialized chapters which follow. In *Part I* Diane Firth (Chapter 2) outlines the state of knowledge concerning pedestrian behaviour and she assesses current information needs and future priorities. Attempts at pedestrian education are reviewed by Amarjit Singh (Chapter 3) who discusses existing programmes designed to modify behaviour, attitudes and knowledge. The problems of evaluating safety programmes are then analysed by Graham Grayson and Ian Howarth (Chapter 4) whose arguments lead to a new set of recommendations for the conduct of evaluative programmes.

In *Part II* Ivan Brown (Chapter 5) identifies aspects of driver behaviour which are particularly associated with risk to pedestrians, and he argues for more research concentration on the behavioural interface between driver and pedestrian. The work on engineering influences reviewed by Steve Ashton (Chapter 6) is not designed to reduce the number of accidents *per se* but to reduce the severity of their consequences by attending to the development of vehicle safety features.

Part III is opened by Noel Sheehy (Chapter 7) who examines the social dimensions to pedestrian accidents and recommends an interactional approach to broaden our perspective on road safety issues, The editors (Chapter 8) critically appraise the various countermeasures introduced into the environment in efforts to minimize road accidents and their effects. The final chapter is by Ian Howarth and Michael Gunn (Chapter 9) who argue for changes in the law. In particular, they maintain that child pedestrian accidents are most likely to be reduced by a change in the legal definition of responsibility on residential roads.

Our view is that there is still a dearth of research on road safety, and our hope is that this volume will encourage fresh research as well as promoting the greater application of existing knowledge. There is a need for research in all of the areas featuring here as chapter topics, and there is a continuing need for an *integrated* approach towards improving road safety: that is, an approach which is not discipline-bound and which does not focus on a few isolated factors to the exclusion of others contributing to accidents.

UWIST, Cardiff   Tony Chapman
March 1981   Frances Wade
                                                       Hugh Foot

Pedestrian Accidents
Edited by A. J. Chapman, F. M. Wade and H. C. Foot
© 1982, John Wiley & Sons Ltd.

Chapter 1

Pedestrian Accidents: General Issues and Approaches

H. C. Foot, A. J. Chapman and F. M. Wade

A primary goal of scientific research is to discern patterns of interaction between events in order to achieve control over those events. Thus a fundamental assumption in the application of the scientific method is that naturally-occurring phenomena are non-random. Why, then, study *accidents* and, in particular, *pedestrian accidents*? According to the Oxford English Dictionary, the two principal ingredients of an accident are that it is an *unexpected event* and that its occurrence is attributed to chance. By definition, therefore, it would seem that accidents are unsuitable for scientific study because they are apparently subject to random fluctuation. Yet the very existence of this review volume indicates that there is a substantial community of researchers which does not believe that the study of accidents is a futile endeavour. Attempts to discern patterns and relationships in the events surrounding pedestrian accidents represent an implicit denial both that accidents are by nature haphazard and that some means of control over them is not possible.

Deaths and injuries inflicted apparently randomly by external agents have not always been classified as accidents. According to a *Bill of Mortality* for 1665 (cf. Howe, 1972) accidental deaths were recorded simply by reference to the nature of the event causing death: for example, 'fall from a scaffold', being 'frighted'. These and other categories of affliction include events which would certainly be classified as accidents in more modern taxonomies.

Let us pursue the notion that accidents are not purely capricious events. With reference to both the unexpected and random nature of an accident, it is beyond dispute that to neither the victim nor the immediate family is the actual occurrence or specified timing of the accident predictable. However, at a statistical level over an entire population, it is possible to predict very closely the annual pedestrian accident rates, and to forecast the groups of pedestrians which are most likely to be afflicted as well as the conditions under which accidents are most likely to occur. At the same time neither the randomness nor the unexpectedness of accidents is uniquely associated with accidents, or more specifically, with injuries produced by external, mechanical agents. Injuries which result from biological agents such as harmful bacteria or viruses carry all the hallmarks of accidents; that is, they are equally unexpected and apparently random. Yet these injuries are classified as *diseases* and their aetiology may be regarded, as in accident causation, as the result of freak combinations of events which expose the victim to the harmful agent.

The consequence of this traditional differentiation between mechanical and biological injury is more than purely lexical: the distinction actively fosters the view that an accident is a fortuitous event which cannot be forestalled, to the extent that society has learned to accept and tolerate accidents as 'facts of life'. In contrast society is committed to an active policy designed to eradicate all diseases, given sufficient resources. We would argue that the term 'accident' is highly value-laden: it implies a sense of inevitability (bad luck, act of God), which is counterproductive to any attempt by society to prevent the occurrence of accidents.

Despite these misgivings about the connotations of the term 'accident', there is no other word in common English usage which can readily substitute for it. We would certainly shrink from suggesting an alternative, because of convention and the formal history of gathering accident statistics. In this chapter we present an analysis of pedestrian accidents and an overview of research theory and methodology that has been developed to investigate patterns of pedestrian accidents. In the first part of the chapter recent pedestrian accident statistics draw attention to some of the key contributing variables on which research has primarily focused. In the second part, a review of the major research strategies used in the study of pedestrian accidents is provided. In the third part, theoretical perspectives towards accident aetiology and prevention are outlined. The chapter concludes with the results of a survey of views about road safety expressed by police officers, road safety officers, teachers and parents.

PEDESTRIAN ACCIDENT STATISTICS

In Britain, road accident statistics are compiled by the Government Statistical Service from reports submitted by the police to the Department of Transport and to the Scottish Development Department. This annual exercise is a survey based upon the entire population of road accidents reported to the police.

The main classification of road accidents is by road user (age and sex) and severity of injury. A *road accident* is defined as involving one or more vehicles on the public highway (including footpaths) and resulting in at least one human casualty; that is, a personal injury accident. A *casualty* is defined as a person killed or injured as the result of an accident. The road user category of *pedestrian* includes 'children riding toy cycles on the footpath, persons pushing bicycles or other vehicles or operating pedestrian controlled vehicles, those leading or herding animals, occupants of perambulators or invalid chairs, people who alight from vehicles and are subsequently injured and persons pushing or pulling a vehicle' (Department of Transport, 1980, p. vi). Adults are classified as those aged 15 years or over, and the adult category is subdivided into those aged 15, 16, 17 to 19, 20 to 29, 30 to 39, 40 to 49, 50 to 59, 60 to 69 and those over 70 years. *Children* are those under 15 years of age, and they are subdivided into three age ranges: 0 to 4, 5 to 9 and 10 to 14 years. *Severity of injury* comprises three classes: a *fatal injury* is one from which death occurs as a result of a road accident within 30 days of the accident; a *serious injury* is one for which a person is detained in hospital as an in-patient, or sustains one or more of the following injuries irrespective of hospital detention—fractures, concussion, internal injuries, crushings, severe cuts, lacerations and severe general shock requiring medical treatment; and a *slight injury* is of a minor character such as a sprain, bruise, or a cut or laceration not judged to be severe.

Table 1.1 Long-term casualty statistics: 1938 to 1952 and 1969 to 1978

Year	Popula-tion (millions)	Licensed road vehicles (millions)	Road casualties		Pedestrian casualties			
					child		adult	
			all (1,000s)	fatal (1,000s)	all (1,000s)	fatal (actual)	all (1,000s)	fatal (actual)
1938	46.2	3.1	233	6.6	NR	870	NR	2,176
39	46.5	3.1	NR	8.2	NR	850	NR	3,647
40	46.9	2.3	NR	8.6	NR	972	NR	3,752
41	46.9	2.4	NR	9.1	NR	1,231	NR	3,550
42	47.1	1.8	148	6.9	18.9	1,112	34.0	2,538
43	47.4	1.4	123	5.7	16.8	993	27.4	2,065
44	47.7	1.5	131	6.4	18.1	1,134	27.6	2,180
45	47.8	2.4	138	5.2	21.6	1,053	26.7	1,549
46	47.9	3.0	163	5.0	23.5	828	32.3	1,661
47	48.2	3.3	166	4.8	23.5	767	32.4	1,613
48	48.7	3.5	153	4.5	22.4	834	30.6	1,543
49	49.0	3.8	177	4.7	23.7	746	29.3	1,569
1950	49.2	4.1	201	5.0	23.6	674	31.8	1,579
51	48.9	4.3	216	5.2	25.3	707	34.5	1,692
52	49.1	4.6	208	4.7	23.9	611	30.5	1,452
1969	53.7	14.3	353	7.3	38.5	635	44.9	2,319
70	53.9	14.5	363	7.4	39.7	616	45.6	2,309
71	54.1	15.1	352	7.6	37.9	651	43.2	2,286
72	54.2	15.7	360	7.7	39.3	662	44.6	2,418
73	54.4	16.6	354	7.4	36.4	600	43.6	2,206
74	54.4	16.8	325	6.8	33.0	505	41.4	2,135
75	54.4	17.1	325	6.3	30.4	427	38.8	1,917
76	54.3	17.4	340	6.5	28.9	405	37.8	1,928
77	54.3	—	348	6.6	30.3	440	38.9	1,869
78	54.3	17.3	350	6.8	28.9	463	39.5	1,957

Compiled from the Department of Transport (1980), RoSPA (undated) and RoSPA (1980). NR, not recorded.

Road accident statistics: long term trends

Road accident and casualty figures in Great Britain have been recorded since 1909 and 1929 respectively (RoSPA, 1980). Table 1.1 presents data for the 15-year span from 1938 to 1952, and the 10-year period from 1969 to 1978. These selected data serve to illustrate the main patterns of road usage and road casualties. While the national *population* increased steadily from 46.2 million (1938) to 54.3 million (1978) and the number of *licensed road motor vehicles* rose from 3.1 million (1938) to 17.3 million (1978), with a slight decrease during the period 1940 to 1945, road casualties steadily increased from something like 150,000 per annum in the 1940s to about 350,000 per annum in the 1970s. The casualties resulting in death have been subject to more fluctuation, although an increase is still apparent. The peak period was during the early 1970s when fatal accidents were running at approximately 7,500 per annum falling to approximately 6,600 per annum during the late 1970s.

Pedestrian casualties of all severities for children and adults show a similar pattern: overall, the trend is an increase in the total number of pedestrian casualties, peaking in the early 1970s. Examination of *fatal* pedestrian accidents, however, reveals a different picture for adults and children: because there are more fatal adult casualties, their general trend matches the trend just outlined for all ages combined; but child pedestrian fatalities have consistently decreased, and the rate has halved since 1945. This decrease is in contrast to the growth of licensed motor traffic (a six-fold increase since 1945) and the increase in the total number of road casualties (doubling since 1945).

Table 1.2 1978 pedestrian deaths in comparison to other deaths

Totals	Sex	Age					
		0–4	5–9	10–14	15–19	20–59	60 and over
Pedestrian	Males	69	138	78	69	386	584
deaths	Females	44	78	56	55	206	657
Other road	Males	15	25	90	901	1,969	423
deaths	Females	15	14	26	162	510	247
Deaths from	Males	5,818	691	697	1,987	57,786	260,958
all causes	Females	4,399	454	482	784	34,984	281,984
Percentages							
Pedestrian deaths	Males	1.2	20.0	11.2	3.4	0.6	0.2
as percentage	Females	1.0	17.2	11.6	7.0	0.6	0.2
of all deaths							
Other road deaths	Males	0.3	3.6	12.9	45.3	3.4	0.16
as percentage	Females	0.3	3.1	5.4	20.7	1.5	0.08
of all deaths							

Compiled from the Department of Transport (1980).

Pedestrian deaths in relation to other deaths

To place the prevalence of fatal pedestrian accidents into perspective, deaths due to pedestrian accidents should first be seen in relation to other types of road deaths and in relation to the total death toll. Table 1.2 presents the 1978 data, and these trends are very similar to those obtained over the preceding years.

For boys and girls aged less than 5 years, pedestrian and other road accidents are a minor cause of death, comprising only 1.1 per cent of the total number of deaths to this age group. However, the picture changes dramatically for children aged 5 to 9 years. In this age range 20 per cent of all deaths to boys and 17 per cent of all deaths to girls are the result of pedestrian accidents. For older children and adults, pedestrian accidents claim proportionally fewer lives, whereas for those aged 10 to 19 years other road accidents account for a large proportion of the total death toll. For example, 45 per cent of deaths to men aged 15 to 19 years are a result of road vehicle accidents.

Pedestrian casualties during the late 1970s

Pedestrian casualties are typically reported in one of two ways: a *numerical count* of casualties classified by age and sex of the pedestrian and by injury severity; or a *casualty rate* presented in terms of casualties per 100,000 population. The former statistic outlines the extent of pedestrian accident involvement in absolute terms; the latter allows comparisons between age and sex groups in relation to the age and sex composition of the national population.

Table 1.3 presents a summary of the absolute number of child and adult casualties for 1975 to 1978 classified by injury severity. In approximate terms there were just under 70,000 pedestrian casualties per year, 30,000 of which were sustained by children. For each year, 400 to 500 children and nearly 2,000

Table 1.3 1975–1978 pedestrian casualties

	Fatal	Serious	Slight	Total
Children				
1975	427	7,754	22,241	30,422
1976	405	7,461	21,072	28,938
1977	440	7,863	22,071	30,374
1978	463	7,462	20,984	28,909
Adults				
1975	1,917	10,714	26,253	38,884
1976	1,928	10,707	25,195	37,830
1977	1,869	11,183	25,925	38,977
1978	1,957	11,352	26,289	39,598

Compiled from the Department of Transport for 1977, 1978, 1979, 1980.

Pedestrian Accidents

adults were killed; 7,500 children and 11,000 adults were seriously injured and 21,000 children and 26,000 adults incurred minor injuries. A more detailed analysis of the absolute number of casualties incurred by the different age and sex groups is shown in Table 1.4. These figures (excluding those for slight injuries), transformed to casualty rates per 100,000 population, are presented in Table 1.5.

There are several notable features to these more detailed breakdowns, the most striking of which is the sex difference in the number of casualties (of all

Table 1.4 1975–1978 pedestrian casualties by sex, age and injury severity

	Age					
	0–4	5–9	10–14	15–19	20–59	60 and over
Fatal						
Male						
1975	76	149	68	61	410	625
1976	84	120	54	73	425	552
1977	72	156	78	74	394	529
1978	69	138	78	69	386	584
Female						
1975	36	63	35	29	168	625
1976	48	61	38	43	179	656
1977	39	61	34	44	169	659
1978	44	78	56	55	206	657
Serious						
Male						
1975	923	2,539	1,417	845	2,991	1,830
1976	813	2,488	1,410	903	2,895	1,786
1977	796	2,577	1,593	957	3,978	1,836
1978	657	2,368	1,608	1,057	3,261	1,835
Female						
1975	548	1,226	1,101	598	1,779	2,671
1976	466	1,182	1,101	682	1,796	2,645
1977	402	1,293	1,202	739	1,908	2,722
1978	346	1,222	1,260	715	1,864	2,620
Slight						
Male						
1975	2,420	6,799	4,128	2,321	8,240	3,204
1976	2,064	6,311	4,134	2,392	7,646	3,173
1977	1,918	6,785	4.386	2,544	7,760	3,145
1978	1,759	6,217	4,423	2,761	7,957	3,147
Female						
1975	1,506	3,947	3,441	2,078	6,190	4,220
1976	1,356	3,713	3,492	2,082	5,803	4,099
1977	1,180	3,994	3,808	2,325	5,922	4,201
1978	1,121	3,605	3,859	2,438	5,880	4,106

Compiled from Department of Transport (1980).

Table 1.5 1975–1978 pedestrian casualty rates per 100,000 population

	0–4	5–9	10–14	Age 15–19	20–59	60 and over
All severities of injury —						
Male						
1975	174	425	245	153	85	135
1976	160	404	243	157	80	131
1977	159	440	262	163	81	131
1978	147	413	266	176	83	132
Female						
1975	113	248	210	144	58	119
1976	107	237	211	148	57	116
1977	98	261	230	163	58	118
1978	95	246	238	161	58	116
Fatal						
Male						
1975	3.9	6.7	3.0	2.5	3.1	15.7
1976	4.5	5.4	2.3	3.3	3.2	13.8
1977	4.1	7.2	3.4	2.9	2.9	13.1
1978	4.1	6.5	3.4	2.8	2.9	14.3
Female						
1975	1.9	3.0	1.6	1.4	1.3	9.9
1976	2.7	2.9	1.7	2.4	1.4	10.3
1977	2.4	3.0	1.5	2.3	1.3	10.2
1978	2.8	3.9	2.6	2.7	1.5	10.2
Serious						
Male						
1975	47	114	62	41	22	44
1976	44	113	61	43	21	43
1977	45	119	69	42	22	44
1978	39	112	70	48	24	44
Female						
1975	30	58	51	33	13	42
1976	27	57	50	37	13	42
1977	24	63	55	38	14	43
1978	22	61	58	36	14	41

Compiled from Department of Transport (1980).

severities) sustained by children under the age of 10 years: approximately twice as many boys as girls incur pedestrian accidents. The pedestrian casualty rates per 100,000 population indicate that this difference is not a function of the population structure. Another notable aspect of the statistics is the change in the casualty rate with age. Children aged 5 to 9 years are particularly vulnerable: this age group is associated with a rate 5 times that of adults aged 20 to 59 years. The casualty rate is also high for adults aged 60 years and over. Within this age range women actually incur more pedestrian accidents of any severity than men, but the casualty rate per 100,000 population shows that this is a function of the preponderance of women in this age group: in fact the men have the higher casualty rate.

A more detailed examination of the relative vulnerability of those aged 60 years and over shows that they are particularly liable to incur fatal injuries, with fatal injury twice as high as those of young children and 5 times those of younger adults. Thus, although children sustain the highest rate of accidents of all age groups, they are more likely to survive their injuries, whilst the older adults tend to die as a result of injuries sustained in relatively fewer accidents.

A final comment on these statistics relates back to an earlier point about predictability. However pedestrian accidents may afflict individuals, there is a remarkable invariance in the figures from year to year. Both the absolute casualty figures and the casualty rates follow the same patterns between the age/sex groups. For example, from 1975 to 1978 the figures for serious injuries to 10- to 14-year-olds were 1,417, 1,410, 1,593 and 1,608 for boys, and 1,101, 1,101, 1,202 and 1,260 for girls. Similarly, fatal casualties to men aged 20 to 59 years numbered 410, 425, 394 and 386; the figures for 5- to 9-year-old boys were 149, 120, 156 and 138. For women the corresponding figures were 168, 179, 169 and 206; and for girls they were 63, 61, 61 and 78. Thus it should be possible to estimate within relatively narrow tolerance limits the absolute casualty figures for this year and the year after. Out of a total population of 54 million inhabitants it is remarkable that the annual fluctuations in the pedestrian casualty statistics are so small.

The cost of accidents

The Department of Transport annually estimates the total cost of road accidents. Included in this calculation are material losses such as lost production, medical and police costs, and also a 'notional allowance' for the pain and suffering endured by the victim and the family (casualty costs). In this way the total cost for road accidents in 1978 was estimated at £1,614 million. Accidents costs are estimated to be higher than casualty costs because in many instances the accident cost has to include more than a single casualty. Furthermore, some items, such as the cost of damage to vehicles and property and the administration of insurance claims, are specific to accidents and not to casualties. In June 1978 the average cost *per casualty* was estimated as follows: for fatal casualties, £89,300; for serious casualties, £3,770; and for slight casualties, £90. The cost *per accident* was calculated at £99,500 for fatal accidents; £5,320 for serious accidents; and £720 for a slight accident.

Statistics compiled in other countries

So far we have confined the discussion of pedestrian accident statistics to British data as well we might in the light of Kennedy's claim (1980) in the BBC

Reith Lectures that the child pedestrian injury rate in Britain is the highest in Western Europe. While data for other countries are available, direct international comparison of accident statistics is notoriously difficult due to disparities in the definitions used and classificatory systems adopted: for example, classes of injury and age groupings of the injured typically vary between countries.

For example, trends in pedestrian accidents in Australia have been reviewed by Cowley and Solomon (1976). In general, pedestrian casualty rates showed a decline during the period 1963 to 1975; it was suggested that the large increase in motorization during these years could have resulted in a reduction of the number of pedestrians using the streets. For females, those in the middle age range from 17 to 59 years were least at risk; younger and older females were more at risk, with those aged 60 years and over showing the highest casualty rate. However, for males, 17 to 59 was the most vulnerable age range and those aged 16 years and less had the lowest casualty rate of all.

Patterns of accidents in Israel have been described by Hakkert, Mahalel and Livneh (1976). In comparison with the Australian trends the Israeli statistics afford less cause for optimism: between 1951 and 1975 inclusively the number of fatalities increased sharply. A similarly bleak picture has emerged for accidents in some developing countries. Jacobs (1976) and Jacobs and Sayer (1977) studied pedestrian and other road accidents in Kenya and Jamaica and found considerably higher pedestrian risk rates than in Britain. This special vulnerability of pedestrians in developing countries has been confirmed in other studies too. For example, Baker (1977) found that the pedestrian death rate in Rio de Janeiro (Brazil) was approximately four times the rate in Baltimore (USA). Various contributory factors were isolated: traffic lights in Rio were scarcer and night use of the streets by pedestrians was much greater than in Baltimore. Several other environmental hazards were isolated to account for the difference in pedestrian fatalities between the two cities.

In this brief summary of pedestrian accident statistics we have discussed only a few of the possible contributing variables, in particular those relating to age and sex. In the chapters that follow other relevant variables are considered including important temporal factors such as season, day of the week and time of day, and spatial factors governing the characteristic locations of accidents.

RESEARCH STRATEGIES

As a field of enquiry, pedestrian accident research has employed a variety of techniques. Broadly speaking these techniques divide into six main categories as represented in Table 1.6. These comprise experimental studies, field studies, surveys, judgement tasks, computer simulations and theory development. (Although these distinctions do not feature in the annotated bibliography at the end of the book, studies that are primarily experimental in nature or involve

Table 1.6 Classification of research strategies

	Distinguishing features	Focus	Realism versus precision
1. Experimentation	Systematic manipulation		
(i) Laboratory	Psychological processes studied	Behaviour	Rigorous control
(ii) Field	Manipulation in the natural environment	Context	High external validity
(iii) Natural	Manipulation by selecting naturally occurring events	Context	High external validity
(iv) Simulation	Reconstruction of behaviour setting	Behaviour and context	Rigorous control
2. Field studies	Unobtrusive observation		
(i) Participant observation	Observer is active member of system studied	Context	High external validity
(ii) Non-participant observation	Attempt is made to conceal observer	Context	High external validity
3. Survey			
(i) Status	Description of *status quo* in a population	High subject generalization	
(ii) Sample	Relationships investigated between variables in a sample of the population usually relating to attitudes	High subject generalization	
(iii) Other	*Status quo* of population investigated further	High subject generalization	
4. Judgement	Inductive study of complicated unfamiliar stimuli	Behaviour	Rigorous control
5. Computer simulation	Non-empirical organization of information	Context	
6. Theory development	Non-empirical	High subject generalization	

theory development are referenced through the primary classification applied to the bibliography).

The purpose of presenting this breakdown of research techniques is to demonstrate in general terms how research has proceeded by the adoption of differing techniques, and to illustrate the types of questions which they are most suited to address. The intention is not to present an exhaustive list, nor to imply that the studies reviewed can be classified solely in terms of a single research strategy: indeed many studies have adopted multi-strategy approaches.

Experimentation

Traditionally, experimentation proceeds by the experimenter endeavouring to hold constant all potentially relevant features of a situation apart from one, the 'independent variable', which is systematically manipulated. The effects of this manipulation on some measurable aspect of behaviour, the 'dependent variable', are recorded. This description suggests a very simple strategy, although in practice most experimental studies involve simultaneous manipulation of several independent variables, the effects of which, and the interactions between which, are measured on a number of dependent variables. Such manipulations can take place in the *laboratory* or in the *field* or be so arranged as to constitute a *natural experiment* or a *simulation*.

In a laboratory experiment the researcher creates the behaviour setting within which the observed behaviour is to take place, and manipulates the variables of primary interest. The intention of the experimenter is to learn something about the nature of the behavioural *processes* as distinct from the behavioural *systems* in which these processes naturally occur. Since pedestrian accidents happen in the context of an entire behavioural system, it is not surprising that very little research on pedestrian behaviour has been based upon laboratory experimentation.

An example of the field experiment approach is found in the work of Miller and Michael (1964) who investigated the effects of different types of pedestrian warning signs on the speed at which drivers travelled in the vicinity of a school crossing. The signs were varied in their size, location, message and design. Other environmental measures, for example, speed control humps, have been introduced experimentally to explore their effects upon vehicle speed and traffic density in residential estates (Sumner and Baguley, 1979). An alternative approach to the deliberate manipulation of independent variables is the use of the natural environment, whereby researchers select for study naturally occurring events in the environment which require no intervention or manipulation on their part. This strategy is commonly used to assess the effects of environmental variables on pedestrian and driver behaviour. Since environmental measures are man-made interventions which are intended to have some impact on behaviour, the distinction between the field and the natural experiment is somewhat blurred. However, many environmental features are introduced permanently and in the absence of any intention to evaluate their impact. Thus researchers who observe the effects of changes in the traffic environment implemented by anonymous others (e.g. town planners and civil engineers) may be said to be conducting a natural experiment. Garwood and Moore (1962) compared the use of bridge and subway pedestrian crossing facilities in terms of the ratio of the time spent on each of these crossing routes to time spent on ground level crossings; Allen (1963) compared the delay to drivers and pedestrians at lights-controlled and uncontrolled pedestrian crossings. Natural experiments have also been conducted on the effects upon child pedestrian behaviour of variables such as traffic density (e.g. Grayson, 1975b; Sandels, 1975) and time-of-day (e.g. Sandels, 1975). In Sandels' study, for example, the behaviour of children was observed in areas differing in traffic density, and young children who attended morning school were compared with those attending afternoon school.

Simulation involves the deliberate attempt to construct a behaviour setting which will mirror or typify some particular facets of a naturally occurring system. In the laboratory experiment the setting may be deliberately created to be *unlike* a naturally occurring behavioural system so that behavioural processes can be studied in what is otherwise a neutral, controlled situation. In contrast, the simulation is created to be *like* some naturally occurring behavioural system, taking account of and paralleling its uncontrollable features. These distinctions are discussed in greater detail by Runkel and McGrath (1972).

Pedestrian research abounds with examples of simulated studies. They range from simple low-cost simulations to elaborate reconstructions of settings involving high expenditure of time, effort and money. In a study of children's kerb behaviour, Pease and Preston (1967) simulated a street environment by the simple expedient of a chalk line drawn on a classroom floor. Children were instructed to imagine that the line was the kerb and were asked to cross the 'road' firstly before and secondly after an imaginary vehicle had passed. England (1976) reported a much more elaborate simulated environment in which a life-size road system complete with lights-controlled and uncontrolled pedestrian crossing facilities was described. This system was used to assess children's use of such facilities. Other simulations involve the use of film of moving traffic scenes (real or model) such as that adopted by Routledge, Repetto-Wright and Howarth (1976a) to investigate gap acceptance by pedestrians.

Simulators are also employed to assess the effects of educational measures. Typically these involve large-scale 'traffic garden' simulated environments which contain roads, kerbs, road markings and traffic signs scaled down to child-size proportions (Colborne, 1971; Nummenmaa and Syvänen, 1974; Sandels, 1975). Alternatively, education evaluation studies have required children to operate dolls in small-scale models of street environments: the actions of the doll are taken to represent those of the child (Firth, 1973; Sandels, 1975). Automobile simulators are used to study aspects of the driving task in relation to general driving skills (e.g. Denton's, 1971, study on the perception of speed), and in relation to specific pedestrian hazards (Barrett, Kobayashi and Fox, 1969). Another area in which simulators are used is to assess the effect of vehicle design on pedestrian injury by using appropriately weighted anthropomorphic pedestrian dummies and standard production cars fitted with experimentally modified body features (see Chapter 6).

Field studies

Some data-gathering research strategies consist entirely of systematic observation of behaviour within natural behavioural systems. The aim is to conduct the observations as unobtrusively as possible in order to minimize disturbance of the events under scrutiny. Participant observation has been distinguished from other strategies of observation (cf. Weick, 1968). In participant observation, control may be exerted over who and what is to be observed, but in general the aim is to learn as much as possible about the naturally occurring behavioural system of which the researcher is a participant member. A record of what has been observed is made discreetly in order that the other participants remain unaware of the scrutiny to which they are subject. Some research on pedestrian behaviour has adopted this type of strategy: studies of the use of streets as play areas have been undertaken in which the observers act as pedestrians, patrolling predetermined routes whilst recording the activities of other pedestrians encountered (Chapman, Foot and Wade, 1980; Chapman and Wade, 1982; Department of the Environment, 1973). Other studies of pedestrian behaviour have used audio-recording techniques for data collection, with observers following child subjects home from school in order to determine the exposure of children to risk (Routledge, Repetto-Wright and Howarth, 1974a, 1974b, 1976b).

The distinction between participant observation and other techniques of observation is somewhat arbitrary and largely a matter of the physical distance between the observer and the observed. The examples above are illustrative of participant observation methods because no attempt was made to conceal the observers from the subjects: observers were intended to be accepted as ordinary pedestrians. In contrast, other techniques of observation involve the recording of behaviour in situations where the observer is totally concealed (cf. Rennie and Wilson, 1980). Some observers have collected ciné-film recordings taken from concealed sites (e.g. Dipietro and King, 1970; Grayson, 1975b); others have taken video-recordings, sometimes in combination with one-way viewing mirrors (Jennings, Burki and Onstine, 1977; Routledge *et al.*, 1976a). Where film and video-recordings are not used for subsequent analysis, other devices have been adopted for recording events as and when they occur. Routledge *et al.* (1976a) used on-site event-recorders for tabulating particular pedestrian behaviours. Observers in a study by Quenault (1968) gave a running commentary into an audio-tape-recorder or used pre-categorized mark sheets to record the hazard avoidance behaviours of drivers.

Survey techniques

A distinction has been made between *status surveys* and *survey research* (e.g. Kerlinger, 1965). The status survey comprises routine fact-gathering in order to establish the status quo of whole populations (e.g. the National Census). In contrast, the survey research strategy (also termed the 'sample survey') investigates samples of populations with the aim of discovering relative incidence, distribution and interrelations among variables. Both types of survey technique are used extensively in pedestrian accident research. Government reports, cited earlier, of pedestrian accident statistics and accident rates per 100,000 population are examples of status surveys: the aim is to present the distribution of pedestrian accidents as they are found in the entire population of such accidents. What constitutes an 'entire population' may be defined in various ways to encompass events taking place in particular cities, whole nations or throughout the world. Status surveys pertaining to pedestrian accidents are typically produced by the Department of Transport and the Economic Commission for Europe. The surveys contain data broken down according to variables such as age, sex, time-of-day, type of accident and annual trends, but no attempt is made to draw inferences from the statistics. The function of such surveys is purely descriptive.

Survey research techniques occupy a prominent position in data-gathering exercises relating to pedestrian accidents. Characteristically data collected through sample surveys are in the form of opinions, attitudes or beliefs of the respondents about themselves and their behaviour, other people, or about aspects of the world in general. Such attitudes may be overtly and directly expressed or tapped less directly through the administration of suitable psychological tests.

Several studies using sample survey methods have investigated the relationship between accidents (including those incurred by pedestrians) and social factors such as the home environment and the quality of family relationships. These studies have typically involved the administration of psychological tests to sample and control groups (Burton, 1968; Krall, 1953; Langford, Gilder, Wilkin, Genn, and Sherrill, 1953) and the gathering of information concerning the incidence of illness, parental separation or maternal work outside the home and other physical and social factors (Backett and Johnston, 1959; Ekström, Gästrin and Quist, 1966; Krall, 1953; Read, Bradley, Morison, Lewall and Clarke, 1953). Other survey research studies have investigated attitudes towards road safety education and its prevalence in schools, either by using postal questionnaires (Russam, 1975; Singh, 1976) or by conducting personal interviews (Firth, 1973; Sadler, 1972).

Some survey studies combine the use of status and sample surveys where, for example, the incidence of pedestrian accidents within an entire population is obtained coupled with additional sample survey information relating to the particular variables in which the researcher is interested. Grayson's (1975a) Hampshire study concerning the distance from home of children at the time they sustained pedestrian accidents is an example of this dual approach.

Judgement tasks

The final category of empirical strategy to be discussed is the judgement task, the most familiar form of which is the psychophysical experiment. A judgement task can be distinguished form the laboratory experiment in that, although they both commonly take place in a laboratory, judgement tasks are by nature inductive and are concerned with describing parameters and establishing thresholds. This contrasts with the laboratory-based experiment which is typically characterized by the hypothetico-deductive approach whereby relationships are deduced from appropriate manipulations. Like laboratory experimentation, judgement tasks are rarely used in pedestrian accident research, although Sandels (1975) reported two such studies which were specifically related to pedestrian behaviour. Children and adults were compared in their abilities to locate the source of a sound, and to detect stimuli in peripheral vision. The research application of such measurement techniques is illustrated by the judgement task used by the UK Transport and Road Research Laboratory (TRRL, 1978): this is a visual sensitivity function test which assesses a driver's ability to detect particular road hazards.

Computer simulation and theory development

Computer simulation and theory development are research strategies for organizing, processing and extrapolating information. The relationship between the empirical methodologies already outlined and these two non-empirical strategies is entirely symbiotic: the one cannot exist without the other. Theory and computer simulation are dependent for their continued existence upon the support of empirical data; and it is necessary to have a theory of the system in question before data collection can commence, since an empirical study must be accompanied by some preconceptions about the factors to be studied and why they merit attention (cf. Chapman and Jones, 1980).

The ways in which pedestrian accident data have been organized and used in support of various theories are discussed in the next section of this chapter. Computer simulation is an additional method of organizing information in which the relationships between variables can be explored by the researcher manipulating the data input and observing the output. For example, computer simulations of pedestrian and vehicle delay at zebra and pelican crossings have been successfully undertaken (e.g. Cresswell and Hunt, 1978; Griffiths, Hunt and Cresswell, 1976).

Comparisons of research strategies

An obvious dimension along which the various research strategies may differ is in terms of their focus (see Table 1.6 above). Field studies, field experiments, natural experiments and empirical/computer simulations emphasize the context in which behaviour takes place and are concerned with studying complete behaviour systems. They contrast with laboratory experiments, judgement tasks and some surveys, in which behaviour is either studied out of context or the setting is of secondary importance to the processes being investigated. A focus on behaviour, particularly on the rigorous control and measurement of behaviour, is found in the laboratory experiment, judgement task and simulation. Subject generalization is a hallmark of the formal theory and survey strategies in comparison with the other research techniques which inevitably sample the activities of relatively few subjects.

A second salient dimension of description concerns the balance between validity or realism and precision of control. Field studies and field and natural experiments are strategies which investigate naturally occurring behaviour systems in a relatively unobtrusive manner; studies based on these strategies usually have a high degree of external validity. In contrast laboratory experiments and simulations represent strategies which, although they permit more rigorous control and precise measurement, usually have less external validity than field studies and field and natural experiments, as a consequence of their obtrusive measures and contrived settings. Researchers must weigh up, in terms of their own objectives, which is the more important for them: precision, control and a high quality of measurement or realism to ensure a greater degree of external validity.

UNDERLYING THEORIES AND PROCESSES

In this section the main theories underlying pedestrian accidents are briefly reviewed.

Epidemiological approach

It was argued earlier that the use of the term 'accident' is misleading because of the fatalistic attitude it engenders and the consequent disinclination it produces to seek preventative measures. The differentiation between mechanical and biological injury is seen as spurious and as an impediment to research.

The idea that accidents might be regarded in the same way as diseases is not new. It was first propounded by Gordon (1948) and has been reiterated by several theorists, in relation to accidents in general (Anonymous, 1978; Baker, 1972; Low, 1969), road accidents (Mackay, 1972, 1973) and pedestrian accidents in particular (Havard, 1973; Read *et al.*, 1963; Wade, Chapman and Foot, 1979). The definition of disease proposed by Clark (1967) permits the inclusion of pedestrian accidents as a disease entity: 'a failure of the adaptive mechanism of an organism to counteract adequately the stimuli and stresses to which it is subject, resulting in a disturbance in function or structure of some part of the body' (p. 4). A pedestrian accident can be regarded as the consequence of maladative behaviour by the pedestrian in response to external environmental stressors.

Epidemiology is the study of the distribution of disease in human populations, and its major purpose is to investigate factors underlying that distribution which might lead to suitable preventive measures. Previous advocates of the use of epidemiology in the study of accidents have emphasized the multi-factorial perspective offered by adopting such a framework. For example, Gordon (1948) suggested that causation is more than purely a function of the agent involved, which might be a biological organism in the case of an infectious disease, or a moving vehicle in a pedestrian accident; causation is a combination of at least three factors: the host, the agent and the environment, and no single one of these factors, according to Gordon, is primarily responsible. Baker (1972) has similarly argued that progress in the control of non-biologically inflicted injury has been impeded by the emphasis upon changing human behaviour (training people to recognize and avoid hazard) rather than by devising environmental interventions to separate the host from the harmful effects of the agent. The practice of preventive medicine in other areas of disease control has relied heavily on the latter course of action where attempts to change human behaviour have been found to be ineffective. To illustrate this assertion, Baker points out that mass pasteurization of milk is a successful environmental measure to control tuberculosis whereas exhortation to individuals to boil their milk supplies fails.

In addition to the potential practical utility of adopting the multifactorial epidemiological approach, this framework also provides a unifying theme for integrating much of the work within the field of pedestrian accidents. This claim may be examined by considering in turn the formal sequence of stages that characterizes an epidemiological approach (MacMahon, 1967). The first stage, *descriptive epidemiology*, entails the examination of the frequency and distribution of a disease in terms of personal, temporal and spatial features. Personal factors include age, sex, marital status, ethnic and socioeconomic group; descriptions of time-based factors include changes over decades, seasonal, weekly and daily fluctuations; and descriptions of place include variation by country, regions and towns, and variations within a local community. The second stage, *hypothesis formulation*, involves the use of descriptive data in formulating hypotheses linking population characteristics and exposure factors to disease frequency. In the third stage, these hypotheses are tested using methods formally termed *analytic* and *experimental* epidemiology, involving the design of correlational or experimental studies: analytic studies utilize cohort or case-history methodologies, and experimental investigations include controlled laboratory research, and evaluation of preventive or public health measures.

With regard to the study of pedestrian accidents, this framework is rarely formally utilized. The purpose of many studies has been primarily to collect descriptive data (e.g. Grayson, 1975a; Preston, 1972; Sandels, 1975) or to amass evidence to test hypotheses (sometimes implicit) concerning disease frequency and population characteristics and/or exposure (e.g. Backett and Johnston, 1959; Routledge *et al.*, 1974a). Whether or not the language of formal epidemiology is used in studies of pedestrian accidents is of little consequence. However, it is of consequence to appreciate that empirical studies of pedestrian accidents can be encompassed within the same framework as that which is advocated by medical researchers in the investigation of 'standard' disease entities.

Accident proneness

In addition to analytic and experimental epidemiological studies designed to test general hypotheses concerning pedestrian accidents, there are several hypotheses relating to pedestrian accidents which derive from particular conceptual standpoints. A frequently propounded specific perspective involves the notion of 'accident proneness'. Early work on accident proneness (in relation to industrial accidents) emphasized the statistical notion that a minority of individuals sustained a proportionally greater number of accidents than would be expected on a purely random basis (Greenwood and Woods, 1919). More prevalent, however, is the view that the high frequency of accidents incurred by a few individuals may be accounted for by reference to their abnormal personality characteristics. Alexander and Flagg (1965) described a typical accident-prone person as one who has developed an unusual degree of resentment against external coercion and authority as a result of a strict upbringing. Typically, accidents are said to occur when the victim tries to expiate unconscious feelings of resentment and guilt towards parents through self-inflicted punishment. Resentment and guilt are thus seen to be common afflictions amongst accident-prone individuals.

Krall (1953) and Burton (1968) have examined the concept of accident proneness in children. Both researchers compared accident victims with control groups matched for age, sex and intelligence. Subjects in Krall's study were children who had experienced at least three accidents of some kind, including pedestrian accidents. The hypothesis tested related specifically to frustration-induced aggression in accident victims as a result of a repressive, authoritarian home environment. The children were observed in a structured play environment with a 'family' of dolls. Significantly more aggressive acts were observed amongst the accident-repeating children relative to the accident-free children. The accident group also solicited affection more frequently and, in numerical terms, uttered more commands, threats and prohibitions than the control group, although these differences were not statistically significant. Krall interpreted her findings overall as supporting the notion that accident-repeating children tend to come from socially disorganized home environments. Alternative interpretations are plausible, however: a high frequency of verbal aggression and solicitance of affection could indicate a well-organized, democratic social unit where expression of emotion rather than repression is encouraged.

Burton's accident group consisted of children who had only sustained one recent pedestrian or cycling accident. Her dependent measures were anxiety, assertiveness and guilt as assessed through various projective personality measures which were administered to the children and mothers in both accident and control groups. The accident children were found to be more unsettled, assertive and hostile, and they had more temper tantrums and sought more attention than the control children. The mothers of the accident victims reported more stress in pregnancy and conflict in handling their children as infants than the control mothers. No apparent increase in guilt was found but Burton interpreted these findings as supporting the hypothesis that accident victims are more anxious and assertive than the accident free children. The mothers of the accident victims were found to be more assertive than the mothers of control subjects but were no more dominant, punitive or aggressive. Burton's interpretation for her accident children may to some extent be confounded by the after-effects of recent hospitalization (which many of the children experienced as a consequence of their accidents). Similar after-effects might also account for differences between the mothers of accident and control children.

Exposure-coping

In addition to the development of the clinical concept of accident proneness, the early statistical notion of 'accident liability' has also received more recent attention. With reference to childhood accidents of all types, Manheimer and Mellinger (1967) defined accident liability in terms of two concepts: the extent to which a child is exposed to hazard, and, once exposed, the extent to which the possession of certain (not necessarily abnormal) psychological and physical attributes leads to an impaired ability to cope with hazard. These concepts are best illustrated with reference to the data collected by Manheimer and Mellinger. Statistical analysis of the accident experience of 8,874 children aged from 4 to 18 years revealed 3 groups of children differing in relative accident liability (high, medium and low rates) which persisted over time. A detailed follow-up study of children so classified indicated that the higher the children's accident liability, the more likely their mothers were to consider them daring, active, exploring and extraverted—characteristics which are often held in high esteem but which encourage exposure to hazard. High liability children also tended to possess characteristics such as aggressiveness, impulsiveness and inattentiveness which were deemed to render them less able to cope with hazard. Mellinger and Manheimer (1967) also identified maladjustment as a factor contributing to accident liability. Maladjusted individuals have a heightened liability resulting from difficulties in coping with the conflict between the recognition of hazard and the impulse to indulge in risky behaviour—the impulse borne, for example, out of gaining and maintaining peer respect.

Both the clinical concept of accident proneness and the exposure-coping model are of limited practical utility. The identification of high-risk individuals can only be considered useful when there are suitable techniques available either for modifying high-risk behaviour or for altering aspects of the environment that such individuals find hazardous. In relation to some diseases there may be immense value in identifying high-risk individuals (e.g. the immunization against rubella for women of child-bearing age). However, the feasibility of initiating behaviour changes specifically among high accident-liability individuals is more difficult to envisage: any attempts to restructure fundamental patterns of behaviour (e.g. through publicity or education) can only be aimed at the population as a whole or at particular classes of road users, such as pedestrians or motorcyclists.

Cognitive–developmental and social learning theory approaches

A commonly expressed hypothesis with regard to pedestrian accidents (among children, in particular) is that it is heedless behaviour on the part of the individual, stepping out or dashing into the road, which precipitates the accident (cf. RoSPA, 1976). The results of the survey described in the final section of this chapter indicate the extent to which blame for accidents is attributed primarily to the child. Yet while such heedless behaviour is almost universally recognized and ascribed, two disparate assumptions have been drawn from it. On the one hand, many hold the view that children are by nature heedless, immature and lacking in judgement, and they maintain consequently that it is not feasible to attempt to change their behaviour; countermeasures must proceed through changes in the pedestrian-traffic environment. On the other hand, there is the view that children are admittedly ill-equipped but that it is viable, through appropriate educational channels, to teach them to behave in a safer manner on the roads. Later in this chapter we draw attention to the paradoxical nature of these positions which in essence represent a facet of the 'nature–nurture' controversy. The nature position may be harnessed in more theoretical terms to the cognitive-developmental perspective, and the nurture position to the social learning perspective. The utility of these two perspectives lies in their potential for understanding the vulnerability of children in sustaining pedestrian accidents.

Cognitive-developmental theorists hold that children 'act in a manner determined by their age and degree of development' (Sandels, 1975, p. 129), and thus are rendered more liable to accidents. In support of this claim Sandels undertook, for example, a series of laboratory experiments in which it was found that children were inferior to adults in their ability to locate the source of a sound and in the efficiency of their peripheral vision. Lakowski and Aspinall (1969) have argued that young children have essentially tunnel vision, and that there is a large but orderly increase with age in peripheral sensitivity between the ages of 6 and 22. The use of laboratory-based studies of perceptual abilities to support a theoretical position in relation to children's road crossing behaviour can be criticized on the grounds that they lack external validity. However, studies of pedestrian behaviour *per se* represent a more direct approach to the study of age differences in pedestrian accidents and these have suggested that the road crossing strategies of children and adults are markedly different in quality. Adults typically assess the traffic situation in advance of crossing, thus minimizing kerb delay; and they tend to walk into the road before it is clear, in anticipation of a gap in the traffic. In contrast, children do not make such advance assessments, delay longer at the kerb, and tend to run across the road (Grayson, 1975b; Routledge *et al.*, 1976a). The interpretation of these findings proposed by Howarth and Repetto-Wright (1978) succinctly represents the cognitive-developmental view, namely that road crossing skills exhibited by adults are too sophisticated to be taught to young children. This view contrasts with the learning-oriented perspective adopted in earlier studies by these researchers (Routledge *et al.*, 1974b, 1976b) in which pedestrian behaviour was investigated in order to 'identify dangerous behaviour and teach children to avoid it, and to identify safe behaviour and teach children to adopt it' (cf. Howarth and Repetto-Wright, 1978, p. 12). Indeed, this philosophy implicitly underpins all road safety education.

With reference to the sex differences in the pedestrian accident rates the cognitive-developmental position is characterized by the survey findings of Sadler (1972) and by our own survey findings in the section that follows, namely that boys are seen, by nature, as more active, more unthinking and more heedless than girls. These attributions are mirrored by a substantial body of developmental research evidence which indicates that girls in early and middle childhood are generally more advanced than boys physically, psychologically and socially (cf. Mussen, Conger and Kagan, 1974). Consequently, it might be argued, girls suffer fewer accidents than boys because they bring to the pedestrian task a more sophisticated repertoire of skills. It is very unlikely that the sex differences are as easily dismissed as this. Reference to statistics compiled in other countries shows that young boys are not always at greater risk than young girls, as was mentioned earlier in the chapter.

According to social learning theory the sex differences in accident rates is ascribed to differential reinforcement of sex-typical behaviour. Preference for certain activities and toys becomes manifest through explicit and implicit training by parents of sex-appropriate roles. In relation to pedestrian activities, Newson and Newson (1976) found that a higher proportion of 7-year-old boys than girls was described by their mothers as 'outdoor' children; there was a greater expectation of girls than of boys to give notice of intended journeys, and boys were said to play in the street to a greater extent than girls, a finding endorsed by Sadler (1972) and by Chapman *et al.* (1980). The Newsons interpret their findings unequivocally in terms of social learning processes: 'these results confirm beyond any reasonable doubt that by the age of seven, and in a whole variety of ways, the daily experience of little boys in terms of where they are allowed to go... and to what extent they are kept under adult surveillance is already markedly different from that of little girls' (Newson and Newson, 1976, p. 100). Although other studies of pedestrian activities have found no sex difference in the way children are treated (e.g. in adult accompaniment from school, Routledge *et al.*, 1974a) the sex difference in the accident statistics may be a function of differential styles of treatment and 'guided' experience.

Social cognition

A serious criticism of the social learning account of pedestrian activity is that it is too simplistic: it describes prevalent patterns of behaviour without acknowledging the purposive features of behaviour. Social cognition is concerned with the influence which social learning exerts upon the structure of the individual's repertoire of cognitive abilities; and, reciprocally, upon the manner and degree to which the cognitive development of the individual promotes different kinds of learning experiences. The unit of analysis is the individual in the context of others: the individual as communicator. Applied to the study of pedestrian accidents the social cognition perspective veiws pedestrian and vehicular traffic as a complex communications system, the conduct of which is sanctioned by sophisticated social controls (cf. Chapman, Sheehy, Foot and Wade, 1981). Road users are seen as communicators who have learned a set of rules (explicit or implicit) which describes how they and others should conduct themselves during pedestrian–driver encounters. A pedestrian accident can thus be conceptualized as the outcome of a failure by one communicator to abide by the rules understood by the other communicator which regulate role relations and behaviour characteristic of that situation; alternatively, it may be conceptualized as a misunderstanding by one party of the rules governing the mutual interaction of both parties (cf. Chapman, Foot, Sheehy and Wade, 1981).

Sociological perspectives

Accident research has also been undertaken from a sociological perspective (e.g. Hacker and Suchman, 1963; Klein, 1969). In considering accidents of all types, Hacker and Suchman advocated that sociological analysis be brought to bear upon the relationship between attitudes toward safety and accident rates. They cited work by Porterfield (1960) in which it was suggested that the coexistence of high homicide, suicide and accident rates reflects the operation of societal norms which place a low value on human life. Hacker and Suchman also suggested that concepts from the sociology of deviance can be applied in accident research: departure from certain institutionalized safe modes of behaviour may be regarded as aberrant. For example, an accident, like an illness, may be viewed as a reaction to stress which enables the individual to evade social responsibilities. This notion of deviance is based on a theory propounded by Merton (1938) which holds that society values certain goals such as wealth, leadership, academic achievement and athletic prowess. Individuals who accept but cannot attain these goals legitimately are likely to achieve them by deviant means. Klein (1969) also recognized the analogy between Merton's notion of deviance and accidents, and in addition suggested that an accident can be regarded as an alternative form of deviant behaviour whereby members of a subculture recognize that they cannot achieve society's goals, and actively reject them. This involves a notion similar to that embodied in the theory of differential association (Sutherland and Cressey, 1955); delinquency is viewed as a learned style of behaviour, acquired from others, wherein deviant or accident behaviour is held in high esteem by members of a peer group. Such behaviour becomes a goal in itself rather than a 'legitimate' means to evade unattainable goals.

Cybernetic models

This review of theoretical perspectives is not complete without reference to systems of thought in which man is regarded as a cybernetic machine regulated by intervening variables such as information processing, probability judgements, decision-making and risk-taking. Older and Grayson (1974) analysed the pedestrian crossing task into 6 sub-stages with reference to some of these processes. In their skills analysis the task comprises location selection, observation, perception (or information selection), judgement (or information processing), decision and locomotion. This framework highlights the importance of the observation stage—few accidents result from judgement failures. The model is useful to the extent that it defines the sequence of events in the road crossing task but is limited in explaining the complex integration of psychological components from the point of initial sensory input to the output decision.

In other models of road accident causation the motorist has been represented as a 'bio-robot'—part man and part machine (Cohen, 1966; Cohen and Preston, 1968). The lack of homeostatic self-correcting systems in the bio-robot is held to be responsible for road accidents, a predicament which could be improved by environmental measures such as better lighting and signals, clearer lane demarcation, and the segregation of pedestrians and vehicles. However, these types of countermeasure derive more obviously from the concept of 'information simplification' than from 'homeostatis' (Brown, 1962, 1965a, 1965b).

Theories and processes: some concluding comments

To conclude this review of theoretical perspectives, a re-emphasis of the value of the epidemiological approach is, in our view, merited. Whereas most other theories of accidents are of a relatively piecemeal nature, the epidemiological model does appear to embrace, within a single framework, many of the key concepts and processes focused upon by other viewpoints. In addition epidemiology provides a properly balanced research paradigm with equal emphasis upon 'diagnosis' at the outset and 'treatment' at the end. The social cognition model also has much to commend it, particularly in terms of defining drivers' and pedestrians' understanding of their relative roles and tasks. Many of the other perspectives considered in this section have been concerned with more particular aspects of the whole problem.

Criticism has been levelled at adopting a disease-oriented approach. Cohen (1966), for example, has argued that the relationship between the pedestrian and the vehicle bears little formal resemblance to that between an individual and an infectious agent. Hacker and Suchman (1963) have pointed out that the agent in accidents cannot be meaningfully separated from the environment, although in our view it may be equally implausible to separate out an infectious disease from the environmental conditions which fostered it. At root, and in terms of consequences for the individual, there may be very little difference between mechanically and biologically induced injuries, and this point alone lends favour to the conceptual representation of an accident as a disease state. In practical terms, as argued at the beginning of the chapter, the implications of viewing accidents in this light for *prevention* are considerable.

A SURVEY OF ATTITUDES ON CHILD PEDESTRIAN SAFETY

At various points in this chapter allusions have been made to society's attitudes towards accidents and, by implication, road safety. As a prelude to the preparation of this book we conducted a survey of attitudes towards certain aspects of road safety, partly to assess whether our conclusions drawn from the literature about society's attitudes towards road safety were justified, and partly to gauge opinions current at the time of writing.

Over the past decade, and largely through the efforts of publicity and education, there has been increasing public sensitivity both to the prevalence of pedestrian accidents and to the need to take preventive action especially in relation to children. In his preface to the *Children and Traffic* series, Jolly (1977) has written: 'In modern society the traffic accident has replaced malnutrition and disease as the biggest single threat to young life and limb' (p. 4), although as we have implied in the opening paragraphs of this chapter society has generally failed to acknowledge accidents in the way it has acknowledged disease. However, the message is being taken seriously by engineers and planners: crossing patrols have been widely introduced outside schools and at other busy crossing sites used substantially by children. New and improved pedestrian facilities have undoubtedly helped reduce the death and injury tolls; there is greater protection for pedestrians crossing at surface levels and better provision for segregating pedestrians from traffic altogether. The progress made in these directions is discussed in Chapter 8.

Coupled with the implementation of environmental countermeasures is the realization that more and better education is needed. Russam (1975) has stated that '. . . it is increasingly being argued that what is also needed is a new professional teaching effort to ensure that lessons in traffic safety should be a normal regular part of a child's education for citizenship of the modern world' (p. 1). To this end the Schools Traffic Education Programme (STEP) has recently being making headway in providing safety education courses for teachers. Despite this, road safety education in Britain, if it is offered at all, is still a relatively haphazard contribution to the school curriculum. Much of the road safety material that is available is either not known or not used by schools. Talks by police and road safety officers are infrequent and much depends upon the whims of individual teachers whether they choose to incorporate road safety materials or examples into their teaching of other curriculum subjects. Jolly (1977) has advocated an integrative approach and his curriculum reform assumes not that road safety should be taught as a subject in its own right but that safety material should be injected in appropriate and relevant ways into regular school subjects.

Irrespective of how road safety is to be taught, recognition of the need for such education raises fundamental questions concerning whose responsibility it should be and what attitudes exist amongst those who are in a position to undertake it. Several surveys have been conducted with particular samples aimed at establishing what educational attitudes and practices exist. Sadler (1972), for example, conducted a comprehensive survey of the attitudes of over 2,000 mothers towards the road safety of children, and Colborne and Sargent (1971) examined the extent of road safety education in schools from a sample of over 2,200 primary and secondary schools in England, Wales and Scotland.

Our survey was conducted during late 1979 and early 1980. It was prompted by the desire to examine and compare attitudes of those primarily concerned with children's road safety out of either personal or professional interest. The four groups that were selected were parents, teachers, police and road safety officers: these are the major teaching groups and they all feature in Colborne and Sargent's survey as sharing some responsibility for road safety training.

The survey was not a comprehensive nationwide exercise. It was designed as a small-scale study, on a local basis primarily. It was aimed not so much at assessing the detailed knowledge and attitudes of any particular section of the population (as, for example, was Sadler's survey of mothers), but at trawling for any relatively gross differences in knowledge and attitudes amongst the selected groups. The questionnaire was brief and tapped a number of attitudes relating to blame, vulnerability, accident locations, sex differences, responsibility for education, practical solution and the *Green Cross Code*. The nature of the questions is apparent from the results section which follows the description of the samples. Forms of questions included a variety of Yes/No, ranking and open-ended types.

Samples

Sample sizes were variable; in part this was because of the relative scarcity 'on the ground' of members of some of the professional groups, especially road safety officers, relative to the other groups. In addition the questionnaire was circulated by post or through institutional channels* from which returns were characteristically variable. Completed questionnaires were returned by 436 respondents.

Parents. The sample of 204 parents (83 men, 121 women) was drawn exclusively from the Cardiff and South Glamorgan area and was a relatively homogeneous group with respect to social class: they were middle and lower-middle class as defined by geographical area and type of housing. All parents had at least one child of primary school age (5–11) but they may also have had other children. Only one copy of the questionnaire went to each household, so in no case did both father and mother respond independently.

Teachers. Sixty teachers (17 men, 43 women) of similar background and social class to the parents were drawn primarily from Cardiff and from a few schools in England. They were teachers in primary and secondary schools.

Police Officers. There were 143 police officers (127 men, 16 women) from relatively mixed social backgrounds and sampled mainly from South Wales and the South-West of England (in particular the Gwent and Somerset and Avon Constabularies and the Police Training Centre in Cwmbran).

* We are much indebted to all respondents who completed the questionnaire. We should particularly like to acknowledge the cooperation of police officers in the Gwent and Somerset and Avon Constabularies and at the Police Training Centre in Cwmbran. In addition we are grateful for the help of teachers from Lakeside Primary School, Cardiff, and from Dell, Elm Tree, Fen Park, Meadow, Pakefield and Whitton Primary Schools in Lowestoft and from Elm Tree and Pakefield Middle Schools in Lowestoft and Hobart High School in Loddon.

Road Safety Officers. Twenty-nine road safety officers (26 men, 3 women) drawn from a wide area in South Wales were included in the sample. Like the police officers they had varied social backgrounds.

It must be pointed out that many of those in two of the three professional groups were themselves parents (50 per cent of the police officers and 62 per cent of the road safety officers), and it is very probable that their reactions to some of the questions on the questionnaire were prompted partially by their experiences as parents as well as by their professional knowledge and expertise. Those with the professional experience of teaching, or of coping with, the victims of road accidents know more of the impact of road safety education and in what ways children in general are capable of risking themselves wittingly or unwittingly. Some exploration of the relative influence upon attitudes of professional and parental roles is possible from the data collected in the survey because comparisons were made within each professional group of those who were parents and those who were not. Responses from men and women were also differentiated and analysed separately.

Results

Each of the main issues addressed in the questionnaire is analysed and discussed in turn and comparisons are made between groups.

Reasons and blame for child pedestrian accidents. In view of some of the more recent thinking concerning accident causation in relation to children and in particular in relation to legal issues governing the apportionment of responsibility (see Chapter 9), two questions concerning the reasons for child pedestrian accidents and the blame for them were incorporated into the questionnaire. One particularly interesting question, as Howarth and Gunn (Chapter 9) point out is that if children are immature, inexperienced and lacking in road sense, then how can they be held responsible for accidents that occur to them as an apparent consequence of these inadequacies? Children can no more be held responsible for their lack of judgement than mentally handicapped individuals can be held responsible for being retarded. The responsibility surely rests with those who have the knowledge and judgement to shield children from exposure to the traffic environment with which they cannot cope. Also, as Howarth and Gunn argue, once children have put themselves at risk through their lack of experience (e.g. by running into the road without looking) they can no more help the consequent outcome of that action (being run down) than the car drivers can help striking them. Nevertheless, it is quite clear from the responses received that children *are* blamed for their lack of maturity. There was total agreement amongst respondents in all four groups that in the league table of blameworthiness, the children are regarded as most at fault, followed in sequence by the parents, the driver of the car and teachers.

Table 1.7 Attributions of responsibility for road accidents by parents, teachers, police and road safety officers

	Parents	Teachers	Police officers	Road safety officers
Child's lack of care/attention	32	37	23	50
Child's impetuousness and distractability	19	31	18	28
Child's unawareness of danger	9	12	16	22
Lack of education	15	22	9	17
Lack of supervision by parents	19	8	15	17
Lack of judgement/road sense	7	6	9	11
Insufficient care and attention by drivers	13	8	5	6

Figures represent the percentage mention by each group.

Listed in Table 1.7 are the most commonly mentioned reasons for accidents. It can be seen both how similar the four groups are in their views and how dominant are reasons attributable to inadequacies of the child relative to inadequacies on the part of others in supervising or instructing them.

Surprisingly few respondents mentioned any causal factors associated with drivers. Only 13 per cent of parents alluded to insufficient care and attention or speeding on the part of drivers, and the corresponding percentages of respondents in the professional groups who mentioned these factors were even smaller. Attributions of blame to environmental factors such as the inadequate provision of crossing facilities, and to physical factors such as parked cars were also infrequent in all groups.

In relation to differences within groups there were no overall differences between men and women respondents, nor (in the case of the three professional groups) between parent and non-parent respondents. Non-parent road safety officers were the only respondents who attributed as much blame to parents as to children, but this was not reflected by the road safety officer parents, nor by any other groups of non-parents. The general verdict appears to be, therefore, that children involved in accidents have only themselves to blame. It may well be that this kind of reaction, which the law of the land appears to endorse, is no more than a defensive reaction against having to blame any other section of society. Whom can we blame if we cannot blame the child?

The age of vulnerability to pedestrian accidents. Estimates of the age at which children are most likely to be involved in pedestrian accidents are fairly congruent with the statistical evidence which shows that children of 5–7 years are at the most vulnerable age. Median age estimates were 6.7 years for the parents and for the teachers, 7.5 years for police officers, and 8.0 years for road safety officers. Parents' estimates (across all groups) yielded a median of 6.8 years which was appreciably younger than the median of 7.6 years yielded by non-parents. This tendency for parents to attribute greater vulnerability to slightly younger children than did non-parents was reflected in the data for all three professional groups. Similarly women gave younger age estimates (6.8 years) than men (7.3 years), a tendency also reflected in each of the professional groupings. The reasons given by respondents to justify their estimates of age of maximum vulnerability were very similar between groups. Children's unawareness of danger, their immaturity, asserting their independence, and lack of parental control were amongst the most frequently cited points; but, while these may be good reasons for accidents occurring, they do not adequately explain why respondents selected one particular age in preference to another.

The age of initial exposure to roads.   An important question concerned the age at which children should first be permitted to cross certain types of road unaccompanied. Substantial agreement between the groups was evident here, with the chosen age increasing progressively from culs-de-sac in residential areas to main roads in town centres (see Table 1.8). The data from the road safety officers are worthy of note: on the one hand, they deemed culs-de-sac as suitable for unaccompanied children only after the age of 7 (considerably older than the youngest age tolerated by the other groups); while, on the other hand, they regarded main roads in town centres as suitable for unaccompanied children as early as 9.5 years (considerably younger than the youngest age tolerated by the other groups). These findings suggests that this sample of road safety officers' perceptions of children's development in relation to road usage may be at variance with the perceptions of the other groups: possibly they see the transition from immature, inexperienced road usage to mature judgement as a faster developmental process, occupying a narrow age-band.

Another intriguing aspect to these data is that non-parents are more cautious

Table 1.8 Recommended age (in years) of initial exposure to roads of varying types as expressed by parents, teachers, police and road safety officers

	Parents	Teachers	Police officers	Road safety officers
Cul-de-sac, residential area	6.0	6.1	6.5	7.1
Side street, residential area	7.3	7.2	7.4	7.8
Country lane	7.9	8.1	8.6	8.5
Main road, residential area	9.1	8.4	9.1	8.6
Side street, town centre	9.7	9.0	9.1	8.6
Main road, town centre	10.8	10.2	10.3	9.5

than parents in permitting children on to the roads for the first time. Non-parents expect children to be about 6 months older than they are expected to be by parents, before they are regarded as fit for unaccompanied exposure to culs-de-sac and side streets in residential areas. This is somewhat difficult to reconcile with the finding already mentioned that non-parents see the slightly older children as more vulnerable to accidents.

Accident locations.   Respondents were asked to indicate where they thought children would be most likely to have a pedestrian accident. For the 10–16 year age bracket there was unanimity between all groups that main roads in city centres are the most likely places, followed in turn by main roads in residential areas, country lanes and culs-de-sac. For the younger 3–9 age group, members of which typically have accidents closer to home, parents and road safety officers were more appreciative than police officers and teachers that accidents are more likely to occur in the quieter residential areas than in busy town centres. There were no systematic differences in the views expressed according to parental status and sex of respondents.

Accidents amongst boys and girls.   All groups identified the greater vulnerability to accidents of boys (estimated 80 per cent) relative to girls (4 per cent). Sixteen per cent of all respondents saw boys and girls as equally vulnerable. All of the road safety officers judged boys as more at risk, possibly a function of their knowledge of the accident statistics. A higher proportion of teachers and parents (20 per cent) than of the other professional groups (10 per cent) assessed the involvement of boys and girls in accidents as equal. A higher proportion of women (22 per cent) than men (12 per cent) was also likely to regard boys and girls as equally vulnerable. Reasons for the differences in vulnerability were similar between groups and included greater adventurousness, greater amount of active street play and less overall care and attentiveness on the part of boys. Road safety officers stressed the impetuousness of boys and their engagement in acts of daring on the streets.

The responsibility for road safety education.   An interesting outcome was the differing views on responsibility for road safety education (see Table 1.9). Parents, teachers and police officers agreed that the primary responsibility lies with the parents, whilst the road safety officers saw it as lying with teachers and only secondarily with parents. Police officers regarded themselves as playing a more crucial role in education than any other group regarded them, and they also saw road safety officers as playing a less crucial role than any other group saw them. By the same token road safety officers judged the police as having less status than themselves. Amongst police and road safety officers in particular this mirror-image perception of their relative importance is rather unexpected and we proffer no suggestion as to why it should exist. In relation to parents

Table 1.9 Judgements of primary responsibility for road safety education (in rank order)

		Judges			
		Parents	Teachers	Police officers	Road safety officers
	Parents	1	1	1	2
	Teachers	4	3	2 =	1
	Road safety officers	2	2	4	3
Educators	Police officers	3	4	2 =	4
	School crossing patrols	5	5	5	5 =
	Older children	6	6	6	5 =

and teachers, the present findings corroborate those amongst mothers in Sadler's (1972) survey and, amongst teachers in Colborne and Sargent's (1971) survey, that parents have the main responsibility for teaching children road safety.

In terms of the school's responsibility, not surprisingly over 98 per cent of all respondents thought that some form of road safety material should be taught in schools. There were some discrepancies between groups in the extent to which such education should feature in the school curriculum. Road safety officers were the most favourably disposed towards regular inputs into the curriculum: 80 per cent of them viewed road safety either as a subject in its own right or as integrated into other school subjects and taught at least once a week. The other groups favoured rather more occasional inputs: police officers saw it as a subject to be taught on average once every two to three weeks; parents about once a month and teachers about twice a term. Possibly the teachers were more aware than other groups of the competing demands upon teaching time. Their apparently greater reluctance to devote formal teaching hours to the subject should be tempered by their frequent suggestion that they should give constant reminders about road safety, not necessarily in the classroom. Also, Colborne and Sargent have reported that teachers in 59 per cent of secondary schools tend to include road safety material from time to time when teaching other topics.

Practical solutions for reducing pedestrian accidents for children. Types of solutions offered by the groups fell into three main categories: (i) those placing the emphasis upon better *education* at school, better instruction by parents, greater discipline and supervision generally, and better publicity through the media; (ii) those concerned with *environmental ameliorations*: the provision of more crossings, subways, protected barriers, speed control humps, playgrounds and recreational facilities; (iii) those concerned with *law enforcement* and more stringent legal sanctions against driving offenders, for example, for speeding and illegal parking. In general terms the solutions of type (i) were proposed twice as frequently as solutions of types (ii) or type (iii). Neither the police nor road safety officers placed any emphasis upon strengthening legal powers; solutions of this type were barely mentioned by either group in contrast to the frequent mention by parents and teachers.

The effectiveness of the Green Cross Code.   To assess overall attitudes by the groups to the *Green Cross Code* respondents rated its effectiveness as a teaching aid for children on a bi-polar scale from very ineffective to very effective. There was a general tendency for all groups to rate the *Code* as being more effective than ineffective: parents, teachers and police officers held similar views of its moderate effectiveness. Road safety officers were markedly less favourably disposed towards it. Parents across all groups were less impressed by it than non-parents.

Respondents were also asked to indicate which three most important rules children should be taught about crossing roads safely. Whatever the attitudes of individual respondents towards the *Green Cross Code* may have been, an overwhelmingly high proportion of them in all four groups have 'stopping', 'looking' and 'listening' (the three basic elements of the *Code*) as the three main ingredients of safe crossing, closely followed by the need to cross at a place where visibility is good and where cars are not parked. There were no noticeable differences between the groups. Knowing the *Green Cross Code* itself was mentioned only by police and road safety officers whose general attitude towards the *Code*, as has just been mentioned, was least enthusiastic.

The survey: some concluding comments

Caution must be exercised in interpreting and generalizing these results in view of both the nature and size of the samples. The picture that emerges, however, is a largely fatalistic one: children are seen as vulnerable and at risk in modern urbanized communities; accidents are to a large extent inevitable and are an unfortunate price that society pays for organizing itself on the basis of immediate, door-to-door mobility. The main antidote envisaged is the regular injection of education. Such education, however, may be seen as little more than a palliative: in teaching the child, society may see itself as discharging a duty and absolving itself of any further responsibility for what happens to that child subsequently. The paradox is that at the same time society acknowledges that children are not capable of sound judgement and cannot be expected to cope with complex traffic environments. Indeed, although this is going far beyond the data collected in this survey, there is always the possibility that, in teaching children to cross roads at all, we are making an assumption that it *is* acceptable to expect children to be able to cope with traffic environments. Perhaps, if we are to teach them anything it should be at the very least to recognize those crossing situations in which under no circumstances should they even attempt to cross the road except in the custody of an adult or sophisticated road user.

CONCLUSION

In addition to presenting these current views about child pedestrian safety, this introductory chapter has attempted to provide a general overview of pedestrian accident research to pave the way for the more specialized individual review chapters that follow. The basic 'problem' of pedestrian accidents has been mapped out with reference to prevalent attitudes towards accidents and the statistical evidence available. Many of the key research issues to be tackled in the book have also been pinpointed and the main research strategies reviewed. Various theories and conceptualizations espoused by those working in the field have been outlined, and an appeal has been made for a more integrated and balanced approach to research.

REFERENCES

Alexander, F., and Flagg, G. W. (1965). The psychosomatic approach. In B. B. Wolman (Ed.), *Handbook of Clinical Psychology*. New York: McGraw-Hill.

Allen, B. L. (1963). Pandas versus zebras—comparative study of control at a pedestrian crossing. *Traffic Engineering and Control*, **4**, 616–619.

Anonymous (1978). Road accidents: the unnecessary epidemic? *British Medical Journal*, October, 1178.

Backett, E. M., and Johnston, A. M. (1959). Social patterns of road accidents to children: some characteristics of vulnerable families. *British Medical Journal*, **1**, 409–413.

Baker, S. P. (1972). Injury control—accident prevention and other approaches to reduction of injury. In P. E. Sartwell (Ed.), *Preventive Medicine and Public Health*. New York: Appleton–Century–Crofts.

Baker, S. P. (1977). International differences in pedestrian fatalities. In A. S. Hakkert (Ed.), *Proceedings of the International Conference on Pedestrian Safety*, Volume 2, 1–5. Haifa: Michlol.

Barrett, G. V., Kobayashi, M., and Fox, B. H. (1969). Feasibility of studying drivers' reaction to sudden pedestrian emergencies in an automobile simulator. *Human Factors*, **10**, 19–26.

Brown, I. D. (1962). Measuring the 'spare mental capacity' of car drivers by a subsidiary auditory task. *Ergonomics*, **5**, 247–250.

Brown, I. D. (1965a). A comparison of two subsidiary tasks used to measure fatigue in car drivers. *Ergonomics*, **8**, 467–473.

Brown, I. D. (1965b). Effects of a car radio on driving in traffic. *Ergonomics*, **8**, 475–479.

Burton, L. (1968). *Vulnerable Children*. London: Routledge and Kegan-Paul.

Chapman, A. J., Foot, H. C., Sheehy, N. P., and Wade, F. M. (1982). The social psychology of pedestrian accidents. In J. R. Eiser (Ed.), *Social Psychology and Behavioral Medicine*. Chichester: Wiley.

Chapman, A. J., Foot, H. C., and Wade, F. M. (1980). Children at play. In D. J. Oborne and J. A. Levis (Eds.), *Human Factors in Transport Research* Volume 2, *User Factors: Comfort, the Environment and Behaviour*. London: Academic Press.

Chapman, A. J., and Jones, D. M. (1980). *Models of Man.* Leicester: The British Psychological Society.

Chapman, A. J., Sheehy, N. P., Foot, H. C., and Wade, F. M. (1981). Child pedestrian behaviour. In H. C. Foot, A. J. Chapman and F. M. Wade (Eds.), *Road Safety: Research and Practice.* Eastbourne: Praeger.

Chapman, A. J., and Wade, F. M. (1982). Recreational use of the street by boys and girls: an observational-developmental study. In G. Breakwell, H. C. Foot and R. Gilmour (Eds.), *Social Psychology Laboratory Manual.* Leicester: The British Psychological Society.

Clark, D. W. (1967). A vocabulary for preventive medicine. In D. W. Clark and B. MacMahon (Eds.). *Preventive Medicines.* Boston: Little, Brown and Co.

Cohen, J. (1966). Patterns of accidents and possibilities of prevention. In *Proceedings of the Second Congress of the International Association for Accident and Traffic Medicine,* Stockholm: International Association for Accident and Traffic Medicine.

Cohen, J., and Preston, B. (1968). *Causes and Prevention of Road Accidents.* London: Faber and Faber.

Colborne, H. V. (1971). Two experiments on methods of training children in road safety. *Ministry of Transport, Road Research Laboratory, Laboratory Report 404.* Crowthorne: RRL.

Colborne, H. V., and Sargent, K. J. A. (1971). A survey of road safety in schools: education and other factors. *Ministry of Transport, Road Research Laboratory, Laboratory Report 388.* Crowthorne: RRL.

Cowley, J. E., and Solomon, K. T. (1976). An overview of the pedestrian accident situation in Australia. In A. S. Hakkert (Ed.), *Proceedings of the International Conference on Pedestrian Safety.* Volume 1, 101–109. Haifa: Michlol.

Cresswell, C., and Hunt, J. G. (1978). Site evaluation of a zebra crossing simulation model. *Traffic Engineering and Control,* **20**, 467–470 and 474.

Denton, G. G. (1971). The influence of visual pattern on perceived speed. *Department of the Environment, Transport and Road Research Laboratory, Laboratory Report 409.* Crowthorne: TRRL.

Department of the Environment (1973). *Children at Play.* Design Bulletin 27. London: Her Majesty's Stationery Office.

Department of Transport (1980). *Road Accidents Great Britain, 1978.* London: Her Majesty's Stationery Office.

Dipietro, C. M., and King, L. E. (1970). Pedestrian gap acceptance. *Highway Research Record,* **308**, 80–91.

Ekström, G., Gästrin, U., and Quist, O. (1966). Traffic injuries and accident proneness in childhood. In *Proceedings of the Second Congress of the International Association for Accident and Traffic Medicine.* Stockholm: International Association for Accident and Traffic Medicine.

England, E. S. (1976). Children's strategies for road crossing in an urban environment. *Unpublished Master of Science Dissertation,* University of Salford, United Kingdom.

Firth, D. E. (1973). The road safety aspects of the Tufty Club. *Department of the Environment, Transport and Road Research Laboratory, Laboratory Report 604.* Crowthorne: TRRL.

Garwood, F., and Moore, R. L. (1962). Pedestrian accidents. *Traffic Engineering and Control,* **4**, 274–276 and 279.

Gordon, J. E. (1948). The epidemiology of accidents. *American Journal of Public Health,* **39**, 504 and 515. Reprinted in W. Haddon, E. A. Suchman and D. Klein (Eds.), *Accident Research: Methods and Approaches.* New York: Harper and Row.

Grayson, G. B. (1975a). The Hampshire child pedestrian accident study. *UK Department of the Environment, Transport and Road Research Laboratory, Laboratory Report 668.* Crowthorne: TRRL.

Grayson, G. B. (1975b). Observations of pedestrian behaviour at four sites. *Department of the Environment, Transport and Road Research Laboratory, Laboratory Report 670.* Crowthorne: TRRL.

Greenwood, M., and Woods, H. M. (1919). The incidence of industrial accidents upon individuals with special reference to multiple accidents. Reprinted in W. Haddon, E. A. Suchman and D. Klein (Eds.), *Accident Research: Methods and Approaches.* New York: Harper and Row.

Griffiths, J. D., Hunt, J. G., and Cresswell, C., (1976). Warrants for zebra and pelican crossings using a minimum waiting cost criterion. *Traffic Engineering and Control*, **17**, 59–62.

Hacker, H. M., and Suchman, E. A. (1963). A sociological approach to accident research. *Social Problems*, **10**, 383–389.

Hakkert, A. S., Mahalel, D., and Livneh, M. (1976). Trends and patterns of pedestrian accidents in Israel. In A. S. Hakkert (Ed.), *Proceedings of the International Conference on Pedestrian Safety.* Volume 1, 1F1–1F10, Haifa: Michlol.

Havard, J. D. J. (1973). Child pedestrian casualties as a public health problem. In *Proceedings of the Third Congress of the International Federation of Pedestrians.* Scheveningen, September.

Howarth, C. I., and Repetto-Wright, R. (1978). The measurement of risk and the attribution of responsibility for child pedestrian accidents. *Safety Education*, **144**, 10–13.

Howe, G. M. (1972). *Man, Environment and Disease in Britain. A Medical Geography Through the Ages.* Harmondsworth, Middlesex: Penguin.

Jacobs, G. D. (1976). A study of accident rates on rural roads in developing countries. *Department of the Environment, Transport and Road Research Laboratory, Laboratory Report 732.* Crowthorne: TRRL.

Jacobs, G. D., and Sayer, I. A. (1977). A study of road accidents in selected urban areas in developing countries. *Department of the Environment, Transport and Road Research Laboratory, Laboratory Report 775.* Crowthorne: TRRL.

Jennings, R. D., Burki, M. A., and Onstine, B. W. (1977). Behavioral observations and the pedestrian accident. *Journal of Safety Research*, **9**, 26–33.

Jolly, K. W. (1977). *Children in Traffic*, Books 1–3. London: Macmillan Education.

Kennedy, J. (1980). Unmasking Medicine. BBC Reith Lectures. *The Listener*, November.

Kerlinger, F. N. (1965). *Foundations of Behavioral Research.* New York: Holt, Rinehart and Winston.

Klein, D. (1969). Some applications of delinquency theory to childhood accidents. *Pediatrics Supplement*, **44**, 805–810.

Krall, V. (1953). Personality characteristics of accident-repeating children. *Journal of Abnormal and Social Psychology*, **48**, 99–107.

Lakowski, R., and Aspinall, P. (1969). Static perimetry in young children. *Vision Research*, **9**, 305–312.

Langford, W. S., Gilder, R., Wilkin, V. N., Genn, M. M., and Sherrill, H. H. (1953). Pilot study of childhood accidents: preliminary report. *Pediatrics*, **11**, 405–415.

Low, M. (1969). Welcoming remarks. *Pediatrics Supplement*, **44**, 791–792.

Mackay, G. M. (1972). Traffic accidents: a modern epidemic. *International Journal of Environmental Studies*, **3**, 223–227.

Mackay, G. M. (1973). The epidemiology in injury—a review. *Proceedings of the International Conference on the Biokinetics of Impacts.* Amsterdam, June.

MacMahon, B. (1967). Epidemiologic methods. In D. W. Clark and B. MacMahon (Eds.), *Preventive Medicine.* Boston: Little, Brown and Co.

Manheimer, D. I., and Mellinger, G. D. (1967). Personality characteristics of the child-accident repeater. *Child Development*, **38**, 491–513.

Mellinger, G. D., and Manheimer, D. I. (1967). An exposure-coping model of accident liability among children. *Journal of Health and Social Behaviour*, **8**, 96–106.

Merton, R. K. (1938). Social structure and anomie. *American Social Review*, **3**, 672–682. Reprinted in R. K. Merton (Ed.), *Social Theory and Social Structure*. Glencoe: Free Press, 1957.

Miller, F. D., and Michael, H. L. (1964). A study of school crossing protection. *Traffic Safety Research Review*, **8**, 51–56.

Mussen, P. H., Conger, J. J., and Kagan, J. (1974). *Child Personality and Development*. London: Harper and Row.

Newson, J., and Newson, E. (1976). *Seven Years Old in the Home Environment*. London: George Allen and Unwin.

Nummenmaa, T., and Syvänen, M. (1974). Teaching road safety to children in the age range 5–7 years. *Paedagogica Europaea*, **9**, 151–161.

Older, S. J., and Grayson, G. B. (1974). Perception and decision in the pedestrian task. *Department of the Environment, Transport and Road Research Laboratory, Supplementary Report 49UC.* Crowthorne: TRRL.

Pease, K., and Preston, B. (1967). Road safety education for young children. *British Journal of Educational Psychology*, **33**, 305–312.

Porterfield, A. L. (1960). Traffic fatalities, suicide and homicide. *American Social Review*, **25**, 897–901.

Preston, B. (1972). Statistical analyses of child pedestrian accidents in Manchester and Salford. *Accident Analysis and Prevention*, **4**, 323–332.

Quenault, S. W. (1968). Development of the method of systematic observation of driver behaviour. *Ministry of Transport, Road Research Laboratory, Laboratory Report 213.* Crowthorne: RRL.

Read, J. H., Bradley, E. J., Morison, J. D., Lewall, D., and Clarke, D. A. (1963). The epidemiology and prevention of traffic accident involving child pedestrians. *Canadian Medical Association Journal*, **89**, 687–701.

Rennie, A. M., and Wilson, J. R. (1980). How drivers respond to pedestrians and vice versa. In D. J. Oborne and J. A. Levis (Eds.), *Human Factors in Transport Research*, Volume 2, *User Factors: Comfort, the Environment and Behaviour*. London: Academic Press.

RoSPA. (1976). Why young children dash into the road. *Safety Education*, Autumn, 25.

RoSPA. (1980). *1978 Road Accident Statistics*. Birmingham: Royal Society for the Prevention of Accidents.

RoSPA. (undated). *Road Accident Statistics, 1938–1952*. London: Royal Society for the Prevention of Accidents.

Routledge, D. A., Repetto-Wright, R., and Howarth, C. I. (1974a). A comparison of interviews and observations to obtain measures of children's exposure to risk as pedestrians. *Ergonomics*, **17**, 623–638.

Routledge, D. A., Repetto-Wright, R., and Howarth, C. I. (1974b). The exposure of young children to accident risk as pedestrians. *Ergonomics*, **17**, 457–480.

Routledge, D. A., Repetto-Wright, R., and Howarth, C. I. (1976a). The development of road crossing skill by child pedestrians. In A. S. Hakkert (Ed.), *Proceedings of the International Conference on Pedestrian Safety*, Volume 1, 7C1–7C9. Haifa: Michlol.

Routledge, D. A., Repetto-Wright, R., and Howarth, C. I. (1976b). Four techniques for measuring the exposure of young children to accident risk as pedestrians. In A. S. Hakkert (Ed.), *Proceedings of the International Conference on Pedestrian Safety*, Volume 1, 7B1–7B7. Haifa: Michlol.

Runkel, P. J., and McGrath, J. E. (1972). *Research on Human Behavior. A Guide to Method.* New York: Holt, Rinehart and Winston.

Russam, K. (1975). Road safety of children in the United Kingdom. *Department of the Environment, Transport and Road Research Laboratory, Laboratory Report 678.* Crowthorne: TRRL.

Sadler, J. (1972). *Children and Road Safety: A Survey Amongst Mothers.* London: Her Majesty's Stationery Office.

Sandels, S. (1975). *Children in Traffic.* London: Elek.

Singh, A. (1976). Road safety education in primary and middle schools. *Department of the Environment, Transport and Road Research Laboratory, Supplementary Report 207UC.* Crowthorne: TRRL.

Sumner, R., and Baguley, C. (1979). Speed control humps on residential road. *Department of the Environment, Transport and Road Research Laboratory, Laboratory Report 878.* Crowthorne: TRRL.

Sutherland, E. H., and Cressey, D. R. (1955). *Principles of Criminology.* Chicago: Lippincott.

TRRL. (1978). A new rapid test of visual contrast sensitivity function for drivers. *Department of the Environment, Transport and Road Research Laboratory, Leaflet 696.* Crowthorne: TRRL.

Wade, F. M., Chapman, A. J., and Foot, H. C. (1979). Child pedestrian accidents: a medical perspective. In D. J. Oborne, M. M. Gruneberg and J. R. Eiser (Eds.), *Research in Psychology and Medicine,* Volume II, *Social Aspects, Attitudes, Communication, Care and Training.* London: Academic Press.

Weick, K. E. (1968). Systematic observational methods. In G. Lindzey and E. Aronson (Eds.), *The Handbook of Social Psychology* (*Second Edition*), Volume 2. Reading, Massachusetts: Addison Wesley.

Part I

The Pedestrian

Pedestrian Accidents
Edited by A. J. Chapman, F. M. Wade and H. C. Foot
© 1982, John Wiley & Sons Ltd.

Chapter 2

Pedestrian Behaviour

D. E. Firth

This chapter seeks to put pedestrian behaviour into perspective in terms of the whole field of road and road user research. Such an approach allows for an appraisal of the current state of knowledge, information needs and assessment of priorities for the future. To a limited extent, areas discussed and research cited overlap with other chapters in the book. Where this overlap occurs details are not given, but how each factor influences behaviour will be specified in order to arrive at a comprehensive representation of the field of study.

THE NATURE OF PEDESTRIAN BEHAVIOUR

A dictionary definition of a pedestrian would be: someone who travels from place to place on foot. Pedestrian behaviour, then, is how the pedestrian actually performs on these journeys. Pedestrian behaviour is complex and to a great extent the basic motor actions necessary for the journey—walking and running—are irrelevant to the present discussion.

On any journey, obstacles are encountered, decisions made and appropriate reactions elicited. For any road user the situation is further complicated by the fact that a large part of the environment with which he/she interacts is not static. The starting point and the goal may well be identical on several journeys but many obstacles encountered will not be: motor vehicles and other pedestrians can move about within the overall constraints of the built environment. In behavioural terms, the result is a complex series of responses performed in an attempt to cope with the ever-changing situation.

In some situations, where static or slow moving obstacles predominate, an error of judgement by the pedestrian has few serious consequences. In others, where the pedestrian encroaches into the domain of fast moving obstacles, even a slight error can result in severe injury or death to the pedestrian. Accident statistics illustrate these points well. There are, for example, few accidents in shopping precincts, in pedestrian-only areas and in roads with restricted traffic flow. Those that there are, are usually slight. In the road itself, however, both the number and severity of accidents dramatically increase.

Pedestrian behaviour research is concerned with the reactions of pedestrians in negotiating the road environment and the variables which influence those reactions. Major emphasis is placed on the act of road crossing and the behaviour leading up to this, because of the large numbers of accidents associated with this part of the overall task.

THE IMPORTANCE OF PEDESTRIAN BEHAVIOUR

The study of pedestrian behaviour is important in its own right. As in any other research area, empirical studies increase our knowledge of the environment in which we live. So the study of the behaviour of the pedestrian will increase our knowledge of the traffic environment.

It is important to pay particular attention to pedestrians as a road user group because they are the most vulnerable in terms of accident statistics. Pedestrians have a higher accident rate than any other group. It is only by studying their behaviour in detail that an attempt can be made to ascertain to what extent behaviour contributes to these accidents.

Pedestrian accidents are not only large in number, they also follow predictable patterns. Some types of accidents are more frequent than others, certain areas of the road are more often the site of these accidents and specific age groups are disproportionately represented in the accident statistics as compared with predictions from general population figures. It is the existence of these patterns which give pedestrian behaviour research its impetus. Attempting to identify any behavioural differences between groups of pedestrians and ascertaining their influence on accident causation is both a logical and important facet in explaining the accident patterns which do exist. However, it is unlikely that a complete explanation of the accident statistics will lie in pedestrian behaviour: drivers and the road environment itself may also be to blame. Nevertheless, the study of pedestrian behaviour is a good starting point for any investigations of the problems. As a group, pedestrians are an easily identifiable sector of the road user population and are readily available for research purposes. Everyone at some time is a pedestrian, there are no tests to pass, limited learning of specific skills, and very few restrictions in behaviour. In addition, the group incorporates a wider age range than found for any other road users. All these factors add to the importance of the study of pedestrian behaviour as a piece of the jigsaw which makes up a picture of the road. Having ascertained the nature and importance of pedestrian behaviour it is necessary to discuss the ways in which it can be investigated.

METHODS USED IN THE STUDY OF BEHAVIOUR

There are many different ways of classifying the methods used in the study of pedestrian behaviour. Each classification has its advantages and disadvantages. The classification used here relates to four basic approaches to the topic, the main techniques applicable to each approach and the sorts of findings associated with each. The opening section of this volume gives a broad discussion of the methodology involved in the whole field of pedestrian research. Here, a brief résumé only of those methods most relevant to pedestrian behaviour research are given.

Studies based upon statistical evidence

General accident statistics in Great Britain are compiled from police records (Stats 19 forms). These are subsequently analysed into different road user groups taking into account other factors such as time of day of the accident; they are then expressed as proportions of the general population. The final figures are published yearly by the Department of Transport (e.g. Department of Transport, 1980). Most countries collect comparable data, and the patterns emerging in relation to high risk groups are very similar for Western Europe. These accident statistics have two major functions in terms of pedestrian behaviour. First, they form the basis and orientation for behavioural studies by identifying factors requiring more intensive study. For example, they highlight the vulnerability of certain groups—the elderly, children under 15 years, and boys are more frequently involved in accidents than other groups. A large number of studies of behaviour has been directed towards these vulnerable age groups to investigate any behavioural differences which may exist. Similarly, statistics show that the act of road crossing is the most likely of all pedestrian behaviours to lead to an accident and that crossing the road in built-up areas is more dangerous than in rural areas. The behavioural researcher, then, begins his/her investigations armed with the information provided by accident statistics and the questions posed by them. The second function of the statistics is that they form the goal of behavioural research which seeks to explain accidents at least in part, in terms of behaviour and either directly or indirectly to reduce those accidents. In this context, accident statistics are a means of validating pedestrian behaviour research. The argument is circular and has in many ways limited the scope of pedestrian behaviour research. A discussion of the merits of this reliance on accident data is reserved for the final part of this chapter. The present section is concerned solely with how accident statistics are used as a guide to the areas of pedestrian behaviour that deserve attention.

In terms of pedestrian behaviour such statistics, although useful, are limited in the amount of information they contain. Any source of information based on subjective reporting of events after they have occurred must be superficial. For this reason, some studies have been undertaken to provide more details of accident situations. Such studies, mainly involving surveys, have been able to throw more light on pedestrian behaviour prior to the accident than is possible from general statistics. For example, Grayson (1975a) in a detailed study of 474 accidents involving child pedestrians, found that looking behaviour immediately prior to road crossing was an important factor. In this study, 90 per cent of children had either not looked before crossing the road or had looked but not noticed the striking vehicle. Other factors, such as journey purpose and distance from home were also shown to be important. Sandels (1974) attempted to point out important behavioural factors in children's accidents. She showed that many accidents to young children (of pre-school and primary school age) occurred as the child tried to cross the road when masked by a stationary vehicle. Dashing or running into the road is another major feature of young children's behaviour prior to an accident. Sandels attempts to explain the reasons for this behaviour in terms of social factors (going towards or away from another person), preoccupation in play, interest in an object at the other side of the road, and being in a general hurry. Although a number of studies of accidents have used child pedestrians as the major target group, other studies have concentrated on the elderly pedestrian (Transport and Road Research Laboratory, 1972). They show that the elderly (usually defined as those aged 60 years and over) differ from other adults in that they are more likely to have looked but not seen the striking vehicle. However, the differences are small and in general the types of accidents involving the elderly are considered to be very similar to those involving adults between 15 and 59 years of age.

Preston (1972), in a study of the distribution of child pedestrian accidents, reported to the police in Manchester and Salford in 1969, found that certain types of area had a greater concentration of accidents than others. She suggested that areas of old, overcrowded houses with limited play areas were those generally having high accident rates. The behavioural implications of this and similar studies are not immediately apparent. On the one hand, children from such areas could well be involved in accidents because they are allowed to play (and, indeed, have to if there is no alternative) in traffic areas and so are more often exposed to the risk of an accident. On the other hand, the actual road behaviour of such groups may also differ from that of children using more protected areas for play purposes. Which of these explanations is correct is impossible to state without more detailed studies of behaviour *per se*, but it would seem probable that those pedestrians more often exposed to traffic would be more likely to be involved in a traffic accident.

Exposure is discussed elsewhere in this volume (Chapter 4); however, it is necessary briefly to consider the concept at this point in the discussion of pedestrian behaviour.

Howarth, Routledge and Repetto-Wright (1974b) have provided a survey of exposure studies to date. Theirs was the first major attempt to point out the importance of the concept in relation to road accidents. It is argued that accident studies which do not account for exposure can only give clues about the extent of certain types of accidents and point to general priorities for future studies. Only by combining accident and exposure research can more insight into possible causal factors be obtained. That is, accidents should, where possible, be expressed in terms of unit exposure to risk rather than as a proportion of overall population figures. Interest in exposure has grown in recent years, not only because of its importance in forming a complete picture of accident statistics, but also as a possible explanation for the statistics. Studies of exposure to date have made use of many different means of defining the term: for example, time spent out-of-doors, time spent in the street, time spent in the road and the numbers of vehicles encountered. Some studies have indicated that including measures of exposure, far from explaining why accidents occur, can increase the estimated risk of an accident. For example, Routledge, Repetto–Wright and Howarth (1974a) showed that, for each road crossed, the younger the child is, the more likely he/she is to be involved in a pedestrian accident.

A recent study by Todd and Walker (1980) showed that this was also true for the elderly. They tried several measures of exposure and, for each one, accident rates for the elderly pedestrian (as compared to those for younger adults) increased dramatically rather than reduced. To a lesser extent, the same was found to be true for male/female rates. Few studies of exposure have found male/female differences of sufficient magnitude to account for the high accident rates to male pedestrians in some age groups. However a study by Chapman, Foot and Wade (1980) indicates that boys up to 17 years of age were more often to be found in the road environment than were girls of the same age. As a whole, though, studies of exposure have been contradictory and inconclusive. Clearly, further research is required in this area, and we require the development of a generally accepted and reliable method of measuring exposure.

There are other aspects to exposure which should be mentioned. The first is that exposure, as well as being associated with risk, may have a positive connotation. Grayson and Firth (1972) point out that exposure can be associated with learning to cope with the traffic environment, a factor which has been almost totally neglected in pedestrian research. The second aspect relates to the study of pedestrian/vehicle conflicts. When studies of exposure incorporate a measure of the number of cars encountered, then a conflict rating can be calculated. Conflicts occur when some sort of avoidance action on the part of the pedestrian or vehicle prevents an accident occurring (e.g. a near miss). The study of such situations is a new field of concern. Calculations are based on the number of cars encountered by a pedestrian and criteria such as sudden avoidance action and change of direction are used to describe a situation in which an accident could have occurred but was somehow avoided (Guttinger, 1976). Because an action by the pedestrian is often involved, conflict studies are very important to pedestrian behaviour, but to date very little research has been undertaken.

Another major group of studies using accident statistics comprises case study investigations. Research in this area has often been concerned with children who are accident repeaters (either generally or specifically in relation to traffic accidents), or have taken a road accident group and compared them with a control group of non-accident victims. Although some of the findings have been useful in relation to the overall accident situations and the personality and social correlates of accident repeaters, such studies have only slight application to pedestrian behaviour *per se*. The reader is referred to Wade, Foot and Chapman (1979) and Chapter 7 for further information on these factors which are beyond the scope of the present discussion. In summary, accident statistics and detailed studies of accidents are useful approaches to pedestrian behaviour research but limited in scope. Even if a particular behaviour was identified as being a probable causal factor in accidents, it may be that this behaviour is exhibited in non-accident situations also. The only way to ascertain whether or not this is so is to study road behaviour itself.

Behavioural and observational approaches

Direct empirical research on the actions performed by pedestrians is probably the most obvious starting point for studies of pedestrian behaviour. Recently, a great deal of research effort has been devoted to this area, possibly because of the limited amount of information accident research can give on behavioural aspects of the problem. The prime concern of direct studies of traffic behaviour has been to isolate any age and sex differences in pedestrian behaviour. Studies have made use of a variety of observation techniques in both the natural road environment and under simulated traffic situations.

Some investigations have made use of observers to categorize pedestrian actions; for example, Sandels (1975) and Michalik (unpublished). Both these studies were concerned primarily with the behaviour of young children. Sandels concluded that the traffic behaviour of four- to seven-year-olds was unreliable and could be categorized as generally unsafe. In particular, four-year-olds displayed what appeared to be poor road behaviour more consistently than older children. Examples of poor behaviour included dashing into the road, not looking before crossing and running across the road. Michalik, on the other hand, found that the traffic behaviour of individual children of five to six years of age, was homogeneous: that is, the children tended to behave in a similar manner on different occasions, provided there were no dramatic changes in the situation. However, behaviour was influenced by momentary social situations so that children in pairs of the same age showed more risky behaviour than individual children. A great deal of information can be acquired using observers as these studies show. Observers may follow children along certain routes (e.g. Routledge *et al.*, 1974a) walk through specific areas monitoring the number of children encountered (e.g. Chapman *et al.*, 1980) or restrict themselves to observing a particular area of the road (e.g. Sandels,

1975). Within these broad strategies, different categories of road user and varying actions may be noted. Despite these possibilities, the information gleaned from such techniques is limited. In the first instance they are subjective, relying solely on the individual observing the events. Observer bias is a well known phenomenon in a variety of settings, not simply those concerned with pedestrian behaviour. In addition there are the problems of defining the categories of behaviour to be observed on an *a priori* basis and of ensuring they are not ambiguous. Lastly, another major note of caution must be related to the amount of information which can be recorded at any moment in time by a person who must be inconspicuous to the subject of the observation. The effect of many of these problems may be minimized by careful planning, training observers, the use of several observers and reducing the number of items to be recorded, but they cannot be eliminated totally.

More recently, the use of film techniques has gained impetus in the field of pedestrian behaviour research. In the last ten years, both video-taping and time-lapse photography have been used in the field. These methods of recording, by their very nature, provide a greater amount of information than can be gained from using one or two observers. They also allow for accurate timing of a greater variety of individual actions, several views of one situation when more than one camera is used, and they enable many different researchers/ observers to see and analyse the same event: they are a more or less permanent record of a transient situation. However, such techniques are not the perfect answer to the problems encountered above. Reliability is still a problem. Although the use of films is objective because it overcomes the observer bias at the point of data collection, there is still a certain amount of subjectivity in the analysis of the data. Two analysts rarely produce identical records of a single film. Careful training of analysts and/or the use of more than one per film can reduce the bias at this stage. In addition, the categories selected from which measures of behaviour are derived need careful planning. Film techniques tend to concentrate on specific observable actions rather than judgements such as 'poor', or 'unsafe', but only overt responses can be measured, overt items must be inferred. This is particularly apparent for items such as head movements. A specific movement of the head by the pedestrian is recorded as an act of looking for traffic. It does not require a specialist on pedestrian behaviour to point out that observing traffic can be performed without the need for a specific head movement or that, conversely, a head movement is not necessarily synonymous with looking and seeing a moving vehicle. The reader is referred to Rennie and Wilson (1980) for a comparison between methods of recording. In spite of these drawbacks, film techniques are the most useful of all techniques for recording pedestrian behaviour. They are less labour intensive than the use of observers in the field and cameras can be much less conspicuous than a five to six foot individual armed with a clip board and pen. In recent years, studies using films of behaviour have greatly increased our knowledge of pedestrian actions.

Grayson (1975b), in an important study mentioned earlier, showed that different overall road crossing strategies are adopted by different age groups of pedestrians. This study made use of time-lapse photography, monitoring items such as kerb delay, head movements, time taken to cross the road, and crossing direction. For most of these items there was a difference between children and adults so indicating that the two groups approach the task of crossing the road with a different strategy. No overall strategy differences between males and females were observed.

The elderly (60 years and over) have been shown to adopt a similar road crossing strategy to that of children (Wilson and Grayson, 1980). In a study of adults filmed again by means of time-lapse cameras, differences were found between the elderly and other adults in many pedestrian actions. Although taken individually these differences were only small, the overall approach of the elderly to road crossing was more like that of children than to the 15 to 59 years age group. Other studies have used filming techniques to monitor pedestrian behaviour in relation to specific tasks such as the use of crossing facilities (e.g. Firth, 1979).

Investigations using filming have not all been carried out in the natural road environment. Sometimes it is necessary to use simulated traffic situations, when for example, very specific actions are to be observed. In such cases, field observations may be so time consuming and expensive as to be virtually impossible. Several degrees of simulation have been used, together with a variety of observational measures. Some studies have also made use of verbal reports of behaviour as an additional data source; for example Firth (1979) in a study of children's use of pelican and zebra crossings. This study used both field observations and observations under simulated conditions as well as verbal report. Firth (1973) and Fisk and Cliffe (1975) used observations of children's behaviour under simulated conditions to establish the effectiveness of road safety education. Limbourg and Günther (1975) studied the behaviour of children aged four to nine years of age in laboratory situations, and Gorges, Bauerfeld and Schlägel (1976) constructed traffic situations from paper, chair, toy traffic-lights, and other simple materials with which to assess the behaviour of young children up to seven years of age. All these studies pointed to areas of concern in children's road behaviour. For example: younger children selected the shortest and quickest route to a pre-determined destination and were unable to understand the importance of obstacles restricting their sight (Limbourg and Günther, 1975); almost all the children crossed the road at a green traffic light and fewer than half stopped before crossing and looking round carefully (Gorges, Bauerfeld and Schlägel, 1976). Recording behaviour under conditions far removed from those encountered in the natural environment can then be useful and increase our knowledge of some aspects of pedestrian behaviour.

Results, though, must be treated with caution and generalizations to actual road behaviour should be generated cautiously. Russam (1975) also indicated the need for caution in interpreting the findings from simulated traffic situations.

The observational approach to pedestrian behaviour has been (and will continue to be) invaluable to pedestrian research. The emphasis, though, is on studying 'normal' behaviour and it is a point of contention whether such studies should or could relate to accident situations. Accidents are comparatively rare events and even intensive filming at a particular site is unlikely to reveal an accident.

Experimental approaches

It has already been stated that observers can only monitor observable or overt responses. These are the result of a number of covert events which can be investigated in situations far removed from the traffic environment and which are used by the pedestrian in many circumstances, not just in the road crossing task. Laboratory experiments other than those associated with observations of traffic behaviour are therefore important in the field of pedestrian research. The third approach to the research has been to investigate covert events and the relative abilities of groups of individuals to perform them. At first glance it may be difficult to see how, for example, controlled laboratory experiments on perception increase our knowledge of pedestrian behaviour. However, if a pedestrian cannot perceive the road situation and monitor the changes which occur, he/she will not be able to decide when or if to cross the road. Such studies, then, have a valuable part to play in providing information about the pedestrian and the judgements made by him/her.

Particular attention has been directed towards isolating any age differences in these abilities and to identify relevant developmental trends. Avery (1974) reviewed the development of abilities essential to the pedestrian task, for example, perception, attention, memory, logical reasoning and reaction time. In this review, the author demonstrated that for most of the abilities mentioned, there is evidence of a developmental trend in that performance generally increases with age. Research evidence on some items, such as hearing, was acknowledged as being sparse, and several areas requiring further research were identified. A great deal of the evidence quoted by Avery is from the general psychological literature, for example, Maccoby (1969) on the development of attention. Although the findings from this and other similar laboratory studies are generalizable to pedestrian performance, the mechanics of attention and its importance in relation to the specific task of road crossing can only be inferred. Some research has, however, been carried out with reference to the pedestrian situation. Salvatore (1974) for example, shows that both age and sex are important factors in the evaluation of the speed of moving vehicles. In addition Martin and Heimstra (1973), show that age is a key factor in how children perceive hazard (including traffic hazard) in potential accident situations.

Countermeasures

Countermeasures are attempts to increase road user safety through the effects of education, propaganda, legislation and changes in the road environment. Often, a modification in some aspect of road user behaviour is the direct aim of these countermeasures, but sometimes, intermediary goals (for example, attitude changes) are their prime purpose. A great deal of research effort has been directed to the study of countermeasures and their effectiveness. Regarding pedestrian behaviour, the effect of countermeasures is important because most pedestrians perform the act of crossing a road armed with information from countermeasures. In addition, those aspects of behaviour most readily affected by different countermeasures increase our understanding of behaviour *per se*.

Education is obviously an important countermeasure. It is primarily aimed at children who form a high accident group; and, if it is successful at a young age, it may carry over to the adult pedestrian of the future. However, the wealth of research in varying aspects of road safety education is beyond the scope of the present chapter. A more detailed discussion of education and other countermeasures can be found in Chapter 3 of this volume. However, it is important here to mention those investigations which have implications for behaviour. The OECD report on education (1978a) summarizes the studies to date and concludes that road safety education in kindergartens and primary schools can be effective but is dependent on exactly what is taught and the methods of teaching. Many of the studies cited in this report make use of tests of knowledge rather than observations of behaviour as criteria for effectiveness. The exception is a study by Schioldborg (1974) who found that most children scored better on knowledge tests than on measures of pedestrian behaviour observed during kindergarten journeys. This is an important point regarding pedestrian behaviour because it implies that poor behaviour in children may be due to factors other than not knowing the correct way to behave. This is supported by Pagett and Waller (1975) who found improvements in the road safety knowledge of children aged eight, eleven and fourteen, six months after a road safety teaching programme. Using limited film data, no similar improvements in observed road crossing behaviour were found.

Propaganda is another countermeasure to attract a great deal of research. In 1968, Wiener reported a study of elderly pedestrians' response to an enforcement campaign. The study showed a dramatic reduction in 'jaywalking' behaviour during the campaign and for four months afterwards. This finding, that propaganda can and does affect pedestrian behaviour, is common to most studies in the area. The OECD report (1978b) contains a review of the relevant literature and concludes that in general there is no question about the ability of mass media communications to modify pedestrian behaviour. Many different propaganda approaches using different target audiences and behavioural items are cited in support of this argument. In some cases, a propaganda campaign in conjuction with an enforcement campaign was undertaken.

This introduces the third countermeasure, legislation. Pedestrians are rarely the object of specific legislation and so studies in this area are not as frequent as in others. Nevertheless, those studies that there are indicate that, along with education and propaganda, legislation can also be used to modify pedestrian behaviour. Jacobs (1966), for example, showed that the use of guardrails, legislation and police enforcement combined to reduce the ratio of pedestrians crossing the roads away from designated crossings.

The provision of designated crossing facilities for pedestrians is probably the most popular environmental countermeasure aimed at pedestrian safety. Footbridges, subways, pelican and zebra crossings are all regarded as safe places for pedestrians to cross the road, but to be of value they must be used by the pedestrian and used effectively. Mackie and Older (1965) and Jacobs and Wilson (1967) showed that the risk of an accident to a pedestrian is lowest on a designated crossing facility, but crossing within 50 yards of such a facility greatly increases the risk. The likelihood of a pedestrian accident is much higher near a crossing facility than on any other section of the road. Pedestrians must, then, be directed towards using crossing facilities for greater safety. A more detailed account of the effect of environmental changes is given in the OECD report (1977) and in Chapter 8. All four approaches to the study of pedestrian behaviour and the methods used which are discussed in this section are of value in increasing our knowledge. The findings of the various studies are organized to facilitate an assessment of the current state of the art.

A CONCEPTUAL FRAMEWORK

Recently, several researchers have recognized the need for imposing some sort of structure or framework on the field of pedestrian research. The scope of the resultant frameworks varies according to the principal concern of their designers, but are aimed at providing guidelines for future research. Some of the studies are concerned only with pedestrian behaviour and others include behaviour as part of a framework covering other areas of pedestrian research.

Heimstra, Nichols and Martin (1969) developed an experimental methodology for analysing child pedestrian behaviour. This was the first systematic description of child traffic behaviour in terms of directly observable variables. Measurement of items such as stopping before crossing, head movements and walking speed, was considered to be essential for building up a picture of behaviour. The categories for observation mentioned in this study have been used by subsequent researchers and developed to accommodate different groups of pedestrians and additional measures. Although important, this study is too limited for our needs here. A more flexible structure capable of encompassing the whole research area, not just those parts which are directly observable is necessary for our purposes.

An attempt to provide such a structure was made by Grayson and Firth (1972). This unpublished work is cited in the OECD report on road safety education (OECD, 1978a). Although primarily concerned with child pedestrian behaviour the authors point out that only minor modifications would be necessary to extend the points of reference to encompass other age groups. The approach taken was one of task analysis, building up an overall framework in relation to the specific tasks which the pedestrian is required to perform. One particular task, that of road crossing, is considered in more detail. This is because, in the complex of tasks the pedestrian performs, road crossing is probably the most difficult and is most highly represented in accident statistics. The road crossing task is analysed in terms of six stages and the operations involved in each of these are specified. Lastly, the variables likely to influence each operation are discussed.

Older and Grayson (1974) produced a modified version of the Grayson and Firth task analysis, to include all age groups of pedestrians. Again, operations and stages were specified concentrating on the act of road crossing. Figure 2.1 is a diagrammatic representation of the stages identified. The authors pointed out that to some extent the division of the task into these stages is an arbitrary one. The stages are a representation of the *ideal* sequence of events. This sequence may be altered in any road crossing situation: for example, some of the stages may be

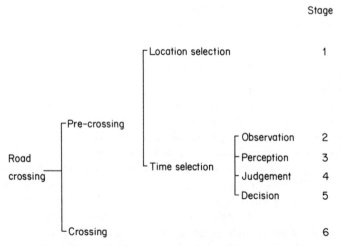

Figure 2.1 The road-crossing task (Reproduced by permission of the Director Transport and Road Research Laboratory, CROWN 1974)

repeated several times before crossing takes place. Alternatively stages may be amalgamated or omitted altogether depending on the conditions prevailing. The task itself is acknowledged to be more complex than the analysis would indicate. In this framework the variables affecting the task are divided into three categories: individual differences (personality, perceptual and cognitive abilities), external factors (environmental cues and social influences) and classification variables such as age and sex of the pedestrian.

Another framework was postulated by Avery (1974). This framework gives an account of the development of the psychological processes involved in road crossing and identifies nine stages in the task. Again the author points out that the situation described is ideal and that stages may be omitted or combined. Snyder and Knoblauch (1971) produced an elaborate model of pedestrian accident causation, covering both driver and pedestrian behaviour. Their model identifies the psychological processes involved on the part of both groups of users as well as their interactions. Other attempts to provide a framework have concentrated on other aspects of pedestrian research. Munsch (1973), Kroj and Pfafferott (1975) and van der Molen (1975) all provided models relating to educational objectives, whilst Routledge (1975) was concerned with pedestrian exposure to the traffic environment.

Despite this recent upsurge of interest in designing models for pedestrian research, none of the attempts so far made is entirely satisfactory from a behavioural point of view. No one study totally sums up all pedestrian skills and analyses all the actions involved in pedestrian behaviour. Nevertheless, some models do provide a useful framework in which to describe pedestrian behaviour research. The next section discusses the current state of knowledge concerning pedestrian behaviour using the framework described by Older and Grayson (1974). This work, although by no means a complete analysis of pedestrian behaviour, is most valuable for this purpose because of its fairly simple and flexible approach to the problem.

CURRENT STATE OF KNOWLEDGE

The stages and operations outlined in Figure 2.1 opposite form the basis for this section. First of all, the six stages of the task are discussed in terms of research findings to date. Lastly there is a section concerned with the variables which have been shown to influence these stages.

Location selection

This stage describes the act of deliberately selecting a specific place to cross the road. It is treated as a single stage in our framework, although it is made up of several sub-tasks and abilities. Grayson (1975b), in his study using time-lapse films, recorded the behaviour of 1,790 pedestrians in the real road environment and found that adults, rather than selecting a specific place to cross, seemed to choose a time to cross. Children, on the other hand, tended to select a location before crossing. Although the majority of observations in this study were carried out on roads having no crossing facilities, there was a traffic island at one of the four sites chosen. Using an island as a central traffic refuge effectively simplifies the pedestrian task. Each part of the road can be treated as a separate crossing with traffic travelling in only one direction. In these terms, the traffic islands can be thought of as a relatively safe place to cross the road. The study showed that only two out of every five adults selected this location as a crossing place, whereas two out of three children did so.

Other studies on location selection have been concerned with pedestrian usage of crossing facilities: for example, zebra and pelican crossings. In such cases where there is no physical separation of vehicles and pedestrians safety is dependent on effective behaviour on the part of the pedestrian. There are several factors which influence pedestrian usage of zebra and pelican crossings. Lovemark (1969) showed that the likelihood of a facility being used was affected by traffic volume and the distance a pedestrian had to walk in order to reach the crossing. In addition, certain features of the design of the facility itself are important. Jacobs (1966) showed that guardrails limiting pedestrian choice of crossing places facilitates usage of designated crossings.

England (1976) cited a study carried out at the Transport and Road Research Laboratory concerned with children's use of crossing facilities. This study made use of observations of the behaviour of seven- to eleven-year-old children in a simulated but full-size road situation. The children were filmed on roads supplied with either a pelican or a zebra crossing, and the findings showed, that unless specifically instructed to use the crossings, few children did so. Children's use of zebra and pelican crossings in the natural traffic environment has, however, been found to be much higher (Firth, 1979). Both the simulated and actual road observations cited above indicate that even when children did use the facilities, and location selection could be seen as perfect, safety was not ensured. The way in which the crossings were used left a great deal to be desired in terms of carrying out the remainder of the pedestrian task. For example, many of the children neither looked at the pedestrian lights nor waited for them to change when using pelican crossings. Similarly children at zebra crossings did not always look for traffic before crossing.

Footbridges and subways form another category of crossing facilities aimed at increasing pedestrian safety. In this category, however, there is physical separation of pedestrians and vehicles. The road crossing task is therefore effectively by-passed if pedestrians use these facilities in order to reach the other side of the road. Research carried out at the Transport and Road Research Laboratory on pedestrian usage of this category of facility has shown that, overall, subways are typically used more often than footbridges. Design features of the facilities themselves were, however, found to be important in attracting users (studies sponsored by the UK Transport and Road Research Laboratory, cited in OECD report on the pedestrian road environment, 1977).

Location selection, then, is an important stage in the road crossing task. It is advisable that the location offering the maximum safety is positively selected by the pedestrian. The fact that pedestrians often ignore designated crossing facilities is problematic, but studies on education and propaganda have shown that pedestrian behaviour can be directed towards the use of such places to cross the road with some degree of success. As a stage, location selection is often omitted, or a place may be selected which is not the one offering the greatest safety to the pedestrian crossing the road. Neither of these actions is in itself crucial to safety. Selecting a *time* to cross the road is more important in terms of safety than is selecting a *place* to cross. If time selection is carried out ineffectively, then an accident is the likely outcome, irrespective of where the crossing actually takes place. In view of this, time selection is discussed in more detail than location selection. For discussion purposes the overall process of time selection is divided into four identifiable operations: observation, perception, judgement and decision. These are treated as stages although the division is to some extent arbitrary. Many of the operations overlap, but they are all basic to the act of time selection and have often been researched separately.

Time selection—observation

The operation involved here is overt search behaviour by the pedestrian. It is often classified as being identical to the head movements monitored in observation studies. In order to select a time to cross the road, the pedestrian needs information about the environment. Observation is the operation carried out by the individual in an attempt to gain that information. Observation or looking behaviour may be deliberate or incidental. In the latter case environmental cues trigger a subsequent search response. The importance of these searches in relation to accidents has been pointed out by Grayson (1975a) and by the Transport and Road Research Laboratory (1972). Grayson in his study of 474 road accidents involving children, showed that 39 per cent of the children were reported as not to have looked at all before crossing the road. The 1972 Transport and Road Research Laboratory report was concerned with accidents to elderly pedestrians, and showed that just over 70 per cent of accident victims over sixty years had not seen the striking vehicle. This was largely as a result of the elderly not looking before crossing. A breakdown in the observation stage, then, is often associated with accidents, but what part does observation play in non-accident situations?

Grayson (1975b), showed that as well as differing in terms of location selection, young children and adults adopted different approaches to time selection. A diagrammatic representation of these two approaches or strategies is shown in Figure 2.2 (p. 61). The figure shows that adults made their observations of the situation on approach to the kerb, and exhibited little or no kerb delay. Young children, on the other hand, stopped at the kerb and then assessed the situation. Kerb delay in this group was much longer than for adults. Transition from one strategy to the other appeared to take place at about eleven or twelve years of age. Similar differences in road crossing strategies were shown by Wilson and Grayson (1980) for pedestrians over sixty years of age and other adults. The elderly pedestrian was found to display a strategy more in line with that of children than with younger adults. Both these studies used measures of head movements as an indication of observation behaviour.

There are three possible reasons why there should be an age difference in search behaviour. The first is that children and the elderly may require more information than adults on which to base a decision. Second, they may not internalize as much information per observation (or head movement) as adults. Third, they may need more time to differentiate relevant from irrelevant information. Which of these explanations is correct, or whether some combination of factors is involved, is difficult to say. Older and Grayson (1974) suggest that the first statement may be the explanation for the differences observed on the basis of signal detection research. In addition, Liss and Haith (1970) found that in a location task involving visual search, five-year-olds were slower than adults in information processing. Thus, it may be that children and the elderly need to spend longer searching for relevant information and processing it, than do adults aged fifteen to fifty-nine years. Generally, they make allowances for this in the road crossing task, but as accident studies show, on occasions when they do not, an accident is likely to result.

Time selection—perception

The operations involved here are a direct consequence of observation, but are separated from it because they are covert rather than overt events. Initial processing of the information input from observation is important to this stage. Both visual and auditory senses are included. The majority of studies relating to this stage are from the general literature, but one or two investigations have been specifically concerned with perception as part of the road crossing task.

Avery (1974) reviewed the relevant literature on visual perception in relation to child pedestrian behaviour. This review suggests that factors such as speed of eye movements, attention and memory may be of importance in producing differences between adults and children on visual tasks. Age, however, is shown to have little effect on visual acuity beyond the age of about five years. Sandels (1975), in a study specifically related to the pedestrian task, suggested that children are more limited than adults in their ability to detect peripheral movement. However, this study was limited by low subject numbers and naïve methodology. There is comparatively little information on the development of the auditory perception which is of value to pedestrian behaviour. That which there is suggests that children are not as efficient in localizing sounds as are adults (Sandels, 1970) and they are more likely to be distracted by irrelevant sounds (Gibson, 1968). An error in the perception stage of the road crossing task has been shown to be important in road accidents involving both the elderly and children. The study of accidents to the elderly, mentioned already, showed that the elderly were more likely to have looked (carried out the observation stage) but less likely than other adults to have seen (inefficient perception) the striking vehicle (Transport and Road Research Laboratory, 1972).

Grayson's study of accidents to children also suggested a genuine cause for concern about the ability of children to perceive a moving vehicle. Twenty-one per cent of the children in the Grayson study were also reported to have looked but not seen the striking vehicle. This problem is not related to faulty judgement in any way and cannot be explained adequately by any research findings to date. Grayson describes the problem as being one of 'lack of attention'.

Time selection—judgement

This operation involves completing the processing of information from the previous stages. In addition, the information is organized into a form that the pedestrian can utilize as a basis for his/her decision about when to cross the road. Judgements of speed, distance, time and gap estimation are important here.

In a study by Salvatore (1974), children of various ages were given a task involving judgements of speed of moving vehicles. The results suggest that in addition to vehicle characteristics (including the auditory factor of vehicle noise), the age and sex of the child were mediating factors in the accuracy of the judgement. There was also an interaction of the two factors in that very little difference between the sexes was found in the 5- to 6-year-old group. Overall, girls displayed more caution than boys in that they tended to overestimate the speed of oncoming vehicles, and evaluated high speeds more correctly. For all three categories of speed used in the study, though, boys gave better estimates. Age was positively related to the estimates, the older children judging low and moderate speeds more accurately. The situation was more complex in relation to high speeds: judgements of these were very often wrong. These results, though, must be viewed in the light of the overall methodology of the study, which is open to criticism; for example, the children were required to categorize speed into three somewhat arbitrary categories of 'fast', 'medium' and 'slow'.

Lovell, Kellett and Moorhouse (1962) showed that age had a considerable effect on what can be described as the logic of velocity perception. In this study children were required to make a relative speed judgement, and say why and how a particular conclusion had been reached. It was not until children reached 9 years of age that 75 per cent of them could make correct judgements (and justify them logically) about the faster of two trains when both started and arrived at the same time, but one took a longer route. The authors concluded that even if a child makes correct judgements, he/she is not necessarily able to think of speed in terms of distance per unit time. The ability to judge distance has also been shown to be related to age. Zeigler and Leibowitz (1957) in a matching task using objects at various distances showed that children aged seven to nine years did not perform as well as adults.

In the pedestrian task perception and judgement are important, but exactly what sort of judgement is required is difficult to define. The speed of a moving vehicle may not in itself be important. Similarly neither may be the perception of distance in terms of how far the vehicle is from the pedestrian. The important factor seems to be the judgement of the time of arrival of a vehicle in relation to the pedestrian's own speed. A judgement of this type was elicited from the children involved in the Lovell *et al.* study. These children were asked *why* two trains would arrive at the same time. The authors point out, however, that such a judgement of speed per unit time may not be related to judgements made at the roadside. How time of arrival estimates are made during the road crossing task is not known, but the consequence of the estimates has been studied in terms of gap acceptance. Moore and Older (1965) indicated that time-gap estimations, and their relationship to the pedestrian's own time to cross the interception path, were important in road crossing. Dipietro and King (1970) also investigated pedestrian gap acceptance and the variables affecting it. Lastly, Older and Grayson (1974) cited a study of gap acceptance in children using video films. This study showed that older children accepted smaller gaps in traffic—the actual time interval between two vehicles during which the child crossed the road. However, these older children allowed longer safety gaps—the interval of time between the child crossing the path of the oncoming vehicle and this vehicle crossing the path of the child. The implication was that young children spend longer at the kerb even when presented with an adequate gap between vehicles.

Vehicles travelling in both directions need to be judged before road crossing can take place; therefore the pedestrian must remember information from one side of the road before proceeding with judgements about the other side. Equally, the amount of information from each side is likely to be quite large and some of it needs to be stored in memory before subsequent judgements are made. In her review of the faculties involved in the pedestrian task, Avery (1974) showed that short-term memory in children is poorer than in adults, and concludes that this is probably due to storage problems. The differences are unlikely to be due to differences in rates of forgetting. Belmont and Butterfield (1969) in a review of the relevant literature concluded that when learning is held constant, different age groups have similar rates of forgetting. Long-term memory and experience of the road environment are other factors which must influence the judgement stage. Adults, by virtue of greater experience in the road environment, should perform better than children. As Grayson and Firth (1972) pointed out, exposure in terms of traffic experience can have a positive effect on behaviour in addition to the possibility of being associated with accidents. Why elderly pedestrians, who have a great deal of experience, should figure so highly in the road accident statistics is a point for conjecture. As Grayson (1980) argues, the adage that the elderly have accidents because of declining faculties finds little support in the empirical evidence to date. Rather, the elderly compensate for any difficulties they may experience by adopting different road crossing strategies.

Time selection—decision

Stage 5 is the culmination of the previous four stages—the decision about whether or not to cross the road. Judgements are made in order to facilitate this operation. If the decision is *not* to cross the road, then the whole process will begin again, the new crossing taking place either at the same location or at a different location. The covert part of the decision stage involves past experience and both long- and short-term memory. Pedestrians sort and order the judgements in the light of past experience and all the information they have in their memory store: for example, information from education, propaganda and legislation. They then make a decision and act on the result. The overt or observable part of this stage entails the moment chosen for, and the act of, crossing the road or, alternatively, the act of abandoning the task.

In view of the covert nature of this stage, no direct observations can be made of it. The result of the operations involved can, though, be observed. Consequently the gap acceptance studies are also pertinent for this stage as well as for the judgement stage. The evidence from these field studies has already been discussed. Also relevant are studies of logical reasoning which are of a more general nature than those associated with speed/time estimation. Piaget (1953) and his associates have had a great deal of influence in this field of study. Piaget argued that logical reasoning develops with age. Children who have not yet attained a certain level of development cannot cope with problems requiring logical reasoning which adults find very simple. Bryant (1974), however, carried out a series of experiments which indicated that children far below the necessary developmental level in Piagetian terms could solve problems using logical reasoning. In these studies, the children solved problems similar to those used by Piaget. In order to do so, however, the children had to be given the relevant strategy for approaching the tasks. Bryant suggested that the poor performance given by children on such tasks was due to misunderstanding the problem itself and also what it was that the experimenter was asking them to do. Once these points were explained and the child was given adequate guidance even very young children could learn to solve problems.

The road crossing task can be thought of as a problem solving situation. Rarely are any two road crossings identical because of the changes which occur in the road environment—vehicles move. Some sort of logical reasoning is important in ordering information, selecting relevant information and subsequently using this as a basis for action. In the light of the above studies on logical reasoning it is not surprising that children sustain more road accidents than do adults. It is interesting here to remember that observation studies of road crossing behaviour have indeed shown that children adopt a different and more simple strategy than that used by adults. The strategy adopted by the elderly, however, is more difficult to reconcile in terms of the development of logical reasoning.

Road crossing

The final stage in the task is the act of crossing the road. At its most simple it involves merely the motor activity of walking, but it can be more complex. Older and Grayson (1974) point out that in heavy traffic sequential crossings can take place. In such crossings, the total road area is sub-divided into smaller units and only part of the road is crossed at any one time. Negotiating traffic in this way involves a series of observations, judgements, decisions and sometimes avoidance responses. Adult pedestrians, are more frequently observed adopting this type of behaviour than are children. Grayson (1975b) in his observation study of pedestrians in a variety of situations shows that the difference in strategies between adults and children extends into this final stage in the road crossing task. Children tend to walk across the road at right angles whilst adults frequently cross diagonally. In addition children are more likely to run across the road. Adults display what seems like dangerous behaviour. They are more likely to start crossing before the road is clear, moving into the road closely behind the passing vehicle. Far from being the dangerous manoeuvre it first appears, this is a very efficient one because it maximizes the time before the arrival of the next vehicle. Adults then, may choose smaller gaps in traffic in which to cross, but they effectively have more time in which to make the crossing.

Figure 2.2 illustrates this point. Grayson concluded that the major difference between children and adults lies in how the stages in the road crossing task are put together rather than in differences in the individual stages. The behaviour of children can be considered to be inefficient in terms of the criteria described above, but it is far better according to the criteria laid down for safe road crossing. Children's behaviour is more like that advocated by road safety

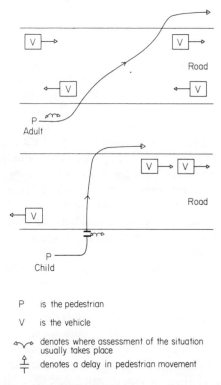

P   is the pedestrian

V   is the vehicle

denotes where assessment of the situation
usually takes place

denotes a delay in pedestrian movement

Figure 2.2 Road-crossing strategies in
adults and children

education literature than is that of adults. In fact, the literature is designed specifically to discourage the adoption of adult strategies by young children. It is in this final stage of the road crossing task that the majority of accidents take place because it is here that the pedestrian moves into that part of the road designed for vehicle usage. However, the reasons for such accidents may well lie in the operations involved in previous stages: road crossing itself is totally dependent on these prior events. The time taken in the execution of stages 1 to 5 (Figure 2.1) is seldom more than a few seconds and is often less than the total time taken in the execution of stage 6. In stage 6, however, the pedestrian is most at risk because he/she is operating in that part of the environment designed for vehicles. A pedestrian has to negotiate roads in order to get from one place to another. The only choice involved is *when* and *where* to cross the road.

Variables influencing the stages

This section is concerned with the variables which influence the road crossing task. Since it is virtually impossible to isolate every factor involved, discussion centres on the variables most important to the execution of the task. This approach also allows for a summary of our present state of knowledge on pedestrian behaviour.

The variable which has attracted most research is that of age. Age differences have been found in the execution of each stage in the road crossing task. In addition, it has been shown that the overall road crossing behaviour of children is different from that of adults (cf. Routledge, Repetto-Wright and Howarth, 1976). Similarly the behaviour of elderly pedestrians differs from that of other adults (cf. Grayson, 1980). Despite these findings, which all point to the fact that adults between 15 and 59 years of age are better equipped for coping with the pedestrian task than are younger and older groups, age differences in behaviour alone are not sufficient to explain why children and the elderly are represented disproportionately in the accident statistics. The situation is very complex. According to road safety rules, children and the elderly display more 'safe' road crossing behaviour than do adults in general. However, this seems to be a compensating behaviour. Studies of perception and judgements indicate that the high-risk pedestrian accident groups need to adopt this approach in order to compensate for the fact that they are not such efficient information processors as are adults. Whether it would be possible or even desirable to train children to use a more efficient crossing strategy is a moot point. Specialists in road safety education tend to opt for a more conservative training scheme, beginning with keeping the child away from the roadway and culminating with the sophisticated adult strategy. There are many intermediary items each graded for use with children of varying ages (Sheppard, 1980). These integrated road safety schemes are of recent innovation and not enough research has yet been carried out to ascertain their value in relation to road accidents.

Sex of child is a variable which has been shown to relate to child pedestrian behaviour. Salvatore (1974) found sex differences in his study of speed estimation. In this study the effect of sex alone was difficult to isolate, however, because of the many other confounding variables involved. Sandels (1975) suggested that more boys than girls behaved in an *unsafe* way in relation to traffic. Behaviour was designated as unsafe if, for example, pedestrians ran into the road, did not look and so on. Finlayson (1972) in a study using filmed observations of children on school journeys also concluded that the poor behaviour was more often exhibited by boys than girls, using similar criteria. Sex has been found to be related to exposure as well as to behaviour. Routledge *et al.* (1974b) in their brief review of exposure studies, concluded that there was only a slight difference between the rates of exposure for boys and girls. In the study by Chapman *et al.* (1980), however, boys up to the age of 17 were found in the traffic environment significantly more frequently than girls. Once in this environment the activity patterns of the two groups were similar. In general, most studies of road behaviour have been unable to find sex differences in behaviour of a sufficient magnitude to account for the very real difference in accident rates between boys and girls. In terms of adult pedestrian behaviour little research effort has been directed towards sex differences.

Another variable likely to affect pedestrian behaviour is personality. Studies by Krall (1953) and Manheimer and Mellinger (1967) concentrated on the characteristics of child accident repeaters, but these studies tell us little about how personality characteristics affect pedestrian behaviour *per se*. The study by Finlayson (1972), however, attempted to relate observed road behaviour to personality factors. She suggested that in children aged five to ten years personality factors such as *tension* and *excitability* corresponded to unsafe or unpredictable behaviour. The somewhat subjective classification of behaviour and relatively small sample used in this study reduce the impact of these findings. In addition, Eysenck (1962) suggested that personality factors such as extraversion, also relate to both driver and pedestrian behaviour. Personality is an important factor in behaviour in general, and probably therefore has a part to play in pedestrian behaviour, but so far the links established have been tenuous. Even if the effect was more rigorously supported, exactly what use could be made of such findings in increasing pedestrian safety is difficult to imagine.

The social environment of a pedestrian engaged in the crossing task is an important influencing variable (see Chapter 7). Grayson (1975b) showed that children in groups made fewer head movements, had a shorter kerb delay and generally did not exhibit such a high degree of safe pedestrian behaviour as did individual children. Michalik (cited in the OECD report on education, 1978b) and Dipietro and King also pointed to differences between group and individual behaviour. Attention is yet another important variable in pedestrian performance. Studies of both accidents and behaviour have indicated that lack of attention is often shown by children. Grayson (1975a) in his accident survey showed that 39 per cent of the children studied had not looked at all before crossing the road. This is an example of lack of attention and is likely to be similar to the *unsafe, unpredictable* and *heedless* behaviour described in other studies. If a child is involved in playing a game in the traffic environment it is very likely that he/she will display some sort of lack of attention to the road crossing task if required to cross the road during the game. The term *attention* is used in relation to pedestrian behaviour in a general way, rather than the more rigorous psychological use of the term.

The effect of countermeasures for pedestrian safety such as propaganda, legislation, environmental measures and education all have an effect on pedestrian safety. These areas of study are all discussed elsewhere in this volume. It is sufficient here to point to their influence on other variables important to pedestrian behaviour; for example, knowledge, past experience and attitudes. A note of caution must however be applied: although these factors are important, none of them has a one-to-one relationship with behaviour in the natural environment. A high level of knowledge of safe behaviour does not necessarily equate with actual performance. As Schioldborg (1974) pointed out, children's knowledge of safe pedestrian behaviour is considerably better than either behaviour *per se*, or the accident statistics would suggest.

Lastly, a group of less concrete variables is also important to pedestrian behaviour. Firth (1975) carried out a study of children's conceptualizations of road safety. She showed that children up to the age of 14 years seemed to attach very little importance to road safety in a free-response situation. The children were invited to make up a story telling an alien everything about roads so that he could 'find his way about safely' next day. Safety was mentioned only briefly by the children involved in the study. This lack of emphasis may be related to the fact that children have only a limited grasp of cause and effect. Bobroff (1960) showed that children up to 10 years of age could follow the rules of a game, but did not fully comprehend the goal and function of the rules. They did not, for example, appear to realize the extent to which the rules governed the behaviour of participants. This factor has not been studied in a pedestrian behaviour context but it could be very important to it. In a similar way, the awareness and perception of hazard by pedestrians could have implications for road behaviour. Martin and Heimstra (1973), found that perception of hazard in children was not well developed. In addition hazard perception was found to be influenced by many other factors. Unfortunately this study made use of only one road scene in the stimuli, and the response required from these children was a simple sorting response into somewhat arbitrarily defined categories of hazard.

IMPLICATIONS FOR THE FUTURE

The last section summarized our current state of knowledge of pedestrian behaviour in terms of the stages involved and the variables affecting those stages. Subdividing the pedestrian task into its component parts in this way enables us to identify more readily those areas where our knowledge is scant and it also illustrates just how complex pedestrian behaviour is. Firstly, the review shows obvious gaps where information about operations and stages is non-existent, of a mediocre quality or insufficient to allow for firm conclusions to be drawn. For example, research evidence on the perception, judgement and decision stages is superficial. In addition, exactly how these abilities operate in the context of road crossing is intuitive rather than proven.

Future research in these areas should, where possible, be directed towards the actions required by the pedestrian. It is only in this way that maximum value will be achieved from them. Studies should be concerned with *why* child pedestrian behaviour is different from that of adult pedestrians. Is it because the child pedestrian is compensating for a deficiency in his/her processing ability, or is there some other reason? In the same way it is important to investigate *how* and *why* certain variables affect the road crossing task. Simply to point out that they do, with little or no reference to the mechanics involved, cannot lead to a full understanding of the situation. Other factors which could well be important in pedestrian behaviour—for example, safety motivation, attitudes towards road safety and accident awareness—have virtually been ignored in the past. To continue to ignore them would result in an incomplete picture of the pedestrian. It may be that the influence of age and sex on these variables could go some way towards explaining the difference in accident rates of the different groups.

The complexity of pedestrian behaviour is readily apparent. No one study to date has effectively summarized all the skills and abilities involved. Pedestrian research is, in relative terms, a fairly new field of study, but it is now time to take stock of exactly what has been gained and what can be hoped for in the future. Grayson (1980) in a paper concerned specifically with elderly pedestrians suggested that in the past there has been too much conjecture and attempts have been made to find simple answers to our very complex situation. He concluded that future research should go back to first principles and pay greater attention to problem definition. These statements apply equally well to the whole of the pedestrian population.

It has been pointed out that the primary goal of pedestrian behaviour research is to reduce the number and severity of road accidents. How far has the research to date achieved this aim? The answer is that no study of pedestrian behaviour has been able to account for why certain types of accident are more common than others or why some groups of pedestrians are represented disproportionately in the accident statistics. The reasons for this lack of success are numerous. For example it may be because the measurements of behaviour at present used in observation studies are not adequate. A combination of measures may be more informative as may a more qualitative approach to behavioural assessment. Another reason involves the fact that accidents and normal behaviour may be unrelated. It is therefore unsound to seek to validate the study of pedestrian behaviour solely with reference to accidents. A third possibility is that studying pedestrian behaviour in isolation can never provide the answer to the accident problem. The pedestrian does not function in a vacuum so it may be that studying the interactions between pedestrians and vehicles may be a more fruitful line of research. Increasing interest in the study of pedestrian/vehicle conflicts should throw some light on this area. Pedestrian behaviour research, then, has so far provided few real answers to the questions posed by accident statistics. On the other hand neither have exposure studies. Should pedestrian behaviour be ignored in the future?

Firth (1980) suggested that pedestrian behaviour research is important in its own right. She argued that the apparent total reliance on accident statistics found to date has unnecessarily limited the field of study. It has effectively perpetuated a fragmented and often intuitive approach to pedestrian behaviour. In order to overcome these problems it is necessary to put a new perspective on the research. First of all it is necessary to develop a meaningful and integrated research framework including all aspects of pedestrian research. Future priorities for investigation of the present gaps in our knowledge can then be assessed. Using such an approach may well incidentally uncover information about accident causation. Without an overall systematic approach, future research will only provide partial answers to questions of great social importance. As Russam (1977) pointed out, a large part of the road layout is likely to remain virtually unchanged for several years to come. We should therefore try to learn as much as possible about these roads and road users.

REFERENCES

Avery, G. C. (1974). The capacity of young children to cope with the traffic system: a review. Traffic Accident Research Unit, Department of Motor Transport, New South Wales, Australia.

Belmont, J. M., and Butterfield, E. C. (1969). The relations of short-term memory to development and intelligence. In L. P. Lipsitt and H. W. Reese (Eds.), *Advances in Child Development and Behavior*, Volume 4, 29–82. New York: Academic Press.

Bobroff, A. (1960). The stages of maturation in socialized thinking and in ego development of two groups of children. *Child Development*, **31**, 321–338.

Bryant, P. (1974). *Perception and Understanding in Young Children*. London: Methuen.

Chapman, A. J., Foot, H. C., and Wade, F. M. (1980). Children at play. In D. J. Oborne and J. A. Levis (Eds.), *Human Factors in Transport Research*, Volume 2, *User Factors: Comfort, the Environment and Behaviour*. London: Academic Press.

Department of Transport, (1980). *Road Accidents Great Britain 1978*. London: Her Majesty's Stationery Office.

Dipietro, C. M., and King, L. E. (1970). Pedestrian gap acceptance. *Highway Research Record*, **308**, 80–91.

England, E. (1976). Children's strategies for road crossing in an urban environment. Unpublished Master of Science Dissertation, University of Salford, United Kingdom.

Eysenck, H. J. (1962). The personality of drivers and pedestrians. *Medicine, Science and the Law*, **3**, 416–423.

Finlayson, H. M. (1972). Children's road behaviour and personality. *British Journal of Educational Psychology*, **42**, 225–232.

Firth, D. E. (1973). The road safety aspects of the Tufty Club. *Department of the Environment, Transport and Road Research Laboratory, Laboratory Report 604*. Crowthorne: TRRL.

Firth, D. E. (1975). Roads and road safety—descriptions given by four hundred children. *Department of the Environment, Transport and Road Research Laboratory, Supplementary Report 138 UC*. Crowthorne: TRRL.

Firth, D. E. (1979). Children's use of crossing facilities. *Traffic Education*, **4**. 18–20.

Firth, D. E. (1980). Methodological problems in pedestrian research. In D. J. Oborne and J. A. Levis (Eds.), *Human Factors in Transport Research*, Volume 2, *User Factors: Comfort, the Environment and Behaviour*. London: Academic Press.

Fisk, A., and Cliffe, H. (1975). The effects of teaching the Green Cross Code to young children. *Department of the Environment, Transport and Road Research Laboratory, Supplementary Report 168 UC*. Crowthorne: TRRL.

Gibson, J. J. (1968). *The Senses Considered as Perceptual Systems*. London: Allen and Unwin.

Gorges, R., Bauerfeld, F., and Schlägel, T. (1976). Examination of traffic behaviour of children at the age of 5 and 7. *Zeitschrift für Verkehrserziehung*, March.

Grayson, G. B. (1975a). The Hampshire child pedestrian accident study. *Department of the Environment, Transport and Road Research Laboratory, Laboratory Report 668*. Crowthorne: TRRL.

Grayson, G. B. (1975b). Observations of pedestrian behaviour at four sites. *Department of the Environment, Transport and Road Research Laboratory, Laboratory Report 670*. Crowthorne: TRRL.

Grayson, G. B. (1980). The elderly pedestrian. In D. J. Oborne and J. A. Levis (Eds.), *Human Factors in Transport Research*, Volume 2, *User Factors: Comfort, the Environment and Behaviour*. London: Academic Press.

Grayson, G. B., and Firth, D. E. (1972). A conceptual framework for child pedestrian research. *Department of the Environment, Transport and Road Research Laboratory, Unpublished Technical Note 748*. Crowthorne: TRRL.

Guttinger, V. A. (1976). Veiligheid van kinderen in woonwijken, ded 2: toepassing van de konflictmethode in een veldonderzoek. Leiden: Nederlands Instituut voor Praeventieve Geneeskunde TNO.

Heimstra, N. W., Nichols, J., and Martin, G. (1969). An experimental methodology for analysis of child pedestrian behaviour. *Pediatrics Supplement*, **44**, 832–838.

Howarth, C. I., Routledge, D. A., and Repetto-Wright, R. (1974). An analysis of road accidents involving child pedestrians. *Ergonomics*, **17**, 319–330.

Jacobs, G. D. (1966). Pedestrian behaviour on a length of road containing guardrails. *Traffic Engineering and Control*, **7**, 556–561.

Jacobs, G. D., and Wilson, D. C. (1967). A study of pedestrian risk in crossing busy roads in four towns. *Ministry of Transport, Road Research Laboratory, Laboratory Report 106*. Crowthorne: RRL.

Krall, V. (1953). Personality characteristics of accident repeating children. *Journal of Abnormal and Social Psychology*, **48**, 99–107.

Kroj, G., and Pfafferott, I. (1975). Empirische Grundlegung der Verkehrserziehung. *Zeitschrift für Verkehrserziehung, September*, 5–15.

Limbourg, N., and Günther, R. (1975). Dimensions of children's traffic environment. *Zeitschrift für Verkehrssicherheit*, **21**.

Liss, P. H., and Haith, M. H. (1970). The speed of visual processing in children and adults: effects of backward and forward masking. *Perception and Psychophysics*, **8**, 396–398.

Lovell, K., Kellett, V. L., and Moorhouse, E. (1962). The growth of the concept of speed: a comparative study. *Journal of Child Psychology and Psychiatry*, **3**, 68–96.

Lovemark, O. (1969). Method for the planning of pedestrian traffic systems in mixed street. *PLANFOR Report Number 16*, Helsingborg, Sweden.

Maccoby, E. E. (1969). The development of stimulus selection. In J. P. Hill (Ed.) *Minnesota Symposium on Child Psychology*, Volume 3, 68–96. London: Oxford University Press.

Mackie, A. M., and Older, S. J. (1965). Study of pedestrian risk in crossing busy roads in London inner suburbs. *Traffic Engineering and Control*, **7**, 376–380.

Manheimer, D. I., and Mellinger, G. D. (1967). Personality characteristics of the child accident repeater. *Child Development*, **38**, 491–513.

Martin, G., and Heimstra N. W. (1973). Perception of hazard by children. *Journal of Safety Research*, **5**, 238–246.

Michalik, C. (unpublished). An empirical study on pre-school road safety education. Cited in *Organisation for Economic Co-operation and Development Special Research Group on Pedestrian Safety*, 1978a.

Moore, R. L., and Older, S. J. (1965). Pedestrians and motor vehicles are compatible in today's world. *Traffic Engineering*, **35**, 20–23 and 52–59.

Munsch, G. (1973). Wege zur Bildung des Verkehrssinnes. Allegmeiner, Deutscher Automobil Club, in der *Schriftenreihe Jugendverkehrserziehung*, Heft.

Older, S. J., and Grayson, G. B. (1974). Perception and decision in the pedestrian task. *Department of the Environment, Transport and Road Research Laboratory, Supplementary Report 49 UC*. Crowthorne: TRRL.

Organisation for Economic Co-operation and Development Special Research Group on Pedestrian Safety (1977). *Chairman's Report and Report of Sub-Group I—The Pedestrian's Road Environment. Department of the Environment, Transport and Road Research Laboratory*. Crowthorne: TRRL.

Organisation for Economic Co-operation and Development Special Research Group on Pedestrian Safety (1978a). *Chairman's Report and Report of Sub-Group II—Road Safety Education. Department of the Environment, Transport and Road Research Laboratory*. Crowthorne: TRRL.

Organisation for Economic Co-operation and Development Special Research Group on Pedestrian Safety (1978b). *Chairman's Report and Report of Sub-Group III—Mass Media Communications for Pedestrian Safety. Department of the Environment, Transport and Road Research Laboratory*. Crowthorne: TRRL.

Pagett, S., and Waller, P. (1975). *The Evaluation of the North Carolina K-9 Traffic Safety Curriculum*. The University of North Carolina Highway Research Center, Chapel Hill, North Carolina, USA.

Piaget, J. (1953). *Origins of Intelligence in the Child*. London: Routledge and Kegan Paul.

Preston, B. (1972). Statistical analysis of child pedestrian accidents in Manchester and Salford. *Accident Analysis and Prevention*, **4**, 323–332.

Rennie, A. M., and Wilson, J. R. (1980). How drivers respond to pedestrians and vice versa. In D. J. Oborne and J. A. Levis (Eds.), *Human Factors in Transport Research*, Volume 2, *User Factors: Comfort, the Environment and Behaviour*. London: Academic Press.

Routledge, D. A. (1975). The behaviour of child pedestrians: an approach to the problem of child pedestrian accidents. *Unpublished Doctoral Dissertation*, University of Nottingham, United Kingdom.

Routledge, D. A., Repetto-Wright, R., and Howarth, C. I. (1974a). A comparison of interviews and observation to obtain measures of children's exposure to risk as pedestrians. *Ergonomics*, **17**, 623–638.

Routledge, D. A., Repetto-Wright, R., and Howarth, C. I. (1974b). The exposure of young children to accident risk as pedestrians. *Ergonomics*, **17**, 457–480.

Routledge, D. A., Repetto-Wright, R., and Howarth, C. I. (1976). The development of road crossing skill by child pedestrians. In A. S. Hakkert (Ed.), *Proceedings of the International Conference on Pedestrian Safety*, Volume 1, 7C1–7C9. Haifa: Michlol.

Russam, K. (1975). Road safety of children in the United Kingdom. *Department of the Environment, Transport and Road Research Laboratory, Laboratory Report 678*. Crowthorne: TRRL.

Russam, K. (1977). The psychology of children in traffic. In R. H. Jackson (Ed.), *Children, the Environment and Accidents*. London: Pitman.

Sandels, S. (1970). Young children in traffic. *British Journal of Educational Psychology*, **40**, 111–116.

Sandels, S. (1974). Why are children injured in traffic? Can we prevent child accidents in traffic? *Skandia Report II*. Stockholm: Sweden.

Sandels, S. (1975). *Children in Traffic*. London: Elek.

Salvatore, S. (1974). The ability of elementary and secondary school children to sense oncoming car velocity. *Journal of Safety Research*, **6**, 118–123.

Schioldborg, P. (1974). Barn trafikk og trafikkopplaering; en analyse av Barnas Trafikklubb, *Pjychological Institute*, University of Oslo, Norway.

Sheppard, D. (1980). The development of methods for teaching pedestrian skills to children. In D. J. Oborne and J. A. Levis (Eds.), *Human Factors in Transport Research*, Volume 2, *User Factors: Comfort, the Environment and Behaviour*. London: Academic Press.

Snyder, M. B., and Knoblauch, R. L. (1971). Pedestrian safety: the identification of precipitating factors and possible countermeasures. *Operations Research Report Number FH. 11-7312*. Washington DC: United States Department of Transportation.

Todd, J. E., and Walker, A. (1980). *People as Pedestrians*. London: Her Majesty's Stationery Office.

Transport and Road Research Laboratory (1972). Accidents to elderly pedestrians. *Department of the Environment, Transport and Road Research Laboratory, Leaflet 323*. Crowthorne: TRRL.

van der Molen, H. H. (1975). Charakkerisierung and Auswertung von verkehr sur-terrichtsexperimenten mit kindem. *Werkqroep verkehrskunde Report. VK-75-09*. University of Groningen, Holland.

Wade, F. M., Foot, H. C., and Chapman, A. J. (1979). The social environment and child pedestrian accidents. *Learning*, **1**, 39–40 and 48.

Wiener, E. L. (1968). The elderly pedestrian: response to an enforcement campaign. *Traffic Safety Research Review*, **12**, 100–110.

Wilson, D. G., and Grayson, G. B. (1980). Age-related differences in the road crossing behaviour of adult pedestrians. *Department of the Environment, Transport and Road Research Laboratory, Laboratory Report 933*. Crowthorne: TRRL.

Zeigler, H. P., and Leibowitz, H. (1957). Apparent visual size as a function of distance for children and adults. *American Journal of Psychology*, **70**, 106–109.

Pedestrian Accidents
Edited by A. J. Chapman, F. M. Wade and H. C. Foot
© 1982, John Wiley & Sons Ltd.

Chapter 3

Pedestrian Education

A. Singh

The problem of pedestrian safety is one of considerable magnitude and growing public concern. Many public safety and health sources have developed action programmes with a view to improving pedestrians' safety, and a number of primary accident prevention efforts have been mounted. These efforts, for the most part, fit into the general categories of legal, engineering and educational programmes, including face-to-face and mass media communications. Historically, nearly all the national and local efforts have taken the form of (1) legislation and enforcement with regard to mandatory and prohibited behaviour, or (2) technical improvements to the pedestrian's road environment (pedestrian crossings: locations, forms, signs, signals, and markings, lighting, etc.). Pedestrian fatalities, however, have not been manifestly reduced, suggesting that the legal and engineering approaches are not sufficient.

The overwhelming majority of pedestrian accidents can be ascribed to human error. In fact, the records suggest that 9 out of 10 accidents come under this group. Successful prevention thus includes the establishment of educational and training programmes which provide knowledge, skills, values, beliefs and attitudes which help people develop safe pedestrian practices. Educational and mass media communications programmes for the promotion of pedestrian safety are a rational alternative or complement to the legal approach and would seem to be a feasible means of improving pedestrian safety. The critical question, then, is whether these can be or have been shown to result in a reduction of accidents.

It is our intention to review and discuss existing educational and mass media communications programmes designed to modify road user behaviour, attitudes and knowledge so that pedestrian safety is promoted through an improvement in the behaviour of road users. While at present we know that many types of programmes and philosophies exist, we rarely know their effects since only a few have been evaluated (see Chapter 4). The organizer of a programme for pedestrian safety is usually in the position of having to choose a method on the basis of personal preference, or current policy with no indication of whether it will produce the desired effects.

Nearly all educational programmes designed to influence the behaviour of pedestrians are directed at young children. Programmes aimed at improving adult pedestrians' behaviour are found within the framework of pedestrian safety campaigns. By presenting relevant research in this field, and analysing the known effects of various components of educational and informational activities, pedestrian safety educators may have a more secure foundation on which to design or choose their programmes.

PEDESTRIAN EDUCATION IN SCHOOLS AND AT HOME

Although pedestrian safety education does not have to be seen as an exclusively school-based venture, there are good grounds for regarding the educational system as the major potential source of information. This stems from the unique role of the school as the single agent to which everybody in society has access. It is also true that it is often easier to change the habits of institutions than those of individuals so that to see all schools giving pedestrian safety instruction is a viable goal, whereas to see all parents instructing their children is not. Pedestrian safety education, however, is neither recognized nor recognizable in the school curriculum in the sense that mathematics or science is recognized and recognizable. By tradition, it is the headteacher who decides the curriculum in the school and consequently it is he/she who decides whether or not road safety education is taught.

In 1968 a survey into the extent and type of road safety education undertaken in schools was carried out by the Transport and Road Research Laboratory of the Department of Transport with the cooperation of the Department of Education and Science and the Scottish Education Department (Colborne and Sargent, 1971). The survey findings which were based on a random sample of 1,277 primary schools and 936 secondary schools in about a 90 per cent return revealed that only 39 per cent of primary schools and 17 per cent of secondary schools had a planned programme of road safety. The picture was still more gloomy as regards the time set aside specifically for this topic: this happened in just 16 per cent of primary and 4 per cent of secondary schools. In schools where some time was set aside for road safety teaching the time was about half an hour or less per week. A variety of methods for teaching children how to cross roads was used. Six per cent of the primary schools in the sample had Tufty Clubs. The incidental teaching of road safety in primary schools seemed to have occurred in various activities such as craft work, science and projects, but there was no evidence of what proportion of this kind of work was concerned with road safety. Road safety talks given by police, road safety officers and other people to children in primary schools formed a large part of the instruction that did take place. The teachers in the survey schools were on the whole favourably impressed with the talks given by police and road safety officers at their schools: 83 per cent thought that the children had found the talks interesting and 73 per cent thought the talks had been effective. However, the data on preparatory and follow up work in connection with these talks suggest that little was being done to reinforce the work of the visiting speakers.

In 1974 another survey among a random sample of British primary and middle schools was undertaken by the University of Reading to collect up-to-date information about current practices and trends in road safety education curricula (Singh, 1976). From this survey it was found that little change had taken place. Thirty-seven per cent of schools claimed to have included within their school curricula road safety teaching intended to prepare pupils for safe behaviour on the roads. The same percentage of them reported that road safety teaching was done incidentally and 28 per cent were against its inclusion in the normal school curriculum. It was also found that almost all the headteachers thought that the children were interested in talks given by outside speakers and that the talks given by them were effective. The survey revealed that education for safe behaviour on roads occurs in many different ways which can be classified as follows: (1) incidentally in classrooms, morning assembly, playground and elsewhere on the premises; (2) as separate lessons from time to time on specific aspects; (3) as part of integrated work on various topics such as local roads, transportation, and people who assist in the crossing of roads; (4) as a subject in its own right; and (5) as talks and demonstrations by police and road safety officers.

Despite the fact that nearly half of all pedestrian casualties on our roads are children under 15 years of age, we note that the current status of road safety education is dismal. Most schools operate without any clear-cut policy concerning their aims and goals, primarily because of the widely varying attitudes concerning child pedestrian safety. Education for pedestrian safety tends to fall into the 'no man's land' between the school and the home, or within the school, it tends to be everyone's concern but no-one's responsibility.

In her survey of current approaches to road safety education in 239 secondary schools, Stephens (1978) found that topics related to road safety were taught in 56 per cent of schools, but the proportion of schools having a planned programme for teaching it was similar to those found in the survey by Colborne and Sargent (1971).

The situation revealed by these three surveys is that education for pedestrian safety is sporadically implemented according to the goodwill of headteachers, and due to initiatives from particular teachers, or police and road safety officers. Road safety is organized occasionally or systematically in about 70 per cent of primary schools and probably in 50 per cent of secondary schools. About one-third of schools appear to show little interest in road safety education, while in another third the subject is treated seriously, headteacher and staff working together to an agreed overall plan.

Some people take the view that the responsibility for road safety training of children of school age rests with the parents. The majority of headteachers of the schools surveyed in 1968 (Colborne and Sargent, 1971) indicated that they thought parents should play the main part in the road safety of children between the ages of 5 and 11. Only 11 per cent thought the school should play the main part and 10 per cent thought that it should be the responsibility of the police.

That this responsibility is accepted, in the main, was shown in a national survey of 2,125 mothers with children aged between 2 and 8 years (Sadler, 1972). The majority of mothers of children aged 5 to 8 accepted that theirs was the main responsibility for teaching children how to use the roads in safety and most of them had already taught even the youngest children (those aged 2) something about crossing roads. The type of instruction given by the parents varied a little with the age of the child, but hardly at all between children who were or were not able to cross roads by themselves. The pattern of instruction seems to be that at an early age children are taught to cross one or two particular roads at first, but as they grow older they are taught to cross several roads. By the age of 5, the age at which most children start school in the United Kingdom, most mothers will have introduced their children to several different road crossings. There is however a sizeable minority, about a quarter, of children who even by the time they are 8 years of age have still been taught to cross only one or two specific roads. Women with driving-licences seem to place more emphasis on their children stopping at the kerb, walking quickly when crossing the road and crossing away from parked vehicles. However, the most surprising findings of this survey were that 19 per cent of mothers of three-year-old children endeavoured to teach their children to cross very busy roads and 13 per cent thought that their two-year-olds could cross a road which they themselves classed as 'very busy'.

Although parental responsibility for the road safety of children has recently been stressed in a national road safety propaganda campaign, the fact remains that many parents do not always know what or how to teach, no matter how seriously they take their responsibility for teaching their children pedestrian safety. They may not always appear to understand that a child's ability to appreciate training and put it to effective use varies widely with age, temperament and mental attitudes.

AUDIO-VISUAL AND PRINTED PEDESTRIAN EDUCATION MATERIALS

There has been an increase recently in the number of printed and audio-visual materials on pedestrian safety topics; indeed, most pedestrian education programmes utilize one or more of these materials (cf. Colborne, 1971b; Firth, 1973; Nummenmaa, 1970; Nummenmaa, Ruuhilehto and Syvännen, 1975; Nummenmaa, and Syvännen, 1974; Pease and Preston, 1967; Sheppard, 1975a,b) and hence their effectiveness must depend upon them at least indirectly. This makes it of importance to know how well they achieve the objectives set for them—or other objectives.

There has been a number of films and filmstrips specially made for pedestrian safety and packages of slides plus a large number of commercially made feature films. Nearly all have been developed with some sort of pedestrian safety education in mind, but none with any evaluation of how well their objectives are achieved.

A number of curriculum guides have also been developed for classroom use under the supervision of a teacher (cf. Ingram, 1978; Jolly, 1977a,b,c; Lewis, 1979; Schools Council Project (5–13), 1977; Schreiber and Lukin, 1978; Sheppard, 1975a,b). Numerous articles for teachers, police and road safety officers suggest concepts that should be stressed, aspects of presentation which may be helpful, and various methodological approaches. These concepts range from giving the facts about pedestrian safety as they are known and nothing else (e.g. McGivern, 1975; Northern, 1975; Roberts, 1973, 1977) to advising that providing information about pedestrian safety is actually the least important aspect of pedestrian education (e.g. Cain, 1978; Clarke, 1978; Fisk, 1974; Glover, 1976; Jolly, 1977a,b,c; Stokes, 1976). Some reports instruct the teacher on how to think about child pedestrian safety (e.g. Cain, 1978; Darlington, 1977; James, 1978; Turton, 1977); what to include and leave out (e.g. Fisk, 1974, Harries, 1979; James, 1978; Kemp, 1979); and how to conduct a programme (e.g. Chambers, 1976; Darlington, 1976, 1977; Elswood, 1970; Meadows, 1977; Turton, 1977). These and other articles of the same type contain useful ideas for teachers; however, most have undergone no testing procedures and so it is impossible to determine their merits.

Printed materials include: fact sheets briefly describing the hazards of traffic environment; tables listing the various types of pedestrian accident(s); the causes and possible effects of accidents on individuals and society as a whole; long and short pamphlets cautioning about dangers of crossing roads unsafely; books for school children and their parents; study guides for teachers and pupils; a programmed road safety education textbook; work-books for pupils; comics; and so on.

Evaluations of audio-visual and printed materials for pedestrian safety education purposes are rarely attempted at the time of production; moreover, much of this material, especially when on film, is quickly outdated. Fortunately, a few evaluations are now being made of these materials, but the nature of these evaluations is still rather limited.

Studies of films and other audio-visuals

Pease and Preston (1967) carried out an evaluation of a road safety propaganda film *Mary Had a Little Lamb*, produced by the Petroleum Films Bureau. This film had been popular with children of 5 to 7 years for over a decade by the time of the investigation. It is a delightful film, telling the story of a school girl's pet lamb who is nearly run over and so learns the *kerb drill* at school, and is thereafter safe while crossing the road. The kerb drill exemplars in this film face their audience as they look left and right, and hence, as the investigators state, 'Children without well established relational notions of direction may be induced, under such circumstances, to re-adapt a static conception of direction, since the verbalization of direction in the film does not coincide with the direction which a relational child would attribute to the exampler's action' (p. 310). Children (average age, 5 years and 6 months) in the experimental and control groups were tested before and after seeing the film in order to assess their concept of direction as it related to the *kerb drill,* and to observe their behaviour when an imaginary car passed while they were performing the *kerb drill* at the side of a simulated road laid out in the class-room. It was found that seeing the film had not improved children's concepts of directionality and that, to many of them, 'right' and 'left' referred to parts of the environment rather than relations to themselves. When the children were interrupted while performing their *kerb drill* by a supposed car, most of them either continued the *kerb drill* from the point they had reached, or crossed the 'road' without further looking. Before they had seen the film, only 7 out of the 42 children took adequate precautions after the 'car' had passed; but then only 9 children did so afterwards. The difficulty with directions, as explained by the experimenters, was due to the fact that the exemplars in the film faced the audience when performing the *kerb drill* and this added to the children's confusion. They thus concluded that the showing of *Mary Had a Little Lamb* did not significantly affect the ability of children to verbalize the *kerb drill* and that the *kerb drill* was seen by the children mainly as a safety rule to be gone through before crossing.

Studies of films and slides conducted in the University of Tempere (Norway) have also shown that films showing correct pedestrian behaviour can be effective in increasing children's knowledge of pedestrian behaviour. For example, in a study of 6-year-olds by Nummenmaa (1970) one group of children was presented with the film twice in two sessions, a second group saw the film once over four successive days, a third group saw the film twice over four successive days in each of the two weeks, a fourth group saw the slides twice over four successive days in each of the two weeks, and a fifth group was a control group which received no treatment. The evaluation of the films was carried out by means of a knowledge-test film consisting of 50 items of traffic behaviour, and by observing traffic behaviour. Nummenmaa found that children exposed to the film, which presented correct behaviour with careful verbal instructions, displayed greater knowledge and slightly better crossing behaviour in a road crossing test than children who did not see the film.

Encouraged by these results, Nummenmaa and Syvänen (1974) carried out another experiment in which the instructional films and slides were supplemen-ted by practical training of the crossing behaviour on the real road. The experimental group was shown the same instructional films for three successive days. The children were taken to the street, and the same skills were taught there by their parents during the same three successive days. The results on the knowledge and skills tests were similar to those found in the earlier study. The results of the observations made in the children's 'traffic garden' showed that the experimental group was very much better all around and incorrect behaviour was indeed rare in all situations, as compared with the control group. The combination of the film instruction with practical training on real roads carried out by parents has thus been decisive. 'Practically everyone in the experiment', the authors wrote, 'always stopped at the kerb while only about two thirds of the controls did so. The only feature where the experimental group made mistakes was looking behind before crossing' (p. 160) on which they scored 80 per cent correct, whereas the control group scored 20 per cent correct.

In many respects, the Tempere studies are exemplary, but again, everyday crossing behaviour was not assessed after the training in these studies. Thus, whether the child's pedestrian safety behaviour has changed as a result of the training remains to be investigated objectively: none of the studies discussed here shows that training by films and slides affects everyday crossing behaviour.

Sheppard (1969) studied two road safety films about crossing the road; these were designed for infants (5- to 7-year-olds) by the Royal Society for the Prevention of Accidents (RoSPA). The first film was shown to 23 children, aged from five to five-and-a-half years, and afterwards each child was questioned individually about the film. From their replies, Sheppard concluded that parts of the film were difficult for the children of this age group to understand, and especially the section at the end of the film which attempted to repeat what the children had seen. As a result of these comments, a second film was made by RoSPA and the film was tested by Sheppard on children of approximately 5 years of age. The results showed that the second film was suitable for children of this age. Thus, the first film was discarded and the second film, entitled *Crossing the Road*, was made available for use in schools.

McGarvie, Davies, and Sheppard (1980) conducted an evaluation of a relatively long road safety film for children of primary school age. 'The film, *Mind How You Go* was produced by the Central Office of Information for the Department of Transport and features as presenter Valerie Singleton who was, at the time it was issued (in 1973), a children's television personality and who still appears regularly on television' (p. 1). The hero, Graham is 8 years old and the film shows him going to school, the events at school and at a school visit to the zoo and his return home before going to the circus in the evening. The film was shown in three primary schools to groups of 12 children at a time. The age groups were 6 to 10 years. In all 90 boys and 90 girls were interviewed separately. The results showed that nearly all the children found this film very enjoyable. All of them knew it was a road safety film and many mentioned the *Green Cross Code* specifically. However, there was some confusion about the film techniques and conventions for showing Graham turning into a clown in his imagination and recalling events that had occurred earlier in the day. A large proportion of children did not see the safety implications of these points. McGarvie *et al.* thus concluded that it would be useful if 'the teacher notes could stress the necessity for ensuring that children have grasped these essential messages: discussions or follow up activities are already advocated in the notes and these could be an appropriate way to do this' (p. 14).

This study does provide valuable information on the reaction to a road safety film *Mind How You Go* but tells little about its direct effects. Unfortunately, no information is available to determine changes in knowledge level or road crossing behaviour.

Colborne (1971b) carried out two experiments to compare different methods of training children aged seven in safe road behaviour. The road crossing task was: (1) crossing well away from parked vehicles; and (2) the correct way to cross between two parked vehicles, when there was no alternative place to cross. In the first experiment, two main methods of instruction were used, one consisting of the showing of two slides of a little girl crossing a road in which vehicles were parked, and the second making use of small model pedestrians and cars. Before and after the instruction all the children were tested in a 'traffic garden'—a miniature road layout enclosed by a fence where there was no traffic other than bicycles, and toy go-karts, marked out in one way systems, crossroads, roundabouts, etc. with small scale traffic signs and overhead traffic lights. The 'after-tests' were administered 1–2 weeks after the instruction. The results of the tests of correct crossing between parked cars showed that slides were more effective than miniature models. It was also found that both teaching methods produced an improvement in so far as the children crossed farther away from the parked car after training. However, the investigator failed to establish which method was the more effective.

In her second experiment, Colborne compared the results of teaching children to cross at a junction controlled by traffic lights, by practical instruction in a traffic garden and by theoretical instruction in the classroom. Her 110 child subjects were tested individually in the traffic garden approximately one week after training. The children who had been trained in the traffic garden did better in a practical test than children trained by theoretical instruction in the classroom. The results of a picture test which the children were asked to do approximately three months after the tests suggested that the children trained by the more practical method had remembered the training better.

Cyster (1980) conducted a pilot study on the use of video-recording in traffic education in primary schools and found that seeing themselves and their friends on television and their ability two or three weeks later to recount in detail what they had seen had created a deep and lasting impression in young children aged 5 to 11. Road safety officers who reported the extent and methods of video-recording use for teaching road safety in primary schools in England and Wales indicated that showing local scenes and seeing themselves and their friends on video-tape have a great impact on young children (Cyster, 1980). Although the pilot study is still in progress, available results suggest the potential value of video-recording to the teaching of road safety in primary schools.

Colborne and Sheppard (1966) studied the meaningfulness of a traffic poster aimed at children aged 5 to 7 years. The purpose of the poster was to indicate that the child should not cross the road, even if he/she saw his/her mother on the other side. About one-half of the seven-year-olds understood the message, but only a few of the five-year-olds. When the original poster was broken into a sequence of five different pictures, the message was grasped better by children of both ages. However, this work did not deal with actual behaviour.

A study by Firth (1973) of a *Tufty* pedestrian safety poster also showed that some children had difficulty in correctly interpreting a road situation shown in an oblique view, from above, though such a design might have been depicted to pose fewer interpretation problems than a composite plan view. For road safety propaganda aimed at young children, Firth wrote, 'Tufty would be useful because he is at least popular with the children and he is well-known in relation to road safety. This would make Tufty a useful medium for propaganda aimed at this age group' (p. 23). The study also showed that children as young as 5 years are quite capable of discussing pictorial learning aids and thereby obtaining more information from them. Firth (1973) thus suggested that pictorial learning aids will have greater educational impact if they are designed taking children's preferences into account as well as basing them on what children can understand. She, like Vernon (1962), concluded that teachers should discuss or preferably teach the content of the pictorial learning aids to children under 7 years of age, otherwise the posters would be ignored. Sheppard (1975), in her study of children's comprehension of road safety posters and pictorial aids, also found that, without explanation, comprehension was often very limited, particularly for children aged 4 and 5 years. Children found themselves confused by dotted lines to represent paths taken by objects or people, and with the over-use of inessential detail. They understood the posters using oblique viewpoints and realistic drawings better than those using aerial views and unrealistic drawings.

Davies (1979) investigated the acceptance and use of the *Green Cross Man Wallchart* which was distributed to schools as part of a campaign in 1976 to enhance children's safety on the roads. The Wallchart features the *Green Cross Man* (GXM) and presents in comic-strip form the sequence of actions in the *Green Cross Code*. Forty-three per cent of teachers who had seen the Wallchart said they had used it. The reactions of the teachers to the Wallchart and the teaching notes were favourable, but there were criticisms of the use of capital letters. One-third of teachers of 5- to 7-year-old children said that the words used would not be within the vocabulary of the children they were teaching. Only about half of the teachers who had seen the Wallchart knew that there were accompanying notes for teachers. The study concluded that despite some of the criticism made about it, the Wallchart was used extensively in schools and its arrival had stimulated a lot of teachers to do road safety teaching. However, there was no assessment of children's reactions to the Green Cross Man Chart, nor its effects on their road crossing behaviour.

The Tufty Club materials

The 'Tufty Club' was founded in 1961 by RoSPA to promote pedestrian safety among children. Initially it was intended for children of less than five years of age, but, since its early beginnings, it has attracted many children of primary school age. Tufty is a squirrel who figures in story books, greeting cards, colouring sheets and safety pamphlets. With his animal friends he becomes involved in many dangerous situations in which he nearly always sets a good example of safe behaviour, in contrast to his playmates.

A small-scale study was carried out by Colborne (1971a) to investigate the claims that young children would not accept an animal character and that Tufty is therefore unsuitable as a pedestrian safety symbol. The study was confined to the pre-school age group which was questioned about animal characters and their activities. She found that all but one of the children identified Tufty by name from a painting, and Tufty's mother was also identified. When the children were asked what Tufty was doing and then what Tufty's mother was doing, and why, all the children said that Tufty was running into the road, many of them implying great disapproval of this. All but one said that Tufty's mother was catching or holding him, and explanations for this ranged from the vague (e.g. 'he's naughty') to the specific (e.g. 'he might get run over'). Colborne concluded that the use of an animal character to convey one basic item of pedestrian safety had been successful even though a complete understanding of the intended message was rare.

Firth (1973) provided a detailed evaluation of printed Tufty stories for teaching pedestrian safety to children belonging to Tufty Clubs. She investigated, among other things, how many people had heard of the Club and how they came to know about it. The opinions on aspects of pedestrian safety of 203 mothers of members were compared with those of 283 mothers of non-members. The pedestrian safety knowledge of member and non-member children was assessed in interviews, using a model technique, and the opinions of road safety officers, Tufty Club leaders, playgroup leaders, and headteachers who said that they had read a Tufty book were also investigated. A major part of the study consisted of comparing children's responses before and after the Tufty book was read to them by their mothers. Results showed no significant difference between the member and non-member children on a behavioural test of crossing. Neither were there any within-group differences when the children ($N = 54$) were asked to show how a model of a boy and a model of Tufty would cross a model road. There was, however, some evidence to show that members could understand and remember the pedestrian safety messages included in the available stories. Headteachers, road safety officers and playgroup leaders had generally favourable opinions of the Tufty materials but some of them expressed doubts about the use of animals to convey road safety messages in stories. The children's road crossing knowledge improved significantly after the book had been read to them.

The Green Cross Code

Because of changes in the volume and speed of traffic together with the criticisms that children tended to learn the *kerb drill* by rote and tended to misinterpret it, research at the Transport and Road Research Laboratory was carried out to develop a new crossing code (Sargent and Sheppard, 1974). Some 400 mothers of young children, 227 road safety officers and 177 teachers were asked to indicate the relative importance for safety they would ascribe to each of the 20 items concerned with crossing the road. There was considerable agreement about priorities and, based on this, some alternative forms of a new crossing code were devised. A total of 294 children aged 6 were questioned at the side of the road to see whether they could understand the terms 'traffic', 'kerb', 'pavement' and other items.

As a result of these two exercises, the *Green Cross Code* was drawn up, with its six carefully-phrased injunctions:

> *First find a safe place to cross, then stop.*
> *Stand on the pavement near the kerb.*
> *Look all round for traffic and listen.*
> *If traffic is coming, let it pass, look all round again.*
> *When there is no traffic near, walk straight across the road.*
> *Keep looking and listening for traffic while you cross.*

The code was tested with 170 children aged 7 and 8 years at the roadside. They were asked to justify their choice of a safe place to cross, and to say whether they knew of other safe places where one could cross. Their ability to read the Code was also tested. The study concluded 'that given guidance and instruction, children between 7 and 8 years of age would be able to follow the instruction given in the Green Cross Code and they would be able to read it without very much difficulty, but it is possible that even after instruction the task of identifying safe places to cross may still prove very difficult for them' (p. 12). During the three months following the introduction of the *Green Cross Code* in 1971 there was an 11 per cent reduction in child pedestrian casualties, but it is not known to what extent this reduction in accident rate was due to the effective teaching content or due to the intensive nature of the publicity campaign. There were also decrements in adult pedestrian casualties.

Since the publication and launch of the *Green Cross Code* it has been widely used to give the main principles in safe road crossing. Morris (1972) describes the results of interviewing some 600 children on their understanding of road crossing situations. His results indicated that despite the success of the Code there was a continuing need for basic teaching of the Code. Despite the determined efforts to find the best wording by listing alternative phrases for the *Green Cross Code*, Sheppard (1975a) later found that nearly a third of the words in it were incorrectly read, or were not read at all, by 20 per cent of children tested.

Fisk and Cliffe (1975) investigated the effects of the *Green Cross Code* being taught to young children aged 5 to 8 years given by a qualified and practising teacher who was also aware of the complexities of road safety education. There were 3 age groups, 5- to 6-year-olds, 6- to 7-year-olds and 7- to 8-year-olds, and a group of 26 children with an average age of 6 years comprised a no-treatment control group. Each of the 3 experimental groups was taken through the *Green Cross Code* in a lesson lasting approximately 20 minutes. The subject matter was the *Green Cross Code* and it was similar for each group; its introduction and expansion was adjusted to the age and development of the group. Both experimental and control groups received a pre- and post-test on knowledge of the *Green Cross Code* and road crossing behaviour; and, as expected, the experimental groups showed an improvement in road crossing and knowledge, but the improvement was not statistically significant for the younger children. These results led Fisk and Cliffe to conclude that either more lessons, at a younger age, are required or a different approach is required in order to achieve any significant improvement in the 5-year-old's road crossing behaviour. They also suggested that practical methods of teaching, on the basis of the *Green Cross Code*, needed to be developed to reach this younger age group. However, it is regrettable that this study made no mention at all of the different teaching methods used to teach the *Green Cross Code* to the 3 experimental groups when the results were discussed.

Kerr (1980), after having discussions with children aged 10 and 11, found that children appeared to know the *Green Cross Code* rules but did not use them. Sheppard (1977) discovered that the majority of the School Crossing Patrols reported that they taught the children how to cross a road safely but not all of them had used the recently developed teaching schemes such as the *Green Cross Code*. This could be, according to Sheppard, 'because they do not favour this Code' (p. 6). Working with infant children, Preston (1980) brought to light a very important failing in the *Green Cross Code* as compared with the old *kerb drill*. The idea that one must always stop, before going into the road is vital, and is not covered by the new Code. Preston thus felt that 'the idea of stopping should not be secondary to a desire to cross the road because many accidents occur when the child inadvertently steps or runs into the road, without any intention of crossing the road' (p. 4). She also discovered that young children were still learning the *Green Cross Code* largely by rote, and did not understand the reasons for the advice. It seems evident that there is a need to conduct further studies on the *Green Cross Code* to find out if the Code needs to be changed.

Pedestrian education programmes

Even though a large number of programmes have been implemented, the number having undergone even a rudimentary evaluation is not more than a few dozen. The number of programmes receiving any sort of published evaluation with the basic features of careful experimentation is probably less than a dozen; those receiving a comparison against a no-treatment control group is no more than six. Even fewer than six have studied effects on road crossing behaviour. Research on pedestrian safety education, especially evaluations, is often not reported in standard scientific journals but is in reports of limited circulation by the Transport and Road Research Laboratory (TRRL), Crowthorne, Berkshire, England.

We all assume that education in fact 'educates'; that is, it achieves its goals of changing knowledge, attitudes and behaviour in a positive manner. Governments and funding organizations (e.g. Schools Council, Nuffield Foundation, Ford Foundation) have required that evaluation be built into grants for educational programmes, but the results are rarely made public. There can be no doubt that evaluation studies using controlled comparisons offer the best hope for finding effective programmes, but these studies can be of several types (see Chapter 4). Some involve comparisons between different educational programmes while others compare a programme group with a 'no-treatment group'—a group which received no formal education programme, although pupils in it may have been exposed to a variety of facts and attitudes about pedestrian safety. Little is known about the nature and quality of this informal education. In the field of pedestrian safety education, all the studies belong to the latter approach. Printed pedestrian education materials are probably more often used than audio-visual materials for teaching children; almost all programmes involve some print reading either by the children or the teachers involved. Unfortunately far fewer results are available for print effectiveness than for films or audio-visuals.

Teaching pedestrian skills—a graded structure

In 1975 Sheppard developed a graded scheme of educational objectives for child pedestrian education with progressive steps matching different stages of children's conceptual development (Sheppard 1975b). The structured scheme of pedestrian teaching, as shown in the Appendix (pp. 103–104), is an example of a scheme consisting of specific objectives in terms of knowledge, abilities and skills, given in great detail for various road and traffic situations. However, at what ages these objectives are to be taught, as Sheppard himself admits, remains to be seen; and much research is still needed in this area. Sheppard's scheme of pedestrian teaching can, nevertheless, be evaluated experimentally as far as its relevance and feasibility are concerned for any particular age group.

Road safety and moral education

Ingram (1978) has developed a road safety programme using the experiences of children as the basis for materials. The *Road Safety and Moral Education* programme provides starting points for work based on pupils' own traffic experiences which were described by children of the ages 5 to 15 in their answers to two requests: '1. Write about a time when you were in or near traffic and you were frightened, angry or unhappy. 2. Write about a time when you were in or near traffic and you did not know the best thing to do. You may draw a picture or diagram if you wish' (p. 26). Ingram selected a number of stories from the survey which were then illustrated and put into books, together with questions and suggested activities. The *Road Safety and Moral Education* programme provides a scheme of work which is a new and useful way of supplementing existing road safety training material. It is a behavioural approach to pedestrian safety education and essentially its rationale is that pedestrian safety education should be related to life experiences, attitudes and values and should be discussed in relation to other moral and social problems. In this sense the material provides an opportunity for an exchange of ideas and experiences between teachers and pupils, the aim of which is to develop among children a more thoughtful and considerate approach to the way they behave and react to others on the roads (Ingram, 1978).

Children and traffic

One curriculum guide which has received considerable attention and publicity is the *Children and Traffic Series*. This is a set of books published in 1977 on behalf of the University of Reading with the permission of the Transport and Road Research Laboratory (Jolly, 1977a,b,c,d). For the Series, specific learning activities and practical experiences were designed for children aged five to thirteen, tried out with a small number of children by the teachers in the project team, revised, re-tested in local schools and revised again. The final draft of the Series was tried out in 108 classes in 60 schools with over 2,000 pupils across the country.

The books are for teachers and are designed to give them help in providing activities and experiences through which their children's knowledge and awareness of the world of traffic could be improved. It was held by the project team that teachers can and should be responsible for thinking out and guiding the road safety activities of their children.

Each book is concerned with one of three particular aspects of road safety education. Book 1—*On the Pavement*—is intended to improve infants' (5- to 7-year-olds') knowledge and awareness of the traffic and roads, postponing the direct teaching of even the most elementary road crossing skills until this has been improved (Jolly, 1977a). Book 2—*The Young Traveller*—which is aimed at the 7 to 9 age group, continues the task of improving the children's background knowledge of their environment (Jolly, 1977b). Book 3—*Preparing for the Road*—is designed primarily to meet the needs of pupils in the upper age ranges of primary and middle schools. At this stage children are frequently expected to cope independently with almost all types of traffic conditions. The suggested activities and practical experiences in Book 3 are meant to develop further the children's understanding of their road environment and to study problems which are of special importance to young pedestrians and cyclists (Jolly, 1977c).

Each book discusses what needs to be taught; it explains when the various ideas and topics might be introduced, and it suggests how the subject matter could be studied within the framework of the existing curriculum. All of the suggested learning activities are closely related to the normal, essential work embodied in the traditional curriculum, according to Jolly (1977a).

The author of the books strongly recommends 'that the work related to the *Children and Traffic* series be integrated into the school's normal programme of work regularly throughout the year rather than concentrated into one relatively short period of intensive study' (1977a. p. 10). He also places more emphasis on small group activities and discussions, and includes such innovative methods as role-playing, role simulation and habit formation. In general, however, these latter methods would require a great deal of teacher training since they call for skills which most teachers simply do not have.

Singh (1979) conducted an evaluation of the final draft of the *Children and Traffic* series in 108 classes in 60 primary and middle schools across the country (mentioned earlier). The teachers were asked to use the books in the Series for two school terms. Data were collected on the teachers' and the pupils' reactions to the materials and on how the materials were used in the classes. Knowledge tests were administered as pre-tests and post-tests to both trial and control classes to obtain information about the children's progress towards achieving the objectives. A post-programme questionnaire assessed the pupils' reactions to the materials. There were significant gains in road safety knowledge test scores in both groups in post-tests, but the trial classes showed greater gains in all three samples. The difference between pre- and post-test means for the trial group at each age level was in excess of half a standard deviation. Eighty out of the 99 trial classes in three trial samples improved their cognitive road safety test score by more than five standard score points compared with only 10 classes out of the 75 control classes (Mean of 50 and standard deviation of 10). These findings were statistically and educationally significant. It was thus concluded that the project's material was effective in changing the knowledge of children at all age levels. Pupils had very favourable reactions to the programme, feeling that it had increased their knowledge about pedestrian safety, helped them to be safer on the roads, equipped them to deal with traffic problems better, and was an effective learning technique. Teachers found the Series to be helpful in planning class activities, small group and individual activities and in identifying objectives. The content of suggested activities was described as 'interesting' and 'stimulating' and the aim of teaching road safety concepts and skills to children as 'excellent'. In conclusion, it seems that the *Children and Traffic* Series fulfilled a genuine need and that it made a valuable contribution to road safety education.

Schools Council Project: Health Education (5–13)

A second widely-used curriculum is the *Schools Council Project: Health Education* (*5–13*) which was published in 1977 after three years of development. It is in the form of two teachers' guides which include road safety education components: *All About Me* for teachers of 5- to 8-year-olds and *Think Well* for teachers of 9- to 13-year-olds. Chapter 6: *Keeping Safe* is mainly concerned with providing the skills and awareness that children increasingly need to keep safe on the roads but without necessarily attacking their sense of adventure. The teaching suggestions follow a sequential pattern from vocabulary development and familiarization with roads to practical work in the playground and at the roadside on the *Green Cross Code*. The aims are: '(a) to develop positive attitudes towards road safety rules; (b) to develop an appropriate road-related vocabulary; and (c) to train children in safe road crossing behaviour' (Stephens, 1978, p. 18).

The guide for teachers of older children, Unit 8 *Skills and Spills* deals with safety education and sets out to create in children an awareness of the potential dangers they face, mainly on roads but also at home and at school. The Unit aims: '(a) to increase knowledge of safety rules, (b) to develop an understanding of road user behaviour, (c) to develop an awareness of the nature and consequences of risk taking, and (d) to develop positive attitudes towards road safety training' (p. 18).

The guides suggest that information on pedestrian safety should be included in regular school subjects such as health, social training, etc., rather than as an independent course; their aim is to help teachers impart information so that pupils can cope successfully with their present and future lives. A variety of methods for presenting road safety education programmes is suggested. Sample courses of study are included for pupils of various age groups, and teachers are provided with a greater variety of material from which they may organize their own programmes. Practical suggestions for classroom work are offered, and the guides also provide a certain amount of pupil material including a book of spirit masters.

Stephens (1978) reported a detailed, special and separate evaluation of the road safety components of the two teachers' guides, *All About Me* and *Think Well*. The aim was to investigate the effects of the teaching on children's vocabulary development, attitudes and roadside behaviour. The method employed was to test children before and after teaching had taken place over one term (12 weeks). One hundred and sixty-two children of 5 to 8 years who received teaching from the first guide were tested using roadside and classroom tests. Seventy-five children in the same school who had received no road safety teaching based on the guides were tested to obtain comparison scores. One hundred and fifty-three children of 9 to 13 years who received teaching from the second guide were tested using classroom questionnaires only, and 32 children were tested to obtain comparison scores. The roadside test for younger children consisted of different tests for experienced and inexperienced road users. Children's road crossing behaviour was observed and recorded. The results indicated that there were significant differences in safe behaviour and other responses between those children who had experienced teaching from the guides and those who did not. The children who had experienced teaching based on the guides particularly showed better vocabulary development and safer road crossing behaviour. Stephens thus concluded that the road safety components of these health education guides for teachers were effective in increasing knowledge and road crossing behaviour.

Both the Jolly and the Schools Council programmes advise that specialists be used for certain topics, but in a role secondary to that of the teachers. However the problem involved in the use of traditional specialists, for pedestrian safety education, is one of availability; police officers and road safety officers are sometimes difficult to involve initially, and securing their services for long-term programmes is almost impossible; thus programmes relying on such personnel are usually short—often only a few hours per year. Also it is often necessary to hold lecture series with large pupil assemblies when specialists are used and this makes it difficult to hold adequate question and answer sessions.

'Road Safety and Me'

The exploratory part of a research programme on communicating road safety information to the young pedestrian carried out in New South Wales, Australia in 1975 (Schreiber and Lukin, 1978) indicated that children under 8 years were seriously handicapped in the traffic environment because of their physical immaturity and lack of experience in assessing traffic situations and that there was a need for new resource material for children and adults. Schreiber and Lukin recommended that future material should show people in realistic traffic situations, with the road safety message presented in a simple, direct manner. Based upon this research, the Australian Department of Motor Transport has produced an audio-visual road safety resource kit, entitled *Road Safety and*

Me, in conjunction with the Teaching Resources Aids Development of the New South Wales Department of Education (Schreiber and Berry, 1978). The kit consists of four film strips with accompanying audio-cassettes, an audio-cassette on everyday sounds (including traffic sounds), ten 49 cm × 49 cm colour photographs to stimulate classroom discussion, pupil worksheets, and a teacher's manual which includes suggested physical activities to promote children's motor ability.

Prior to the publication, the kit was evaluated both by the 40 teachers who used it and by behavioural scientists from the Traffic Accident Research Unit who observed the way in which it was used in the classroom and the way in which children responded to the material. The teachers received the kit enthusiastically. Some of them made a number of suggestions to improve further the technical standard of the kit. The behavioural scientists observed that some teachers did not use the resource material to facilitate greater understanding of the traffic environment, nor did they appear to understand the importance of promoting physical skills as a means of increasing a child's ability to cope in the traffic environment. Schreiber and Berry thus suggested that attention should be given to promote teacher training so that teachers become familiar with the aims of the material and the demands it puts on them for the material to function effectively prior to its use. They also suggested that the manual should be modified to take into account the teacher's need for more specific instruction on the ways in which the kit's material should be integrated to promote discussion. The study, however, did not assess children's reactions to the material nor the effects on their everyday road crossing behaviour.

Norwegian traffic safety materials

Schioldborg (1974, 1976) evaluated the printed traffic safety materials used in the Norwegian Traffic Club by comparing members' and non-members' road safety knowledge, road crossing behaviour and accident rates. Parents' attitudes were also compared for members and non-members, because member parents were actively encouraged by the Traffic Club to supplement the printed materials by practical training in the traffic situation. The results of the road safety knowledge test clearly indicated a superior performance by the members of the Traffic Club. The behavioural results were inconclusive. When club members were alone they behaved significantly more correctly than when they were in company, whereas this difference was not found in non-members. Members differed significantly from non-members on the item 'Look only to one side or not at all when crossing an unmarked intersection'; but no difference was found on other items. The accident rate for members was significantly lower than for non-members. Over the whole country members had a 20 per cent lower accident rate, and in Oslo a 40 per cent lower accident rate, than non-members. This non-significant effect of training on the pedestrian behaviour of the children supports the view expressed by many writers (e.g. Gerber, Huber and Limbourg, 1977; Rothengatter and Brakenhoff-Splinter, 1979) that parents are poorly informed about the abilities and the development of abilities and that many do not know what to teach about pedestrian safety or whether the teaching is adequate.

Behaviour modification techniques

The effect of behaviour modification techniques on children's road crossing behaviour has been demonstrated in a number of studies. Using children up to 12 years of age in Salt Lake City, Utah, Reading (1973) demonstrated that if a child, showing safe crossing behaviour is rewarded with words such as 'That was a good job of crossing the street' and by giving the child a sweet, a smile, and a 'good pedestrian certificate', the advocated traffic behaviour could be developed in the child to occur in real traffic. However, whether the desired behaviour can be stabilized after the programme has been terminated remains to be investigated. Ducker (1975) compared the effectiveness of three experimental Threat Detection Training Programmes which employed behaviour modification techniques to teach safe road crossing behaviour to children in the 5 to 9 age group. The three programmes were: '1. *The Basic Programme*—involved having teacher introduce the programme and the safe road crossing sequence, and then provide reinforced practice of the sequence using practice games and simulated roads in-class. 2. *The Simulator Programme*—was similar to the Basic programme except that the in-class practice sessions involved the playing of the practice games in a traffic flow simulator. 3. *The Film Programme*—was also basically similar to the Basic programme except that the programme and the safe road crossing behaviour sequence were introduced and demonstrated using a film featuring a child-prestigious personality (Captain Kangaroo)' (p. 15). One behavioural pre- and two post-tests were conducted to determine improvement in road crossing behaviour as a result of each of the three programmes. The first post-test occurred within several days following the final training session of the programme. The second post-test was conducted 26 to 28 days after the first and provided data relating to programme permanency. The results clearly showed that while each of the three experimental programmes had made reductions in unsafe road crossing, the Simulator and the Film programmes were significantly better than the Basic programme in this regard and not greatly different from one another. When Ducker examined the programme permanency, he found that the sample tended to revert to unsafe behaviours regardless of the programme they had received. However, despite these reversals, the net reduction in unsafe road crossing behaviour attributable to the Film and Simulator programmes was still considerable. The results also showed that the behaviour modification technique had a greater and longer effect on the children's behaviour if the demonstration of the required behaviour was performed by a popular 'personality' rather than performed by the teacher on a simulated road laid out in the school playground. Page, Iwata and Neef (1976) demonstrated the same phenomenon with a group of retarded persons. After being taught pedestrian skills they succeeded in generalizing the learned behaviour to the real traffic situation.

In another experimental study Rothengatter and Brakenhoff-Splinter (1979) trained children aged 4 how to cross a quiet road without parked cars and in the vicinity of parked cars. The results on pre-tests indicated that crossing between parked cars was considerably more difficult to perform for children than crossing on quiet roads without parked cars. The children showed no significant increase of correct performance on the quiet roads but transfer effects of the training were evident when they were asked to cross the road between parked cars. These results suggest that the effect of a behaviour modification technique is dependent on the task involved. The Limbourg and Gerber (1978) study in which behaviour modification principles were applied to develop a new programme for parents to teach their children how to cross the road also suggested a positive effect of the training.

In a review of the literature on the effectiveness of traffic education, Rothengatter (1978) stressed the importance of modelling and imitation learning principles of social theory (Bandura, 1977) as effective methods of modifying behaviour of children. He concluded that reinforcement technique is effective 'if the behavioural elements of the required behaviour are already present, but may have to be supplemented by practical training or demonstration if the behaviour is to be elicited as is the case in younger children' (p. 13). Other authors (e.g. Gerber, Huber and Limbourg, 1977; Limbourg and Gunther, 1978) have advocated the application of this technique on theoretical grounds.

Problems and limitations of evaluative research on pedestrian education materials

Although some studies have been carried out to investigate the effect of films, posters and other audio-visual materials, no studies have investigated the effects of them on children's normal, everyday crossing behaviour. Evaluation of audio-visual materials for pedestrian behaviour purposes are much needed both at the time of production and after the production. There are two procedures, one advocated by a scientific review panel concerned only with the scientific accuracy of the material and another by a panel of teachers which can be used to review films and other audio-visuals. The scientific review will assess accuracy, factual presentation and scientific acceptability, and only if the criteria are met is a film seen by a panel of teachers who then determine whether the central message is effectively conveyed and whether the material is credible, timely, persuasive and educational. As both reviews represent value judgements rather than objective statements, majority decisions can be used to clarify films as 'acceptable' or 'unacceptable'. These types of reviews at least can ensure that invalid and out-of-date material does not make its way into the school. Availability of these ratings could help teachers to choose films more effectively for their educational programmes for pedestrian safety. Evaluation of the actual effects of the audio-visual and printed materials on attitudes, beliefs and/or behaviour related to pedestrian safety has been rare and has often not been addressed to the most important questions. And there is evidence (cf. Colborne, 1971b; Nummenmaa, 1970; Nummenmaa, Ruuhilehto, and Syvänen, 1975; Nummenmaa and Syvänen, 1974; Sandels, 1975) that the contents of printed materials on pedestrian safety are soon forgotten or are not effective in changing children's everyday crossing behaviour. The anticipated value of printed materials is that they improve children's crossing behaviour and safe use of roads. No film or printed material has actually shown that it can achieve or contribute to this aim.

Another problem with printed and audio-visual materials is that the effects which they are to produce are rarely specified. We need a fuller exploration of their aims, evaluation of how well they are achieved, and clear information on how they contribute to the overall field of pedestrian education. At present, no confidence can be placed in the educational value of a large number of available materials for children; and, given the extensive use of these, it should be no surprise that many pedestrian safety teaching materials achieve little, if any, beneficial effect.

In general, the results of educational programme evaluation studies involve such a variety of approaches and findings that analysis is difficult. While their educational impact merits analysis a variety of problems remain and many types of programmes have not been studied. Problems of design and measurement also hamper evaluation studies.

If the purpose of pedestrian education programmes is to generate changes in knowledge about pedestrian's safety, then they are an overwhelming success. All programmes which have assessed the effects on knowledge have found positive results. Generally, there can be little doubt that a wide variety of educational efforts can create knowledge gains, and these efforts may involve teachers, curriculum guides, road safety officers, police, playgroup supervisors or parents. However, it is uncertain how long such knowledge may be retained and how it might improve children's behaviour on the roads.

Conclusions are more difficult if attitude changes are considered to be a necessary part of the training process. The *Reading Study* (Singh, 1979) and the *Schools Council Project: Health Education (5–13)* (Stephens, 1978) found positive attitude changes. On inspection, programmes producing positive attitude change are most likely to be of long duration and to involve a predetermined attitude change orientation as opposed to merely presenting information. These important factors would, of course, require careful testing in a series of experimental studies.

The question whether a pedestrian education programme really changes children's *behaviour* on the roads is an especially difficult one to answer. The research carried out so far is limited, and much more research is needed. At present, it can be stated that pedestrian education courses of many types can increase knowledge levels and a few of them are capable of modifying pedestrian behaviour. The whole research area requires far more study and experiment along the following lines: (1) more validity and reliability checks on evaluation scales; (2) more study of the influences on 'no-treatment groups'; (3) true experimental as opposed to quasi-experimental designs, involving random assignment to 'no training' and training groups; (4) studies of different types of programmes across a variety of age groups; and (5) studies of successful programmes to determine what aspects (i.e. source, message, methodology, etc.) contribute their effects on attitudes and road crossing behaviour.

PEDESTRIAN EDUCATION THROUGH THE MEDIA

The use of mass media communications for the promotion of pedestrian safety has concerned road safety researchers for a long time. There are newspapers, radio, television, magazines, books, audio-tapes, films, pamphlets, brochures, posters, stickers and even personalized mail if it is forwarded in bulk. We shall, however, limit ourselves to those channels that have been employed to promote pedestrian behaviour, and driver behaviour believed to be relevant to pedestrian safety, and whose influences have been assessed in evaluative research.

Wilde, L'Hoste, Sheppard and Wind (1971) reviewed the state of affairs in *Road Safety Campaigns: Design and Evaluation* on behalf of the Organisation for Economic Co-operation and Development (OECD), and found that little research had been done on evaluating the effectiveness of mass media communications for safety. They wrote: 'From the available literature it becomes readily evident that the amount of scientific information on safety communications is rather limited indeed and that it contrasts sharply with the social importance of the issues involved as well as with the total number of campaigns launched in various countries at different times. However, if there is one thing that emanates clearly from the experience hitherto obtained, it is that the area is characterized by many serious problems, both with regard to the design of safety publicity campaigns, as well as concerning the accompanying research efforts dealing with the assessment of campaign effectiveness. The success of a safety campaign cannot be assessed by the number or magnitude of newspaper articles, letters to the editor, comments in Parliament or small-talk between friends and neighbours and similar forms of public or official reactions triggered by the campaign efforts, nor by the flattering congratulations extended to those who organized campaigns for their commendable efforts. The energy of a fire does indeed depend upon the fire, not

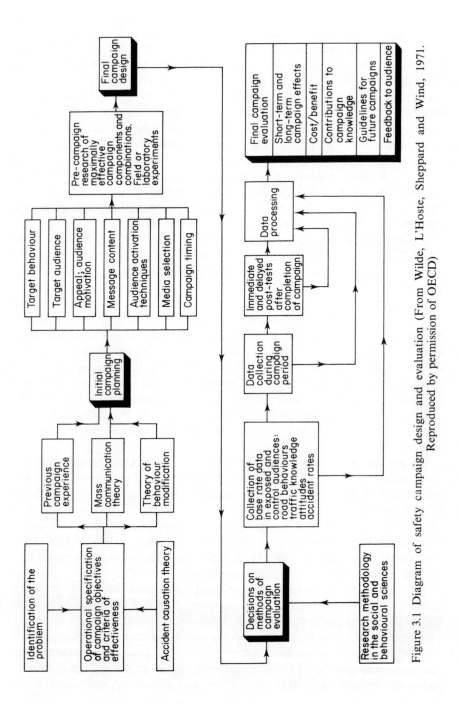

Figure 3.1 Diagram of safety campaign design and evaluation (From Wilde, L'Hoste, Sheppard and Wind, 1971. Reproduced by permission of OECD)

upon the amount of smoke. The true effectiveness of a safety campaign is its power actually to reduce accident tolls and to increase the frequency of those road behaviours which are compatible with safety. That changes in behaviour on the road and reductions in accident rates are the only meaningful criteria for campaign success may appear obvious enough, if one is truly interested in the promotion of traffic safety rather than in curtains of smoke which cover up the real issues. And yet, in the recent past, many a safety campaign has been evaluated in ways which betray this fundamental conceptual error' (pp. 9–10). They thus recommended: 'No major safety campaign should be launched without being accompanied by appropriate scientific research. Those who produce campaigns should plan sufficiently ahead so that adequate time for preparatory research and pre-tests is provided' (p. 10). The OECD Report thus presented a model design for publicity campaigns and the attendant evaluating research, as shown in Figure 3.1.

A 3-month publicity campaign was started in April 1971 to launch the *Green Cross Code*. The campaign was aimed chiefly at parents through press and television, and at children through television, posters, cinema and a brochure. The detail of the Code was given in the brochure which had a tear-off slip, returnable to the Department of the Environment. There was a wide demand for the brochure and over 7,000,000 were distributed throughout the United Kingdom. Parents were asked to certify on the tear-off slip that their child understood the Code and had taken the parent over a road at least 3 times. A proficiency card was then returned to the child and in the 3 months of the campaign over 100,000 of these were issued. The total media expenditure was £570,000 covering television, posters and announcements in cinemas. An analysis of replies showed that the average member of the audience had five opportunities to see the publicity on television and fourteen opportunities in the press.

The evaluation of the campaign was carried out at three levels: road-side observations, knowledge, and accident reductions. From these data and behavioural observations, it was concluded that the campaign had a significant effect upon the target behaviour: an increase in the frequency of children 'stopping at the kerb' was from 41 to 44 per cent and in those who looked both ways from 50 to 54 per cent. When children aged 5 to 9 were asked what they should do when crossing a road, their responses 'cross in a straight line' showed an increase from 21 to 59 per cent, and 'look all round' from zero to 17 per cent. The answer 'look right, left and right again' which was a feature of the *kerb drill*. fell from 75 to 53 per cent. Applying conservative criteria, this publicity was associated with an 11 per cent reduction in child casualties. The greatest reduction in accidents was observed between the ages of 5 and 9, the special target audience. Some decrements in adult pedestrian casualties were also identified. Finally, when the researchers calculated the savings in medical and other expenditures and compared the mass education programme, it was claimed that the monetary savings in a 3-month period were greater than the costs of the programme.

In 1975, the Department of the Environment (as it was then known) launched a joint television and leaflet campaign aimed at parents of children aged 2 to 9 years. The parents were interviewed before and after the campaign and they were also given guidance on supervision and road safety instruction. The guidance was carefully graded to be suitable for parents of children in three separate age groups: 2 to 4, 5 to 6 and 7 to 9 years. The emphasis was on supervision and keeping children away from the road for the parents of the younger group, on parents setting a good example and explaining to their children what they were doing when crossing roads for the parents of the 5- to 6-year-old group, and on teaching children how to cross busier roads, judging distance and speed, and teaching the *Green Cross Code* for the parents of the older group. An analysis of results showed that there was an increased awareness of the need for parental supervision and instruction for parents of children aged 2 to 4 years. The proportion of mothers claiming to have given road safety education during the previous 6 months was similar before and after the campaign, but there was a slight increase in the proportion of mothers who said they had carried out instructions on how to cross a road safely both in the home and at the roadside. Unfortunately accident rates before and after the campaign had not been compared.

Wuhrer (1970) evaluated a similar comprehensive safety programme conducted in a selected geographical area in Germany in 1967. This programme included elaborate safety education and publicity including changes in the physical environment, about 7 miles of pavements were built as well as children's playgrounds. The police force was made to appear as frequently and conspicuously on the road as possible. The campaign resulted in a 13 per cent drop in fatal and injurious accidents while no such decrease was observed in four neighbouring areas not covered by the campaign. Wuhrer attributed this success to the joint action and close co-operation of a number of organizations and authorities dealing with traffic safety. Again, however, it was not possible to link this beneficial effect upon accidents to special causal factors.

A study at the Jefatura Central De Trafico in Spain (1964) measured the effects of a very intensive pedestrian safety campaign by means of questionnaire responses of over 3,000 self-selected respondents, and by means of actual observation of pedestrian behaviour at sites before, during and after the campaign. The questionnaire data showed that posters, strips and loudspeaker vehicles were more effective in influencing the behaviour of pedestrians than were radio and press, thus suggesting that communications presented in the very situation of traffic are superior. Roadside observations showed an increase in the frequency of pedestrians crossing correctly at intersections with lights (from 41 per cent before the campaign to 59 per cent during and afterwards). At crossings with markings in the pavement, but not lights, the percentages of pedestrians crossing correctly was 38 per cent before the campaign, 50 per cent during the campaign and 54 per cent afterwards, 'correct crossing' being defined as staying within the limits of the markings. Finally, at places without lights or markings, the percentages of correct crossings defined in terms of looking (head turns) before going across were respectively 44 per cent, 98 per cent and 95 per cent.

McInerney (1959) studied the effect of a year-long publicity campaign mounted in New York City to alert the public to the dangers of careless pedestrian and motorist behaviour and to make the public aware of safe pedestrian and driver conduct. The campaign made use of newspaper advertisements, television and radio messages, billboards, subway and bus cards, bulletin board posters for company offices, fender stickers, light pole posters, mail imprinting, leaflets distributed to homes through community groups and jay-walker cards distributed by Boy Scouts. McInerney found that this publicity *per se* had little effect until the police enforcement came into action. In the first few weeks of police enforcement of the anti-jay-walking law, traffic fatalities of pedestrians dropped from 201 to 174 as compared with the previous year. Injuries dropped from 17,000 in 1957 to 15,000 in 1958. These results suggest that where publicity and police action are combined a reduction in accidents can occur.

Blomberg and Preusser (1975) conducted several smaller-scale experiments on the effect of mass communication messages upon pedestrian safety among children as well as adults. In the first experiment, a 2-minute film showing stopping at the kerb before crossing and perceptual search routines was shown to children of primary school age in Pittsburgh, Pennsylvania. The main points of the film were discussed with the children before they were shown the film a second time. The discussion continued until consensus on the correct answers was reached by the entire class. The results of the before-and-after comparisons showed that both stopping at the kerb and the extent of visual search going across were positively and significantly affected by the communication.

The next experiment by Blomberg and Preusser was conducted with a group of adults. The message content of stopping before crossing and visual scanning was modified for an adult audience. Single-page pamphlets containing three multiple-choice questions on the front and the correct answers and their justification on the back were handed out to customers in a bank in Stanford, California, who were either asked to complete the questions and check the correct answers before leaving the bank (experimental group) or to take the questionnaire home, read and complete it there, and then return it by mail (control group). In order to identify the members belonging to experimental and control groups outside the bank, they were given a small gift and some literature in either a white or yellow shopping bag. Although both stopping and appropriate search behaviours were slightly more common in the experimental group, the difference with the controls was not significant. However, in both target behaviours women were performing significantly better than men. The authors thus concluded: 'It appears from these data that adults crossing at controlled intersections stop or at least pause before entering the travelled portion of the roadway but do not adequately search for oncoming traffic. Rather, they rely on the intersection controls to ensure that no cars are coming. Alternatively, at the midblock location the search behavior was adequate, but many adults did not stop at the outside edge of the parked cars' (p. 20).

In their third experiment Blomberg and Preusser investigated the effect of a message aimed at reducing the tendency of bus passengers to cross a street in front of a bus after disembarking. The passengers, while still on the bus heard the message from loudspeakers installed throughout the passenger compartment. The behaviour of passengers after disembarking was observed and compared with the controls across the four bus stops and different times of day. No significant difference in walking in front of the bus was identified. However, some significant differences were observed when different times of day and different bus stops were considered separately, indicating that the message had a positive effect under specified conditions of time and place.

Blomberg and Preusser conducted a further experiment with children and their parents. The target behaviour was not to cross in front of a stationary vehicle. Information was collected pertaining to the extent children were accompanied by adults and the frequency of adults and children crossing the road in front of or behind an ice cream van or not crossing at all after they had bought the ice cream. The driver of the ice cream van gave an envelope containing the message to a child customer telling him/her to take it to his/her parents. One week later, on the second day of testing, the ice cream vendor truck followed the same route while playing a jingle on its outside loudspeakers every 30 seconds whenever he stopped the van. The same types of information were collected on this second day. Children were also asked what the jingle meant and adults were asked whether they had received a letter from the ice cream company during the previous week. It was found that the frequency of both adults and children crossing behind the van increased, but this was significant only as far as the children were concerned. The interview data revealed that almost half of the children did not fully understand the meaning of the jingle and almost 90 per cent of the parents said they had not received the letter. Blomberg and Preusser commented that a high degree of accident reduction could be achieved if children and parents were to be repeatedly exposed to the messages.

Wiener (1968) observed the percentage of legal and illegal crossings made by elderly pedestrians at selected corners before, during and after a heavily published anti-jay-walking campaign. The results showed a significant increase in legal crossings during the campaign, but four months after the campaign the percentage of legal crossings was the same as before the campaign, unless a police officer was present on the corner. The pedestrians were found to have a favourable attitude toward anti-jay-walking law enforcement. Denham (1957) conducted a much harsher combination of education and enforcement experiment on the effect of mass communication messages upon pedestrian safety. The pedestrian was informed that a pedestrian control project was in operation and that a fine for jay-walking in Miami would be strictly imposed. During the first month pedestrian accidents were reduced by 23 per cent over the same month of the previous year, and pedestrian violations were reduced by 55 per cent. After four months, accidents were reduced by 19 per cent and violations by 23 per cent. These results indicate that the threat of legal action, as long as it is enforced, is one of the strongest motivations for safe pedestrian behaviour.

Numerous experiments have also been conducted on the effect of mass media publicity focusing upon driver behaviours that are known to have implications for pedestrian safety. For example, Blomgreen, Scheuneman and Wilkins (1963) studied the effect of a slogan, 'A good driver is courteous—he signals' posted at the exit of a shopping plaza in Evanston, Illinois. They found that signalling frequency was under the direct influence of the communication, that it persisted to some extent after removal of the poster and that it tended to generalize to the next intersection. The increment in signalling frequency was found to be equal for left and right turns. Brown, Kane, MacEachern and Petrachuk (1973) studied the effect of two different motivating appeals upon 'turn-signalling' behaviour. Posters either said: 'Avoid accidents, signal your turns', or 'Be courteous, signal your turns', and were identical in other respects. They were posted at two exits of a shopping plaza located in the outskirts of the built-up area of Kingston, Ontario. When drivers were exposed to the 'avoid accident' poster, signalling rate rose to 73 per cent from 61 per cent. The 'courtesy' poster raised signalling rate to 76 per cent. No significant difference between the two appeals was observed. Gill, Mercer and Ward (1974) came to a similar conclusion when they conducted an identical study at the same location a year later; that is, the 'courtesy' appeal was superior to that of the 'avoid accidents' appeal in promoting the driver behaviour, but the difference failed to reach statistical significance.

Other studies (e.g. Carr, Goldberg and Farber, 1974; Department of Transport, Ottawa, 1970) have reported marked attitude and knowledge changes resulting from mass media publicity, but no changes occurred in accident rates. Piccolino (1968) found a zero order correlation between judgements of the effectiveness to be expected from various messages and the behaviour change they produced in drivers; this indicates that the cogency of the variables increases as one goes down the list. Mass publicity messages in other studies (e.g. Wilde *et al.*, 1971; Blomberg and Preusser, 1975; Wilde, Cake and Le Brasseur, 1974) have shown a greater modifying effect if the message was behaviour-oriented, concrete, unambiguous and instructive (Figure 3.1).

Ben-David, Lewin and Haliva (1970) and Ben-David, Lewin, Haliva and Tel-Nir (1972) conducted three experiments on the effect of different motivating appeals in warning letters addressed to private motorists in Israel. 'Correct stopping at intersection stop signs' was a single target behaviour in their first experimental study. There were two target behaviours: 'correct stopping at stop signs' and 'correct lane choice' with regard to in-pavement direction arrows in the second experiment; and 'a larger range of driver violations' was considered in the third experiment. Randomly selected groups of drivers whose behaviour had been observed, received either a low threat, a medium threat, or a high threat letter, or no letter at all. If an offence was seen to be repeated by a driver, a letter similar to the first was sent to him/her. In the third experiment, in addition to private drivers, drivers of taxis, buses and commercial vehicles were also included. The results indicated that the advisory letters with specific reference to violations were the prime motivator for reduction in errors. This led them to conclude that a low threat communication is an effective means of bringing driver behaviour back into focal attention. Accidents were not treated as a dependent variable in their studies.

The OECD sub-group on Mass Media Communication for Pedestrian Safety (1978b), who reviewed some 30 reports on the subject, some of them are also discussed in the present text, found two reports which were evaluated on their ability to reduce accidents (Blomberg and Preusser, 1975; Morris, 1972). Seven studies (Blomgreen, Scheuneman and Wilkins, 1963; Brown, Kane, Mac-Eachern and Petrachuk, 1973; Morris, 1972; Piccolino, 1968; Reading, 1973; Singer, 1963; Walsh and Nickson, 1972) used behavioural indices as a measure of effect and it was found that mass media communications were capable of modifying pedestrian and driver behaviours. Four studies (Blomberg and Preusser, 1975; Denham, 1957; Ben-David, Haliva, Friedman, Snyder and Tel-Nir, 1973; McInerney, 1959) that added physical or enforcement changes to mass media publicity showed a demonstrable effect upon accident rates of pedestrians or drivers. There is also evidence to suggest that both drivers and pedestrians can be reached easily through posters, stickers, signs, and loud-speaker vehicles.

Studies give no information, however, regarding the optimal duration of a publicity programme, the degree of repetitiveness in message presentation, and finally the amount of publicity which is necessary in order to obtain an effect. The literature also gives no information on the belief and attitude systems that are associated with particular actions such as going across a street either at a pedestrian crossing or elsewhere. These factors need to be investigated before mass media messages can be designed in a purposeful manner. Finally, the researcher, in addition to studying changes in accident rates should also study information, attitude and behaviour change, in order to determine the nature of the process between the stimulus and the end effect. The *ability* to behave safely should be distinguished from the *desire* to behave safely (OECD, 1978b).

EDUCATION OF PARENTS AND TEACHERS FOR
CHILD PEDESTRIAN SAFETY

Parents

When children are young, parents have a prime responsibility for giving them both road supervision and pedestrian training. They have countless opportunities to give pedestrian training on the roads as they accompany their children on journeys to and from schools, shops, etc. Research on socialization has shown that different social agents of behaviour modification are relevant in different stages of development. For the stage of development at which children learn to use the roads safely as pedestrians, the parents are the most relevant agents of behaviour modification. However studies by Sadler (1972) and Sandels (1975) have shown that although mothers accept that they have prime responsibility for teaching children road safety, the majority have no knowledge of rules pertaining to the psychological principles of learning. Many have no idea that they contribute to modifying the behaviour of their children because they have no intention at all of initiating the learning process; this applies particularly to learning by imitation. Their studies suggest that parents need to be educated about how to determine the developmental stage and experience of their child. They should also be taught how to recognize what a child is already able to perform in order to establish at which point training should start. The general aim should be to enable parents to use educational techniques adapted to the developmental stage of their child and to observe the results of the learning processes initiated by these techniques.

The OECD Special Research Group on Pedestrian Safety (1978a) recommended that parents should be informed of their children's limited abilities as road users and that they should be encouraged to increase the safety of their children both by supervision and training. Traffic clubs could be used to increase parental involvement. Theoretical training needs to be reinforced by practical training of children in real traffic. Such training should be carried out by teachers and parents.

Several other studies (Osborne, 1975; Sandels, 1975) and reports (Department of Education and Science, 1977) have emphasized the need of young people for pedestrian training. Again and again the parent is named as the ideal pedestrian educator, and Sandels suggests the various ways in which the parents can train their child to use roads safely as a pedestrian. Thus parents should be encouraged and informed to give their children better road supervision and training.

In Germany, the development of the education of parents has been in progress for some time as a special subject of adult education, and a host of suitable techniques is provided to influence parents to display the kind of educational behaviour desired (Heinrich, 1979). In the UK more than 13,000 local Tufty

Clubs are in existence where parents receive instruction on how to give pedestrian training to their children. A study at the Transport and Road Research Laboratory has recently been carried out to investigate the potential of setting up a British Traffic Club for pre-school children aged three to four and a half years (Downing, 1980). The initial findings, Downing reports, 'are promising and suggest that Traffic Clubs for pre-school children may be an effective road safety measure, and one which appeals to a large number of pre-school children and their parents' (p. 10). In the Scandinavian countries the national clubs for pre-school children are founded on the assumption that their success would be greater if parents could be persuaded to participate in the practical on-the-road training of their children. Parents are given booklets which give guidance on what instruction to give the children and on the expected abilites of children at different age levels. The material is sent out every 6 months, recommending repetition exercises and practical tests. In Germany, the sponsors of the traffic club for pre-school children are currently concerned with working out suitable training aids for parents.

Numerous studies (e.g. Nummenmaa, 1970; Nummenmaa and Syvänen, 1974; Sandels, 1975; Singh, 1979; Stephens, 1978) have repeatedly confirmed that there may be many ways, methods and institutions to teach children the rules of the road they have to know and to make them aware of the dangers traffic participation involves, but it is practical on-the-road training which will impart the experience really necessary for their safety. Thus, for very obvious reasons, the tasks of practical training must be assumed by parents. It is very likely that integrated schemes involving police, road safety officers, and teacher and parent instruction in pedestrian safety will be more successful in increasing children's safety on the roads than unintegrated schemes. In the Scandinavian countries, attempts at integrated road safety training schemes are being made in which parents are being asked to give practical instruction on the roads. Parents can be reached through school teachers or by road safety organizations and mass media.

As evidenced in Sadler's study, parental acceptance, already high, can be ensured only through adequate 'public relations'; in other words, by making available to the public the pedestrian safety materials which they can use to teach their children how to use roads safely as pedestrians. Through Parent Teacher Associations, as well as the mass media, parents could become more widely acquainted with ways in which they can act as partners with schools in educating children for road safety.

Teachers

Before a child begins his schooling his parents are responsible for the child's pedestrian training. However, it is widely considered that the school must take on part of the responsibility for pedestrian training when the child enters the formal educational system. Schools could help children to acquire the concepts, skills and values needed as a sound basis for a lifetime of safe and efficient use of our ever-changing and complex traffic environment. The second conference of 'government experts on road safety education in schools' (Council of Ministers of Transport, 1971) recommended in its conclusions that every effort should be made to give children a road safety education which is as effective as it can be and which best matches each stage of their development. Road safety education should be taught as a compulsory subject, systematically and continuously in kindergartens, primary schools and secondary schools and it should be an integral part of the curriculum, but it can of course also be made a separate discipline. If traffic education is included throughout the school years matched to increasing levels of sophistication, school teachers would reinforce the efforts of parents and others such as RoSPA and road safety officers and police officers, and transmit knowledge about the psychological, moral, social and physical consequences of human behaviour on the roads.

Acceptance by the teaching profession of the responsibility for pedestrian safety education must clearly depend upon appropriately educated teachers. They must know what to teach and how to teach it. This aspect of teacher training is little documented and, to clarify the situation, a survey is needed to know about the extent of both in-service courses and courses for trainee teachers, what training and how much is given, and what effect this has on the quality of pedestrian safety instruction given in schools. The second conference of road safety experts, just mentioned, states that exhortations to teachers to undertake road safety education are of little value unless they are given concrete information on which to work. Teachers require suitable audio-visual and other teaching aids to improve their techniques.

In 1975, RoSPA published a booklet *Suggestions for Teaching Road Safety* which aimed to make teachers more aware of road safety problems and the need for road safety education in the school curriculum. The booklet also gives guidance on methods of teaching road safety. Some in-service training courses for teachers have been run by the Department of Science and Education and these were very valuable, but surely it would be better to begin training teachers in road safety education when training them for their career as a whole.

CONCLUSIONS

As a result of the above-mentioned researches it is safe to say that the last ten years have generally increased our knowledge of the attitudes of children to pedestrian safety and pedestrian safety education and the effect of those attitudes on learning safe road behaviour, of the reactions of children to teaching, of the amount they are retaining of what is taught, and of their road safety practices. However, there is almost no empirical evidence as to the effectiveness of these education and informational programmes, including face-to-face and mass media communications, in changing the road behaviour. Changes in cognitive states do not necessarily result in behavioural changes. The problem of relating pedestrian safety teaching to road behaviour is very considerable, but no teaching programme can be said to be completely effective if evaluation in this is not attempted. Tied to this issue is the necessity to study programme effects over time, as it is possible, for example, that the effects of one approach are immediate but temporary, while another approach may result in delayed but permanent effects. The opinion and suppositions regarding different effects of different pedestrian education programmes remain empirically unsupported as there has been no research evaluating the effectiveness of one approach over another. Furthermore, in those evaluated programmes which have utilized more than one approach (Ducker, 1975) only one main effect (the programme) was considered. Studies are needed of the benefits of teacher training courses including those based on curriculum guides or special workshops and of the value of curriculum guides in preparing teachers and others for pedestrian safety work. More still needs to be known about the effects on behaviour, attitudes, and on knowledge of the various audio-visual, mass media and print materials used in pedestrian education and information programmes. More knowledge of the formation of attitudes of parents, teachers and young people towards pedestrian safety practices would be welcome.

Perhaps the most urgent need is the fashioning of a research technique which would test and evaluate the new meterials that many teachers and road safety specialists are using and which are being recommended for providing pedestrian training. We need answers to the question 'What kinds of educational and informational programmes for pedestrian safety have what kinds of effects on what kinds of people?' If the effectiveness of different methods does vary according to readily definable audience types, then differential programming, rather than one programme for all subjects would be incumbent on the educator. Perhaps it is into these fields that future research in the subject can be expected to move.

APPENDIX: PEDESTRIAN TEACHING—
A GRADED STRUCTURE

1. Keep away from path, road.
2. Know road is dangerous.
3. Use path and stay on it.
4. Recognize traffic.
5. Learn safest place to cross on one local quiet road the child will have occasion to use.
6. Learn where traffic may come from, on to section of road where the child will cross.
7. Learn to stop, near to kerb, before crossing.
8. Learn that one must ALWAYS look and listen.
9. Learn to recognize absence of traffic on this road.
10. Learn how to cross when there is no traffic on this road, at a quiet time.
11. Learn how to cross where there is

no traffic on this road, at a busy time.
12. Repeat items 5, 6, 9, 10, 11 on one other local quiet road the child will have occasion to use.
13. Repeat items 4, 6, 9, 10, 11 on all other local quiet roads the child will have occasion to use.
14. Learn how to modify place if parked vehicles present, on all these roads.
15. Learn to keep looking and listening while crossing these roads.
16. Learn *Green Cross Code*.
17. Learn dangers of distractions.
18. Learn to look especially for 2-wheeled vehicles on roads.
19. Learn dangers of alighting from and crossing near buses.
20. Learn how to recognize school crossing patrol.
21. Learn how to cross where this patrol is.
22. Learn how to cross from the edge of parked cars.
23. Learn how to recognize zebra crossing.
24. Learn how to judge where the traffic situation permits crossing safely on a zebra.
25. Learn how to cross on a zebra crossing.
26. Learn how weather can influence stopping distances.
27. Learn how to choose safe places to cross on unfamiliar straight roads with no protected places.
28. Learn how to cross using safe gaps when traffic is coming on these roads.
29. Learn how to choose safe places to cross on unfamiliar roads when side roads exist.
30. Learn how to cross using safe gaps when traffic is coming on these roads.
31. Learn how to cross using safe gaps at junctions when traffic is coming.
32. Learn how to cross using safe gaps at night.
33. Learn how to achieve conspicuity and its importance.
34. Learn to recognize pelican crossings.
35. Learn how to cross at pelican crossings.
36. Learn how to cross at light-controlled junctions.
37. Learn how to maximize the gap in the traffic.
38. Learn how to cross at a safe time, at a convenient safe place.

REFERENCES

Bandura, A. (1977). *Social Learning Theory*. Englewood Cliffs, NJ: Prentice-Hall.
Ben-David, G., Haliva, Y., Friedman, P., Snyder, M., and Tel-Nir, N. (1973). The influence of personal communication on urban driving behaviours. *Paper presented at the First International Conference on Driver Behaviour*. October. Zurich.
Ben-David, G., Lewin, I., and Haliva, Y. (1970). The influence of advisory letters in changing the driving behaviour of private motorists in Israel. *Accident Analysis and Prevention*, **2**, 189–206.
Ben-David, G., Lewin, I., Haliva, Y., and Tel-Nir, N. (1972). The influence of personal communication on the driving behaviour of private motorists in Israel. *Accident Analysis and Prevention*, **4**, 269–301.

Blomberg, R. G., and Preusser, D. (1975). Identification and test of pedestrian safety messages for public education programmes. *Report Number DOT-HS-099-3-705.* Washington DC: United States Department of Transportation.

Blomgreen, G. W., Scheuneman, T. W., and Wilkins, J. L. (1963). Effect of exposure to a safety poster on the frequency of turn signalling. *Traffic Safety Research Review,* 7, 15–22.

Brown, I., Kane, J., MacEachern, L., and Petrachuk, D. (1973). The effect of two appeals upon turn signalling behavior. *Unpublished Report.* Kingston, Ontario: Queen's University.

Cain, D. (1978). A child's safety is our responsibility. *Traffic Education,* 3, 14–18.

Carr, B. R., Goldberg, H., and Farber, C. M. L. (1974). The Canadian breathalizer legislation: an inferential evaluation. *Proceedings of the Sixth International Conference on Alcohol, Drugs and Traffic Safety, Toronto,* 8–13.

Chambers, F. (1976). How to plan a primary school project. *Safety Education,* 138, 23–24.

Clarke, D. E. (1978). Under fives—the Birmingham approach. *Traffic Education,* 3, 24–25.

Colborne, H. V. (1971a). Road safety and pre-school children. *Safety Education,* 121, 11–12.

Colborne, H. V. (1971b). Two experiments on methods of training children in road safety. *Department of the Environment, Road Research Laboratory, Laboratory Report 404.* Crowthorne: RRL.

Colborne, H. V., and Sargent, K. J. A. (1971). Survey of road safety in schools: education and other factors. *Ministry of Transport, Road Research Laboratory, Laboratory Report 388.* Crowthorne: RRL.

Colborne, H. V., and Sheppard, D. (1966). Testing a poster for infants. *Safety Education,* 107, 8–10.

Council of Ministers of Transport (1971). *Second Conference of Governmental Experts on Road Safety Education in Schools.* Vienna: Council of Europe.

Cyster, R. (1980). The use of video recording in traffic education in primary schools. *Traffic Education,* 5, 5–6.

Darlington, J. O., (1976). Education in road safety in the county of Hereford and Worcester. *Safety Education,* 136, 20–21.

Darlington, J. O. (1977). Teach the teachers and they will teach the child. *Traffic Education,* 2, 12–13.

Davies, R. F. (1979). The Green Cross Man Wallchart: distribution, acceptance and use amongst teachers. *UK Department of Environment, Transport and Road Research Laboratory, Supplementary Report 518.* Crowthorne: TRRL.

Denham, P. M. (1957). Miami's pedestrian control programme. *Traffic Digest and Review,* 5, 1–3.

Department of Education and Science (1977). *Health Education in Schools.* London: Her Majesty's Stationery Office.

Department of Transport, Road and Motor Vehicle Traffic Safety (1970). *Report on Publicity Effects concerning Certain Items in the Highway Code.* Ottawa.

Downing, C. (1980). Pre-school children and their parents. *Unpublished Report, Department of Environment, Transport and Road Research Laboratory,* Crowthorne: TRRL.

Ducker, R. (1975). *Threat Detection Training Programmes for Child Pedestrian Safety.* Volumes I and II. Washington: National Highway Traffic Safety Administration.

Elswood, D. (1970). A road safety project for 8–12s. *Safety Education.* 119, 8–9.

Firth, D. E. (1973). The road safety aspects of the Tufty Club. *Department of the Environment, Transport and Road Research Laboratory, Laboratory Report 604.* Crowthorne: TRRL.

Fisk, A. (1974). Suggestions for a syllabus of road safety education in nursery and primary schools. *Safety Education*, **132**, 14–15.

Fisk, A., and Cliffe, H. (1975). The effects of teaching the Green Cross Code to young children. *Department of the Environment, Transport and Road Research Laboratory, Supplementary Report 168 UC*. Crowthorne: TRRL.

Gerber, D., Huber, O., and Limbourg, M. (1977). *Verkehrserziehung in Vorschulalter*. Cologne: Bundesanstalt für Strassenwesen.

Gill, L. L., Mercer, S. W., and Ward, S. (1974). The effect of two appeals upon turn signalling behavior: a cross validation. *Unpublished Report*. Ontario: Queen's University.

Glover, E. M. (1976). Mind that child! *Safety Education*, **136**, 15.

Harries, D. E. (1979). Stop! Look! Listen! *Safety Education*, **4**, 21–23.

Heinrich, H. C. (1979). Behavioural counter-measures—education. *Symposium on Safety of Pedestrians and Cyclists, Road Research*, Paris: Organisation for Economic Co-operation and Development.

Ingram, V. (1978). Road safety and moral education. *Traffic Education*, **4**, 29–30.

James, W. J. (1978). Road safety education in school for partially sighted children. *Safety Education*, **143**, 31–32.

Jefatura Central De Trafico (Madrid) (1964). The pedestrian walk. *International Police Chronicle*, **12**, 13–56.

Jolly, K. W. (1977a). *Children and Traffic, Book 1—On the Pavement*. London: Macmillan Education.

Jolly, K. W. (1977b). *Children and Traffic, Book 2—The Young Traveller*. London: Macmillan Education.

Jolly, K. W. (1977c). *Children and Traffic, Book 3—Preparing for the Road*. London: Macmillan Education.

Jolly, K. W. (1977d). Teaching the 4Rs: trends in curriculum reform and their implications for the future of road safety education in schools. *Safety Education*, **140**, 3–5.

Kemp, A. (1979). Traffic and safety education in middle schools. *Traffic Education*, **4**, 13–14.

Kerr, S. (1980). Traffic education means life. *Traffic Education*, **5**, 27–29.

Lewis, G. D. (1979). The Tamworth child pedestrian proficiency scheme. *Traffic Education*, **4**, 16–17.

Limbourg, M., and Gerber, D. (1978). Das Tubingen Eltern Trainingsprogramm für die Verkehrserziehung von Kindern im Vorschulalter. *Unpublished Report*. Cologne: Bundesanstalt für Strassenwesen. (Cited in Rothengatter, T. *The Influence of Instructional Variables on the Effectiveness of Traffic Education*. Paper presented at the Organisation for Economic Co-operation and Development, Brussels, Workshop on Road Safety Education.)

Limbourg, M., and Günther, R, (1978). Erleben and Verhalten von 4 bis 9 Jahrigen Kindern im Strassenverkehr, *Zeitschrift für Verkehrserziehung*, 1977, **1**, 3–9. (Cited in Rothengatter, T. *The Influence of Instructional Variables on the Effectiveness of Traffic Education*. Paper presented at the Organisation for Economic Co-operation and Development, Brussels, Workshop on Road Safety Education.)

McGarvie, A., Davies, R. F., and Sheppard, E. J. (1980). A study of a road safety film for children. *Department of the Environment, Transport and Road Research Laboratory, Supplementary Report 578*. Crowthorne: TRRL.

McGivern, D. (1975). A student road safety project. *Safety Education*, **135**, 7–8.

McInerney, T. J. (1959). The pedestrian safety campaign in New York city. *Traffic Quarterly*, **13**, 283–293.

Meadows, A. (1977). Traffic education in Kent schools. *Safety Education*, **140**, 24–25.

Morris, J. P. (1972). *Road Safety Publicity: Quantifying the Effect of Public Service Advertising*. London: The Advertising Association.

Northern, N. M. (1975). Road safety education for younger pupils. *Safety Education*, **135**, 5–6.

Nummenmaa, T. (1970). Development of structured descriptions of events in childhood. *Unpublished Research Report 44, Department of Psychology*. Tampere, Finland: University of Tampere.

Nummenmaa, T., and Syvänen, M. (1974). Teaching road safety to children in the age range 5–7 years. *Paedogogica Europaea*, **9**, 151–161.

Nummenmaa, T., Ruuhilehto, K., and Syvänen, M. (1975). Traffic education programme for pre-school aged children and children starting school. *Report Number 17*, Helsinki: Central Organisation for Traffic Safety.

Organisation for Economic Co-operation and Development (OECD) Special Research Group on Pedestrian Safety (1978a). *Chairman's Report and Report of Sub-Group II: Road Safety Education. Department of the Environment, Transport and Road Research Laboratory*. Crowthorne: TRRL.

Organisation for Economic Co-operation and Development (OECD) Special Research Group on Pedestrian Safety (1978b). *Chairman's Report and Report Sub-Group III: Mass Media Communications for Pedestrian Safety. Department of the Environment, Transport and Road Research Laboratory*. Crowthorne: TRRL.

Osborne, E. A. (1975). Road safety. Sharing the responsibility. *Safety Education*, **134**, 6–7.

Page, T. J., Iwata, B. A., and Neef, N. A. (1976). Teaching pedestrian skills to retarded persons: generalization from the classroom to the natural environment. *Journal of Applied Behavioral Analysis*, **9**, 433–444.

Pease, K., and Preston, B. (1967). Road safety education for young children. *British Journal of Educational Psychology*, **33**, 305–312.

Piccolino, E. B. (1968). Depicted threat, realism and specificity: variables governing safety poster effectiveness. *Dissertation Abstracts International*, **28B**, 4330.

Preston, B. (1980). Teaching the Green Cross Code. *Traffic Education*, **5**, 3–4.

Reading, J. B. (1973). Pedestrian protection through behaviour modification. *Traffic Engineering*, **43**, 14–16 and 19–23.

Roberts, I. G. (1973). Road safety in Hertfordshire schools. *Safety Education*, **128**, 16–18.

Roberts, I. G. (1977). Road safety in middle schools in Hertfordshire. *Traffic Education*, **2**, 24–26.

Rothengatter, T. A. (1978). Learning foundations of traffic education. *Report VK 77-01, Traffic Research Centre*, Groningen: Rijksuniversiteit Groningen.

Rothengatter, T. A., and Brakenhoff-Splinter, J. (1979). Training road crossing behaviour for children. *Report VK 79-02, Traffic Research Centre*, Groningen: Rijksuniversiteit Groningen.

Royal Society for the Prevention of Accidents RoSPA (1975). *Suggestions for Teaching Road Safety*. Birmingham: Royal Society for the Prevention of Accidents.

Sadler, J. (1972). *Children and Road Safety: A Survey Amongst Mothers*. London: Her Majesty's Stationery Office.

Sandels, S. (1975). *Children in Traffic*. London: Elek.

Sargent, K. J. A., and Sheppard, D. (1974). The development of the Green Cross Code. *Department of the Environment, Transport and Road Research Laboratory, Laboratory Report 605*. Crowthorne: TRRL.

Schioldborg, P. (1974). Children, traffic and traffic training: an analysis of the children traffic club. *Unpublished Report, Psychological Institute*, Oslo, Norway.

Schioldborg, P. (1976). Children, traffic and traffic training. *Paper presented at the Fifth Congress of the International Federation of Pedestrians.* June Geilo, Norway: International Federation of Pedestrians.

Schools Council Project (1977). *Health Education (5–13).* London: Nelson.

Schreiber, J., and Berry, C. (1978). Communicating road safety to the young pedestrian—evaluation of road safety resource material for infants schools. *Traffic Accident Research Unit.* Rosebery, New South Wales, Australia: Department of Motor Transport.

Schreiber, J., and Lukin, J. (1978). Communicating road safety to the young pedestrian: an exploratory research programme. *Traffic Accident Research Unit.* Rosebery, New South Wales, Australia: Department of Motor Transport.

Sheppard, D. (1975b). Teaching pedestrian skills. a graded structure. *Safety Education,* **133,** 5–7.

Sheppard, D. (1975b). Teaching pedestrian skills: a graded structure. *Safety Education,* **135,** 13–17.

Sheppard, D. (1977). Ways in which school crossing patrols instruct children about crossing roads. *Department of the Environment and Department of Transport, Transport and Road Research Laboratory, Laboratory Report 779.* Crowthorne: TRRL.

Sheppard, E. J. (1969). A study of two road safety films. *Safety Education,* **115,** 19–20.

Sheppard, E. J. (1975). Comprehension by children of aerial views in road safety teaching aids. *Department of the Environment, Transport and Road Research Laboratory, Supplementary Report 152 UC.* Crowthorne: TRRL.

Singer, R. E. (1963). Action for pedestrian safety and control. *International Road Safety Traffic Review,* **11,** 17–20, 22–24, 29.

Singh, A. (1976). Road safety education in primary and middle schools. *Department of the Environment, Transport and Road Research Laboratory, Supplementary Report 207 UC.* Crowthorne: TRRL.

Singh, A. (1979). Children and traffic: evaluation of the effects of traffic education on the knowledge and attitudes of children aged 5–13. *Traffic Education,* **4,** 8–12.

Stephens, M. (1978). Health and traffic education 5–13 and 13–18. *Traffic Education,* **3,** 18–20.

Stokes, J. (1976). Safety—a school project. *Safety Education,* **138,** 8–9.

Turton, M. (1977). Road safety for infants. *Traffic Education,* **2,** 24–26.

Vernon, M. D. (1962). *The Psychology of Perception.* Harmondsworth, Middlesex: Penguin.

Walsh, L. B., and Nickson, F. (1972) *Pedestrian Safety for Urban Streets.* Volumes I, II, and III. San Jose, California: City of San Jose Pedestrian Safety Project.

Wiener, E. L. (1968). The elderly pedestrians: response to an enforcement campaign. *Traffic Safety Research Review,* **12,** 100–111.

Wilde, G. J. S., Cake, L. J., and Le Brasseur, R. (1974). Mass media safety campaigns: an annotated bibliography of recent developments, 1970–1973. *National Highway Traffic Safety Administration Report Number NHTSA-4–7304A.* Washington DC: United States Department of Transportation.

Wilde, G. J. S., L'Hoste, J., Sheppard, D., and Wind, C. (1971). Road safety campaigns: design and evaluation. Paris: Organisation for Economic Co-operation and Development.

Wuhrer, H. (1970). Nr. Sicher (Numbersafe) ADAC, Munich. (Cited in Wilde, G. J. S., L'Hoste, J., Sheppard, D., and Wind, C. (1971). *Road Safety Campaigns: Design and Evaluation.* Paris: Organisation for Economic Co-operation and Development.)

Pedestrian Accidents
Edited by A. J. Chapman, F. M. Wade and H. C. Foot
© 1982, John Wiley & Sons Ltd.

Chapter 4

Evaluating Pedestrian Safety Programmes

G. B. Grayson and C. I. Howarth

'Yes, but does it work?' In this chapter we examine this seemingly innocuous question and its implications, and show that the question is in fact a very complex one that raises issues fundamental to pedestrian safety research. It would be appropriate at this early stage to define 'evaluation'. This is not easy; it would appear that evaluation is one of those terms that is frequently used but inadequately defined. Despite this, there is a recognizable structure in all evaluation, and it is possible to describe a set of procedures that can maximize the information obtained from the evaluative process.

These procedures follow fairly directly from the structure of applied research which, to be effective, must always pass through the following sequence at least once (see Howarth, 1980a, for further discussion):

(a) *Define the objectives* to be achieved. If there is more than one objective, ask whether they compete with each other, and if they do, decide an order of priority.
(b) *Investigate the resources* available to achieve the objectives. Decide which resources are most relevant and useful.
(c) *Devise and implement a strategy* whereby the resources can be used to achieve the objectives.
(d) *Evaluate* the effectiveness of the strategy in terms of the degree to which it achieves the objectives.

Very few safety programmes pass through the full sequence and then stop. Some safety programmes begin, remain, and end at stage (c). When this happens the strategies used are ill-considered, and their efficacy unknown. However, when a programme has been carried through to the evaluation stage it is unusual for it to stop there, for the success or failure of the programme also evaluates the ideas developed at the earlier stages. It is therefore quite likely, and indeed desirable, that evaluation be followed by a reconsideration of the objectives, or the resources, or the strategies used, leading to a modification of the programme and to further evaluation in a continuing recurrent process.

It is desirable at this point to distinguish between safety measures which act directly on the road user, and those which act through changes in the environment. The latter are largely engineering measures which are localized, and for that reason have effects which are relatively easy to monitor. However, the evaluation of both engineering measures and those which are aimed directly on the road user often suffers from important shortcomings. For example, the evaluation of engineering measures has tended to concentrate on producing evidence of effectiveness, and has contributed less to our understanding of the operation of countermeasures. By contrast, those measures that aim to influence the road user directly are usually very much harder to assess in terms of accident reduction, but more readily provide information on the ways in which countermeasures work—or do not work—in practice.

A further distinction is that between pedestrian safety research and pedestrian safety programmes. Research is concerned with the identification of possible ways of reducing pedestrian casualties; programmes are concerned with the implementation of these ideas. Our aim in this chapter is to demonstrate that evaluation is capable of linking these two activities, and of making a positive contribution to both. Historically, evaluation has been accorded a low standing in safety research and safety programmes, particularly those aimed directly at the road user. The reasons for this are complex. In the early days, enthusiasm for the design and introduction of safety measures left little time or appetite for evaluative procedures. Moreover, there has been a tendency for talent and achievement to be recognized more readily in the formulation and development of countermeasures than in the more prosaic business of evaluation. Perhaps even more pervasive has been the tendency to view evaluation from a political standpoint (we hasten to draw attention to the fact that 'political' here has a small 'p'). In this context evaluation is all too readily seen as an almost subversive activity that could rock the boat. For example, if a safety measure costs £ X, then to expend that amount of money is a public demonstration of one's confidence in it, particularly if X is a large number. But to pay, in addition, for evaluation by increasing the expenditure to £ X + £ Y, even if Y is only small, is to suggest that there is some doubt about the need to spend £ X on the programme itself, and to raise the fearful prospect that the result may show that the initial outlay was wasted.

Finally, if safety programmes are to be evaluated efficiently, the normal rules of scientific evidence and inference must be followed as far as possible. These often conflict with concepts of justice and fairness which are important elements in any stable society. For example, the effectiveness of a safety measure may be difficult to evaluate if it is applied simultaneously to all parts of the country, since any changes it may produce will be difficult to disentangle from the effects of other simultaneous factors such as the weather, the price of oil or the temporary impact of publicity given to the measure during its introduction. Much better information could be obtained if the measure were applied, initially, to only a part of the country, so that one could compare, for example, accident rates in those parts of the country to which the measure is applied with the rates in those parts of the country where the measure has not yet been implemented. Unfortunately, if there is strong public belief in the measure this will be regarded as unfair to the people initially deprived of it; whereas if the measure imposes penalties, or in some way inconveniences the people to whom it is applied, the uneven application of it will be regarded as unjust to those who suffer it in the test period.

Safety research takes place within a social framework, and it would be pointless to pretend that this fact does not influence the way in which it operates. Thus there is a very human tendency to give potentially unfavourable evaluation a low priority in safety programmes, or to give undue emphasis to trivial, but apparently favourable results. The practice of evaluation may be deterred by a growing appreciation of the complexity of its problems. We now consider the nature of these in greater detail, and argue that, despite their complexity, these problems can be overcome. When they are, evaluation can be the most valuable element in any safety programme. Not only does it provide the essential feedback loop that enables us to decide whether to continue or to abandon a safety programme, it also acts as a link between pedestrian safety programmes and safety research, since it is an essential element in both. It provides a better understanding of the basic issues in research, and also in the design of safety programmes. If the results are illuminating, or even surprising, then this is an effective stimulus to the development of new ideas. At a more mundane level, evaluation can lead to a continual improvement in safety measures. A large part of this chapter is taken up with an examination of the problems that must be dealt with if evaluation is to be done properly. These are questions of methodology, and it is important to make clear that methodology is being referred to here not in the narrow sense of concern with statistical procedures and experimental design, but in its true meaning as the study of the methods of scientific enquiry. In this latter sense, the proper definition of problems is deemed to be just as important as the techniques used in the solution of problems. With this distinction in mind, the first part of the examination is concerned with the nature of the questions that can be asked, and in particular with the measures that can be involved.

THE MEASUREMENT OF RISK

Evaluation is not only of practical value: it is also intellectually rewarding. The greater the effort put into it, the greater the information which can be extracted. The minimum requirement for an evaluation programme is to get an answer to the question 'Does it work?' But with more effort one can get useful answers to the subsidiary questions 'Why or how does it work?' and 'For whom does it work?' But whatever the question being asked, the answer depends upon estimates of risk. In the simplest case one tries to estimate whether the risk of an accident has been reduced for the whole population considered; for example, have zebra crossings reduced (or increased) the total number of pedestrian accidents? But it is obviously more useful if one can estimate separately the risk of crossing on the zebra and the risk of crossing elsewhere, and further estimate whether any change is due to changes in travel patterns, or to changes in the risk of individual road crossings, or both. It is also helpful to have separate estimates of risk for different sections of the population; are pelican crossings, for example, equally helpful to the young, the middle-aged and the elderly?

In many cases it is actually easier to estimate the effect of a safety measure on a rather restricted measure of risk than it is to measure its effect on the accident rate for the total population. This is the case with uncontrolled crossings, where it has been shown that these reduce the risk of crossing the road at the sites where they are located, but the overall effect as far as lengths of road are concerned is much less clear, a situation found both in this country and abroad (Older and Grayson, 1976).

Whatever the question being asked, there is an appropriate estimate of risk, where risk is defined as the ratio of the number of accidents to exposure:

$$\text{Risk} = \frac{\text{Number of accidents}}{\text{Exposure}}$$

To be meaningful, the number of accidents and the exposure measure must be related to the same data base. But even with this restriction there are an enormous number of different measures of exposure one can use. For example, in most countries accident statistics are presented per 100,000 population; that is, the number of accidents is divided by the number of people in the total (or the relevant) population and then multiplied by 10^5. This enables international comparisons to be made which can tell us, for example, whether an average member of the population is more likely to die as a pedestrian in one country than in another. But this estimate will *not* tell us whether it is safer to cross the road in one country than in the other, since the greater likelihood of accidents may be the result of a much greater number of road crossings rather than a reflection of the danger of individual crossings, which may indeed be safer in the country with the greater number of road crossings.

Unfortunately, in the case of pedestrians we do not usually have any information about their average exposure in terms of roads crossed, or of miles travelled. This is in marked contrast to what we know about vehicular transport, where almost all advanced countries make some estimate of vehicular miles (although this is sometimes only estimated from petrol sales), and the average occupancy of the vehicles concerned. From these estimates of exposure we can calculate the risk per mile of different kinds of transport, and monitor and interpret the changes in risk that have occurred over time. In the case of pedestrians we have few estimates of the average pedestrian miles, or of the average number of roads crossed. Hence, although there has been a fall in pedestrian accidents in Great Britain during the past 10 years (see Chapter 1), we do not know whether this is because pedestrian travel has become safer, or, alternatively, because it has become more dangerous, but with a disproportionate reduction in the amount of pedestrian travel.

This lack of relevant and regular exposure data means that there is no single large scale pedestrian safety programme about which one can be certain that it has had an overall effect on *safety* in the sense in which that term is usually understood. There are some programmes that have been associated with a reduction in the total number of accidents (e.g. the *Green Cross Code*), but whether these are due to a reduction in exposure or a reduction of risk we do not know. Equally there are some programmes (e.g. in relation to zebra and pelican crossings) that we can be reasonably sure have decreased the risk at particular sites. But whether they are associated with an overall reduction in pedestrian risk, again we do not know.

There are three major exceptions to this general lack of interest in measures of pedestrian exposure. On a national level, the largest investigation undertaken in this country to date is the survey of pedestrian activity carried out by the Office of Population Censuses and Surveys (Todd and Walker, 1980). This survey, which was confined to adults, had two main aims: (a) to collect detailed information on pedestrian movement in order to derive exposure measures, and to examine differences in these measures between sub-groups of the population; and (b) to compare these measures with the appropriate accident data in order to obtain measures of risk, and again to examine the distribution of risk over the population. Three exposure measures were obtained from the survey data: roads crossed, distance travelled, and time spent walking. When related to accident data, each measure produced a corresponding risk estimate—risk per road crossing, risk per kilometre, and risk per hour on foot. The survey not only provided accurate and reliable estimates of the *quantity* of exposure, but the amount of detail obtained made it possible to derive some measure of the *quality* of exposure; for example, in terms of class of road, use of crossing facilities, location of road crossing, and so on. On both these levels the survey yielded a wealth of valuable information. However, its value is limited by being restricted to one point in time, and it cannot therefore be used to any real extent in evaluation work. As Howarth (1980b) has pointed out, only when such data are available in a consistent and repeated form will exposure and risk measures be able to play their full part in the assessment of particular safety programmes, as well as the monitoring of long-term trends.

On a more local level, Howarth and his associates have developed four different techniques for studying pedestrian exposure and have compared the results obtained from these in the city of Nottingham (Routledge, Repetto-Wright and Howarth, 1976). The four methods were:

(a) Ask parents about their children's pedestrian travel.
(b) Ask the children themselves to report what they did in the previous twenty-four hours.
(c) Follow children home from school and record their road crossings.
(d) Place observers at a sample of road sites and observe the number of road crossings made by different types of pedestrians.

Methods (a), (b) and (c) were applied to a sample of children and by comparing them one can detect under- or over-estimation of the amount of travel in the first two methods, which depend upon purely subjective assessments. In fact method (c) produced the highest estimate of children's exposure to traffic, which was slightly under-estimated by the children themselves, and slightly more so by their parents. Method (d) applied to a sample of roads rather than to a sample of pedestrians. The degree of agreement between methods (c) and (d) is an excellent validation of the observational methods on which both are based. Methods (c) and (d), as well as being the most accurate, also gave more detailed information, since the observers could record where the road crossings occurred (for example, whether they were at road junctions or pedestrian crossings, and whether they were close to parked cars), the behaviour of the pedestrians and the traffic density at the time.

Methods (a), (b) and (c) enable one to estimate mileage travelled as well as the number of roads crossed, while method (d) only provides an estimate of the number of roads crossed, and not of mileage travelled. In method (d) other information about the pedestrians, such as their age and sex, or the purpose of the journey must be estimated by the observers (rather inaccurately in some cases), or the pedestrians must be stopped and questioned to elicit the extra information. These extra procedures make the whole exercise more difficult and expensive.

On an even more local level, many studies have used observation to estimate exposure at particular road crossing sites where the exposure of pedestrians to traffic is high or where some specific safety measure is being applied. A number of such studies were carried out by the Road Research Laboratory in the 1960s (see Chapter 6); perhaps the best known is that of Mackie and Older (1965). It is interesting that in all these investigations the concern was directly with the measurement of pedestrian risk, and the notion of exposure was only implicit. The procedure used was to compare the numbers of pedestrians crossing various sections of selected lengths of road with the numbers of injury accidents involving pedestrians recorded on the same lengths of road. Proximity to road junctions and to pedestrian crossing facilities were major variables in the analysis, and it was these studies that were responsible for the identification of those sections of road adjacent to crossings as being areas of high risk to pedestrians. It was this finding that led subsequently to the introduction of the zigzag markings that are now a standard feature of zebra crossings.

These investigations, and others of a similar nature that have been carried out elsewhere, are essentially normative in purpose, and are only of incidental value in evaluative work. Furthermore, they are site specific. This means that even if the technique were to be used to estimate the effect of a particular safety measure, it could only do so over short lengths of road representing a very small sample of pedestrian movements. The assumption is widely held that safety measures have little or no effect on overall patterns of pedestrian movement; this assumption should be more often questioned. The techniques used by Todd and Walker (1980) and by Howarth and his associates are the only ones by which effects on overall patterns of travel can be directly assessed.

In addition to direct methods of estimating exposure by asking people or observing them, there are also a number of indirect methods. Grayson (1979) has estimated exposure and risk by comparing the number of pedestrian accidents that occur on the pavement (assumed to be unaffected by pedestrian behaviour, and hence to provide an estimate of exposure), with the number of accidents in the roadway. By a similar but more complex estimation procedure Wass (1977) has estimated exposure from a combination of different accident statistics.

Even when exposure is estimated directly, accident statistics must be used to calculate risk. Numbers of accidents can, in theory, be obtained from the accident data which are recorded in all advanced countries; but, unfortunately, there are many deficiencies in the way these enter the official statistics. Accidents are usually recorded by people such as the police and members of the medical profession, whose primary concerns are more pressing. They tend to be recorded some time after the event has occurred, and the gory consequences have been cleared away. It is well-known that many of the accidents that are entered in hospital records are not reported to the police, and *vice versa*. Under-reporting is particularly prevalent for accidents with mild consequences. Serious accidents, and particularly fatal accidents, are more meticulously recorded. Hence, where feasible any evaluative procedures should be based on fatal and serious accident statistics. But even for these, some details of the accident may not be recorded very accurately. For example, parked cars that may have been present at the time of the accident may have been moved before the accident information was recorded. An additional complication is that the conventions for filling in the form may not always be interpreted in the same way. These problems are well-known, and continual efforts are made to remedy them.

In summary, the most convincing answer to the question 'Does it work?' should be provided by good estimates of risk based on reliable accident statistics and accurate measures of exposure. Without these, evaluative programmes can have little authority.

OTHER METHODOLOGICAL PROBLEMS

Having looked at the questions that need to be asked, it is now time to turn to the more technical problems involved in providing answers to the questions.

These technical problems are not specific to accident research, for they involve the basic rules of scientific evidence and inference, and as such are common to many branches of applied science. They will be dealt with under three headings: (a) problems of control; (b) statistical problems; and (c) problems of interpretation. All forms of evaluation attempt to demonstrate that a particular treatment brings about a particular result—ideally, a reduction in accidents. Whether the result is to be attributed to the treatment under consideration, or to some other factor is a problem of control. Whether the result can achieve an acceptable standard in the light of the laws of probability is a statistical decision problem. Whether one can maintain that the effect will continue to occur at different times and in different circumstances is a problem of interpretation.

Problems of control

In the laboratory, the rules of experimental design are embodied in the controlled experiment, where the effect of one factor on another can be established by exercising strict control of the situation. This approach—the essential feature of the scientific method—lies behind the enormous advances in knowledge that have occurred in the physical and biological sciences. The application of this approach to the behavioural and social sciences has not always been so successful. There are good reasons why this should be so. Perhaps the most important is the influence that belief can have on the effect of a particular programme. If people believe in something, then it tends to work—at least in the short term. There are many examples of this powerful but confusing phenomenon, ranging from the placebo effect in medicine to the 'Hawthorne' effect in industrial relations. Safety programmes are not immune to the influence of this phenomenon, and it is not uncommon to find programmes that have an initial impact which subsequently fades away (e.g. most propaganda campaigns, the breathalyzer and possibly the *Green Cross Code*). The effect of belief is always difficult to control, but it may be measurable.

A second major difficulty in achieving a proper controlled experiment is the sheer practical difficulty of gaining adequate control of all the variables. Despite these difficulties, the degree of control achievable in the laboratory experiment is held as the ideal by many workers; for example, Tarrants and Veigel (1978) recommend that 'all projects selected for effectiveness evaluations should be designed as experiments and should follow general scientific rules of experimental design' (p. 38). In the real world, of course, most evaluation falls short of this ideal. Strategies for coping with the difficulties encountered in field studies of safety programmes are discussed in a report of the Organisation for Economic Co-operation and Development (OECD, 1981), while Howarth (1980a) has produced a more theoretical treatment.

Road accidents are both stable and unstable. In some respects, particularly in national statistics and in the long term, they show great regularity. In others, particularly at a local level, and in the short term, they vary considerably in response to a wide variety of influences—diurnal, seasonal, locational and many others, both known and unknown. It is very easy to misinterpret the effect of a safety programme if it is applied in phase with one of these naturally occurring influences. When this happens a real change in accident rates occurs, but it may well be due to some influence other than the safety programme itself. For example, Schioldborg (1976) has described the results of a safety education programme aimed at pre-school children in Norway. Among those children taking part in the programme, pedestrian accidents per child were 20 per cent less than those among children not receiving the programme. At first sight this seems an impressive result, considerably greater than most of those achieved in the past by propaganda and educational programmes. But the children who took part were not randomly assigned to treatment and non-treatment groups. The children were volunteered by their parents, and only the volunteers received the treatment. Hence, no valid conclusions can be drawn. Indeed it is perfectly possible that this form of safety training, like some others, actually increases children's liability to accidents. The kind of parents who volunteer their children for a safety education programme are likely to be safety conscious even in the absence of the educational programme. We know that after safety education the children had, on average, fewer accidents than other children in Norway. What we do not know are the comparative accident rates before the safety programme. If the difference between the two groups was initially more than 20 per cent, we would conclude that the safety programme had actually increased risk. The problem might have been overcome in three ways, either by measuring accident rates of treated and untreated groups before and after the programme, or by assigning half the volunteers to an untreated (or delayed treatment) group, or by finding a more appropriate comparison group. Best of all would be to use a combination of these.

There is nothing new in this emphasis on control. Indeed, it has been implicit in all empirical science since the time of Galileo, and was first stated explicitly and formally by John Stuart Mill (1891) in his *System of Logic*. One of the canons expounded by him was the *Method of Difference* which states 'if a case in which an effect occurs, and one in which it does not occur, are exactly alike except for the presence or absence of a single factor, then the factor is probably the cause of the effect' (p. 256). In the classical laboratory experiment referred to earlier, the procedure adopted to ensure that the cases are 'exactly alike' is to take a homogenous sample and then to allocate the subjects at random to either a 'treatment' or a 'control' group. Differences between the results for the two groups are then taken as a measure of the effectiveness of the treatment.

In applied work, and in road safety research in particular, it is often difficult to allocate people at random. The next best (as was suggested in relation to the Norwegian study), is either to use the subjects as their own controls in a before-and-after study (but in that case treatment is confounded with time), or to find a *matched* control group (but in that case one is always in doubt about the adequacy of the match). A specially powerful example of the use of matched controls is the use of *matched pairs*. This requires that for every member of the treatment group, a control is found that matches as closely as possible in all the variables which may be deemed relevant. This is difficult to achieve in practice, and is not without problems at a theoretical level (Meehl, 1971).

Even these accommodations to the rules of scientific inference are often missing from safety research, and misleading inferences are drawn from inappropriate comparisons, or from studies of a whole population where many explanations can be found for any observed changes over time. At a local level there is often no possibility of obtaining a control group, but a large number of small before-and-after studies are better than one large one, since it is unlikely that they will all be affected in exactly the same way by the passage of time. At a national level, as when major propaganda or educational programmes are mounted, the before-and-after comparisons are so weak that no strong conclusions can be drawn. In such studies the need for control groups is very great, but unfortunately the resistance to them is very strong. As described earlier, the use of untreated groups may raise ethical problems as well as purely practical ones.

The ethical problems raised by the unequal treatment of different people can be matched by the ethical problems of mounting an expensive campaign without any sure knowledge of whether it will make things better rather than worse, and with no possibility of finding out. These are discussed further in Chapter 3. But the practical problems are more difficult to argue away. How are the treatment and control groups to be kept separate and distinct throughout the whole exercise, and—even more important—how are we to ensure that they are comparable to begin with? For example, in the case of television safety campaigns, it is possible to make use of the regional television networks to give different treatments to different regions. But it could be argued that the very existence of the regional networks is a result of real differences between the regions. These difficulties do not excuse our abandoning the rules of scientific evidence as formulated by John Stuart Mill. We should always strive to make our inferences as powerful as possible, and the power of these inferences depends upon our ability to overcome the practical difficulties of applied research. The power of science lies not in the certainty of any single inference, but in the cumulative effect of many inter-related studies. As each evaluation makes us reconsider our objectives, our resources and our strategies, so our understanding increases, and with it our ability to make things happen as we would wish them to happen.

So far we have tended to assume that the only desirable result of a safety measure is a reduction in accidents, and that is why we have based our discussion on the measurement of risk. While this may be the primary aim of any safety measure, there is no reason why it should be the sole aim. Safety at the expense of quality of life is likely to be unacceptable, rejected, and therefore self-defeating.

Statistical problems

This topic has been dealt with at length elsewhere. Probably the best and most recent treatment is in OECD (1981), and no extended discussion is attempted here. Instead we draw attention to two statistical points of particular relevance to the practice of evaluation. The first of these is the question of significance. Safety research has long suffered under the tyranny of statistical significance. If there is a certain irony in that it has been hoist with its own petard, it can derive some consolation from the fact that it is not alone, for other sciences are in similar situations (psychologists' discomfort with the concept of IQ is a case in point). Having patiently persuaded customers and practitioners over the years of the necessity of applying esoteric mathematical procedures in order to establish 'significance', safety workers now evince alarm when those same people equate significance with truth or validity. Slavish adherence to the tenets of statistical significance produced crude and arbitrary methods of evaluation. If a safety measure achieved a certain level (i.e. was 'significant'), then it was accepted without reservation. If it fell below this level—albeit an arbitrary one—then it was consigned to the flames. It is of course desirable that certain standards should obtain to ensure that data are treated with both respect and caution; it is equally *undesirable* that these standards should become the sole determinants of success or failure, or worse, that they should be held to decide between truth or falsity. To establish a level of significance is to do no more than to place marker flags on the continuum of probability; it is only an aid to decision making, and not a substitute.

The second point to be raised briefly is derived from the first. When using statistical techniques in order to test hypotheses, there are two forms of mistake that can be made. The first is to find an apparent effect, when in reality one does not exist. The second is to fail to detect an effect when it does exist. Formally, these are known as Type I and Type II errors respectively. The emphasis on significance described above has led to an excessive concentration on the avoidance of Type I errors; technically speaking, hypothesis testing then becomes a highly conservative affair. It could be argued that this is unsatisfactory, particularly in the early stages of countermeasure development and testing. It is likely that a fair number of promising safety measures have been abandoned in the past because they did not satisfy statistical standards intended mainly to avoid making mistakes. Hauer (1978) gives a good discussion of this point, and stresses the practical necessity of specifying the costs and values of the various outcomes if real benefit is to be gained from hypothesis testing.

Interpretation problems

If methodological standards were scrupulously observed, and statistical techniques were impeccable, then interpretation would be easier, but not altogether without difficulty. Adequate control and proper statistics merely enable us to deduce that an effect is related to and perhaps caused by a particular treatment. Our expectations that the treatment will have a similar effect on other occasions, or that the treatment can be modified while still remaining effective, or that it can be improved upon—these are all matters of interpretation, and depend upon our theoretical understanding of what is going on. Many studies merely evaluate a particular safety programme, but in so doing contribute little to our theoretical understanding. They are obviously less valuable than those studies which, by increasing our understanding, suggest what we should do next.

However, in the real world it is more common to find deficiencies in methodology and in statistics that make interpretation a complex and difficult task. There is then the possibility of being unduly influenced by expectation or by common sense. This is not to suggest that common sense is necessarily bad, simply that it should be used with discretion. The point here is that interpretation always takes place within a particular environmental framework, and should be recognized as being affected by it. This can be seen in its most extreme form when cross-cultural factors come into play. Wilson and Older (1970) studied the effects of doubling the number of crossing facilities in two English towns, and demonstrated that this could be done without adversely affecting road uses safety or behaviour. This they interpreted as a positive result. However a later Canadian review (Lea, 1978) interpreted the absence of any marked changes as evidence that crossing facilities did not contribute to safety. This is only one example from many that could be given to show that evaluation is not a precise and objective procedure, but one which is influenced by a variety of external factors—cultural, political, personal and practical. One of these is fashion. Bandwagons are not uncommon on both local and national levels; safety research workers who are concerned about objectivity should be very cautious about boarding such vehicles. Scientific caution based on adequately controlled studies, proper statistical inference, and a coherently developed theory, is to be preferred. The ride is initially slower and less exhilarating, but ultimately goes much further. Most bandwagons crash.

THE USE OF INDIRECT MEASURES

Even this brief discussion of methodology has shown that evaluation is a complex process fraught with difficulty. But in small-scale studies of safety there is an additional problem created by the fact that accidents are rare events. So in the short term the number of accidents occurring may be too small to make any reliable inference. This has led to a demand for alternative indirect methods of evaluating safety measures by the use of what may be called 'accident surrogates'; that is, events which are not accidents, but which are related to and predictors of accidents, and which are common enough to be readily observed. The commonest of these is the 'conflict' or near accident. Different definitions and criteria of conflicts have been used, but all of them produce much more data than accidents themselves. Hence evaluation of a safety measure can be done more quickly on the basis of conflict studies.

But conflicts have another useful property. They occur so frequently that they can be observed directly by safety workers. In contrast, accidents are so rare that they are very seldom observed by a safety researcher. The authors of this chapter have been studying pedestrian accidents for many years, but neither have they nor has any of their colleagues ever observed an accident in the course of their studies. The characteristics of real accidents and the events leading up to them must always be studied retrospectively, through the filter of fallible, shocked and often biased memory. Since near accidents may share many of the characteristics of real accidents, and may be preceded by similar chains of events, one may hope to learn something about real accidents by observing near accidents or conflicts.

So one hopes that an adequate answer to the question 'Does it work?' can be obtained by looking for a reduction in conflicts, and that the more detailed questions 'Why, or how does it work?' and 'For whom does it work?' can be answered by studying the effect of the safety programme on the characteristics of observed conflicts. Whether this hope will ever be justified is a matter of interpretation, and a hypothesis which must itself be evaluated. Unfortunately, no adequate evaluations have yet been carried out for pedestrian/vehicle conflicts.

In the case of vehicle/vehicle conflicts a number of different studies have shown correlations between conflicts and accidents. But these correlations are not very large, and may well be due to variations in traffic density. Pedestrian/vehicle conflict studies are beginning to be reported (e.g. Guttinger, 1980), but attempts to validate them as predictors of real accidents are still rare. An obvious way to do this would be to see whether observed conflicts show the same relationship to age as real accidents do. The Accident Research Unit at the University of Nottingham intends to conduct a study of this kind in the near future. Until there are more validations of this kind, conflict studies will remain even more difficult to interpret than are measures of risk based on accident statistics.

EXAMPLES OF EVALUATION

In this section we look at some practical examples of evaluation in order to draw some lessons for the future. This is not meant to be a textbook of case histories, but more a brief examination of some events in the last decade. The first event to be considered is the decade itself, or rather the reduction in accidents that has taken place over that period. In the last ten years the population of the UK has increased by one million, there are three million more vehicles on the roads, and traffic has increased by some 40 per cent (see Chapter 1). Despite this, pedestrian casualties have shown a marked decrease both in absolute numbers (16 per cent) and in population rates (17 per cent). There is therefore considerable ground for satisfaction in that more people and more vehicles are using the roads more safely, at least as far as pedestrians are concerned. However, the satisfaction would be all the greater if one knew why the reduction in casualties had taken place. There is no shortage of explanations: urban planning techniques, traffic engineering measures, road safety education, publicity and propaganda have all been advanced—usually by their own advocates. What is lacking is any means of judging one claim against another. The result is one with which all should be happy, but for which none can legitimately claim the credit. The retrospective examination of global changes in accident frequencies is no substitute for properly planned and executed evaluation studies.

The possible explanations mentioned above differed in nature and objectives. Two were concerned with modifications of the physical environment, and two aimed to influence the road user directly. These differences have important implications for the practice of evaluation. As Grayson (1981) has pointed out, it is virtually impossible to obtain unequivocal evidence of the effectiveness of some educational measures due to their inability to satisfy methodological requirements.

The assessment of wide-ranging educational principles is a far more difficult task than the evaluation of some traffic engineering measure. A good example in the last decade is the introduction of the *Green Cross Code* in Britain. Taylor (1977) has described the sequence of events in which an extensive publicity campaign was followed by a reduction in child pedestrian casualties that was sufficient to offset the costs of the campaign. This result was widely heralded as demonstrating the effectiveness of road safety instruction and publicity, and an OECD report on the mass media (OECD, 1978) singled out the *Green Cross Code* as probably the only proven measure in the literature. The report also states: 'further work will be necessary in order to establish which particular aspects of the Code make it an effective accident countermeasure' (p. 22). This quotation merits further attention. To begin with, it is mistaken in inferring the success of the campaign from the reduction in casualties; the mere examination of accident data does not allow one to draw firm conclusions of that nature, for it is equally possible that the effect could have been brought about by temporary changes in driver behaviour or in child pedestrian behaviour that may have resulted from the very existence of publicity, rather than from its subject matter. Second, there is the methodological point that, in the absence of a control group it is not strictly possible to conclude that the reduction in the number of casualties occurred as a result of the publicity campaign; it might, for example, be attributable to cyclical variations in the long-term distribution of casualties. Finally, there is the point implied in the quotation. Even if it were possible to link the casualty reduction to the introduction of the Code, one would still not know how or why this had occurred. There are therefore two lessons to be drawn from this example; first, that some form of control is essential; and second, that accident statistics by themselves are only descriptive of situations or changes in situations, and have no explanatory value.

The next two examples of evaluation at work are concerned with 'hardware' countermeasures; that is, modifications of the physical environment. It was suggested earlier that evaluation of the effectiveness of these measures should in principle be an easier task than the assessment of measures operating directly upon the road user. The first example to be given shows that this is not always necessarily the case. It concerns the zigzag markings in the area of the road adjoining zebra crossings. These markings were introduced as a result of a number of studies over the years that had shown that pedestrians experienced very high risks when crossing the road in the close proximity of crossing facilities, and further, that many of the accidents involving pedestrians on or near pedestrian crossings were associated with overtaking vehicles. A pattern of zigzag markings on the road within 20 yards of zebra crossings was therefore designed in order to indicate to drivers that they should not park or overtake within the area, and to pedestrians that they should not cross the road within the same area—except, of course, at the crossing itself. The measure was adopted in Britain early in the last decade, and has attracted much attention overseas. Indeed, one of the recommendations of an OECD report on environmental measures (OECD, 1977) was that similar areas should be introduced more widely. It is all the more unfortunate, then, that evaluation of this measure has proved to be such a difficult task. There are a number of reasons for this. The first is that the measure was introduced over a long period of time (more than two years) for practical and financial reasons, there being at the time over 10,000 zebra crossings in the country. This means that national accident statistics could not be used over that period. Another reason was the advent of the pelican crossing. This more or less coincided with the introduction of zigzag markings, with the result that just as zebra crossings were being equipped with the markings, so small but increasing proportions of them were being converted to pelican crossings. Thus from the outset the number of cases under treatment was never constant, a fact which rendered the use of national accident statistics difficult at best. An additional problem was that the standard accident reporting system in use at the time took 50 yards as the limit for recording an accident as being near to a crossing, whereas the markings occupied only 20 yards of road. It was necessary therefore to undertake specific investigations on a smaller scale, but this immediately comes up against the problem that pedestrian crossings have very low accident rates per crossing installation, in the order of one of two pedestrian accidents per year on average. In practice, there has been no definitive study of the effectiveness of the markings, nor can there ever be one. Although the original problem was identified with care and the countermeasure introduced only after extensive pilot work, evaluation of zigzag markings relies on the results from a number of small-scale studies of behaviour, accidents and risk. None of these is conclusive in itself, but together they allow one to be reasonably confident that the markings are effective.

The fourth example to be discussed is the experimental installation of speed control humps in residential areas (Sumner and Baguley, 1979). Unlike the other examples, in this case the evaluation process was planned from the outset in the light of the specific objectives of the proposed countermeasure. First was the identification of the problem: the high numbers of accidents, particularly to children, on roads in residential areas used by through traffic. Second was the specification of desired changes in behaviour: the reduction of vehicle speeds and the diversion of necessary traffic. Third was the statement of the ultimate objective: that the reduction of accidents on the experimental roads should not be offset by an increase in the surrounding areas as a result of diverted traffic. Finally, there was another issue, that of public acceptability. This has not been considered in most evaluation work in the past, but it is an issue of growing importance, and one which could play a very significant role in the future. By specifying the objectives in this way it was possible to make evaluation a continuing process; first came the assessment of acceptability and behavioural change, and then subsequently the examination of accident data. This distinction between short-term and long-term evaluation is one of the main lessons to be drawn from this example. Another is the importance of specifying and measuring possible side-effects, especially where one of the intentions of the proposed measure is to divert activity to other locations. In these circumstances, the possibility of side-effects needs to be built in to the design of the evaluation process.

Local solutions to local problems often involve the 'black spot' approach. When there are a large number of accidents at a particular place, local pressure may result in an engineering remedy being tried; for example, the installation of a new pedestrian crossing, or new road markings, or changes in the layout of the roads to change the pattern of traffic flow, the installation of traffic islands, or of pedestrian barriers. When this is done, the number of accidents is monitored, and if there is a fall in the number then the measure is justifiably regarded as successful. However, it is unusual for the number of pedestrian road crossings at the site to be monitored, so that the assumption that the safety measure has worked by making the site *safer* is based on the untested assumption that the measure will not have had a marked effect on pedestrian flow at the particular site. Even when pedestrian flow at the site is monitored, the effect of these local measures on overall pedestrian travel patterns is hardly ever studied, and indeed it would be wildly extravagant to attempt to study them for every black spot which is changed. However, there is a suspicion developing that the black spot approach is beginning to produce diminishing returns on the grounds that the accidents which have been prevented at the black spot may be counterbalanced by an increase in accidents elsewhere. It is also possible that the black spot approach is having a generally depressing effect on the quality and quantity of pedestrian travel. Underpasses, pedestrian barriers, and traffic lights all impose a delay, or increase the distance to be travelled to get from A to B. We do not, at the moment, know the overall cumulative effect of these products of the black spot approach. These considerations have led in recent times to the application and evaluation of schemes that are much less site-specific than the traditional black spot approach (Dalby, 1979; Sabey, 1980).

EVALUATING THE EVALUATORS

So far in this chapter we have looked at some of the problems of evaluation and at a few examples of the ways these have influenced the assessment of safety measures in the past. It should, by now, be obvious that the practice of evaluation falls far short of what we are presenting as the theoretical ideal. It is therefore fair to ask if the difficulties of evaluation are such that it is unrealistic to expect evaluation to make a more positive contribution to safety research, and whether the low priority given to evaluation in the past may not have been fully justified because of the practical and theoretical difficulties which evaluation creates. This leads to a more pertinent (and even impertinent) question: 'Is the growing preoccupation of safety workers with evaluations justified, or are they merely creating "jobs for the boys"?'

We have already stated our belief that evaluation can be the most valuable part of any safety programme. We must now try to justify that belief in more detail. The first, and perhaps the most important argument, is a very pragmatic one. Safety measures cost money, and are becoming increasingly expensive to implement. They consume scarce resources, and it is no longer politically acceptable to do this merely on the *assumption* that benefits may result. Sabey (1980) has looked at the implications of these facts in relation to the activities of local authorities, who now have a major responsibility for road safety. The cost-effective approach will be applied to safety measures, as to all other aspects of government activity. Evaluation is an essential pre-requisite of any cost-effectiveness calculation. It follows from this that, whatever the current deficiencies of evaluation, these must be overcome if safety programmes are to be justified in competition with other claims on resources.

However, it is a major part of our argument that evaluation is not just the concern of the Treasurer's Department. If done properly evaluation can provide better understanding (the basis of safety research) and lead to better counter-measures (the basis of safety programmes). To be effective in this latter sense, the evaluation of a countermeasure should go beyond the basic task of establishing whether it has brought about a reduction in accidents. It is for this reason that evaluations should make use of the more detailed and sophisticated estimates of risk described earlier in the chapter, since these measures are essential if one is to attempt some explanation of the result. Grayson (1979) has argued that any measure of risk implies a theory of accident causation, and that more precise measures imply more and more sophisticated theories. For example, the commonest measure of risk, the risk per 100,000 population, which is the one used in most accident statistics, simply measures the risk of accident involvement to a member of the population used in calculating the statistics. This measure of risk can be used to test hypotheses about the relative danger of living in different places. The risk per road crossing, which is calculated by many researchers, implies a theory that pedestrian accidents are more likely to occur on roads rather than elsewhere, and can be used to test hypotheses about the relative risks of crossing different types of road. This type of statistic has been used, for example, to investigate the effect of traffic density on the risk of crossing roads (Jacobs and Wilson, 1967; Howarth, Routledge and Repetto-Wright, 1974). The finding that the risk to pedestrians is roughly proportional to traffic density is both of great theoretical and practical significance, and leads to the development of yet another measure of risk, the risk per potential encounter with a vehicle (Howarth, *et al.*, 1974). This statistic can be used to compare the effectiveness of safety measures in situations where traffic densities may vary greatly.

Even more detailed exposure measures have been obtained by Howarth and his team and by others. Howarth and Repetto-Wright (1978), for example, used observations of the number of road crossings at junctions and not at junctions, and near parked cars and not at parked cars, to estimate the absolute and relative risks of crossing roads in these circumstances. These very detailed measures help us to test the hypotheses that, for example, it is more dangerous for children to cross the road at a junction (for 5- to 7-year-olds it probably is, for older children it is probably safer), and that parked cars increase the risk for young children (they almost certainly do). For adult pedestrians, Todd and Walker (1980) have provided detailed risk estimates that can be used in a similar way. These more sophisticated measures of exposure not only help us to test hypotheses about accident causation, they also solve some of the problems of evaluation and, when incorporated in an evaluative programme, increase the amount of information that can be gleaned from it.

If a countermeasure has been designed with care, it should be possible to state in advance the means by which it will bring about a reduction in accidents, together with hypotheses about possible side-effects, such as the increase in accidents elsewhere, or a reduction in pedestrian travel. The evaluation of these hypotheses should be built in to the evaluation programme as they were, for example, in the research on zigzag markings and speed control humps that was discussed in the preceding section. In planning evaluative research one must anticipate what could go wrong, as well as what should go right.

This emphasis on the development of theory in relation to evaluation is similar to what occurs in epidemiology, so much so that many medical people regard accident research as a branch of epidemiology. Haddon, Suchman and Klein (1964) adopted the medical approach with enthusiasm, and their book contains many examples of well conducted research in this tradition, although few of these were concerned specifically with the evaluation of safety programmes.

However, many safety researchers are reluctant to adopt all the concepts and terminology of epidemiology. For example, the notion of 'cause' is not particularly favoured by accident researchers, particularly on the European side of the Atlantic. In this they may be ahead of epidemiologists, who get themselves into a conceptual tangle when attempting to distinguish between non-causal associations, predisposing causes and precipitating causes. In both accident research and epidemiology it would seem preferable to concentrate on estimating the effectiveness of countermeasures, without worrying too much about the philosophical difficulties inherent in the concept of cause.

Unfortunately, in most evaluative research there has been a tendency to divorce the search for understanding from the search for effective counter-measures. This is particularly the case in the evaluation of measures designed to improve safety by changing attitudes or improving knowledge. For example, most studies of the effectiveness of safety education have concentrated on measuring the degree to which they change attitudes or knowledge (see Chapter 3), rather than on the effect which these programmes have on the incidence of accidents. This is unfortunate since the best designed studies of the effects of safety education on accident rates have been very disappointing. The search for understanding divorced from the evaluation of the primary purpose of safety research can become a very sterile exercise.

RECOMMENDATIONS

It will be obvious from this account that we are not only enthusiastic about the needs and possibilities for evaluation, but that we also hold strong views about the way evaluative programmes should be conducted. A basic aim of safety research is to develop a better understanding of the factors leading to accidents. Grayson (1979) has pointed out that these are so complex that it would be foolish to expect any dramatic insight, but the challenge must be accepted. Properly designed evaluative studies are one of our best sources of increased understanding.

Howarth (1980a) has argued that the structure of applied research must be matched to the structure of the institutions in which it is carried out. In particular, he argues that applied researchers must act as a bridge between pure research and practical affairs. There is a tendency for these elements to operate in isolation, and to communicate only through the most formal and ineffective channels, such as the pages of little-read academic journals, or the ballot box.

We would now like to encapsulate these ideas in six concrete recommendations. The first three are concerned with the institutional structures within which evaluation is conducted and considered; the last three with the manner in which it should be carried out.

1. Communication between politicians, administrators, practitioners, safety researchers, pure scientists and the public should be improved. Conferences, both large and small between these diverse groups of people are sometimes very frustrating because of mutual incomprehension. But the incomprehension is a symptom of what needs to be changed, and is a justification for making yet more attempts to communicate rather than giving up.
2. We strongly support the recommendation in OECD (1978) that the budget of every safety programme should include an element devoted to evaluation. This will increase the likelihood that ineffective programmes will be curtailed and that effective ones will be more widely adopted. It will also increase the effectiveness of communication between all of the parties enumerated above, who are involved with pedestrian safety, since an interest in the effectiveness of safety programmes is shared by all of them.
3. The evaluation of local safety programmes can present opportunities for involving clients and the public in all stages of the programme; the formulation of objectives, the investigation of resources, and the design of strategic interventions as well as the evaluative stage. Local evaluation will be improved to the extent that local people understand what is being attempted and why.
4. All safety programmes must make explicit their definition of the problem. This may seem very obvious but the history of pedestrian safety is replete with examples of countermeasures looking for problems, or of mere recognition of a problem being mistaken for proper analysis. To give one more example, elderly pedestrians have long been identified as a target group for safety programmes. However, there has been very little analysis of why this should be so and of what their problems really are. The tendency in the past has been to apply the countermeasures on the assumption that the problem is one of age alone. Wilson and Grayson (1980) have shown that many of the popularly held stereotypes about the behaviour of the elderly are not confirmed when one examines their behaviour objectively.
5. All safety programmes must identify the ways in which the problem arises and the possible ways of alleviating it. This is effectively to construct a model of accident causation and to derive various hypotheses from it. These hypotheses should be tested by the evaluative procedures, as well as the simple efficacy of the programme in reducing accidents.
6. Nevertheless one should not lose sight of the fact that the primary purpose of accident prevention is to prevent accidents. There should always be a determined effort to answer the question 'Does it work?'. This determination

implies the proper use of scientific method, with adequate controls, careful measurement and appropriate statistics.

Safety programmes are not an end in themselves, and good intentions are no guarantee of success.

ACKNOWLEDGEMENT

We wish to thank Miss Barbara Sabey for reading a draft of this paper and for her helpful comments.

REFERENCES

Dalby, E. (1979). Area-wide measures in urban road safety, *Department of the Environment, Transport and Road Research Laboratory, Supplementary Report 517.* Crowthorne: TRRL.

Grayson, G. B. (1979). Methodological issues in the study of pedestrian behaviour. *Unpublished Doctoral Dissertation.* Nottingham: University of Nottingham.

Grayson, G. B. (1981). The identification of training objectives: what shall we tell the children? *Accident Analysis and Prevention,* **13**, 169–173.

Guttinger, V. A. (1980). The validation of a conflict observation technique for child pedestrians in residential areas. *Proceedings of the Second International Traffic Conflicts Technique Workshop.* May. Crowthorne: TRRL.

Haddon, W., Suchman, E. A., and Klein, D. (Eds.) (1964). *Accident Research: Methods and Approaches.* New York: Harper and Row.

Hauer, E. (1978). Traffic conflict surveys: some study design considerations. *Transport and Road Research Laboratory, Supplementary Report 352.* Crowthorne: TRRL.

Howarth, C. I. (1980a). The structure of effective psychology: Man as problem-solver. In A. J. Chapman and D. M. Jones (Eds.), *Models of Man.* Leicester: The British Psychological Society.

Howarth, C. I. (1980b). The need for regular government sponsored studies of the exposure of pedestrians and cyclists. *Paper presented at the Conference of the International Driver Behaviour Research Association.* June. Aarhus. Denmark: University of Aarhus.

Howarth, C. I., and Repetto-Wright, R. (1978). The measurement of risk and the attribution of responsibility for child pedestrian accidents. *Safety Education,* **144**, 10–13.

Howarth, C. I., Routledge, D. A., and Repetto-Wright, R. (1974). An analysis of road accidents involving child pedestrians. *Ergonomics,* **17**, 319–330.

Jacobs, G. D., and Wilson, D. G. (1967). A study of pedestrian risk in crossing busy roads in four towns. *Ministry of Transport, Road Research Laboratory, Laboratory Report 106.* Crowthorne: RRL.

Lea, N. D. (1978). A study of means to improve pedestrian and bicycle safety. *Report TP 1004.* Ottawa: Transport Canada.

Mackie, A. M., and Older, S. J. (1965). Study of pedestrian risk in crossing busy roads in London inner suburbs. *Traffic Engineering and Control,* **7**, 376–380.

Meehl, P. E. (1971). High school yearbooks, a reply of Schwartz. *Journal of Abnormal Psychology,* **77**, 143–148.

Mill, J. S. (1891). *System of Logic.* London: Longmans, Green and Co.

Organisation for Economic Co-operation and Development (OECD) Special Research Group on Pedestrian Safety (1977). *Chairman's Report and Report of Sub-Report of Subgroup I: The Pedestrian's Road Environment. Department of the Environment, Transport and Road Research Laboratory.* Crowthorne. TRRL.

Organisation for Economic Co-operation and Development (OECD) Special Research Group on Pedestrian Safety (1978). *Chairman's Report and Report of Sub-group III: Mass Media Communication for Pedestrian Safety, Department of the Environment, Transport and Road Research Laboratory.* Crowthorne: TRRL.

Organisation for Economic Co-operation and Development (1981). *Methods for Evaluating Road Safety Measures.* Paris: OECD.

Older, S. J., and Grayson, G. B. (1976). An international comparison of pedestrian risk in four cities. *Proceedings of the International Conference on Pedestrian Safety, Volume1,* 1A1–1A7. Haifa: Michlol.

Routledge, D. A., Repetto-Wright, R., and Howarth C. I. (1976). Four techniques for measuring the exposure of young children to accident risk as pedestrians. *Proceedings of the International Conference on Pedestrian Safety, Volume 1,* 7B1–7B7. Haifa: Michlol.

Sabey, B. E. (1980). Road safety and value for money. *Department of the Environment, Transport and Road Research Laboratory, Supplementary Report 581.* Crowthorne: TRRL.

Schioldborg, P. (1976). Children, traffic and traffic training . *Paper presented at the Fifth Congress of the International Federation of Pedestrians.* June. Geilo, Norway.

Sumner, R., and Baguley, C. (1979). Speed control humps on residential roads. *Department of the Environment, Transport and Road Research Laboratory, Laboratory Report 878.* Crowthorne: TRRL.

Tarrants, W. E., and Veigel, C. H. (1978). The evaluation of highway traffic safety programs. Report DOT-HS-802-525. Washington DC: United States Department of Transportation.

Taylor, H. (1977). Pedestrian safety: the role of research. *Department of the Environment, Transport and Road Research Laboratory, Supplementary Report 319.* Crowthorne: TRRL.

Todd, J. E., and Walker, A. (1980). *People as Pedestrians.* London: Her Majesty's Stationery Office.

Wass, C. (1977). Traffic accident exposure and liability. *Institute of Road, Traffic, and Town Planning Report.* Lyngby, Denmark: Technical University of Denmark.

Wilson, D. G., and Grayson, G. B. (1980). Age-related differences in the road crossing behaviour of adult pedestrians. *Department of the Environment, Transport and Road Research Laboratory, Laboratory Report 933.* Crowthorne: TRRL.

Wilson, D. G., and Older, S. J. (1970). The effects of installing new zebra crossings in Rugby and Chelmsford. *Ministry of Transport, Road Research Laboratory, Laboratory Report 358.* Crowthorne: RRL.

Part II

The Driver and the Vehicle

Pedestrian Accidents
Edited by A. J. Chapman, F. M. Wade and H. C. Foot
© 1982, John Wiley & Sons Ltd.

Chapter 5

Driver Behaviour

I. D. Brown

PROBLEM PEDESTRIANS?

As an individual the driver is, fortunately, seldom if ever involved in an accident with pedestrians, or even a witness to such accidents. He may therefore be completely unaware that the annual toll of pedestrian casualties in the UK is, at about 70,000 per annum, roughly the same as that of car drivers (Department of Transport, 1980; see Chapter 1). In the USA, pedestrians account for about one in five of all fatalities from accidents (National Safety Council, 1976). If the driver concerns himself with accident statistics at all, he may observe that the total number of UK pedestrian casualties fell during the first half of the 1970s and has stabilized during the past five years, in spite of the continued increase in motor traffic (Department of Transport, 1980). Drivers may thus tend to assume that the problem of pedestrian accidents has been brought under control; that accident prevention in this field is largely a question of pursuing proven remedial measures; and thus conclude that the remaining pedestrian involvement in accidents is, in fact, self-inflicted, on the grounds that roads are intended for vehicular traffic and pedestrians must accept increased risk of injury if they refuse to make correct use of the proper crossing facilities.

In addition to ignoring the sobering fact that fatal and serious pedestrian casualties in the UK have levelled out at over 20,000 per annum, such assumptions overlook a number of serious problems for society which are disguised by these summary statistics. Perhaps the most important of these problems is that the number of pedestrian casualties within the age-range 10 to 19 years is on the increase (Department of Transport, 1980). The number of older pedestrians (over 60 years) killed and injured is also high—roughly equal to all the casualties in the 20- to 60-year-old age-range. The road toll is nearly 40 per cent higher for male pedestrians than for females and this ratio is higher among children. Perhaps most disturbing of all is the fact that nearly 6,000 people are killed or injured in the UK each year *while on pedestrian crossings*.

Clearly, these statistics provide no grounds for complacency. Rather, they should be used as evidence that the traffic system is not adequately designed to meet the present needs and capabilities of many road users. In particular, it is clear that our present uncontrolled crossing facilities are not affording adequate protection against errant drivers and that certain categories of pedestrian appear incapable of exercising the skills currently demanded by participation in the road traffic system. Pedestrian accidents and their prevention are thus very much the concern of the *driver*.

Accident statistics should therefore be used to identify specific problems in the *interaction* between the two classes of road user and to provide guidance on alternative accident countermeasures affecting the behaviour of all those involved in such interactions.

This conclusion raises two critical questions: (1) 'Are our current accident statistics adequate for such interpretations of causation and countermeasures?' and (2) 'If not, what additional information is required to facilitate a reduction in the present appalling toll of pedestrian casualties?'

RISK AND REMEDIES

With regard to the first question, it must be understood that official accident statistics usually provide information on the *relative* risks among age, sex, occupational and other subgroups of the road user population. They can also be used to distinguish accident 'black spots' in the traffic environment; that is, sites associated with above-average proportions of casualties. Information at this level of enquiry is therefore used mainly to identify vulnerable groups of road users and weak features in highway design. Direct action can thus be taken to reduce the vulnerability of certain road users, or redesign the environment to reduce known hazards, without reference to *absolute* measures of the accident risks involved.

On the basis of such evidence, the child pedestrian has been identified as a 'high risk' road user: that is, incurring more casualties than other age-groups, per 100,000 in the population. It has also been possible to identify this group's involvement in pedestrian accidents as mainly an urban problem, when children cross roads elsewhere than on a pedestrian crossing. If one tries to control for exposure to risk, by using crude measures such as the amount of walking done by various age groups, children under 10 years of age still have between two and three times the likelihood of accident involvement calculated for the other high-risk group of over-65s (Smeed, 1977).

As a result, accident countermeasures have been concentrated on the design of road safety educational procedures for the younger pedestrian (see Colborne, 1971; Colborne and Sargent, 1971; Firth, 1973; Grayson, 1975a, b; Higgs, 1972; Michon, van der Molen, Rothengatter, Vinjé and Welvaart, 1979; Nummenmaa, Ruuhilehto and Syvänen, 1975; Russam, 1975; Sadler, 1972; Sargent and Sheppard, 1974; Sheppard, 1977; Singh, 1976). Intuitively, it makes good sense to train naïve road users in safety procedures and this policy has therefore been pursued vigorously. But the questions remain; is this the right, or only policy to be followed and, indeed, is it working to reduce pedestrian casualties?

The evidence here is discouraging. Some authorities, for example the Netherlands Institute for Road Safety Research (SWOV, 1977), have concluded that '(measures)...aimed at influencing pedestrians' behaviour by means of guidance, training, information and publicity have so far often not had the desired effect...(of reducing accidents)' (SWOV, 1977, p. 22). Other experts in this field, for example Sandels (1974) in Sweden, have gone so far as to assert that '...children in the ages of 0–10 years are not sufficiently developed biologically to behave in a safe manner in all traffic situations. Children are human beings going through different stages of their development and they can never perform above their present level' (p. 68). In other words, one cannot rely on education alone to reduce the younger child pedestrian's accidents.

On theoretical grounds, one might also question the soundness of certain educational procedures for child pedestrians, such as the *Green Cross Code* (Sargent and Sheppard, 1974), which attempt to inculcate road crossing behaviour that is not exhibited by adults. The adult's pre-crossing behaviour involves a good deal of covert perception and decision making, while on the move (see Chapter 2). By contrast, the *Green Cross Code* teaches the child pedestrian to carry out this pre-crossing activity while stationary at the kerb. In principle this seems a logical method of dealing with individuals whose perception and decision making are not fully developed. However, it has two unfortunate consequences. The child may mimic adult behaviour, regardless of instructions to the contrary, and hence omit those processes he cannot observe. In addition, there is the possibility that the less efficient method of road crossing propounded by the Green Cross Code may be carried into later life, when perceptual and decision skills are fully developed.

EXPOSURE TO RISK

The problem underlying any assessment of alternative countermeasures against pedestrian accidents and, indeed, of evaluating pedestrian risk in the first instance, is related to valid measurement of the pedestrian's *exposure* to the risk of accident (see Chapter 4), since:

$$\text{Risk} = \frac{\text{Accidents}}{\text{Exposure}}$$

More specifically, the pedestrian is mainly (although not solely) at risk when crossing roads. Without a reliable measure of road crossing frequency, we therefore cannot begin to evaluate the various risks to pedestrians. Nor can we, with certainty, begin to design accident countermeasures that address the important risks.

There are of course numerous methodological difficulties in obtaining valid measures of exposure to risk in the traffic system. However, some progress has been made in this field during recent years, notably among child pedestrians, by Howarth and his colleagues at Nottingham University (Howarth, Routledge and Repetto-Wright, 1974; Routledge, Repetto-Wright and Howarth, 1974 a, b; 1976). These investigators have used a number of empirical measures of exposure in order to identify certain subgroups of the pedestrian population, certain aspects of behaviour, and certain features of the traffic environment, which, in isolation or combination, are associated with accident risk. However, it is acknowledged that this information merely provides a valid and reliable description of the child pedestrian problem, in one geographical area. The issue, then, is how to pursue this specific problem and the pedestrian accident problem in general, to a practical solution.

DRIVER/PEDESTRIAN COMPATIBILITY

This enunciation of the pedestrian accident problem shows quite clearly that we have only in recent years been prepared to address it, more appropriately, as a mismatch between the attitudes and behaviour of two interacting groups of road user. For far too long, the participation of drivers in pedestrian accidents seems largely to have been ignored by researchers. Traffic engineers too appear to have regarded the driver as just one component in a flow of traffic which must be disrupted as little as possible by the needs of road-crossing pedestrians. This attitude has led to the continued use of uncontrolled crossing facilities (e.g. the UK zebra crossing), which are misused by drivers and pedestrians alike. It has also led to the use of certain design criteria which effect undesirable compromises between the needs of drivers and pedestrians: for example, light-controlled crossings in which the duration of the 'Walk' period is based on the observed *mean* walking speed. By definition, half the pedestrian population will be inconvenienced by the use of such criteria. Some investigators (e.g. Shinar, 1978) have suggested that this contributes to the elderly pedestrian's over-involvement in accidents and have pointed out the adverse implications for driver behaviour. Research by Zuercher (1976), for example, is adduced to show that drivers are very reluctant to give way to pedestrians who seem likely to cause them above-average delay.

A 'systems' approach to pedestrian accidents would, by contrast, involve the study of the behavioural interface between drivers and pedestrians, at the various sites in the traffic environment where pedestrians cross the road. This approach would take into account the *pre-crossing*, as well as the crossing, behaviour and skills of the pedestrian; the demands on and behaviour of the driver; the physical characteristics of the traffic environment and of vehicles; and the procedural rules and conventions applying to the various types of interaction between road users. Only in this way can better information be provided as to whether accident countermeasures should be directed at the pedestrian, the driver, the traffic system hardware, or some combination of these three components in the system.

A start in this direction was provided by Snyder and Knoblauch's (1971) *post hoc* analysis of 2,157 pedestrian accidents in 13 US cities during 1969 and 1970. Appreciating that the driver's and pedestrian's tasks are broadly similar, in terms of information processing, they categorized their accident sample in terms of the following causal factors, for both driver and pedestrian behaviour:

Course selection.
Visual search and detection.
Evaluation of the situation.
Decision making.
Action.

An additional category took into account the interaction between the driver and pedestrian. Table 5.1 shows the number of times each causal factor was identified in the analysis, its relative frequency of occurrence and the proportion of accidents to which it referred.

Table 5.1 Primary causes attributed to pedestrian accidents

	Causal factor	Number of attributions	Per cent of attributions	Per cent of accident sample
Pedestrian	Course	1206	30.6	55.9
	Search and detection	1166	29.4	54.1
	Detection	238	6.0	11.0
	Evaluation	158	4.0	7.3
	Decision	17	0.4	0.8
	Action	19	0.5	0.9
Driver	Course	181	4.6	8.4
	Search and detection	510	12.9	23.6
	Detection	292	7.4	13.5
	Evaluation	82	2.1	3.8
	Control/action	75	1.9	3.5
	Driver/pedestrian interaction	9	0.2	0.4
	Total	3953	100.0	—

Based on Shinar's (1978) adaptation of findings by Snyder and Knoblauch (1971) from analysis of 2,157 accidents.

Five outcomes of this analysis are immediately apparent:

1. It is seldom that any pedestrian accident has a single cause. (The total number of causal factors identified is nearly double the number of accidents examined.)
2. The more frequently identified factors are those which ascribe causation to the pedestrian's behaviour.
3. Marginally the most frequent factor in causation was the pedestrian's poor choice of a place or time to cross the road.
4. Of almost equal importance (presumably because these factors are not entirely independent) was the pedestrian's failure to search and detect the oncoming vehicle.
5. The driver's failure to search and detect the crossing pedestrian was a prime factor in his accident involvement.

Clearly one must be cautious in interpreting findings of this nature, since they are based upon a *post hoc* categorization of data which represent the subjective assessments of numerous individuals, perhaps operating under strain in the period following a road accident, who must integrate the evidence from involved and impartial road users. However, as Shinar (1978) pointed out in his evaluation of these findings, the primary problem appears to be the pedestrian's lack of care in crossing the road, which is exactly the conclusion reached by Sabey and Staughton (1975) in their analysis of UK pedestrian accidents. It is not possible to determine the extent to which this lack of care reflects *unawareness* of the hazards associated with road crossing, or *incapacity* to scan the road scene efficiently, or *deliberate risk-taking*. We therefore cannot evaluate the potential savings in pedestrian casualties likely to result from traffic education and legislation, directed at pedestrians alone. Perhaps a more relevant question here is whether the smaller proportion of accidents ascribed to driver behaviour is remediable by similar countermeasures.

However, although it may be necessary to direct preventive measures specifically at the driver and the pedestrian, it is the study of their *joint* contribution to accidents which will provide the understanding of their behavioural mismatch from which such specific countermeasures will follow. This is a clear from a further analysis of the Snyder and Knoblauch (1971) data, providing a rank-ordering of the more common combinations of causal factors. These are reproduced in Table 5.2.

Drivers' contributions to these accident data stand out clearly as a problem of *visual search and detection* of crossing pedestrians. There is no implication in these multicausal collisions of drivers being on an inappropriate course. Nor do their faulty evaluations or actions appear to contribute. In other words, the typical behavioural mismatch occurs when a pedestrian crosses in the 'wrong' place, or at the 'wrong' time, without looking out for oncoming traffic and

Table 5.2 The more frequently observed combinations of causal factors in pedestrian accidents

Causal combination	Per cent of accident sample in which combination observed
Pedestrian course and search/driver detection	13.6
Pedestrian course and search	11.3
Pedestrian search/driver search	9.9
Pedestrian course and search/driver search	6.3
Pedestrian course and detection/driver detection	5.7
Pedestrian search/driver detection	3.9
Pedestrian course	3.7
Driver search	3.6
Pedestrian search	3.6
No factors identified	8.1
Other factors (each combination less than 3 per cent)	30.3

Based on Shinar's (1978) adaptation of findings by Snyder and Knoblauch (1971) from analysis of 2,157 accidents

then collides with a driver who sees the pedestrian too late to take effective avoiding action.

The crucial question here is why the driver's search and detection processes so commonly fail to provide sufficient advance information of the errant pedestrian? We cannot simply dismiss all such accidents as last-minute 'dart-outs' and therefore irremediable, since the potential hazard presented by pedestrians is well-known by most drivers and traffic rules and conventions oblige them to travel at a speed which allows them to stop safely 'within the limits of visibility'. Clearly many drivers are not complying with this basic requirement of road safety.

For an understanding of their problem it therefore seems necessary to examine the task of driving in more detail, in an attempt to draw inferences concerning the weak spots in drivers' information processing. At those points, any interaction with pedestrians will clearly carry an increased risk of accident and the specific behavioural mismatches at these high-risk interactions should point to the remedial measures required to reduce or eliminate the risk.

THE DRIVING TASK

There are six identifiable components of the driving task which have implications for pedestrian safety. Each of them is now discussed in some detail.

Route finding

This usually requires a driver who is unfamiliar with the locality to search the road scene for symbolic or verbal road signs, illuminated signals, or memorized landmarks, in order to proceed along the chosen course to his destination. Such a description of a frequently performed task may seem trite, but this process is in fact quite demanding. Drivers will usually have memorized a verbal or pictorial representation of their chosen route. Route finding thus requires them to make a continuous comparison of this mental representation with the actual road scene. There is no certainty that the real world will have been imaged appropriately from route cards or maps and discrepancies will result in periods of increased mental effort, as the driver attempts to resolve them.

A number of well-known sources of such discrepancy are associated with hierarchical systems of signposting routes. For example, long-distance drivers may memorize a series of town names along their route and suddenly discover at a rural junction that the names of only the adjacent villages are displayed. Another source of discrepancy results from the policy adopted by certain local authorities of using signs to re-route traffic around congested areas, when the driver's map indicates the existence of the more direct route. One more interesting source of discrepancy between the actual traffic environment and the driver's spatial encoding and memory for routes has been pointed out by Lewis (1979). Figure 5.1(a) illustrates the type of motorway sign confronting drivers who wish to exit from the M5 southbound on the M6. As Lewis points out:

> ... this is a particularly difficult junction for those unaccustomed to it, because the need for a grade-separated interchange produces a mismatch between the spatial arrangement of signposted roads and motorists' spatial expectancies. Although the M5 initially forks off to the left, as the sign indicates, it then passes underneath the M6 ... Most users know that they should leave the M6 to the East here

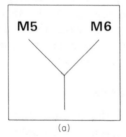 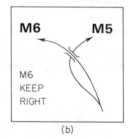

Figure 5.1 (a) The sign for the M5–M6 intersection, mismatching drivers' expectancies. (b) An alternative sign which would illustrate the actual junction geometry. (Reproduced from Lewis, 1979. *Ergonomics*, **22**(2), 117–127 by permission of Taylor & Francis, Ltd.)

and, even now, puzzled motorists can be seen parked on the hard shoulder, poring over their maps, trying to understand what is happening. The sign is not believed because it does not conform to drivers' expectancies. Where such a paradox exists, the decision time allowed for drivers should be increased considerably over that generally recommended . . . (for purposes of traffic system design) . . . and, possibly, reinforcing signs added to eliminate doubts. (pp. 120–121)

Of course, this particular problem will not (or should not) contribute to pedestrian accidents, since it is illegal to walk along, or across, motorways. However, the example serves to illustrate the general point that road design features which fail to match drivers' expectancies will puzzle and distract them, to the possible detriment of their visual search behaviour for potential hazards, including pedestrians. Accident black spots for pedestrians may therefore well be the result of some discrepancy created by road designers, or local authorities, between the route that visiting drivers want and the information they actually get.

An additional problem for route-finding drivers will be remembering where they are along their memorized route and what comes next. This, again, may seem trite, but a good deal of evidence on people's ability to monitor sequences of learned responses shows that errors commonly occur as the result of effectively forgetting where one is in the sequence and thus running off some other string of responses at an inappropriate time in the task. For route-finding drivers, this will result in their searching for a landmark in the wrong place: usually a demanding and time-consuming exercise, which is liable to distract from the task of maintaining appropriate safety margins.

In general, it seems a reasonable prediction that the interactions between pedestrians and route-finding drivers will carry a higher risk of accident than interactions involving drivers who are familiar with the locality. Accident statistics are extremely uninformative on this point and, for any such findings to be useful, it would of course be essential to correct the data for the pedestrian's relative exposure to risk from the two categories of driver. However, in the absence of such data it seems logically sound to limit pedestrian risk from route-finding drivers, by appropriate design of the road system. This would involve, for example, the separation of uncontrolled pedestrian crossing sites from through-routes and other areas where drivers are likely to be distracted by route finding. In this connection a useful additional item of information, collected by the police on their accident report forms, would be the driver's familiarity with the locality. Such data might highlight certain general or specific features of the traffic environment which regularly puzzle or confuse non-local motorists and which are currently overlooked as contributory causes of pedestrian accidents.

Route following

This term may be used to describe the behaviour of drivers passing through a familiar environment. Commuting drivers will represent the extreme of the continuum of familiarity among this population. For the pedestrian, they represent an entirely different source of hazard. Their course and progress will normally be determined by recognition, often subconsciously, of geographical and traffic system features. They will therefore not need to read road signs; their daily experience with their route will often lead to acceptance of tighter schedules; and they will thus tend to drive at higher speeds and be relatively intolerant of delay. It follows that they will be disconcerted by changes introduced into their familiar routes: such as road works, alterations in road priorities, closed streets, and so on. Familiarity with a route through busy urban areas may lead to relative contempt for the rights of pedestrians; and tight schedules often result in inadequate vehicle separation, with a consequent reduction in the crossing time afforded to pedestrians; thus increasing their exposure to risk. Motorists driving in the vicinity of their homes may also be expected to have a relatively high susceptibility to distraction by both overt and covert events, since the objective of their travel will almost certainly occupy more of their cognitive processing time than in the case of long-distance drivers, who are usually more concerned with the process of travelling to their destinations.

These possibilities must, however, remain speculative for the present, since there is no firm evidence on the pedestrian's relative exposure to risk from commuters, as was pointed out earlier. In terms of absolute risk, the commuter clearly presents a problem for pedestrians, particularly children, because of the coincidence between drivers' journeys to and from work and children's journeys to school and their early evening play/errand-running activities, respectively. This is demonstrated by the two peaks in the diurnal pattern of child pedestrian accidents: one around 8 a.m. and the other, more widely distributed but with an even higher peak, between 4.00 and 5.00 p.m. (Department of Transport, 1980). Because of the greater distribution of times at which adults begin their working day, the peaks in the diurnal pattern of adult pedestrian accidents are flatter and more distributed than those for children. However, it is clear for both adults and children that the commuting hours are a hazardous period. In the case of the child pedestrian, it seems unnecessary to require precise information on relative exposure to risk before concluding that the behaviour of younger schoolchildren and of commuting drivers is mutually incompatible. Logical countermeasures would include re-routing commuters well away from schools and, in the case of new schools, integrating them into the residential environment away from motorized traffic. As might be expected, the child pedestrian is frequently at risk from commuters transporting their own children to school. The risk is often compounded by unfortunate design and siting of school buildings which, even now, seem to take little account of the various methods by which children travel to school.

Sabey and Staughton (1975) have reported that drivers travelling too fast for their particular situation (but not necessarily at high absolute speeds) are the second largest source of error in accidents. (The primary source being 'lack of care'.) It would be useful to know whether this contribution of excess speed to accidents is largely a function of overfamiliarity with the route. If it were, potential remedial measures would include the introduction, or, for some countries, the extension of temporary speed restrictions during the commuting hours; greater use of lights-controlled, rather than uncontrolled crossings on commuters' routes; or some other method of removing decisions on road user priorities from the commuting motorist.

Lane tracking

Drivers have to perform a tracking task as they steer their vehicles along the chosen route. The visual demands of steering will naturally be a function of the physical environment (including weather conditions), vehicle design, traffic conditions, speed, and probably a variety of other factors. Demands will also be met differently by different types of driver and this variation is dealt with in more detail later. Suffice it, here, to say that the sources of visual information on which drivers steer their vehicles will quite often be remote, in terms of visual angular displacement, from the sources of information on pedestrian pre-crossing behaviour. Drivers on a straight course will fixate in the region

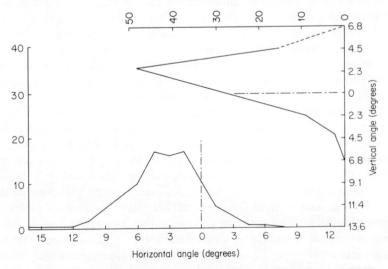

Figure 5.2 Distribution of car drivers' visual fixations (driving on left side of the road). (Adapted from Nagayama *et al.*, 1979)

of the 'focus of expansion': that is, where objects appear stationary and will tend to bias their horizontal scanning fixations towards the opposing stream of traffic. A typical pattern of such visual activity has been presented by Nagayama, Morita, Miura, Watanabem and Murakami (1979) and is reproduced in Figure 5.2.

Such recordings of drivers' eye movements typically show few excursions below about 10° from the horizontal. Steering will be accomplished using visual information on vehicle 'yaw', or heading displacement from the desired track, although the specific cues used will vary with speed, lane-width, preview of the road and various individual factors (e.g. see McLean and Hoffman, 1971, 1972, 1973, 1975). On bends, drivers will switch their visual fixations to a region aligned with the nearside edge of the road and thus be tracking discrepancies between the bend in the road and the curve followed by their vehicle, with only occasional excursions in the direction of vehicle heading.

It follows that pedestrian risk will be a function of these changes in fixation. On straight roads, other conditions being equal, drivers will be more likely to detect pre-crossing pedestrian activity occurring well ahead of their vehicle, near the focus of expansion of the visual scene. The probability of detection will fall the nearer the pedestrian is to the vehicle, because of the greater angular displacement from the driver's direction of gaze. Whether a pedestrian's movements are detected in the driver's visual periphery will depend upon a variety of perceptual factors involving relative motion and conspicuity, and upon the difficulty of the driver's steering task. The latter will also determine whether pedestrians are detected by purposeful scanning fixations directed at their activity, or by certain attention-getting cues in their behaviour. Some of these perceptual factors are considered in more detail later. However, the implications of the present argument for accident countermeasures are relatively clear. Crossings should ideally be sited in situations which are compatible with the direction in which drivers are gazing for current information on vehicle steering demands. On this criterion alone, sites carrying increased risk of accident will be those in the vicinity of moderate curves, where large discrepancies may exist between drivers' lines of sight and their direction of travel.

Current techniques for the continuous recording of drivers' head and eye movements would appear to offer considerable scope here for the identification of environmental and other demands on vehicle steering control, which could be used to site crossings efficiently. Installing facilities where pedestrians already cross by preference or habit may seem logical, but it takes little direct account of the visual demands on drivers. It would also be instructive for pedestrians to know that their risk of collision is raised if they cross from the offside of a turning vehicle, or too close to a fast vehicle on a straight road. The latter point in particular may be difficult for pedestrians to appreciate, if they associate their conspicuity with proximity to the vehicle, rather than to the driver's effective visual field.

Finally, it might also be instructive for drivers if they were informed of these weak spots introduced into their visual scanning behaviour by the demands of vehicle guidance. As Shinar, McDowell, Rackoff and Rockwell (1978) have pointed out, from their studies of individual differences in visual search behaviour, certain individuals have quite rigid, inefficient, scanning patterns when driving. It therefore seems unlikely that self-knowledge alone will lead to more efficient search behaviour on the road. Research seems required on the possibility and methods of training for efficient visual search, before bad scanning habits develop.

Collision avoidance

In a dynamic traffic environment, where individual vehicles are independently controlled by drivers having vastly different levels of skill and ability, and the road is bordered by apparently imponderable pedestrian activity, the avoidance of collision places a virtually continuous demand on the driver. Attention, perception and decision-making will therefore continually be occupied by the detection, prediction and resolution of dynamic interactions between a driver's own course and those of other road users. These detailed information-processing demands are discussed more fully later. The general point here, is that there will be three different determinants of the driver's visual scanning for collision avoidance cues: (a) attention will be *drawn* to unusual and compelling events which require a decision regarding their hazard potential; (b) attention will be *directed* to those parts of the road scene which, on recent or past experience, are expected to produce hazard; and (c) events for which a decision has already been made will need to be *checked* for evidence of the decision's appropriateness. Component (a) of this collision avoidance behaviour will introduce risk for the pedestrian who enters the driver's field of view remote from the latter's direction of gaze. If pedestrians have a clear view of the driver's head and eye movements they can, if sufficiently mature, knowledgeable and cautious, avoid being overlooked by the distracted driver. However, a more hazardous situation exists where components (b) and (c) of collision avoidance behaviour occur. In both cases, but particularly in (c), drivers will be searching for, or checking on, a specific object, event, or action. In other words, they will have a mental representation of these expected targets and may simply be searching for a match to this mental representation in the perceived road scene. If no such match is found information processing may cease, depending upon concurrent environmental demands. The crucial point here is that pedestrians, observing a driver gaze in their direction, may act on the assumption that their presence has been detected and their behaviour taken into consideration in the driver's future course of action. It is clear from the above argument that this assumption may be quite false where pedestrians are not specifically included in the driver's visual search behaviour.

The extent of this general scanning problem seems far from negligible. In a report on 3,704 road accidents investigated in depth by the UK Transport and Road Research Laboratory, Sabey and Staughton (1975) attribute almost 10 per cent (367) to the fact that drivers 'looked but failed to see' the objects with which they collided. Clearly, the 'directed' and 'checking' components of the driver's visual scanning behaviour present a major hazard for other road users, because they may lead not only to the pedestrian being overlooked; such gazing behaviour may actually *mislead* the cautious pedestrian who attempts to 'read' the driver's intentions.

It must be noted that pedestrians will also be susceptible to the 'looked but failed to see' phenomenon. Drivers too may therefore be overlooked, or misled into assuming that they have been seen by the pedestrian gazing in their direction. As Table 5.2 shows, around 6 per cent of road accidents appear to involve a driver and pedestrian both of whom 'looked but failed to see'.

Given the basic nature of the attentional process and the numerous sources of hazard scanned by drivers in the traffic environment, it is difficult to conceive of a general accident countermeasure directed specifically at drivers, to reduce this source of pedestrian risk. Situation-specific remedial measures are, of course, feasible and, indeed, already widely used. They mainly cue the driver to the presence of pedestrians, where a hazard known to the traffic authorities exists. Such measures include symbolic *Children Crossing* signs, flashing lights used during the periods when children are entering or leaving school, and so on. Their obvious purpose is to increase the probability that the signalled object will be incorporated into the driver's visual scanning behaviour. Unfortunately, the appropriate response to such information is largely extinguished among regular commuting drivers and static signs are often insufficiently compelling. There seems scope here for the development of additional devices aimed at cueing the driver more effectively to the presence of specific hazards. In the meantime, drivers and pedestrians alike should be wary of assuming that gazing implies seeing.

Rule compliance

The duties and responsibilities of the driver are defined by legislation and convention. Many of these rules will be memorized and brought into operation by features and events perceived in the road scene. Others will be signalled by a variety of road signs, containing more specific messages. The latter more imperative type of communication, if well-designed, will usually not increase the information-processing load of the driver unduly. It may, however, create frustration among road users if rules are not compatible with the driver's perception of immediate road safety needs. A problem with many rules is that they are designed for 'average', or sometimes 'worst case' situations and individuals. Clearly such rules will be inappropriate, if applied to situations or individuals that are neither 'average' nor 'worst case'.

A common example is a speed-restriction which applies regardless of traffic conditions. When traffic is light and road conditions good, such restrictions are widely ignored by drivers; sometimes excessively so (e.g. see Lines, 1978). There is a dual implication here for pedestrian accident risk. Firstly, pedestrians may falsely assume that motorists are complying with legal speed requirements, and thus adopt inadequate safety margins when crossing in front of errant drivers. Secondly, speeding drivers may be devoting part of their attention to the avoidance of detection in their offence and drivers who are scanning their rear-view mirrors for police vehicles are perhaps not giving pedestrians the attention they deserve!

In terms of attention and perception, the identification of cues signalling rule-changes in the traffic environment can sometimes be quite demanding. This is particularly true for the urban environment, where traffic information is often displayed against a complex background of advertisements and other visual displays. Relevant messages are frequently displayed by subtle means; such as the colour or shape of a road sign, carrying different implications for the mandatory or advisory nature of the information. Symbolic road signs, in general, impose a need to decode the message they attempt to convey. Although considerable research effort was directed at the design of such signs and their messages are now clear to the majority of road users, certain examples nevertheless appear to puzzle many road users (see Mackie, 1967). It follows that the risk of pedestrian accidents will be raised wherever interactions occur during the driver's attempts to search for, comprehend, and comply with displayed information on traffic rules. There are obvious implications here for the siting of pedestrian crossings in the vicinity of other traffic information displays.

A different problem faces drivers who are attempting to implement memorized rules on road user priorities. They will often be faced with the difficulty of recognizing relative spatial positions, perhaps in relation to a specific section of the road system, and then translating this information in terms of a memorized priority rule. Their task in this respect is often eased by the introduction of an over-riding priority rule, such as: 'give way to traffic on the right' (or left, as the case may be). But even apparently simple rules can be surprisingly difficult for drivers to implement, under certain conditions. Thomson (1978), for example, has carried out a sophisticated analysis of the information-processing requirements of alternative priority rule systems at intersections in NewZealand. He found that change in the rules, introduced in 1977 to simplify priorities during such conflicts, produced *greater* uncertainty in the driver's task. As he points out, an increase in the information needed to complete a task leads to increased error and slower responses. It seems to follow that situations in the road system which cause drivers uncertainty about traffic rules will increase pedestrian risk. Where such situations occur is clearly not the place to site uncontrolled crossings. Unfortunately, these situations are often used naturally by pedestrians, for two reasons: (1) they largely occur at unsignalled intersections having no pedestrian crossing provision; and (2) they produce hesitations and gaps among intersecting queues of vehicles, which are taken advantage of by pedestrians, in order to avoid a detour to the nearest marked crossing. This tactic may work well for perceptive adults, but children who mimic such overt behaviour will be at risk from drivers attempting to perceive and resolve fairly complex spatial relationships between vehicles, and with little attention to spare for pedestrians.

In general, it may be concluded that rule compliance by drivers is a potential source of hazard for pedestrians, particularly children, because of its demands upon both wide visual scanning and the resolution of uncertainty. It is difficult to evaluate its importance from detailed analyses of causes attributed to road accidents, because of the covert processes involved; which may be performed subconsciously and are therefore seldom recorded appropriately in formal accident reports. They should, however, be accessible to measurement by more sophisticated techniques for the evaluation of 'mental load' in the driving task (e.g. see Brown, 1961). These may highlight areas of increased pedestrian risk which are inaccessible to direct observation.

Vehicle monitoring

Experienced drivers will continually monitor information on the state of their vehicle. They will process auditory information for defects and occasionally scan their instruments for information on engine state, speed, fuel, etc. Many of these monitoring activities are carried out subconsciously, or are so overlearned that they minimally distract from the main task of scanning the road scene. However, they have some implications for pedestrian safety because they normally involve only small eye movements. A cautious pedestrian, attempting to assess the direction of the driver's gaze, may thus be unaware that the latter is actually checking his/her speed as the pedestrian begins to cross.

In general, the problem of drivers being distracted by vehicle monitoring has declined in recent years, largely owing to better design of vehicle instrument displays. Older analogue displays of oil pressure, water temperature, battery charging current, etc. have largely given way to symbolic indication of engine failures. These less cluttered displays clearly aid visual search for information on vehicle state. They also limit information-processing demands by the two-state, fault/no-fault nature of the evidence they provide. Vehicle monitoring on modern vehicles is therefore likely to contribute very little to pedestrian risk.

DRIVERS' INFORMATION PROCESSING

It is clear from the above task analysis that the information-processing demands of driving are high, especially in those sections of the traffic environment where the driver is likely to encounter pedestrians. These task demands are met largely because many components of driving are overlearned for experienced motorists. Thus the perceptual motor skills involved in vehicle control will usually not occupy a substantial proportion of the experienced driver's processing resources. In addition, the processing of sensory information will be dealt with by attending selectively to the various task demands and by sequencing responses, so that the numerous inputs and outputs comprising the task are distributed over time.

It follows that there are two possible ways in which this information-processing structure of the driver's task could produce mismatches between driver and pedestrian behaviour and thus increase the risk of pedestrian accidents.

1. Inexperience could lead to inadequate structuring of information flow; producing errors of omission and commission as potential hazards are overlooked, or demands peak to a level beyond the driver's response capabilities.
2. Impairment in the state of the driver may, in addition, reduce the quality of sensory information and disrupt the timing of skilled responses.

In either case, it is likely that a high level of concentration will be required on the main components of the driving task. Therefore the driver's 'reserve capacity', which is needed to monitor specific hazards, may be seriously restricted. In extreme cases, given the largely visual input to the driving task, drivers may be performing as if they had 'tunnel vision'. In order words, they may be fixating mainly those regions of the road scene which provide information on vehicle control (speed and steering demands) and these, as we have seen, will limit attention to a relatively small area of the visual field, directly ahead of the vehicle. Clearly this carries increased risk for the crossing pedestrian. In addition, unless drivers are displaying L-plates on their vehicle, or its progress is so erratic that the occupant may be assumed to be, say, grossly intoxicated, pedestrians will be unaware of the risks presented by inexperienced or impaired drivers. They may therefore quite reasonably assume crossing priorities, where these are in their favour, yet not be afforded them. Recovery from the resulting situation is unlikely to be effected skilfully by either an inexperienced or an impaired driver and the risk of accident from this type of encounter may be expected to be high.

There is, in fact, good evidence of the implication of impaired drivers in accidents. Table 5.3 reproduces the breakdown of data reported by Sabey and Staughton (1975) from an in-depth investigation of 2,130 accidents involving 3,757 drivers, 147 pedestrians and 3,909 vehicles. Of the 1,505 drivers in this sample who were judged to be 'primarily at fault' and the 706 judged to be 'partially at fault' (i.e. 2,211 'blameworthy' drivers in all), 632 (28.6 per cent) were considered to be impaired in some way. (A number of them clearly suffering impairment from more than one source, which accounts for the apparent

Table 5.3 Impairment of driver or pedestrian at fault in accidents

	Source of impairment	Number impaired	Per cent impaired
Drivers	Alcohol	463	73.3
	Fatigue	159	25.2
	Drugs	87	13.8
	Illness	33	5.2
	Emotional distress	26	4.1
	Total number impaired at fault drivers	632	—
Pedestrians	Alcohol	4	66.7
	Illness	2	33.3
	Total number impaired at fault pedestrians	6	100.0

After Sabey and Staughton (1975).

discrepancy in the total.) Around 75 per cent of these blameworthy drivers were suffering from alcohol intoxication and 25 per cent of the total were judged to be fatigued. It may be noted in passing that of the 116 pedestrians considered to be blameworthy by these authors, only 6 (5 per cent) were judged to be impaired—4 by alcohol and 2 by illness. Clearly, the drinking driver presents a potential source of risk for other road users and Sabey and Staughton (1980) have subsequently expounded this problem in more detail. Fortunately, since the so-called 'drinking hours' of 11 p.m. to 4 a.m. do not coincide with peak periods of pedestrian activity, especially among the vulnerable group of children, the intoxicated driver is likely to present a much smaller problem than the intoxicated pedestrian, when these drinking road users interact (see Sabey and Staughton, 1980).

Inexperience among drivers may therefore present far more of a problem than impairment, for the pedestrian, although one cannot ignore the relatively high involvement of fatigued drivers in accidents, shown in Table 5.3. Indeed, this may partially account for the flattened peak of child pedestrian accidents during the afternoon and early evening (Department of Transport, 1980), as tired homeward-bound commuters find themselves sharing the road system with 'unpredictable' children running errands and at play. The contribution of inexperience among drivers to accidents in general is not, however, readily apparent from in-depth studies of their errors. Of the sample investigated by Sabey and Staughton (1975), only some 6 per cent of driving errors were directly attributable to inexperience. However, as these authors admit, the boundaries between their classifications of error could not always be clearly defined and an accident could thus be attributed to the various ways in which lack of skill was exhibited rather than to inexperience *per se*. There is certainly evidence of the *younger* driver's overinvolvement in accidents and in convictions for traffic offences (see Pelz and Schuman, 1971). In addition, there is evidence from the comprehensive study of all Swedish child pedestrian accidents during 1968 and 1969 by Sandels (1974) that young drivers, aged 18 to 22 years, were involved in most of the accidents with the younger children below 10 years. This overinvolvement by the younger, presumably less experienced drivers, was attributed mainly to'... speeding, negligence of the rights of pedestrians at marked crossings and a general lack of adjustment to the traffic rules' (Sandels, 1974, p. 38). There was also evidence of 'faulty manœuvring,' 'lack of foresight and imagination', and, as might be expected from such behaviour, a greater tendency for younger drivers to 'hit' child pedestrian casualties rather than be 'run into' by them; thus increasing injury severity.

One can therefore conclude that there is evidence of deficient information-processing among both impaired and experienced drivers, which has implications for pedestrian risk. In addition, the earlier review of the driving task has shown that even competent and experienced drivers may be overloaded with information at times and thus present a potential hazard for pedestrians. It may therefore be instructive to examine the different stages of information-processing in the driving task, to explore the specific problems they present for driver/pedestrian interaction, and thus arrive at some possible accident counter-measures. These stages may conveniently be labelled: (a) expectancy, (b) attention, (c) perception, and (d) decision making, although no sequential dependence among these various stages is implied, as will become clear.

Expectancy

Information processed by the driver obviously derives largely from the road scene. However, it is placed in context with information he has stored in memory, from previous specific and general experience of currently perceived events. In other words, the driver adjusts his behaviour, especially his speed, to the hazards he expects, as well as to those he perceives. This is a common and logical way of performing any skilled task, but it is clearly essential when information-processing demands are high. A driver who made no assumptions about the occurrence of future events or the development of current events would be a serious hindrance to other road users, as observation of any novice driver indicates. However, where drivers' expectancies are incorrect their safety margin will be small, at best, and may well be negative. Pedestrians crossing their path during these decreases or absences of a safety margin will, by definition, be seriously at risk and dependent upon their own actions to prevent a collision.

Watts and Quimby (1980) have identified a number of situations in traffic where negative safety margins are common among drivers. They did this by measuring the behaviour of subjects, recruited from the general motoring public, who drove over a 16 mile route for which detailed accident statistics were available. The latter thus provided a crude measure of objective risk at various sections along the test route. A more precise measure of the drivers' safety margins was recorded for these sections by calculating the difference between the (measured) distance ahead that was visible and the overall stopping distance of the vehicle (determined from the driver's speed and standard values assumed for reaction time and deceleration). The drivers also rated various hazards subjectively, on a driving trial prior to the recording of these objective data. It is interesting to note that there was a significant measure of agreement among these subjective ratings, demonstrating the commonality of drivers' expectancies concerning traffic system hazards.

The situations which were underrated as potential hazards are contrasted with over-rated situations in Table 5.4, reproduced from the authors' report on this study. The differences between the rank ordering of the hazards on subjective and objective risk are also shown, together with the totals of accidents recorded statistically for the route sections in question.

The positive relationship between under-rated hazards and accidents is quite

Table 5.4 Examples of traffic system hazards which are under-rated or over-rated
for accident risk

			Description of hazard	Rank-order difference between subjective and objective risk of hazard
Under-rated hazards (11 accidents in total)		1.	Suburban dual carriageway near a pedestrian bridge.	−26.0
		2.	A rural brow on a single-carriageway road.	−25.5
		3.	A left turn off a rural road.	−25.0
		4.	A de-restricted rural dual-carriageway site near a picnic area	−24.5
		5.	Rural crossroads controlled by traffic lights	−21.0
Over-rated hazards (Zero accidents in total)		1.	Hump bridge on a rural road.	+35.0
		2.	Level crossing on a rural road.	+32.0
		3.	A suburban shopping centre in a 30 mph limit.	+31.0
		4.	Right bend at the end of a rural dual-carriageway.	+28.0
		5.	Right turn on to a rural dual-carriageway.	+24.5

After Watts and Quimby (1980).

clear, demonstrating the important contribution of drivers' expectancies to their information processing and also illustrating the extent to which expectancies are involved causally in accidents. Table 5.4 exemplifies the hazardous potential of driver behaviour for pedestrians, as a function of environmental features of the road system. In a more detailed description of their data, Watts and Quimby (1980, pp. 7—8) also highlight certain specific categories of hazards which are of relevance to the present discussion. For example: a hump bridge, as might be expected because of the restriction in sight distance produced by vertical curves, was associated with a negative safety margin for almost 50 per cent of the drivers tested. Even worse, a left bend in a rural area was found to be associated with a substantial negative safety margin for nearly all the drivers tested. By reference to the subjective risk reported at these and other locations, the authors were able to suggest that certain categories of traffic hazard are, in fact, seriously misjudged. They were therefore able to suggest various accident countermeasures which would involve increasing the perceptibility of the hazards in question. (See also Brown, 1979; Näätänen and Summala, 1976). Whether such countermeasures would be effective for pedestrian safety is uncertain. This doubt is expressed because of a study by Sheppard (1975) of the situations which worry motorists. One situation studied was 'the housing estate, where there are many children about'. Sheppard's findings show that this situation causes drivers far less concern than a number of others in which the driver might be assumed to have more control than in areas frequented by children at play. Perhaps also surprisingly, lesser concern in these situations tended to be expressed by drivers of greater age and experience. This suggests that experienced drivers may, in fact, have false assumptions about their ability to predict the behaviour of child pedestrians, since, as Sandels (1974) has pointed out, much of the child's behaviour is quite unpredictable in the traffic environment.

We can, of course, predict that novice drivers will have certain inappropriate expectancies since experience is, by definition, the acquisition of perceptual anticipation. Interactions between pedestrians and novice drivers will thus tend to be high-risk events. Impaired drivers, too, are likely to have inappropriate expectancies, because of the reduced quality of their sensory input, a decrement in their ability to retrieve memorized information, and a general reduction in the rate at which their expectancies are set up in a dynamic situation. In general then, there are clear implications for the role of drivers' expectancies in the causation of pedestrian accidents. This may partially account for the counter-intuitive finding by Routledge *et al.* (1976) that children are *more* at risk crossing *away* from road junctions than *at* them. Sandels (1974) and SWOV (1977) report similar results. It seems plausible that drivers behave more cautiously at road junctions because that is where, quite reasonably in view of their experience, they expect pedestrians to cross. There are, of course, alternative explanations of this phenomenon; for example, vehicle speeds are generally lower at junctions and therefore the probability of recovery from driver or pedestrian error is higher than on straight roads. The masking of crossing pedestrians by cars parked away from junctions is also a possible explanation of the difference in accident rates. However, neither of the latter explanations is entirely dissociated from the effects of expectancy.

We might therefore tentatively conclude that further studies of the role of expectancy in pedestrian accidents, perhaps modelled on the approach adopted by Watts and Quimby (1980), would be quite informative for the identification of high-risk interactions between drivers and pedestrians. Findings from such research would have three potential areas of application:

1. to the identification of traffic system features which produce negative safety margins among drivers;
2. to the development of training in hazard perception among novice drivers;
3. to the design and introduction of visual displays warning drivers of specific pedestrian hazards.

In general, it would seem more effective to give drivers appropriate expectancies by cueing them with specific hardware devices, such as signs and light signals, rather than relying on early instruction and training in the enormous range of hazards presented by pedestrians.

Attention

As we have seen, attention can be *focused* on events which require fairly continuous monitoring, such as the vehicle cues required for steering; or it can be *distributed* among events for checking purposes; or it can be *attracted* by some compelling object in the visual periphery. The relative extent to which these attentional characteristics comprise the driver's visual sampling behaviour will obviously depend upon his speed and the specific environmental demands. In a busy urban area, attention will be distributed over a wide visual field, as the driver checks for potential hazards arising from ahead, behind, and either side. The probability that novel stimuli will claim his attention momentarily is high. However, steering demands will be lower and, in the extreme, drivers may simply be tracking their distance from the kerb, rather than using higher-order information such as vehicle yaw-rate. At higher speeds, attention will be directed mainly to the focus of expansion of the visual field. For example; Rockwell (1972) has reported that 90 per cent of eye fixations fall within $\pm 4°$ of this region. Mourant, Rockwell and Rackoff (1969) found that drivers travelling on an open road spent about half the time fixating straight ahead, about a quarter looking right or left, and the remaining time looking at other vehicles, environmental features and the road surface. Clearly the amount of attentional checking is much reduced at higher speeds and drivers have little time to spend to task-irrelevant distractions.

Attention is thus distributed over a flattened conical field of view, and this cone will expand and contract as speed falls and rises, respectively. Within that cone the visual field will be sampled in a manner determined by the driver's experience and expectancies (Lovegrove, 1978). Each source of information will be used to predict developments in that region of the visual field and thus determine its future checking requirements. The following general predictions about pedestrian risk can therefore be made:

(a) At lower vehicle speeds, the risk is that pedestrians will be overlooked, as drivers scan some other, perhaps remote, part of the road scene. This risk is compounded by the fact that the environmental features which decrease driving speed (e.g. traffic congestion, road junctions, etc.) will also increase the pedestrian's information processing demands. Thus both driver and pedestrian may overlook the other at a critical point in their interaction. This will be a particular problem where the driver interacts with smaller (i.e. less conspicuous) child pedestrians, whose attentional sampling strategies are not well developed (see Kenchington, Alderson and Whiting, 1977).
(b) At higher vehicle speeds, the risk is that pedestrians may attempt to cross so close to the vehicle that they are outside the driver's effective visual field (i.e. the cone of focused attention). If their pre-crossing behaviour is such that they provide few cues of relative motion in the driver's visual periphery, they will not attract the driver's attention and again may be overlooked.
(c) At any speed, the risk of collision will be increased if pedestrians change their road crossing behaviour, either in direction or speed, after the driver has predicted their trajectory, made due allowance for it and then switched attention to some other competing demand.
(d) Since attentional sampling proceeds on the basis of experience and expectancy, it follows that novice drivers will present pedestrians with a higher risk than experienced drivers. There is support for this view from eye movement studies by Mourant and Rockwell (1972) who found that the visual search behaviour of novices was poorly matched to the demands of driving.

There is evidence that certain other individual differences in attention are important for information processing in driving. This has been demonstrated by Kahneman, Ben Ishai and Lotan (1973), who developed a test in which subjects had to attend selectively to one of two messages presented simultaneously, one to each ear. Key words had to be detected and repeated. The ear to which the subject was required to listen was signalled by a high or a low tone. Thus performance could be measured to provide an index of selective attention and also a measure of the speed at which the subject could switch attention from one source of information to another. In a retrospective study of a group of Public Service Vehicle drivers, Kahneman *et al.* were able to show, as predicted, that individuals' characteristic speeds of attentional switching were negatively correlated with their rate of involvement in traffic accidents. Mihal and Barrett (1976) have produced comparable results from a retrospective study of truck drivers.

Although no causal relationship was established by these results, the findings match our expectancy that individuals will differ in the efficiency with which they search their visual field for potential hazards. Since the correlations reported by these authors involved performance on an *auditory* task of selective attention, the results support the idea that accident liability is a function of the individual's *central* information-processing resources and not simply dependent on peripheral limitations in visual search. The current uncertainty is whether more efficient attentional behaviour can be taught and, if so, how this should be achieved. Clearly this is an area where further research is required, although the methodological problems are somewhat daunting, as with all validation studies of individual differences in performance. However, some effort is certainly required on practical methods of inculcating efficient visual search strategies among trainee drivers, rather than leaving them to learn these the hard way, often at the pedestrian's expense.

The extent of the general problem of attentional errors among drivers may be assessed from the in-depth study of accidents reported by Sabey and Staughton (1975). Their data show that these errors ('lack of attention', 'distraction' and 'failed to look') accounted for 18 per cent of the 3,704 accidents investigated.

The alternative countermeasure to training less-skilled drivers is to introduce more hardware devices into the traffic system which will claim the driver's attention at appropriate points. However, as mentioned earlier, the effectiveness of such attention-getting devices usually declines with prolonged specific experience, and commuters may well have extinguished all responses to static traffic signs designed to highlight critical information. The development of new devices aimed at presenting such information auditorily, within the vehicle, may largely overcome these difficulties.

There remains the problem of the impaired driver, exemplified by Table 5.3. Some evidence (e.g. Hamilton and Copeman, 1970; Hockey, 1970) suggests that attentional sampling will become *more* selective with increasing alcohol intoxication and *less* selective with increasing tiredness. It follows from such findings that intoxicated drivers will present greater risk for the pedestrian who crosses in the periphery of their visual field, or anywhere else remote from sources of visual information currently considered important by the driver. By contrast, tired drivers may overlook pedestrians crossing anywhere in their visual fields, since their attentional sampling will be diffused; that is, it will be less determined by task demands than is usually the case for their normal state of alertness. There is further evidence on this point from studies by Michon and Wertheim (1978), who have reported that drowsiness alters the nature of ocular-motor control of attention. In other words, tiredness actually reduces the efficiency with which the eyes scan the visual world, in addition to any impairment it produces in the effective visual field.

Accident countermeasures aimed at impaired drivers will largely consist of improved methods of detecting their impairment and enforcing associated traffic legislation. There seems little scope for influencing the attentional characteristics of impaired drivers directly and, as indicated earlier, pedestrians can usually not detect the usual driver impairments and can therefore not be expected to increase their own safety margins in such interactions.

Perception

Perceptual demands of driving involve the identification of static features and of dynamic patterns of activity in the road scene. Since drivers are attempting to encode information of immediate relevance for their task, it follows that the efficiency with which they perceive task-relevant events will be a function of their specific skills and experience as a driver. Thus, once again, the pedestrian will be more at risk from the inexperienced driver, who will tend to overlook or misperceive static features of the road scene and also misread the development of dynamic interactions among road users.

One individual characteristic of perception which has been associated with accident liability in research conducted over the past few years, is a function of the driver's 'cognitive style'. This term describes the characteristic manner in which individuals process information about the world. The aspect of cognitive style found to be of particular relevance for road safety is termed 'field dependence' (see Witkin, Lewis, Herzman, Machover, Melssner and Wapner, 1972). This describes the relative ability of the individual to identify the salient features in a complex scene and it is assumed to reflect an individual's capacity to 'overcome the embedding contexts in perceptual functioning' (Goodenough, 1976, p. 53). It appears that this relative ability is a trait which finds expression across a variety of situations in which perception is uniquely important. It may therefore be predicted that 'field dependent' persons, having less capacity for overcoming embedding contexts, will be more liable to accident involvement than 'field independent' individuals, because they will tend to overlook critical features of a busy road scene, and be slow to notice the insidious changes in traffic interactions which signal an impending collision.

Goodenough (1976) has reviewed a number of studies which support this prediction. The field independent driver is, in fact, slow to recognize developing hazards; takes longer to perceive road signs; has difficulty in learning to control a skidding vehicle; and drives much less 'defensively' in high-speed traffic (i.e. exhibits less perceptual anticipation). In addition, there is evidence from Mihal and Barrett (1976) that the field dependent driver has a higher rate of accident involvement. Shinar *et al.* (1978) show that this type of perceptual inadequacy is exhibited as a less effective pattern of visual search than is observed among field independent drivers. Field dependent individuals are found to be less able to adapt to the different visual demands of changing environments; that is, more rigid in their visual search behaviour. On curves, for example, they will continue to scan in the region of the focus of expansion, rather than processing information from the curve, which is the more efficient strategy adopted by field independent drivers. They also exhibit a more concentrated pattern of visual fixations generally, and Shinar *et al.* have likened this to 'tunnel vision'. In sum, it can be said that visual search is a much slower, less efficient, process for field dependent drivers. It has also been found by these authors that these effects of field dependence increase with the driver's age (over the range 20–70 years). This change seems to occur independently of any impairment in reaction time or memory.

To the present writer's knowledge, the direct implications of field dependence for pedestrian risk are unknown. Perceptual inadequacies of this type will obviously tend to produce delayed or inappropriate actions from drivers and accidents will often be attributed to these response errors, rather than to perception *per se*. For example, Sabey and Staughton (1975) attribute only about 3 per cent of their accident sample to perceptual error (defined by them as 'incorrect interpretation'), although various other categories of error ('misjudged speed and distance', 'wrong position for manœuvre', etc.) may well have had a substantial perceptual component. It is nevertheless possible to identify certain situations in which field dependent drivers may contribute to pedestrian accidents. Clearly, they will have greater difficulty than field independent drivers in perceiving the pre-crossing behaviour of pedestrians where the latter occurs against a background of complex pedestrian activity. Their more rigid visual search patterns will increase risk where large visual angles separate the vehicle's direction of travel from the road scene's focus of expansion (mainly on lateral curves). Their slower rate of processing visual information will increase risk generally where traffic presents many competing demands. Of course, it is possible that field dependent drivers adjust their speed to offset their relative difficulty in information processing. They may therefore not inevitably be overinvolved in accidents with perceptual explanations. However, this possibility remains to be investigated: as does the feasibility of retraining the field dependent's visual search behaviour, in order to match it more efficiently to the demands of the driving task.

Of course, the difficulty of perceiving meaningful events in a complex traffic scene is common amongst drivers. Reducing pedestrian risk in road crossing is therefore more than a problem in retraining drivers with specific perceptual inadequacies. Since perception is the *imposition* of a pattern on sensory information, risk could be reduced by increasing the driver's subjective probability of interaction with pedestrians. This will largely be a question of cueing the driver to changes in pedestrian activity, as discussed in the earlier section dealing with 'Expectancy'. In addition, improved perception is naturally a function of increased conspicuity of pedestrians. Personal aids to child pedestrian conspicuity have been discussed by Lewis (1973). However, there remains scope for improving conspicuity by appropriate design of the traffic environment. This would, in principle, require the system designer to provide better contrast between pedestrians and their background, at places where they typically cross. The use of 'sight-screens' and raised pavement at the approaches to uncontrolled crossings may provide viable solutions here.

Perhaps a greater need is for further research on the constituents of 'conspicuity' afforded by different types of pre-crossing behaviour among pedestrians. Routledge *et al.* (1976), for example, have suggested that the pre-crossing behaviour of boys is a possible source of their greater involvement than girls in child pedestrian accidents, since boys and girls demonstrated a comparable exposure to risk in their studies. More recent evidence provided by Chapman, Foot and Wade (1980) suggests that this conclusion may hold only for school journeys. However, if differential pre-crossing behaviour were found to be implicated substantially in the perceptual errors made during driver/pedestrian interactions, it might be possible to manipulate more informative pre-crossing behaviour among child pedestrians, by appropriate training. As suggested in an earlier section on 'Collision Avoidance', it may be informative for perceptual explanations of pedestrian accidents to explore the 'looked but failed to see' phenomenon. This, too, could produce evidence on 'behavioural conspicuity', with implications for training.

Drivers suffering from some form of temporary impairment, from fatigue, alcohol, or other drugs, have impaired perception. Again, there seems little scope for pedestrian accident countermeasures against these typical driver impairments, other than improved detection and the enforcement of legislative controls on the sources of these impairments.

Decision making

Rational decision making requires an individual to balance the perceived costs and pay-offs of alternative courses of action, in order to maximize the expected gain from each response. The quality of drivers' decision making will thus be a function of both their physical and social environments. Unfortunately, both costs and pay-offs associated with use of the road transport system are often difficult to perceive and balance. This is particularly true for perception of the pay-offs likely to accrue from excessive speed. For example, Svenson (1976) has shown that if speed over part of a journey is held at a low level, individuals are extremely poor judges of the higher speeds they need to sustain in order to achieve a given average speed. In practice, time lost due to traffic delays is usually overestimated, as is the effect of high-speed periods on average speed. The overall effect is that delayed drivers speed whenever they can, often unnecessarily, in order to regain lost time; but seldom recover that time as fast as they believe. Presumably, this effect results largely from the fact that time perception depends upon the activity filling the interval in question. Thus time spent in traffic jams appears to pass slowly, because little is happening. High-speed periods will, by contrast, seem shorter than they actually are, because the driver is more involved in the information-processing requirements of fast travel. The upshot is that speeding seldom produces the anticipated pay-off and may often not be worth the risks incurred.

There is a limited amount of empirical evidence supporting this idea that drivers overestimate the pay-offs from high speed. For example, we know that drivers overvalue short journey times in financial terms. When Dawson and Everell (1972) surveyed the paid use of Italian autostrada, as compared with travelling free on a parallel all-purpose road, they found that motorists were prepared to pay more than twice their average hourly income to travel at motorway speeds and thus save an hour of working time. This tendency towards overvaluing speed remained, although at a reduced level, even when motorists travelled during non-working hours and were thus, presumably, paying for the privilege themselves.

There is also evidence that drivers underestimate the costs of speeding. For example: Duncan, Sumner and Shrewsbury (1977) report that more than a third of British drivers exceed the upper limit of 70 mph on motorways. This suggests that they underestimate the penalties for a speeding conviction (see Hogg, 1977).

Even in those situations when drivers are able to assess the relevant costs and pay-offs accurately, a potential source of error is the set of criteria on which these are valued, in order to maximize the expected gain from their decisions. As Brown (1980a) has demonstrated, the costs of specific driver behaviours largely derive from factors intrinsic to the traffic system (e.g. accident involvement, injury, detection and conviction for an offence, etc.) By contrast, the pay-offs largely derive from factors extrinsic to the traffic system (e.g. shorter journey times, greater income, increased business, etc.) Thus costs and pay-offs will be valued on quite different criteria and a rational balance will be difficult to achieve. Driver's decision making, in general, will therefore tend to be irrational and will certainly be impaired where the various costs and pay-offs are imperfectly perceived and inappropriately valued.

As would be expected, novice drivers are likely to make imperfect decisions. This may partly be accounted for by their immature system of values (if they are young). However, only a negligible proportion of all accidents seems to be attributable to decision errors, as such (Sabey and Staughton, 1975); although other causal attributions used in the Sabey and Staughton study obviously include a decision making component (e.g. 'lack of judgement'; 'following too close'; 'irresponsible or reckless'; etc.). Certainly, in relation to the commission of traffic offences, faulty decision criteria appear to play a much smaller part than faulty perception (Brown, 1980a).

Perhaps a major source of error among younger drivers' decisions is their underestimation of the potential costs of certain actions. This will result, at least in part, from their relative inability to identify certain hazards in the traffic environment. In a study of this source of error, Laidlaw (1975) presented drivers with various traffic hazards in a filmed sequence of driving through traffic. Viewers scanned the visual scene as perceived by the driver, through the windscreen. They were required to respond as rapidly as possible to perceived hazards, by signalling their presence and then identifying them orally. It was thus possible to record the proportion of known hazards reported, as a function of driving experience. The results are shown in Figure 5.3, for novice and experienced drivers.

The critical point here, is that although novice drivers were equally as efficient as the experienced group in reporting hazards close to the vehicle, all distant hazards were less frequently reported. Thus distant hazards seem to play little part in the novice driver's decision making. It follows that decisions made by inexperienced drivers will tend to be more *ad hoc*; increasing the probability of 'panic' reactions when errors occur. An extremely relevant finding here, in relation to younger drivers' involvement in pedestrian accidents, is that they

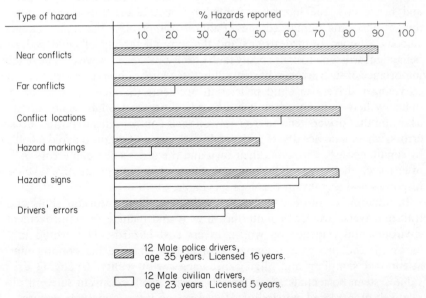

Figure 5.3 Differences in hazard perception by novice and experienced drivers (All differences significant at 1% level, apart from 'Near Conflicts'). (Adapted from Laidlaw, 1975)

make only limited use of other road users' behaviour in the perception of traffic hazard.

The major scope for accident countermeasures in this area of decision making lies with the teaching of appropriate skills to novice drivers. Training schemes in general unfortunately tend to concentrate on encouraging the rapid acquisition of vehicle control skills; thus reinforcing the new motorist's typical view of driving skill as mastery of the machine. Confidence in their ability as a driver will thus, initially, be largely a function of their vehicle control skills and these will thus determine the demands they impose upon themselves in the basically self-paced conditions of driving in traffic. Brown (1980b) has adduced evidence to support the view that, in general, drivers' subjective risk levels are mainly determined by confidence in their use of vehicle control skills to correct decision errors. Novice drivers' decision errors are thus seen to result from an immature and exaggerated form of this generally misplaced confidence. In other words, their 'roadcraft' will be mismatched to their self-imposed demands. Brown (1980c) has modelled these relationships between control skills, confidence and decision skills, to explain the high peak in accident involvement observed some two to three years after an individual begins to drive (see Pelz and Schuman, 1971).

It would thus be predicted that younger novice drivers provide a major risk for pedestrians. This will derive mainly from their relative inability to perceive and hence cost the hazard presented by pedestrians crossing the road at uncontrolled and unmarked sites. Failure to appreciate the rapid changes in velocity attained by pedestrians and the unpredictability of child pedestrian behaviour, will tend to cause many faulty decisions among novices. The practical importance of such errors is possibly illustrated by the observed overinvolvement of younger drivers in child pedestrian accidents (Sandels, 1974). The basic difficulty here is likely to be exacerbated, if Brown (1980b) is correct in his assertion that drivers tend to over-rely on their control skills to correct decision errors, where a novice driver and a child pedestrian attempt to avoid a collision by simultaneously correcting their own and the other's decision errors. All too often, such behavioural encounters result in counterproductive avoidance responses and a collision becomes inevitable.

In addition to more effective methods of teaching decision skills among trainee drivers, accident countermeasures would include the improvement of environmental evidence on which drivers cost hazards. This would involve hardware and procedural changes designed to enhance perception, improve attentional sampling and align expectancies with reality. Changing drivers' value systems to include a greater consideration of pedestrian safety is also a relatively unexplored possibility. However, the latter approach requires attitudinal changes and it is still not clear whether these result from, or are a prerequisite of, behavioural change. In the absence of conclusive evidence that drivers' decisions on pedestrian behaviour can be improved, one must resort to the removal of a need for drivers' decision making about road user priorities, by greater use of signal-controlled crossing facilities.

CONCLUSIONS: CAUSES AND COUNTERMEASURES

The aim of this chapter has been to analyse the various components of the driving task and the specific information-processing skills involved in those components, in order to identify those aspects of driver behaviour considered likely to increase pedestrian risk. The problem is seen to reflect a behavioural mismatch between driver and pedestrian, contributed to by certain inadequacies in traffic system design. Solutions are seen to result from greater attention to the specific difficulties arising at this behavioural interface, rather than from a concentration on driver or pedestrian behaviour and needs in isolation.

Where possible in this review, specific inferences from these behavioural considerations of the driver's task have been related to statistical evidence on pedestrian accidents. In particular, inferred accident causation has been linked with the specific driving errors attributed to traffic accidents in certain in-depth studies of pre-accident behaviour. A major problem here is that drivers' errors are usually not categorized in psychologically meaningful terms by accident investigators. The categories used are also often not mutually exclusive. Thus a description of error as 'improper overtaking', although it clearly identifies the responsible task component, does not distinguish perceptual errors from decision errors. Errors described as 'wrong decision or action' represent a category not exclusive of other errors described as 'following too close'; and so on. The problem, of course, is two-fold: the categories of road-user error employed by accident investigators have to be related to practical accident countermeasures. It may often be easier to go straight from a categorization of error in terms of, say, 'improper overtaking' to a redesign of traffic priorities, than would be the case if the errors in question were related to specific failings in human information-processing. However, it is by no means clear that such task-relevant error descriptors will identify the true source of driver error. This is the other part of the two-fold problem: that *post hoc* attributions of accident causation may emphasize one or more of the secondary errors which often contribute to a driver's accident involvement and ignore the initial, primary error. Thus, although such investigations may often lead to a limited form of *accident* prevention, they may be a relatively inefficient method of preventing driver *error*. A concentration on behavioural errors rather than on their occasional outcome (i.e. accidents) is clearly essential to a scientific approach to accident prevention, since it is necessary to know not only the behaviour which resulted in an accident, if one is to design countermeasures: one also needs control data on the frequency of comparable behaviour which does *not*

result in accidents. Without such control data, the effectiveness of any
countermeasure and its implications for the inconvenience of and acceptability
by the road users affected will be indeterminable.

It seems probable that a concentration on the behavioural interface between
driver and pedestrian may be more informative in these respects than attempts
at causal attribution which fail to isolate the primary mismatch in their
behaviours.

One thing is clear from this and other reviews of pedestrian accident causation:
there is no single major cause of such accidents and there is therefore no single
outstanding countermeasure which can be suggested to reduce pedestrian risk.
Less demanding methods of communicating route information to long distance
drivers may reduce the present attentional and perceptual load this places on
them. Improving the advance signalling of hazards may also limit those
occasions when drivers' expectancies are wrong and they actually adopt negative
safety margins. Such cueing techniques will need to be extremely compelling if
they are to influence the contribution of commuting drivers to pedestrian
accidents. Further research seems required in both these areas, to identify the
more important communications needs of drivers and their inappropriate
expectancies. Improvements in both areas should provide pedestrians with
greater safety margins.

This review and other investigations of pedestrian accidents have identified
the younger novice driver as a particular problem, especially in interactions
with child pedestrians. The implications for driver training seem clear: 'roadcraft' needs to be taught in a structured fashion, so that novice drivers do not
develop a misplaced confidence in their vehicle control skills and thus place
inappropriate demands on their limited decision making abilities in traffic. This
is largely a question of interleaving 'roadcraft' education with the teaching of
control skills. Effectively, it will involve training in hazard perception, especially
the incorporation of road user behaviour into the information processed by
the driver. Instruction in the limited pay-offs likely to accrue from excessive
speed and the costs of such behaviour in the traffic system, are also likely to
be informative and effective in improving the novice driver's decision skills.

Impaired drivers, although overinvolved in accidents in general, are probably
not a major problem for pedestrians, except during the late-night so-called
'drinking hours', and during the late afternoon/early evening when tired
commuters are driving home. Fortunately, the vulnerable child pedestrian is
little exposed to risk from these drivers, although there is clearly a problem
during the overlap between homeward-bound commuters and after-school play
and errand-running. Countermeasures here seem mainly a question of segregating the two road user groups, by greater use of lights-controlled crossing
facilities and, in the longer-term, the redesign of residential areas. Improved
detection and enforcement of legislation on driving impairments are, of course,
an obvious general solution to the problem.

Certain other individual inadequacies among drivers, identified in this review (e.g. reduced attentional selectivity, field dependence) can probably best be dealt with by greater attention to the potential for retraining. This is another area in which further research seems required; both on the implication of such disadvantaged drivers in traffic accidents and on the techniques appropriate to their retraining.

Although the problem of pedestrian accidents has been recognized for many years, at least by certain researchers (e.g. see Moore and Older, 1965), it seems fair to conclude that we are only now in a position to appreciate the actual exposure to risk among these vulnerable road users and thus launch a more scientific attack on the problem of their behavioural interaction with the driver.

REFERENCES

Brown, I. D. (1961). Measuring the spare 'mental capacity' of drivers by a subsidiary task. *Ergonomics*, **4**, 35–40.

Brown, I. D. (1979). Can ergonomics improve primary safety in road transport systems? *Ergonomics*, **22**, 109–116.

Brown, I. D. (1980a). The traffic offence as a rational decision: exposure of a problem and suggested countermeasures. In S. M. Lloyd-Bostock (Ed.), *Psychology in Legal Contexts: Applications and Limitations*. London: Macmillan.

Brown, I. D. (1980b). Error-correction probability as a determinant of drivers' subjective risk. In D. J. Oborne and J. A. Levis (Eds.), *Human Factors in Transport Research*, Volume 2, *User Factors: Comfort, the Environment and Behaviour*. London: Academic Press.

Brown, I. D. (1980c). Experience and exposure are a confounded nuisance in research on driver behaviour. *Paper presented at the International Driver Behaviour Research Association, Symposium on Risk-Exposure Measurement in Road Traffic Safety Research*. June. Aarhus, Denmark.

Chapman, A. J., Foot, H. C., and Wade, F. M. (1980). Children at play. In D. J. Oborne and J. A. Levis (Eds.), *Human Factors in Transport Research*, Volume 2, *User Factors: Comfort, the Environment and Behaviour*. London: Academic Press.

Colborne, H. V. (1971). Two experiments on methods of training children in road safety. *Ministry of Transport, Road Research Laboratory, Laboratory Report 404*. Crowthorne: RRL.

Colborne, H. V., and Sargent, K. J. A. (1971). A survey of road safety in schools: education and other factors. *Ministry of Transport, Road Research Laboratory, Laboratory Report 338*. Crowthorne: RRL.

Dawson, R. F. F., and Everell, P. F. (1972). The value of motorists' time: a study in Italy. *Department of the Environment, Transport and Road Research Laboratory, Laboratory Report 426*. Crowthorne: TRRL.

Department of Transport. (1980). *Road Accidents Great Britain 1978*. London: Her Majesty's Stationery Office.

Duncan, N. C., Sumner, S. L., and Shrewsbury, J. S. (1977). Measurement of the speeds of cars on motorways in 1976. *Department of the Environment, Transport and Road Research Laboratory, Supplementary Report 326*. Crowthorne: TRRL.

Firth, D. E. (1973). The road safety aspects of the Tufty Club. *Department of the Environment, Transport and Road Research Laboratory, Laboratory Report 604*. Crowthorne: TRRL.

Goodenough, D. R. (1976). A review of individual differences in field dependence as a factor in auto safety. *Human Factors*, **18**, 53–62.

Grayson, G. B. (1975a). The Hampshire child pedestrian accident study. *Department of the Environment, Transport and Road Research Laboratory, Laboratory Report 668.* Crowthorne: TRRL.

Grayson, G. B. (1975b). Observations of pedestrian behaviour at four sites. *Department of the Environment, Transport and Road Research Laboratory, Laboratory Report 670.* Crowthorne: TRRL.

Hamilton, P., and Copeman, A. K. (1970). The effect of alcohol and noise on components of a tracking and monitoring task. *British Journal of Psychology*, **61**, 149–156.

Higgs, M. H. (1972). Opinions on the design and measurements of the effect of a road safety leaflet. *Department of the Environment, Transport and Road Research Laboratory, Laboratory Report 483.* Crowthorne: TRRL.

Hockey, G. R. J. (1970). Changes in attention allocation in a multicomponent task under loss of sleep. *British Journal of Psychology*, **61**, 473–480.

Hogg, R. (1977). A study of male motorists' attitudes to speed restrictions. *Department of the Environment, Transport and Road Research Laboratory, Laboratory Report 276.* Crowthorne: TRRL.

Howarth, C. I., Routledge, D. A., and Repetto-Wright, R. (1974). An analysis of road accidents involving child pedestrians. *Ergonomics*, **17**, 319–330.

Kahneman, D., Ben Ishai, R., and Lotan, M. (1973). Relation of a test of attention to road accidents. *Journal of Applied Psychology*, **58**, 113–115.

Kenchington, M. J., Alderson, G. J. K., and Whiting, H. T. A. (1977). An assessment of the role of motion prediction in child pedestrian accidents. *Department of the Environment, Transport and Road Research Laboratory, Supplementary Report 320.* Crowthorne: TRRL.

Laidlaw, J. B. (1975). Effect of driving experience on perception of hazard in the traffic environment. *Unpublished report to the Department of the Environment, Transport and Road Research Laboratory.* Crowthorne: TRRL. (Cited in Brown, 1980c).

Lewis, G. D. (1973). Children's use of aids to conspicuity. *Department of the Environment, Transport and Road Research Laboratory, Laboratory Report 534.* Crowthorne: TRRL.

Lewis, P. A. (1979). System failures on road traffic networks: can ergonomics help? *Ergonomics*, **22**, 117–127.

Lines, C. J. (1978). The effect of motorway signals on traffic speed. *Department of the Environment, Transport and Road Research Laboratory, Supplementary Report 363.* Crowthorne: TRRL.

Lovegrove, S. A. (1978). Approach speeds at uncontrolled intersections with restricted sight distances. *Journal of Applied Psychology*, **63**, 635–642.

Mackie, A. M. (1967). Progress in learning the meanings of symbolic traffic signs. *Ministry of Transport, Road Research Laboratory, Laboratory Report 91.* Crowthorne: RRL.

McLean, J. R., and Hoffman, E. R. (1971). Analysis of drivers' control movements. *Human Factors*, **13**, 407–418.

McLean, J. R., and Hoffman, E. R. (1972). The effects of lane width on driver steering control and performance. In *Proceedings of the Sixth Conference of the Australian Road Research Board*, **6**, 418–440.

McLean, J. R., and Hoffman, E. R. (1973). The effects of restricted preview on driver steering control and performance. *Human Factors*, **15**, 421–430.

McLean, J. R., and Hoffman, E. R. (1975). Steering reversals as a measure of driver performance and steering task difficulty. *Human Factors*, **17**, 248–256.

Michon, J. A., van der Molen, H. H., Rothengatter, T. A., Vinjé, M. P., and Welvaart, A. M. P. (1979). Research on child traffic education. *Information Leaflet Number 7A.* University of Groningen: Traffic Research Centre.

Michon, J. A., and Wertheim, A. H. (1978). Drowsiness in driving. In Commission of the European Communities, *Driver Fatigue in Road Traffic Accidents,* EUR 6065EN. Luxembourg: CEC.

Mihal, W. L., and Barrett, G. V. (1976). Individual differences in perceptual information processing and their relation to automobile accident involvement. *Journal of Applied Psychology,* **61**, 229–233.

Moore, R. L., and Older, S. J. (1965). Pedestrians and vehicles are compatible in today's world. *Traffic Engineering,* **35**, 20–23 and 52–59.

Mourant, R. R., and Rockwell, T. H. (1972). Strategies of visual search by novice and experienced drivers. *Human Factors,* **14**, 325–335.

Mourant, R. R., Rockwell, T. H., and Rackoff, N. J. (1969). Drivers' eye movements and visual workload. *Highway Research Record,* **292**, 1–10.

Näätänen, R., and Summala, H. (1976). *Road User Behaviour and Traffic Accidents.* Oxford: North Holland Publishing Company.

Nagayama, Y., Morita, T., Miura, T., Watanabem, J., and Murakami, N. (1979). Motorcyclists' visual scanning patterns in comparison with automobile drivers. Society of Automotive Engineers Technical Paper Series, Number 790262.

National Safety Council (1976). *Accident Facts.* Chicago: National Safety Council.

Nummenmaa, T., Ruuhilehto, K., and Syvänen, M. (1975). Traffic education programme for preschool aged children and children starting school. *Report Number 17.* Helsinki, Finland: *Central Organization for Traffic Safety.*

Pelz, D. C., and Schuman, S. H. (1971). Are young drivers really more dangerous after controlling for age and experience? *Journal of Safety Research,* **3**, 68–79.

Rockwell, T. H. (1972). Skills, judgements and information acquisition in driving. In T. W. Forbes (Ed.), *Human Factors in Highway Traffic Safety Research.* New York: Wiley.

Routledge, D. A., Repetto-Wright, R., and Howarth, C. I. (1974a). A comparison of interviews and observation to obtain measures of children's exposure to risk as pedestrians. *Ergonomics,* **17**, 623–638.

Routledge, D. A., Repetto-Wright, R., and Howarth, C. I. (1974b). The exposure of young children to accident risk as pedestrians. *Ergonomics,* **17**, 457–480.

Routledge, D. A., Repetto-Wright, R., and Howarth, C. I. (1976). Four techniques for measuring the exposure of young children to accident risk as pedestrians. In A. S. Hakkert (Ed.), *Proceedings of the International Conference on Pedestrian Safety,* Volume 1, 7B1–7B7. Haifa: Michlol.

Russam, K. (1975). Road safety of children in the United Kingdom. *Department of the Environment, Transport and Road Research Laboratory, Laboratory Report 678.* Crowthorne: TRRL.

Sabey, B. E., and Staughton, G. C. (1975). Interacting roles of road environment, vehicle and road user in accidents. *Paper presented at the Fifth International Conference of the International Association for Accident and Traffic Medicine,* September. London.

Sabey, B. E., and Staughton, G. C. (1980). The drinking driver in Great Britain . *Paper presented at the Eighth International Conference on Alcohol, Drugs and Traffic Safety.* June. Stockholm, Sweden: University of Stockholm.

Sadler, J. (1972). *Children and Road Safety: A Survey Among Mothers.* London: Her Majesty's Stationery Office.

Sandels, S. (1974). Why are children injured in traffic? Can we prevent child accidents in traffic? *Skandia Report II.* Stockholm: Skandia.

Sargent, K. J. A., and Sheppard, D. (1974). The development of the Green Cross Code. *Department of the Environment, Transport and Road Research Laboratory, Laboratory Report 605.* Crowthorne: TRRL.

Sheppard, D. (1975). The driving situations which worry motorists. *Department of the Environment, Transport and Road Research Laboratory, Supplementary Report 129 UC.* Crowthorne: TRRL.

Sheppard, D. (1977). Ways in which school crossing patrols instruct children about crossing roads. *Department of the environment, Transport and Road Research Laboratory, Laboratory Report 779.* Crowthorne: TRRL.

Shinar, D. (1978). *Psychology on the Road: The Human Factor in Traffic Safety.* New York: Wiley.

Shinar, D., McDowell, E. D., Rackoff, N. J., and Rockwell, T. H. (1978). Field dependence and driver visual behavior. *Human Factors,* **20,** 553–559.

Singh, A. (1976). Road safety education in primary and middle schools. *Department of the Environment, Transport and Road Research Laboratory, Supplementary Report 207 UC.* Crowthorne: TRRL.

Smeed, R. J. (1977). Pedestrian accidents. In A. S. Hakkert (Ed.), *Proceedings of the International Conference on Pedestrian Safety,* Volume 2, 7–21. Haifa: Michlol.

Snyder, M. G., and Knoblauch, R. L. (1971). Pedestrian safety: the identification of precipitating factors and possible countermeasures. *Operations Research Report Number FH-11-7312.* Washington DC: United States Department of Transportation.

Svenson, O. (1976). Experience of mean speed related to speed over parts of a trip. *Ergonomics,* **19,** 11–20.

SWOV (1977). The pedestrian as a road user. *Institute for Road Safety Research, Publication 1977-IE.* Voorburg: SWOV.

Thomson, G. A. (1978). A model for determining the effectiveness of intersection priority rules. *Accident Analysis and Prevention,* **10,** 313–333.

Watts, G. R., and Quimby, A. R. (1980). Aspects of road layout that affect drivers' perception and risk taking. *Department of the Environment, Transport and Road Research Laboratory, Laboratory Report 920.* Crowthorne: TRRL.

Witkin, H. A., Lewis, H. B., Herzman, M., Machover, K., Melssner, P. B., and Wapner, S. (1972). *Personality Through Perception: An Experimental and Clinical Study.* Westport, Connecticut: Greenwood Press.

Zuercher, R. (1976). Communications at pedestrian crossings. In A. S. Hakkert (Ed.), *Proceedings of the International Conference on Pedestrian Safety,* Volume 1, 7E1–7E7. Haifa: Michlol.

Pedestrian Accidents
Edited by A. J. Chapman, F. M. Wade and H. C. Foot
© 1982, John Wiley & Sons Ltd.

Chapter 6

Vehicle Design and Pedestrian Injuries

S. J. Ashton

It is often stated that, because accidents are caused by people, the correct approach to accidents is to prevent their occurrence by changing people's behaviour. But changing behaviour is difficult. In the majority of pedestrian accidents the pedestrian is at least partly to blame. Three different identifiable groups account for a large proportion of pedestrian casualties, these being young children, intoxicated adults, and the elderly, and it is difficult to see how radical changes in the behaviour of these groups can be achieved. The young child is learning to cope with traffic, and although a child might appear to be able to cope there are occasions when training is forgotten; witness the child who runs out into the road whilst playing, or the child who sees a friend across the road and forgets to look. Whilst the effects of alcohol are well documented the consumption of alcohol is one of the established social traditions of this country, and is unlikely to change. The elderly adult suffers from failing senses; there is deterioration in seeing and hearing; reactions and movement are slower; and hence they have problems in traffic.

Whilst education may reduce accidents by changing people's behaviour, the effects of education are likely to be small compared to those of engineering. Engineering influences pedestrian accidents in two ways. First of all the design of the environment affects the chance of an accident happening. Second the design of the vehicle affects the injuries that are sustained when the accident happens. Recent research (Ashton, 1980) has shown that a reduction of roughly one-third in the number of pedestrians seriously injured, after being struck by the front of a car, could be achieved by improved vehicle design.

PEDESTRIAN INJURY RESEARCH

If vehicles are to be designed to minimize the likelihood of pedestrian injury it is necessary to know what injuries are sustained and how those injuries are caused. The first question is relatively simple to answer by using data from medical records, and indeed many such studies describing the injuries sustained by pedestrians have been made. The second question is more complex and has been studied in three separate ways: first of all by the study of real accidents;

second by carrying out experimental tests in which anthropometric dummies and cadavers are struck by real and stylized vehicles; and, third, by mathematical modelling and computer simulation.

Accident studies

There has been a large number of studies in which medical or coroners' records have been used to describe the injuries sustained by pedestrians and to compare those injuries with the injuries sustained by other road users. A comprehensive review of these studies has been made by Ashton and Mackay (1979a). The results of these studies are generally not directly comparable due to differences in the populations considered and in the methods used to describe the injuries. For instance, Aston and Perkins (1954), Bø (1972), Gratten, Hobbs and Keigan (1976) and Nelson (1974) have described the injuries sustained by all pedestrian casualties, whilst Gögler (1962), Jamieson and Tait (1966) and McNicol-Smith and Letheren (1961) described the injuries sustained by hospital in-patients. Gissane and Bull (1961), Huelke and Davis (1969), Sevitt (1968), Tonge, O'Reilly and Davison (1964) and Tonge, O'Reilly, Davison and Johnson (1972) have all described the injuries sustained by those fatally injured. The severity of the injuries considered has ranged from all injuries to only those responsible for death. In many of the studies only non-minor injuries were considered, but the definitions of non-minor injury varied between the studies. Most, but not all, of the studies have described the injuries in terms of the body areas injured, but the number of regions considered has varied from six to eleven. Even when the same number of regions was used the regions themselves were not the same.

In general, studies using only medical records, whilst describing the injuries sustained, provide little or no information on accident circumstances or injury causation. Police data, on the other hand, can provide information on general accident circumstances but, because of the methods used to record injury severity, cannot be used to consider injuries. Combining data from police and medical records enables the maximum use to be made of existing data sources but the results are limited. A recent study using police, medical and coroners' records has examined the effects of age and accident type on the pattern of injuries sustained by pedestrians (Ashton, Bimson and Driscoll, 1979).

As the police only rarely note the exact location of the pedestrian's contacts with the vehicle or ascertain impact speed, specially structured studies, usually involving in-depth 'at-the-scene' investigation of each accident, are required if pedestrian injury causation is to be studied. In at-the-scene studies a detailed examination of the accident site and the vehicles involved is made as soon as possible—usually within half an hour after the occurrence of the accident. Data available from this type of investigation consist of a series of marks on the vehicle made by contact with the pedestrian, the injuries sustained by the pedestrian, marks on the road surface if any, and usually, although not always, the position of the pedestrian when struck and the final positions of the vehicle and pedestrian.

The first studies considering in any detail the causes of pedestrian injury were carried out in the mid-1960s. These studies, however, were not specifically designed to examine pedestrian accidents but were studies in which all road accidents were considered: pedestrian accidents formed only a small proportion of the accidents studied. Robertson, McLean and Ryan (1966), Wooler (1968) and Jamieson, Duggan, Tweddell, Pope and Zvribulis (1971) described the results of at-the-scene studies of road accidents carried out in Adelaide and Brisbane, Australia. In England the Accident Research Unit at the University of Birmingham carried out at-the-scene studies of road accidents in Birmingham and Worcestershire (Mackay and Fonseka, 1967), and the particular problem of the 'other road users' (i.e. pedestrians, cyclists and motorcyclists) were described by McLean and Mackay (1970). Another study examining the problems of the 'other road users' was carried out in Toronto, Canada, by the Cornell Aeronautical Laboratory (Culkowski, Keryeski, Mason, Schotz and Segal, 1971). In this study the accidents were either investigated by the local police force using specially developed forms, or by a team from the Cornell Laboratory.

Studies specifically designed to examine mechanisms of injury to pedestrians were carried out in the early seventies by the University of Houston, Texas (Tharp, 1974) and by the Transport and Road Research Laboratory in England (TRRL, 1974). Small sample sizes and methodological problems limited the usefulness of the results: in the Houston study 175 accidents involving 190 pedestrians were studied, whilst in the Transport and Road Research Laboratory study 149 accidents were studied. A particular limitation of the latter study was the lack of data on impact speed.

Major studies of pedestrian accidents were initiated in England and in Germany in the mid-1970s, and in the USA in the late-1970s. The Accident Research Unit at the University of Birmingham began an in-depth study of pedestrian accidents at the end of 1973. By the end of 1979 over 700 pedestrian accidents had been investigated, mainly by at-the-scene investigation, the research team being alerted by the police or ambulance service within minutes of an accident's occurrence. In Germany in-depth studies of pedestrian accidents have been carried out in Hanover since 1973, and more recently in Berlin, under the auspices of the Institute of Automotive Engineering at Berlin Technical University (Wanderer and Weber, 1974). Although all types of accidents were studied over 200 of these were accidents where a pedestrian was struck by the front of a car or light van (Appel, Kühnel, Stürtz, and Glöckner, 1978). In the USA the National Highway Traffic Safety Administration has recently funded pedestrian accident studies at a number of centres: the aim is to collect data on approximately 2,000 pedestrian accidents (Daniel, Eppinger and Cohen, 1979).

Smaller studies of pedestrian accidents have also been carried out in France by
The Association Peugeot-Renault (Thomas, Stcherbatcheff, Duclos, Tarrière,
Foret-Bruno, Got and Patel, 1976) and by the Organisme National de Securité
Routière (Ramet and Cesari, 1976).

Experimental test work

The first experimental pedestrian impact tests were carried out at the
University of California in the early sixties when dummies representing a toddler,
a 3-year-old, a 6-year-old child and an average male adult were struck, at
a range of impact speeds between 16 kilometres per hour and 64 kilometres
per hour by three different sized vehicles (Severy, 1965, 1970; Severy and Brink
1966). Following these tests there was little experimental research, except for
some Japanese work (JAMA, 1968; Taneda, Kondo and Higuchi, 1973), until
the early seventies when experimental pedestrian impact tests were carried out
at Wayne State University, Michigan (Padgaonkar, Krieger and King, 1976;
Krieger, Padgaonkar and King, 1976), by the Institute for Automotive Engineering in Berlin (Kühnel, 1974; Kühnel and Raü, 1974), by the Transport and
Road Research Laboratory (Harris 1976; Jehu and Pearson, 1976) and by a
number of vehicle manufacturers such as Fiat (Montanari, 1974), Peugeot-
Renault (Stcherbatcheff, Tarrière, Duclos, Fayon, Got and Patel, 1975a, b)
and Volkswagen (Haar, Lucchini, and Weissner, 1976). By the late seventies
virtually all the European car manufacturers had become involved in experimental test work on pedestrian safety (Department of Transportation, 1979) and
standardized procedures for carrying out pedestrian impact tests are now being
developed.

Whilst these experimental tests, using real vehicles, have shown how pedestrians move when struck and that vehicle shape has an effect on the pedestrian's
trajectory when struck, their use makes the study of the effects of shape on
pedestrian impact motion complex due to the interacting effects of changes in
more than one parameter between vehicles. For instance, the effects of changes
in bumper height may be masked by changes in bonnet height and bumper
lead. To overcome this stylized vehicles have been developed in which only one
parameter need be altered at a time. Impact tests using stylized vehicles have
been conducted in England by Rolls-Royce (Bacon and Wilson, 1976) and by
the Transport and Road Research Laboratory (Harris and Radley, 1979), in
Europe by Berlin Technical University (Kramer, 1974, 1975) and by Volkswagen
(Lucchini and Weissner, 1978) and in the USA by Texas A and M University
(Ross, White and Young, 1974) and by Battelle Laboratories, Columbus
(Herridge and Pritz, 1973).

The question of how accurately experimental tests reproduce real accidents
has been studied by reproducing real accidents experimentally (Kühnel,
Wanderer and Otte, 1975; Stcherbatcheff *et al.*, 1975a). An extensive programme

of reconstructions or real accidents is currently under way in which each accident is reproduced 5 or 6 times with anthropometric dummies and 3 times with cadavers (Cesari, Heger, Friedel, Mackay, Tarrière and Weissner, 1979). Although experimental tests give similar results to real accidents there are variations in the exact locations of the contacts on the vehicle. These variations result from the differences between real people and dummies and cadavers. It is of interest in this context to note that variations in the response of dummies in identical situations have been found (Stcherbatcheff *et al.*, 1975b).

Cadavers have been used in a number of experimental impact tests using both real vehicles (Kreiger *et al.*, 1976; Stcherbatcheff *et al.*, 1975b) and stylized vehicles (Pritz, Weis and Herridge, 1975a, b). They have also been used in studies of leg injury tolerance (Aldman, Lundell and Thorngren, 1979; Burow, 1971; Kramer, Burow and Heger, 1973).

In addition to the full-scale experimental tests that have been carried out there have been tests on specific parts of the vehicle exterior to test their stiffness. Sarrailhe and Hearn (1971) used an impactor to investigate the stiffnesses of the front edges of the bonnets of a number of different vehicles. Drop tests, using a head form, to determine the stiffnesses of the various structures contacted by the head have been carried out by Brun, Lestrelin, Castan, Fayon and Tarrière (1979), Kramer (1979) and Stcherbatcheff (1979). An impactor to test the compliance (stiffness) of the vehicle exterior is being developed by the US government (Eppinger and Pritz, 1979).

Mathematical models

Mathematical models used in the simulation of pedestrian accidents have ranged from relatively simple 3-segment two-dimensional models (Culkowski *et al.*, 1971) to complex 17-segment three-dimensional models (Fowler and Newman, 1980). A two-dimensional model, originally developed by the Highway Safety Research Institute, Michigan, USA (Robbins, Bennett and Bowman, 1973) for occupant simulation is currently being used by Peugeot and Renault for studying the movement of pedestrians (Brun *et al.*, 1979; Stcherbatcheff, 1979). A three-dimensional model, also initially developed for occupant simulation by Calspan (Bartz, 1972; Fleck, Butler and Vogel, 1974), has been further developed for pedestrian simulation by British Leyland (Fowler, Axford and Butterfield, 1976; Fowler and Newman, 1980).

The models are generally validated by comparing their output with the results of experimental tests and real accidents. The more complex simulations give reasonable accuracy although, due to the assumptions made for computational ease, their accuracy becomes less as the simulations proceed. The advantage of computer simulation is that it enables parametric studies to be conducted with relative ease (Twigg, Tocher and Eppinger, 1977) and proposed designs to be evaluated quickly (Kruse, 1976). (See Figure 6.1).

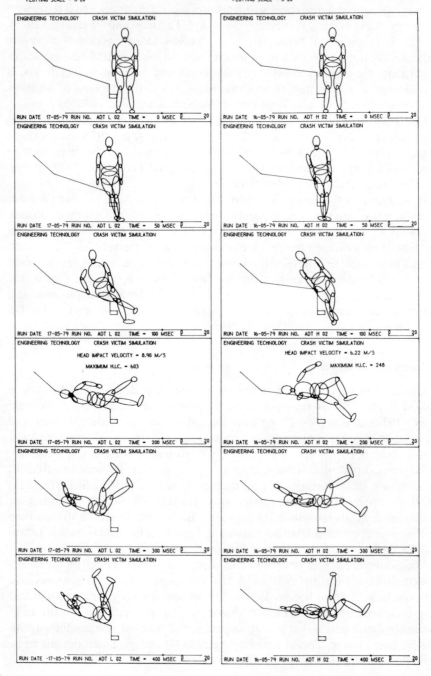

RUN DATE 17-05-79
RUN NO. ADT L 02
ADULT PEDESTRIAN IMPACT
15 M.P.H. 13.5 IN. BUMPER HEIGHT, 6 IN. LEAD, 23 IN. L/EDGE HEIGHT
CONSTANT 0.6G DECELERATION. 6.7056 M/S (15 MPH) INITIAL VELOCITY
OPAT 50TH ADULT MALE
PLOTTING SCALE - 1/20

RUN DATE 16-05-79
RUN NO. ADT H 02
ADULT PEDESTRIAN IMPACT
15 M.P.H. 13.5 IN. BUMPER HEIGHT, 6 IN. LEAD, 32 IN. L/EDGE HEIGHT
CONSTANT 0.6G DECELERATION. 6.7056 M/S (15 MPH) INITIAL VELOCITY
OPAT 50TH ADULT MALE
PLOTTING SCALE - 1/20

ENGINEERING TECHNOLOGY   CRASH VICTIM SIMULATION

RUN DATE 17-05-79 RUN NO. ADT L 02   TIME = 0 MSEC

ENGINEERING TECHNOLOGY   CRASH VICTIM SIMULATION

RUN DATE 16-05-79 RUN NO. ADT H 02   TIME = 0 MSEC

ENGINEERING TECHNOLOGY   CRASH VICTIM SIMULATION

RUN DATE 17-05-79 RUN NO. ADT L 02   TIME = 50 MSEC

ENGINEERING TECHNOLOGY   CRASH VICTIM SIMULATION

RUN DATE 16-05-79 RUN NO. ADT H 02   TIME = 50 MSEC

ENGINEERING TECHNOLOGY   CRASH VICTIM SIMULATION

RUN DATE 17-05-79 RUN NO. ADT L 02   TIME = 100 MSEC

ENGINEERING TECHNOLOGY   CRASH VICTIM SIMULATION

RUN DATE 16-05-79 RUN NO. ADT H 02   TIME = 100 MSEC

ENGINEERING TECHNOLOGY   CRASH VICTIM SIMULATION

HEAD IMPACT VELOCITY = 8.90 M/S

MAXIMUM H.I.C. = 603

RUN DATE 17-05-79 RUN NO. ADT L 02   TIME = 200 MSEC

ENGINEERING TECHNOLOGY   CRASH VICTIM SIMULATION

HEAD IMPACT VELOCITY = 6.22 M/S

MAXIMUM H.I.C. = 248

RUN DATE 16-05-79 RUN NO. ADT H 02   TIME = 200 MSEC

ENGINEERING TECHNOLOGY   CRASH VICTIM SIMULATION

RUN DATE 17-05-79 RUN NO. ADT L 02   TIME = 300 MSEC

ENGINEERING TECHNOLOGY   CRASH VICTIM SIMULATION

RUN DATE 16-05-79 RUN NO. ADT H 02   TIME = 300 MSEC

ENGINEERING TECHNOLOGY   CRASH VICTIM SIMULATION

RUN DATE 17-05-79 RUN NO. ADT L 02   TIME = 400 MSEC

ENGINEERING TECHNOLOGY   CRASH VICTIM SIMULATION

RUN DATE 16-05-79 RUN NO. ADT H 02   TIME = 400 MSEC

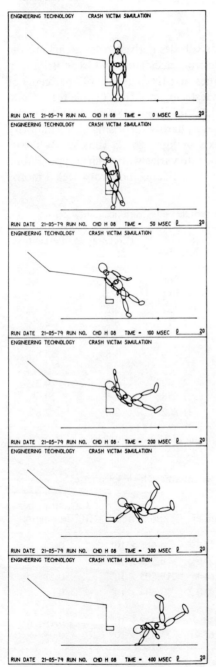

RUN DATE 21-05-79
RUN NO. CHD H 08
CHILD PEDESTRIAN IMPACT
15 M.P.H. 13.5 IN. BUMPER HEIGHT, 6 IN. LEAD, 32 IN. L/EDGE HEIGHT
CONSTANT 0.6G DECELERATION. 6.7056 M/S (15 MPH) INITIAL VELOCITY.
OGLE 6YR OLD CHILD
PLOTTING SCALE - 1/20

Figure 6.1 Examples of computer simulations of pedestrian accidents (Reproduced by permission of I. Mech. E.)

ACCIDENT CIRCUMSTANCES

Vehicles involved

Cars and car derivatives (i.e. light goods vehicles derived from a car) are the vehicles most frequently involved in pedestrian accidents. In Great Britain in 1978 there were 70,295 pedestrian casualties and the majority (91 per cent) of these were involved in single vehicle-pedestrian accidents (Table 6.1). Cars, taxis or light goods vehicles were the vehicles involved in 80 per cent of simple vehicle–pedestrian accidents. This is, however, hardly surprising as the majority of the vehicles on the road are cars, taxis or light goods vehicles. What is, perhaps, surprising is that the involvement rate varies with vehicle type. Public service vehicles in 1978 were roughly 3 times as likely, and two-wheeled motor

Table 6.1. Vehicles involved in single vehicle pedestrian accidents 1978

Type of vehicle	Number	Percentage of total	Percentage fatal
Pedal cycles	568	0.9%	0.4%
Mopeds	911	1.4%	1.3%
Motor scooters	122	0.2%	3.3%
Motor cycles	5,213	8.2%	3.8%
Cars and taxis	46,614	73.2%	3.1%
Public service vehicles	2,410	3.8%	4.8%
Goods vehicles			
<1524 kilogrammes unladen weight	4,349	6.8%	4.2%
>1524 kilogrammes unladen weight	1,658	2.6%	10.6%
Other	1,802	2.8%	2.8%

Source: Road Accidents Great Britain 1978 (Department of Transport, 1980)

Table 6.2. Pedestrian casualties per million vehicle kilometres

Type of vehicle	Number	Vehicle kilometres	Casualties per 10^6 kilometres
Pedal cycles	568	$4,455 \times 10^6$	0.13
Two-wheeled motor vehicles	6,246	$6,828 \times 10^6$	0.92
Cars and taxis	46,614	$219,805 \times 10^6$	0.21
Public service vehicles	2,410	$3,694 \times 10^6$	0.65
Goods vehicles			
<1524 kilogrammes unladen weight	4,349	$22,348 \times 10^6$	0.19
>1524 kilogrammes unladen weight	1,658	$21,510 \times 10^6$	0.08

Source: Road Accidents Great Britain 1978 (Department of Transport, 1980)

vehicles $4\frac{1}{2}$ times as likely as private cars to be involved in pedestrian accidents. Heavy goods vehicles, however, had an involvement rate less than that of private cars (Table 6.2). These differences can be partly explained by vehicle usage patterns: public service vehicles have a high urban mileage whereas heavy goods vehicles have a high rural and motorway mileage; thus public service vehicles are exposed to pedestrians more often than heavy goods vehicles. Involvement rates are not static but change as the environment changes. Smeed (1968) reported that public service vehicles were 6 times as likely and goods vehicles twice as likely to be involved in a pedestrian accident than private cars.

The chance of being killed also varies with vehicle type: roughly 3 per cent of pedestrians struck by cars or taxis are killed compared to 6 per cent of those struck by public service vehicles and 10 per cent of those struck by heavy goods vehicles (Table 6.1). These differences stem mainly from variations in the way the pedestrian moves when struck by the different vehicles. In the USA Robertson and Baker (1976) found that cars with wheelbases longer than 2.95 metres were involved in fatal pedestrian accidents twice as frequently as vehicles with wheel-bases shorter than 2.67 metres.

Location of contacts

The most frequent type of car/pedestrian accident is that in which the pedestrian is struck by the front of a car: approximately 80 per cent of car/ pedestrian accidents being of this type. The exact proportion of accidents where the initial contact is to the front of the vehicle varies with age and injury severity. Adults are less likely than children, and elderly adults less likely than other adults, to have a contact with the side of the vehicle. The nearside of the vehicle is more frequently contacted than the offside, although again there are variations with age; adults being less likely than children and elderly adults less likely than other adults to contact the nearside than the offside. For children there are further variations with the age of the child: the younger the child the more likely is the first contact to be to the nearside of the vehicle (Ashton, 1979). With commercial vehicles, particularly heavy goods vehicles there is a much higher incidence of contacts to the side and the rear, and the consequences of these contacts are often serious in that the pedestrian, on falling to the ground, is at risk from being run over by the rear wheels of the vehicle. Frontal contacts are still, however, the most frequent type of contact with commercial vehicles.

The location of the initial contact influences the severity of the injuries sustained, fatal injuries being more likely to be sustained when the pedestrian is struck by the front of the vehicle than the side. Again age is important: the proportion dying after being struck by the front of a vehicle being greater for elderly adults than for other adults, and greater for adults than for children in general. Younger children are more likely to sustain fatal injuries (Ashton, 1979).

The risk of sustaining serious injuries, when struck by the front of a car, varies with the actual location of the contact; initial contact with the outer thirds of the front structure normally results in more serious injuries than contact with the central section. This stems from the fronts of the wings being stiffer than the centre section and from the fact that the subsequent head contact is likely to be on a relatively stiff structure (the 'A' pillars), and thus serious injury is more likely if the initial contact is to the outer parts of the front structure (Danner and Langweider, 1979).

Action of pedestrian

Contact with the nearside of the vehicle occurs more frequently because a higher proportion of pedestrians are crossing from the nearside than from the offside when struck. The variations in contact location with age may be due to differences in the way pedestrians of different ages cross the road. Ashton, Pedder and Mackay (1977a) reported that 55 per cent of a sample of 336 pedestrians were crossing from the nearside when struck, compared to only 37 per cent crossing from the offside. The other 8 per cent were either in the road, but not crossing, or on the pavement when struck. It was further noted that children were reported as running when struck in 76 per cent of the child accidents, whilst only 25 per cent of the adults and 6 per cent of the elderly adults were reported as running.

Impact speed

Pedestrian accidents, being essentially urban accidents, tend to occur at comparatively low speeds; approximately 95 per cent of all pedestrian accidents occur at speeds less than 50 kilometres per hour and about half at speeds less than 20–25 kilometres per hour. A large proportion of these accidents however result in only minor injuries. It is generally agreed (Ashton and Mackay, 1979b; Jamieson *et al.*, 1971; Tharp and Tsongos, 1976) that, with current car designs, pedestrians struck at impact speeds less than 25 kilometres per hour usually sustain only minor injuries whilst those struck at speeds greater than 30 kilometres per hour usually sustain non-minor injuries. At impact speeds less than 50 kilometres per hour the injuries are likely to be survivable, whilst at speeds greater than 55 kilometres per hour the pedestrians are most likely to be killed (Figure 6.2). These threshold speeds are for the total population and ignore age effects. The 50 percentile impact speed for accidents in which pedestrians sustain non-minor injuries is roughly 35 kilometres per hour, and for fatalities alone 50 kilometres per hour.

There are considerable variations in injury severity for a given impact speed, fatalities having been observed at impact speeds less than 20 kilometres per hour and minor injuries at speeds greater than 40 kilometres per hour. The

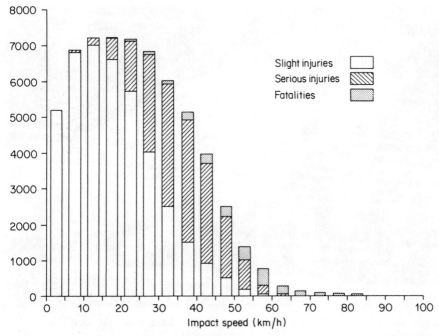

Figure 6.2 Estimated impact speed and injury severity distribution for pedestrians struck by cars and car derivatives

variations in injury severity for a given impact speed indicate that factors other than impact speed are important in determining injury severity.

PEDESTRIAN IMPACT DYNAMICS

For a pedestrian struck by the front of a car or light van, and this is the most common type of pedestrian accident, the first contacts are with the bumper and/or the front edge of the bonnet depending on the shape of the vehicle front structures. The exact locations of these contacts on the pedestrian depend on the relative heights of the pedestrian and vehicle front structures. For instance with a young child the bumper will strike the upper leg and the front edge of the bonnet will strike the torso, whereas with an adult the bumper strikes the lower leg and the front edge of the bonnet strikes the upper leg. At low impact speeds (i.e. less than 20 kilometres per hour) these will frequently be the only contacts and there will be little damage if any to the vehicle, the contacts often resulting in only surface cleaning marks to the vehicle (Figure 6.3 and 6.4).

At higher speeds the pedestrian will angulate and slide over the front edge of the bonnet, the head and upper torso dipping down to strike the vehicle. The exact location of this second contact on the vehicle depends mainly, for

Pedestrian Accidents

Figure 6.3 Cleaning of surface dirt on bumper of vehicle as a result of contact with a pedestrian's legs

Figure 6.4 Cleaning of surface dirt on the leading edge of the bonnet as a result of a low speed pedestrian accident

Figure 6.5 Damage to the front of a vehicle which struck a pedestrian at an impact speed between 60 and 65 km/h

current vehicle designs, on the relative height of the pedestrian and the front of the vehicle, the length of the bonnet and the speed of the vehicle at impact; the slip of the pedestrian increases, for current designs, with increasing impact speed. Children generally strike the top surface of the bonnet with their heads, whereas adult heads strike farther back, often in the windscreen and windscreen frame area. If the impact speed is sufficiently high for there to be a head contact with the bonnet, windscreen or windscreen frame the impact forces are such that there is normally physical damage to the vehicle (Figure 6.5)

At very high impact speeds, and by this it is meant above 60 kilometres per hour, an adult pedestrian will generally rotate about this second, usually head, contact with the vehicle, the body then angulating about the leading edge of the roof and the legs dipping down to strike the top surface of the roof (Figure 6.6).

Due to the forces applied to the pedestrian as a result of the contacts with the vehicle, the pedestrian is accelerated up towards the speed of the vehicle and, should there be braking during the impact (and this is the most common situation) the pedestrian will first attain a common velocity with the vehicle and then, as the vehicle slows at a higher rate than the pedestrian, the pedestrian will fly through the air in advance of the slowing vehicle before being brought to rest after striking the ground. If, however, there is no braking during the accident, or braking does not occur until a very late stage, the pedestrian may

Figure 6.6 Damage to the top of the roof as a result of pedestrian contact. This is the same vehicle shown in Figure 6.5

pass over the top, or down the side, of the vehicle and then contact the ground. Each of these contacts with the vehicle and the contacts with the ground may, and frequently do, cause injury.

The initial contacts between the bumper and/or the front edge of the bonnet result in the pedestrian being pushed forward, and at the same time rotate about a horizontal axis; these two types of motion are called 'translation' and 'rotation' respectively and relative amounts of each determine the actual motion of the pedestrian. Should the first contact be low on the pedestrian's legs the pedestrian will receive a relatively large amount of rotational motion and a small amount of translation, the head moving in towards the vehicle. As the position of the initial contact on the pedestrian's body moves away from the ground the amount of rotation decreases and translation increases until a stage is reached where there is only translation; that is, the pedestrian is just pushed forward. Increasing the height of the contact still further results in there again being rotation as well as translation, but now the pedestrian's head moves away from the vehicle (Figure 6.7). This is, of course a simplified explanation of the way a pedestrian moves at impact and is based on the assumption that a pedestrian is a rigid body. In reality this is not so, and there is the added complication of frictional forces between the feet and the ground. Hence the motion of a pedestrian in a real accident is more complex than this.

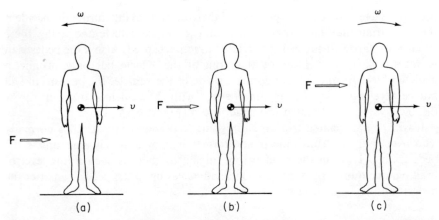

Figure 6.7 Change in pedestrian motion with location of contact: (a) contact below centre of gravity; (b) contact near to centre of gravity; (c) contact above centre of gravity

The pedestrian will finally come to rest some way from the point of impact and this distance, commonly called the 'throw distance', is dependent on the location of the initial contact on the vehicle, the speed of the vehicle at impact and the amount of braking during impact. For pedestrians struck directly by the fronts of vehicles braking at impact there is a good correlation between the 'throw distance' and impact speed, although there are small variations with

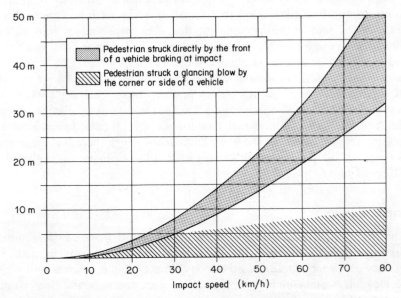

Figure 6.8 Relationship between pedestrian throw distance and impact speed

pedestrian age and vehicle type. Should there be no braking during the accident the pedestrian may be carried some distance on the vehicle and under these conditions 'throw distance' is not related to impact speed. Also if the pedestrian is not struck a direct blow by the front of the vehicle but only sustains a glancing blow from the front corner or side of the vehicle, the pedestrian will not be accelerated up to a common speed with the vehicle and again 'throw distance' will not be related to impact speed (Figure 6.8).

It will be appreciated from the foregoing that pedestrians are not normally 'run over' but are 'run under'. The former is comparatively rare unless the pedestrian is lying in the road before impact or there is such a low level of braking, or no braking, that the vehicle advances upon the pedestrian after the pedestrian has landed on the ground.

PEDESTRIAN INJURIES

Multiplicity of injury

A characterisitic of road accident casualties, and pedestrians are no exception, is the presence of multiple injuries. This is hardly surprising considering the nature of the initial contacts between the vehicle and pedestrian and the subsequent contacts that the pedestrian makes with the ground. The number of injuries sustained varies with overall injury severity and impact speed.

Fonseka (1969), reporting on a sample of pedestrians involved in accidents in Birmingham, England, found that for all severities of injury there was an average of 2.7 injuries per person, but that if only non-minor injuries were counted the average number sustained fell to 2.1. Jamieson and Tait (1966) noted that for a sample of survivors, there was on average 1.66 injuries per person if only non-minor injuries were counted; when fatalities were included with survivors the average number of injuries rose to 2.5 per person. The fatalities alone sustained on average 3.8 serious and fatal injuries per person. Fisher and Hall (1972) found that the number of injuries sustained rose with increasing impact speed; in the 0–16 km/h speed range there was an average of 1.6 injuries per person but this rose to 2.4 injuries per person in the 80–96 km/h speed range.

Location of injuries

The head and the legs are, as might be expected from consideration of pedestrian impact dynamics, the body areas most frequently injured. The frequency with which these and other body areas are injured varies with vehicle type, location of first contact with the vehicle, pedestrian age and overall injury severity.

Ashton *et al.* (1979) noted that, in general, pedestrians contacting the sides of cars sustain fewer serious leg and pelvic injuries than those struck directly by the front of the vehicle. Pedestrians struck by the fronts of buses or heavy goods vehicles tend to sustain fewer serious leg and pelvic injuries and more serious chest, arm and head injuries than those struck by the fronts of cars. Pedestrians struck by motorcycles sustain fewer serious pelvic injuries and more serious arm injuries than pedestrians struck by the fronts of cars.

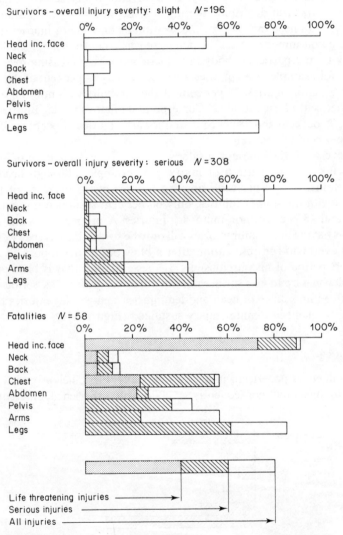

Figure 6.9 Pattern of injury for adults aged 15–59 years struck by the fronts of cars or car derivatives by overall injury severity and severity of injury counted

As accidents in which a pedestrian is struck directly by the front of a car are the most frequent type of pedestrian accident, the effects of age and overall injury severity on pedestrian injuries is now considered by reference to this type of accident.

The variation in the distribution of injuries between pedestrians with different severities of injury can be seen in Figure 6.9 which shows the distribution of injuries for adults aged 15 to 59 years by overall injury severity and severity of injury counted in describing the injuries. Leg injuries were sustained more frequently than head injuries by those sustaining only minor injuries. For those sustaining non-minor injuries the converse was true. In general the likelihood of injury to any particular body area increased with increasing overall injury severity; for example, head injuries were received by 54 per cent of the survivors sustaining minor injuries, 79 per cent of the survivors with non-minor injuries and 95 per cent of the fatalities. Corresponding figures for leg injuries were 76 per cent, 75 per cent and 88 per cent, and for arm injuries 37 per cent, 45 per cent and 57 per cent respectively.

The severity of the injuries considered in describing the pattern of injury also has an effect on the pattern of injury. For example, although head injuries were sustained by 79 per cent, and leg injuries by 75 per cent of the adult survivors with non-minor injuries, only 60 per cent sustained non-minor head injuries and 48 per cent non-minor leg injuries. A proportion of the survivors classed as having non-minor injuries will only be so classified as they were kept in hospital overnight for observation after a blow on the head, possibly resulting in a short period of unconsciousness. If these injuries, that is brief periods of unconsciousness, and also surface injuries are not considered as 'serious' injuries the relative importance of head and leg injuries changes, leg injuries becoming the most frequent non-minor injury sustained (Figure 6.10).

Effects of age

Age influences pedestrian injury in two ways. First, height and weight are related to age, and consequently a child will experience different impact

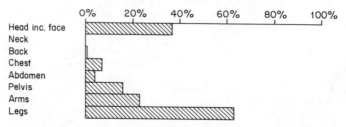

Figure 6.10 Pattern of injury, excluding surface injuries and minor concussion, for adults aged 15–59 years struck by the fronts of cars or car derivatives and who sustained serious injuries

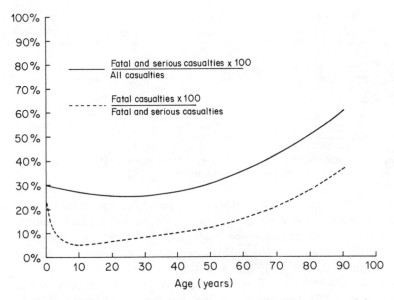

Figure 6.11 Variation with age of the proportion of pedestrians sustaining serious and fatal injuries, and of the proportion sustaining serious and fatal injuries who die

conditions to an adult if both are struck at the same speed by similar vehicles. Second, injury tolerance is a function of age. The bones of the young child (i.e. less than 10 years of age) are more resilient than the bones of an adult. The elderly, as a result of decreasing bone strength, are more likely to be injured than younger persons, and once injured they are more likely to die from their injuries than other age groups.

The effects of age can be seen in the changes with age in the proportions of pedestrians with injuries of different severities (Figure 6.11). In the 5- to 15-year age group approximately 5 per cent of those sustaining a non-minor injury die, compared to 15 per cent for the 61- to-70-year age group and over 25 per cent for the over 80-year-olds. The increase in the proportion sustaining non-minor injuries with increasing age may be partly explained by the lowering of injury tolerance to impact with age but may also be partly due to differences in impact conditions with age; children having a higher incidence of contacts with the sides of the vehicle than adults. It will also be evident from this figure that the very young child (i.e. a child less than 2 years of age) is more likely to be killed than an older child. This is partly due to the very small child receiving a direct blow to the head from the front of the vehicle, and partly due to the increased likelihood of a small child being knocked forward and run over. Fortunately, however, their involvement rate is low: less than 1 per cent of all child pedestrians struck by cars are less than 3 years of age.

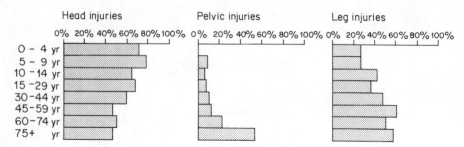

Figure 6.12 Variation in incidence of serious head, pelvic and leg injuries with age for pedestrians sustaining serious injuries

The effects of age are also evident in the pattern of injury, for example there is a lower incidence of non-minor leg and pelvic injuries, and a higher incidence of non-minor head injuries in the young than in the elderly (Figure 6.12).

Two studies have tried to quantify the effects of age on overall injury severity. Götzen, Suren, Behrens, Richter and Stürtz (1976) suggested that the impact speeds for injuries sustained by elderly (i.e. greater than 60 years of age) were approximately 7.5 kilometres per hour slower than the speeds at which younger adults sustained comparable injuries. Ashton (1978) reported that, for adults, an increase in age of $2\frac{1}{2}$ years was roughly comparable with an increase in impact speed of 1 kilometre per hour in its effect on injury severity.

INFLUENCE OF VEHICLE DESIGN

The idea that vehicle exterior shape can influence the injuries sustained by pedestrians was perhaps first propounded by Wakeland (1962) who suggested that automobile designers should be 'keel hauled' over the exteriors of their vehicles to encourage the elimination of sharp protusions. He also suggested that the exterior of the vehicle should be tested with a pendulum device to identify the stiff areas likely to cause trauma and that these areas should then be softened. Wakeland thus recognized that 'shape' and 'stiffness' are important in the causation and severity of pedestrian injuries.

Overall vehicle shape influences pedestrian injuries. A number of studies have compared the injury potential of the Volkswagen 'Beetle' with more conventional square fronted vehicles. Some studies (Hall and Fisher, 1972; Jamieson and Tait, 1966) have suggested that a person is more likely to be seriously injured when struck by a 'Beetle', whilst others (Culkowski *et al.*, 1971; McLean, 1972) have stated that a 'Beetle' is less likely to cause serious injury than a conventional vehicle. These conflicting results are likely, however, to be due to sampling differences as it has also been reported that at impact speeds less than 30 kilometres per hour a 'Beetle' is less likely to cause serious injury than a conventional vehicle, whilst at impact speeds greater than 40 kilometres per hour the converse is true (Appel, Stürtz and Behrens, 1976; Robertson *et al.*, 1966).

The effects of vehicle design on pedestrian injuries is examined below by reference to the factors influencing the severity of the leg and pelvic injuries resulting from the primary vehicle contacts and to the factors influencing the severity of the head injuries resulting from the secondary vehicle contacts.

Leg and pelvic injuries

Ashton, Pedder, and Mackay (1977b) showed that contact with the vehicle was the main cause of serious leg and pelvic injuries, and that the design of current vehicle front structures, which are relatively stiff structures not designed for pedestrian injury mitigation, influences the location and severity of the injuries sustained. Difficulties arise in discussing the effects of vehicle shape on pedestrian injuries aue to the confounding effects of pedestrian height. In order to eliminate the effects of pedestrian height, bumper height and bonnet height can be expressed in the following way:

$$\text{Relative bumper height} = \frac{\text{Absolute bumper height}}{\text{Pedestrian height}}$$

$$\text{Relative bonnet height} = \frac{\text{Absolute bonnet height}}{\text{Pedestrian height}}$$

With current front structures, fractures resulting from bumper contact normally occur at the point of contact (Pritz, Hassler, Herridge and Weis, 1975) except when the bumper contact is very low on the leg when, due to the inertia of the leg, the maximum bending moment occurs above the bumper contact (Bacon and Wilson, 1976; Fiala, Fabricus and Niklas, 1968). Thus bumper height influences the location of the leg fractures; bumpers located at a relative height less than 0.26 pedestrian height result in lower leg fractures, whilst bumpers located at a relative height greater than 0.31 result in mainly knee and upper leg fractures (Ashton, Pedder and Mackay, 1978a). Knee injuries are particularly prevalent when the relative bumper height is 0.26 to 0.35 pedestrian height, when a direct contact on the knee is likely to occur. In absolute terms bumpers located at 45 to 54 centimetres above the ground are more likely to result in knee injuries than lower bumpers. Impact forces near the knee joint result in an increased risk of comminuted fractures (Kramer *et al.*, 1973) and damage to the ligaments of the knee joint (Stcherbatcheff *et al.*, 1975b), and these injuries have serious long term consequences.

The height of the bumper also has an influence on the likelihood of a fracture occurring, the lower the bumper the less chance there is of the bumper contact causing a fracture (Ashton *et al.*, 1977b) as the effective mass of the leg reduces as the contact height is lowered (Bacon and Wilson, 1976).

Bumpers located at say 35 centimetres above the ground would therefore be preferable to bumpers located at 50 centimetres above the ground, although the optimum height depends on the age, and thus height, distribution of the involved population. This applies only to current relatively stiff narrow bumpers and the introduction of other designs such as full face compliant front structures may alter this.

Reducing the stiffness of the bumper has been noted to lower the bumper contact forces, and thus reduce the chance of injury (Pritz *et al.*, 1975) However although increased bumper compliance reduces the bumper contact forces there is a risk of a counteracting effect due to increased ground frictional forces, the foot being held against the ground for a longer time by the compliant bumper. To overcome this Bacon and Wilson (1976) designed a compliant bumper which lifted the leg off the ground as the bumper deformed.

Bumper lead has a large influence on the relative importance of the bumper and the front edge of the bonnet as sources of injury. As bumper lead increases the importance of the front edge of the bonnet as a source of injury decreases. However this interaction between the bumper and the front of the bonnet is also influenced by the relative heights of the two structures. In order to allow for this, bumper lead can be expressed in the following way:

$$\text{Bumper lead angle} = \text{Tan}^{-1} \frac{\text{Bonnet height} - \text{Bumper height}}{\text{Bumper lead}}$$

Ashton *et al.* (1977b) reported that when bumper lead angle is less than 70° nearly all the leg fractures result from bumper contact but that as bumper lead angle increases there is an increase in the number of fractures resulting from contact with the front edge of the bonnet. This is because long bumper leads, or more precisely bumper lead angles of less than 70°, result in virtually all the initial contact forces being applied through the bumper (Bacon and Wilson, 1976). As the bumper lead angle increases there is early contact with the leading edge of the bonnet as well, the bumper contact forces reducing and the front edge of bonnet contact forces increasing, until a situation is reached where virtually all the contact forces are applied by the front edge of bonnet contact. There is thus an optimum bumper lead angle where the initial contact forces are distributed between the bumper and the front edge of the bonnet, and likelihood of fracture from either is minimized. Vehicles with relatively square fronts appear to be less likely to cause leg fractures than sharp fronted vehicles; accident studies (Ashton *et al.*, 1977b) and experimental tests (Bacon and Wilson, 1976) indicate that vehicles with bumper lead angles greater than 80° are less likely to cause leg fractures than vehicles with bumper lead angles less than 70° (Figure 6.13).

When there is a contact with the front edge of the bonnet, the height of the front of the bonnet, as well as the bumper lead angle influences the pelvic and femoral injuries sustained. Schneider and Beier (1974) and Ashton *et al.* (1978a) reported that pelvic injuries were more likely to occur to pedestrians struck by

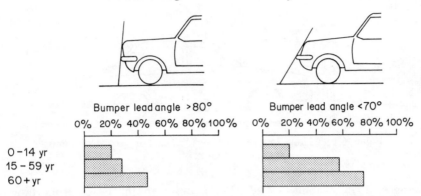

Figure 6.13 Variation in percentage of pedestrians sustaining a leg or pelvic fracture by age and bumper lead angle for pedestrians struck at impact speeds between 21–40 km/h

vehicles with a bonnet front edge height of 75 to 85 centimetres (relative bonnet height of 0.46 to 0.50 pedestrian height), and that reducing the height of the bonnet lessens the chance of pelvic injury. This is because, as the location of the contact moves away from the pelvis down the leg, the forces on the hip joint reduce (Bacon and Wilson, 1976; Kramer, 1975; Stcherbatcheff *et al.*, 1975b). Reducing the stiffness of the leading edge of the bonnet has also been shown to have a beneficial effect on pelvic and upper leg injuries (Harries, 1976; Jehu and Pearson, 1976; Pritz *et al.*, 1975)

Accident studies have shown that the relative locations of the bumper and front edge of the bonnet are of prime importance in determining the nature and severity of the pelvic and leg injuries sustained by pedestrians struck by the front of cars and light goods vehicles. Experimental tests have shown that stiffness is more important than shape in determining the severity of the injuries sustained and that the introduction of 'full face' compliant front structures designed from consideration of human leg and pelvic injury tolerance would result in a reduction in serious leg and pelvic injuries. If vehicles were designed so that the risk of sustaining a leg or pelvic fracture from contact with the front of the vehicle was minimal at speeds below 40 kilometres per hour, and this appears to be technically possible, then there would be a very large reduction in the number with non-minor leg and pelvic injuries. This would result in a reduction in the number with non-minor injuries, after being struck by the front of a car or light van, of about 20 per cent.

Head injuries

Contact with the vehicle has been identified as the main cause of head injuries (Ashton, Pedder and Mackay, 1978b; Stürtz and Suren, 1976; Tharp and

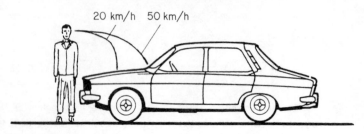

Figure 6.14 Change in location of head impact on vehicle with impact speed

Tsongos, 1976; Thomas *et al.*, 1976), although the exact proportion of non-minor head injuries resulting from vehicle contact cannot be determined as in some situations the head injury could have been caused by either the secondary vehicle contact or the subsequent ground contact.

Following the initial contact of the bumper and/or front of the bonnet with the pedestrian's lower body the pedestrian will either be pushed forward falling to the ground, or bend and slide over the front of the vehicle, the head and upper torso dipping down to strike the vehicle. The likelihood of a secondary head contact with the vehicle increases with increasing impact speed and decreasing front end height, although above 50 kilometres per hour virtually all pedestrians sustain a head contact with the vehicle.

The location of the head contact on the vehicle is determined by pedestrian height, vehicle front end height and bonnet length, and by the amount of slip of the pedestrian over the front of the bonnet. For current vehicle designs the amount of slip tends to increase with increasing impact speed. The head of an adult struck by an average sized car would dip down to strike the bonnet at moderate impact speeds but at higher speeds the increased slip would result in a head contact with the windscreen or windscreen frame (Figure 6.14). The risk of

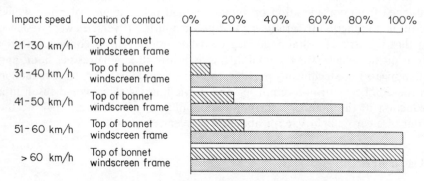

Figure 6.15 Percentage of bonnet and windscreen frame contacts resulting in life threatening or fatal head injuries by location of contact and impact speed

striking the windscreen or windscreen frame reduces with increasing bonnet length and decreasing pedestrian height.

The severity of the head injuries sustained is influenced by the location of the head contact on the vehicle and the speed at which the head strikes the vehicle. Accident studies (Ashton *et al.*, 1978b; Thomas *et al.*, 1976) have shown that contact with the windscreen frame is much more likely to result in serious head injuries than contact with the bonnet (Figure 6.15) and experimental tests (Stcherbatcheff *et al.*, 1975a) have shown that this is because the windscreen frame is considerably stiffer than the bonnet (Figure 6.16 and 6.17).

The risk of sustaining a non-minor head injury from vehicle contact can be lessened by either reducing the stiffness of the structure contacted or changing the location of the head contact so that a less stiff area is contacted. Improbable though it may seem the second strategy is the better of the two. The windscreen frame is a difficult structure to modify radically and although it may be possible to change its design so that contacts with it are unlikely to result in non-minor head injuries at speeds up to 30 kilometres per hour (Stcherbatcheff, 1979) the benefits that would accrue from this alone would be very small (Ashton, 1980). If, however, the location of the head contact could be changed from the windscreen frame to the bonnet greater benefits would be obtainable as it is possible to design the bonnet so that non-minor head injuries are unlikely at

Figure 6.16 Head contact with the lower edge of the windscreen frame which resulted in fatal head injuries

Figure 6.17 Head contact with the top surface of the bonnet which resulted in no head injuries

speeds below 40 kilometres per hour. It may even be possible to design the bonnet such that head contacts at speeds up to 50 kilometres per hour do not result in non-minor injuries (Kramer, 1979).

The provision of a compliant front structure, primarily designed to reduce the likelihood of non-minor leg and pelvic injuries, influences the location of the head contact on the vehicle. The slip of the pedestrian relative to the vehicle becomes virtually zero as a result of the gripping effect of the compliant front structure on the pedestrian's legs (Harris, 1976; Künnel and Appel, 1978; Pritz, 1976, 1977). This reduction in slip results in the head contact being on the bonnet for all but the smallest cars. The elimination of localized stiff areas on the top surface of the bonnet, such as those that occur at the join of the bonnet, wings and scuttle, and the provision of suitable under bonnet clearance will minimize the risk of non-minor head injury from bonnet contact. Thus design of the vehicle exterior can have a significant effect on the severity of the head injuries sustained.

THE FUTURE

Pedestrian accidents, despite being complex multi-impact events, are accidents where changes in vehicle design can influence the injuries sustained. This is now being recognized by motor manufacturers and governments. At the Seventh International Technical Conference on Experimental Safety Vehicles papers were presented by manufacturers describing the construction of experimental safety vehicles (Echavidre and Gratador, 1979; Stcherbatcheff, 1979) and modifications to existing vehicles (Kramer, 1979; Pritz, 1979) designed to lessen the risk of serious pedestrian injury. A paper by Daniel *et al.* (1979) described how the United States government is developing motor vehicle safety standards which would require that vehicles are designed so that there is a reduced risk of pedestrian injury.

So what will the vehicle of the future look like? The exterior shape will not be dissimilar to today's vehicles but the materials from which the vehicle is constructed will differ and there will be small detail differences (Figure 6.18).

The front of the vehicle will have a full face compliant front bumper; this will extend over the whole of the front face from the bonnet down and will probably be made of a skinned foam construction with cut outs for lighting and cooling for the engine compartment. This structure as well as reducing the risk of serious leg and pelvic injuries, will protect the vehicle itself from damage in low speed vehicular accidents.

Figure 6.18 The Chrysler/Calspan Research Safety Vehicle. This vehicle has a full face compliant bumper designed to reduce the incidence of pelvic and leg fractures in pedestrian accidents

The top surface of the engine compartment and wings will have no localized stiff areas, such as the join between the bonnet and wings and the join between the bonnet and scuttle. This will be achieved by either extending the bonnet to cover the whole of the engine compartment and wings, the join between the bonnet and the wings being on the side of the wings, as in the Renault 18, rather than on the top of the wing as is normally the case, or if this is not practicable, the joins will be designed with impact attenuation properties (Bez, Hoefs and Stahl, 1979). The rear edge of the bonnet will probably be extended back to cover the scuttle and the lower edge of the windscreen frame, as in the Leyland Princess and the Triumph TR7. This will mask these stiff areas together with the windscreen wiper arms and bosses. The area under the bonnet will be designed so that as the bonnet deforms as a result of a pedestrian head contact it does not bottom out on under-bonnet structures. The 'A' pillars (i.e. the pillars at either side of the windscreen) will have a smooth exterior shape and will probably be covered with energy absorbing material (Stcherbatcheff, 1979). The windscreen will be a laminated windscreen.

The effect of all these design changes has been estimated to reduce the number of pedestrians seriously injured, as a result of being struck by the front of the vehicle, by about one-third (Ashton, 1980).

REFERENCES

Aldman, B., Lundell, B., and Thorngren, L. (1979). Physical simulation of human leg-bumper impacts. In *Proceedings of the Fourth International Conference on the Biomechanics of Trauma*. Lyon: International Research Committee on the Biokinetics of Impact.

Appel, H., Kühnel, A., Stürtz, G., and Glöckner, H. (1978). Pedestrian safety vehicle-design elements—results of in-depth accident analyses and simulation. In *Proceedings of the Twenty-Second Conference of the American Association for Automotive Medicine*. Morton Grove, Illinois: American Association for Automotive Medicine.

Appel, H., Stürtz, G., and Behrens, S. (1976). Influence of front end design of passenger cars on injuries of pedestrians in car to pedestrian collisions. In *Proceedings of the Conference on the Biomechanics of Injury to Pedestrians, Cyclists and Motor Cyclists*. Lyon: International Research Committee on the Biokinetics of Impact.

Ashton, S. J., (1978). Pedestrian injuries and the car exterior. *Unpublished Doctoral Dissertation*. Birmingham, United Kingdom: University of Birmingham.

Ashton, S. J., (1979). Some factors influencing the injuries sustained by child pedestrians struck by the fronts of cars. In *Proceedings of the Twenty-Third Stapp Car Crash Conference*. Warrendale: Society of Automotive Engineers.

Ashton, S. J. (1980). A preliminary assessment of the potential for pedestrian injury reduction through vehicle design. In *Proceedings of the Twenty-Fourth Stapp Car Crash Conference*. Warrendale: Society of Automotive Engineers.

Ashton, S. J., Bimson, S., and Driscoll, C. (1979). Patterns of injury in pedestrian accidents. In *Proceedings of the Twenty-Third Conference of the American Association for Automotive Medicine*. Morton Grove, Illinois: American Association for Automotive Medicine.

Ashton, S. J., and Mackay, G. M. (1979a). A review of real world studies of pedestrian injury. In *Unfall-und-Sicherheitsforschung Strassenverkehr*. Cologne: Heft 21.

Ashton, S. J., and Mackay, G. M. (1979b). Some characteristics of the population who suffer trauma as pedestrians when hit by cars and some resulting implications. In *Proceedings of the Fourth International Conference on the Biomechanics of Trauma.* Lyon: International Research Committee on the Biokinetics of Impact.

Ashton, S. J., Pedder, J. B., and Mackay, G. M. (1977a). Pedestrian injuries and the car exterior. In *Society of Automotive Engineers Transactions*, Paper 770092. Warrendale: Society of Automotive Engineers.

Ashton, S. J., Pedder, J. B., and Mackay, G. M. (1977b). Pedestrian leg injuries, the bumper and other front structures. In *Proceedings of the Third International Conference on the Biokinetics of Impact.* Lyon: International Research Committee on the Biokinetics of Impact.

Ashton, S. J., Pedder, J. B., and Mackay, G. M. (1978a). Influence of vehicle design on pedestrian leg injuries. In *Proceedings of the Twenty-Second Conference of the American Association for Automotive Medicine.* Morton Grove, Illinois: American Association for Automotive Medicine.

Ashton, S. J., Pedder, J. B., and Mackay, G. M. (1978b). Pedestrian head injuries. In *Proceedings of the Twenty-Second Conference of the American Association for Automotive Medicine.* Morton Grove, Illinois: American Association for Automotive Medicine.

Aston, J. N., and Perkins, T. A. (1954). The clinical pattern of injury in road accidents. *British Medical Journal*, **2**, 200.

Bacon, D. G. C., and Wilson, M. R., (1976). Bumper characteristics for improved pedestrian safety. In *Proceedings of the Twentieth Stapp Car Crash Conference.* Warrendale: Society of Automotive Engineers.

Bartz, J. A. (1972). Development and validation of a computer simulation of the crash victim in three dimensions. In *Proceedings of the Sixteenth Stapp Car Crash Conference.* New York: Society of Automotive Engineers.

Bez, U., Hoefs, R., and Stahl, H. W. (1979). The V-shaped front—its influence on injury severity in pedestrian accidents and side impacts. In *Proceedings of the Seventh International Technical Conference on Experimental Safety Vehicles.* Washington DC: United States Department of Transportation.

Bø, O. (1972). Road casualties—an epidemiological investigation. Scandinavian University Books.

Brun, F., Lestrelin, D., Castan, F., Fayon, A., and Tarrière, C., (1979). A synthesis of available data for improvement of pedestrian protection. In *Proceedings of the Seventh International Technical Conference on Experimental Safety Vehicles.* Washington DC: United States Department of Transportation.

Burow, K. H. (1971). Injuries of the thorax and lower extremities to forces applied by blunt objects. In *Proceedings of the Fifteenth Stapp Car Crash Conference.* New York: Society of Automotive Engineers.

Cesari, D., Heger, A., Friedel, B., Mackay, M., Tarrière, C., and Weissner, R. (1979). A preliminary report about the work of the joint biomechanical research project (KOB). In *Proceedings of the Seventh International Technical Conference on Experimental Safety Vehicles.* Washington DC: United States Department of Transportation.

Culkowski, P. M., Keryeski, J. M., Mason, R. P., Schotz, W. C., and Segal, R. J. (1971). Research into impact protection for pedestrians and cyclists. Report Number VJ-2672-V2, Buffalo, New York: Cornell Aeronautical Laboratory.

Daniel, S., Eppinger, R. H., and Cohen, D., (1979). Considerations in the development of a pedestrian safety standard. In *Proceedings of the Seventh International Technical Conference on Experimental Safety Vehicles.* Washington, DC: United States Department of Transportation.

Danner, M., and Langweider, K. (1979). Collision characteristics and injuries to pedestrians in real accidents. In *Proceedings of the Seventh International Technical Conference on Experimental Safety Vehicles*. Washington, DC: United States Department of Transportation.

Department of Transport (1980). *Road Accidents Great Britain 1978*. London: Her Majesty's stationery office.

Department of Transportation. (1979). *Proceedings of the Seventh International Technical Conference on Experimental Safety Vehicles*. Washington, DC: United States Department of Transportation.

Echavidre, J. P., and Gratador, J. (1979). Peugeot VLS 104 and pedestrian protection. In *Proceedings of the Seventh International Technical Conference on Experimental Safety Vehicles*. Washington DC, United States: Department of Transportation.

Eppinger, R. H., and Pritz, H. B. (1979). Development of a simplified vehicle performance requirement for pedestrian injury mitigation. In *Proceedings of the Seventh International Technical Conference on Experimental Safety Vehicles*. Washington, DC: United States Department of Transportation.

Fiala, E., Fabricus, B., and Niklas, J. (1968). Pedestrian accident tests with catapult. *Report Number 40, Motor Vehicle Institute*, Berlin: Berlin Technical University.

Fisher, A. J., and Hall, R. R. (1972). The influence of car frontal design on pedestrian accident trauma. *Accident Analysis and Prevention*, **4**, 47–58.

Fleck, J. T., Butler, F. E., and Vogel, S. (1974). *An Improved Three Dimensional Computer Simulation of Motor Vehicle Crash Victims*. Buffalo: Calspan Corporation.

Fonseka, C. P. (1969). Causes and effects of traffic accidents. Volume 4. *Report Number 33*, University of Birmingham, United Kingdom: Department of Transportation and Environmental Planning.

Fowler, J. E., Axford, R. K., and Butterfield, K. R. (1976). Computer simulation of the pedestrian impact—development of the contact model. In *Proceedings of the Sixth International Technical Conference on Experimental Safety Vehicles*. Washington, DC: United States Department of Transportation.

Fowler, J. E., and Newman, D. P. (1980). The use of computer simulation for the design of safer vehicles. In *Proceedings of the Conference on progress towards safer passenger cars in the United Kingdom*. London: Institute of Mechanical Engineers.

Gissane, W., and Bull, J. P. (1961). A study of 183 road deaths in and around Birmingham in 1960. *British Medical Journal*, **1**, 1716.

Gögler, E., (1962). *Road Accidents*, Series Chirugica Geigy, Number 5.

Götzen, L., Suren, E. G., Behrens, S., Richter, D., and Stürtz, G. (1976). Injuries of older persons in pedestrian accidents. In *Proceedings of the Conference on Biomechanics of injury to Pedestrians, Cyclists and Motorcyclists*. Lyon: International Research Committee on the Biokinetics of Impact.

Gratten, E., Hobbs, J. A., and Keigan, M. E., (1976). Anatomical sites and severities of injury in unprotected road users. In *Proceedings of the Conference on Biomechanics of Injury to Pedestrians, Cyclists and Motorcyclists*. Lyon: International Research Committee on the Biokinetics of Impact.

Haar, R., Lucchini, E., and Weissner, R. (1976). Automobile and pedestrian—the accident situation. In A. S. Hakkert (Ed.), *Proceedings of the International Conference on Pedestrian Safety*, Volume 1, 4A1–4A6. Haifa: Michlol.

Hall, R. R., and Fisher, A. J. (1972). Some factors affecting the trauma of pedestrians involved in road accidents. *Medical Journal of Australia*, **1**, 313–317.

Harris, J. (1976). Research and development towards protection for pedestrians struck by cars. In *Proceedings of the Sixth International Technical Conference on Experimental Safety Vehicles*. Washington DC: United States Department of Transportation. (Also issued as *Supplementary Report 238. Department of the Environment, Transport and Road Research Laboratory*, Crowthorne).

Harris, J., and Radley, C. P. (1979). Safer cars for pedestrians. In *Proceedings of the Seventh International Technical Conference on Experimental Safety Vehicles.* Washington DC: United States Department of Transportation.

Herridge, J. T., and Pritz, H. B. (1973). A study of the dynamics of pedestrians and generally unsupported transit occupants in selected accident modes. In *Proceedings of the Seventeenth Conference of the American Association for Automotive Medicine.* Lake Bluff, Illinois: American Association for Automotive Medicine.

Huelke, D. R., and Davis, R. A., (1969). A study of pedestrian fatalities in Wayne County, Michigan. *Highway Safety Research Institute Report Number Bio9*, Michigan: University of Michigan.

JAMA (1968). *Experiments on the Behaviour of a Pedestrian in a Collision with a Motor Vehicle—Summarized Report.* Tokyo: Japanese Automobile Manufacturers Association.

Jamieson, D. G., Duggan, A. W., Tweddell, J., Pope, L. I., and Zvribulis, V. W. (1971). Traffic collisions in Brisbane. *Special Report Number 2.* Canberra, Australia: Australian Road Research Board.

Jamieson, D. G., and Tait, I. A., (1966). Traffic injury in Brisbane report of a general survey. *Special Report Series Number 13.* Canberra, Australia: National Health and Medical Research.

Jehu, V. J., and Pearson, L. C. (1976). The trajectories of pedestrian dummies struck by cars of conventional and modified frontal design. *Department of the Environment, Transport and Road Research Laboratory, Laboratory Report 718.* Crowthorne: TRRL.

Kramer, M. (1974). A new test device for pedestrian–vehicle accident simulation and evaluation of leg injury criteria. In *Proceedings of the Eighteenth American Association for Automotive Medicine.* Lake Bluff, Illinois: American Association for Automotive Medicine.

Kramer, M. (1975). Pedestrian vehicle accident simulation through dummy tests. In *Proceedings of the Nineteenth Stapp Car Crash Conference.* Warrendale: Society of Automotive Engineers.

Kramer, M. (1979). Improved pedestrian protection by reducing the severity of head impact onto bonnet. In *Proceedings of the Seventh International Technical Conference on Experimental Safety Vehicles.* Washington DC: United States Department of Transportation.

Kramer, M., Burow, K., and Heger, A. (1973). Fracture mechanism of lower legs under impact loads. In *Proceedings of the Seventeenth Stapp Car Crash Conference.* New York: Society of Automotive Engineers.

Krieger, K. W., Padgaonkar, A. J., and King, A. J. (1976). Full scale experimental simulation of pedestrian vehicle impacts. In *Proceedings of the Twentieth Stapp Car Crash Conference.* Warrendale: Society of Automotive Engineers.

Kruse, W. L. (1976). Calspan/Chrysler research safety vehicle—front end design for property and pedestrian protection. In *Proceedings of the Sixth International Technical Conference on Experimental Safety Vehicles.* Washington, DC: United States Department of Transportation.

Kühnel, A. (1974). Vehicle pedestrian collision experiments with the use of a moving dummy. In *Proceedings of the Eighteenth Conference of the American Association for Automotive Medicine.* Lake Bluff, Illinois: American Association for Automotive Medicine.

Kühnel, A., and Appel, H. (1978). First step to a pedestrian safety car. In *Proceedings of the Twenty-Second Stapp Car Crash Conference.* Warrendale: Society of Automotive Engineers.

Kühnel, A., and Raü, H. (1974). Der Zusammenstoss Fahrzeug—Fussgänger unter

Berucksichtigung der Eigenbewegung des Fussgangers. *Der Verkehrs Unfall*, **1**, 3, and **2**, 25.

Kühnel, A., Wanderer, U., and Otte, D. (1975). Ein Vergleich von Realen mit nachgefahren Fussgängerunfallen. In *Proceedings of the Second International Conference on the Biomechanics of Serious Trauma*. Lyon: International Research Committee on the Biokinetics of Impact.

Lucchini, E., and Weissner, R. (1978). Influence of bumper adjustment on the kinematics of an impacted pedestrian. In *Proceedings of the Third International Meeting on Simulation and Reconstruction of Impacts*. Lyon: International Research Committee on the Biokinetics of Impact.

Mackay, G. M., and Fonseka, C. P. (1967). Some aspects of traffic injury in urban road accidents. In *Proceedings of the Eleventh Stapp Car Crash Conference*. New York: Society of Automotive Engineers.

McLean, A. J. (1972). Car shape and pedestrian injury. In *Proceedings of the Symposium on Road Safety*. Canberra: Australian Department of Transport.

McLean, A. J., and Mackay, G. M. (1970). The exterior collision. In *Automobile Safety Conference Compendium. Publication Number P30*. New York: Society of Automotive Engineers.

McNicol-Smith, J., and Letheren, B. F. (1961). *Alfred Hospital Accident Survey 1960–1961*. Melbourne, Australia.

Montanari, V. (1974). Fiat technical presentation. In *Proceedings of the Fifth International Technical Conference on Experimental Safety Vehicles*. Washington DC: United States Department of Transportation.

Nelson, P. G. (1974). *Pattern of Injury Survey of Automobile Accidents, Victoria, Australia, June 1971–June 1973*. Melbourne, Australia: Royal Australian College of Surgeons.

Padgaonkar, A. J., Krieger, K. W., and King, A. J. (1976). A three-dimensional mathematical simulation of pedestrian–vehicle impact with experimental verification. *Paper 76-WA/Bio-1*. Washington DC: American Society of Mechanical Engineers.

Pritz, H. B. (1976). A preliminary assessment of the pedestrian injury reduction performance of the Calspan Research Safety Vehicle. In *Proceedings of the Sixth International Technical Conference on Experimental Safety Vehicles*. Washington DC: United States Department of Transportation.

Pritz, H. B. (1977). Experimental investigation of pedestrian injury minimization through vehicle design. *Paper 770095*. Warrendale: Society of Automotive Engineers.

Pritz, H. B. (1979). Vehicle design for pedestrian protection. In *Proceedings of the Seventh International Technical Conference on Experimental Safety Vehicles*. Washington DC: United States Department of Transportation.

Pritz, H. B., Hassler, C. R., Herridge, J. T., and Weis, E. B. (1975). Experimental study of pedestrian injury minimization through vehicle design. In *Proceedings of the Nineteenth Stapp Car Crash Conference*. Warrendale: Society of Automotive Engineers.

Pritz, H. B., Weis, E. B., and Herridge, J. T. (1975a). Body-vehicle interaction: experimental study. Volume 1. *Summary Report Number DOT-HS-801-473*. Washington DC: United States Department of Transportation.

Pritz, H. B., Weis, E. B., and Herridge, J. T. (1975b). Body-vehicle interaction: experimental study. Volume 2. *Summary Report Number DOT-HS-801-474*. Washington DC: United States Department of Transportation.

Ramet, M., and Cesari, D. (1976). Bilateral study—100 injured pedestrians connection with the vehicle. In *Proceedings of the Conference on Biomechanics of Injury to Pedestrians, Cyclists and Motorcyclists*. Lyon: International Research Committee on the Biokinetics of Impact.

Robbins, D. H., Bennett, R. O., and Bowman, B. M. (1973): *MVMA Two-Dimensional*

Crash Victim Simulation. Michigan, USA: Highway Safety Research Institute.

Robertson, J. S., McLean, A. J., and Ryan, G. A. (1966). Traffic accidents in Adelaide, South Australia. *Special Report Number 1.* Canberra: Australian Road Research Board.

Robertson, L. A., and Baker, S. P. (1976). Motor vehicle sizes in 1440 fatal crashes. *Accident Analysis and Prevention.*, **8**, 167–175.

Ross, H. E., White, M. C., and Young, R. D. (1974). Drop tests of dummies on a mock vehicle exterior. In *Proceedings of the Third International Congress on Automobile Safety.* Washington DC: United States Department of Transportation.

Sarrailhe, S., and Hearn, B. M. (1971). *Deformation characteristics of cars in tests to simulate pedestrian impact.* Canberra: Aeronautical Research Laboratories, Australian Defence Scientific Service.

Schneider, H., and Beier, C. (1974). Experiment and accident comparison of dummy test results and real pedestrian accidents. In *Proceedings of the Eighteenth Stapp Car Crash Conference.* Warrendale: Society of Automotive Engineers.

Severy, D. M. (1965). Auto-pedestrian experiments. In *Proceedings of the Seventh Stapp Car Crash Conference.* Springfield Illinois: Charles C. Thomas.

Severy, D. M. (1970). Vehicle exterior safety. In *Automobile Safety Conference Compendium. Publication Number P30,* New York: Society of Automotive Engineers.

Severy, D. M., and Brink, H. (1966). Auto-pedestrian collision experiments. *Paper Number 660080.* New York: Society of Automotive Engineers.

Sevitt, S. (1968). Fatal road accident injuries, complications and causes of death in 250 subjects. *British Journal of Surgery,* **55**, 31.

Smeed, R. J. (1968). Some aspects of pedestrian safety. *Journal of Transport Economics,* **2**, 255–279.

Stcherbatcheff, G., (1979). Pedestrian protection, special features of the Renault E.P.U.R.E. In *Proceedings of the Seventh International Technical Conference on Experimental Safety Vehicles.* Washington DC: United States Department of Transportation.

Stcherbatcheff, G., Tarrière, C., Duclos, P., Fayon, A., Got, C., and Patel, A. (1975a). Reconstructions experimentales d'impacts tête-vehicle de pietons accidente. In *Proceedings of the Second International Conference on the Biomechanics of Serious Trauma.* Lyon: International Research Committee on the Biokinetics of Impact.

Stcherbatcheff, G., Tarriere, C., Duclos, P., Fayon, A., Got, C., and Patel, A. (1975b). Simulation of collisions between pedestrians and vehicles using adult and child dummies. In *Proceedings of the Nineteenth Stapp Car Crash Conference.* Warrendale: Society of Automotive Engineers.

Stürtz, G., and Suren, E. G. (1976). Kinematics of real pedestrian and two-wheel rider accidents and special aspects of pedestrian accidents. In *Proceedings of the Conference on Biomechanics of Injury to Pedestrians, Cyclists and Motorcyclists.* Lyon: International Research Committee on the Biokinetics of Impact.

Taneda, K., Kondo, M., and Higuchi, K. (1973). Experiments on passenger car and pedestrian dummy collisions. In *Proceedings of the First International Conference on the Biokinetics of Impact.* Lyon, International Research Committee on Biokinetics of Impact.

Tharp, K. J. (1974). Multidisciplinary accident investigation pedestrian involvement. *Report Number DOT-HS-801-165.* Washington DC: United States Department of Transportation.

Tharp, K. J., and Tsongos, H. G. (1976). Injury factors in traffic pedestrian collision. In *Proceedings of the Conference on the Biomechanics of Injury to Pedestrians, Cyclists and Motorcyclists.* Lyon: International Research Committee on the Biokinetics of Impact.

Thomas, C., Stcherbatcheff, G., Duclos, P., Tarrière, C., Foret–Bruno, J. Y., Got, C., and
    Patel, A. (1976). A synthesis of data from a multidisciplinary survey on pedestrian
    accidents. In *Proceedings of the Conference on the Biomechanics of Injury to Pedestrians,
    Cyclists and Motorcyclists*. Lyon: International Research Committee on the
    Biokinetics of Impact.
Tonge, J. I., O'Reilly, M. J. J., and Davison, A. (1964), Fatal traffic accidents in Brisbane
    from 1935–1964. *Medical Journal of Australia*, **2**, 811.
Tonge, J. I., O'Reilly, M. J. J., Davison A., and Johnson, N. G., (1972). Traffic crash
    fatalities, injury patterns and other factors. *Medical Journal of Australia*, **2**, 5.
Transport and Road Research Laboratory (TRRL) (1974). Pedestrian injuries.
    Department of the Environment, Transport and Road Research Laboratory, Leaflet 317.
    Crowthorne: TRRL.
Twigg, D. W., Tocher, J. L., and Eppinger, R. H. (1977). Optimal design of automobiles
    for pedestrian protection. *Paper 770094*. Warrendale: Society of Automotive
    Engineers.
Wakeland, H. H. (1962). Systematic automobile design for pedestrian injury protection.
    In *Proceedings of the Fifth Stapp Car Crash Conference*. Minneapolis: University of
    Minnesota.
Wanderer, U. N., and Weber, H. M. (1974). First results of exact accident data
    acquisition on scene. *Paper 740568*. Warrendale: Society of Automotive Engineers.
Wooler, J. (1968). Road traffic accidents in Adelaide and Brisbane, Australia. In
    Proceedings of the Fourth Conference of the Australian Road Research Board. Canberra:
    Australian Road Research Board.

Part III

The Environment

Pedestrian Accidents
Edited by A. J. Chapman, F. M. Wade and H. C. Foot
© 1982, John Wiley & Sons Ltd.

Chapter 7

Accidents and the Social Environment

N. P. Sheehy

In one sense examining the social dimensions to pedestrian accidents involves taking on that problem in its entirety. It is possible to maintain that all human learning is of a fundamentally social kind; the acquisition of any item of knowledge is dependent upon the beliefs, values, attitudes and opinions which characterize social relationships and which define both the act of learning and its content. The notion of 'social environment' is usually used in a more restricted sense, however, to signify the acquisition of those behaviours which enable the person to function completely as a member of a social group. It is in this sense that the term 'social environment' is used in this discussion. However, the scope of our subject matter remains considerable. It is possible to view accidents and their causes at many levels, from the intra-individual to the social/ organizational. This allows us a broad range of theoretical perspectives from which to consider the behavioural processes underlying pedestrian accidents, and affords us comparable latitude in the scope of the countermeasures we might choose to adopt.

The literature dealing with the social dimensions to pedestrian accidents suggests a structure at many levels of social activity, but particularly in terms of individuals, groups and the community. This tri-partite structuring of the research literature is entirely pragmatic, however, and has no special significance beyond its face validity.

THE ROLE OF INDIVIDUAL FACTORS

Psychology takes as its starting point the individual and the development of the person. Not surprisingly, therefore, most of the psychological interest in pedestrian accidents has been motivated by a desire to identify those factors of individual personality which accentuate the accident liability of certain people. Two approaches to the study of individual factors can be identified. The first has its origins in personality theory and seeks to identify maladaptive personality complexes which operate in a pathologic manner to increase the accident liability of the person generally. Most of the research in this area has addressed itself towards clarifying constituent features of the so-called 'accident prone' personality. The second line of approach adopts a social learning perspective. It emphasizes the role of development in fostering the growth of the person, and the ways in which developmentally-bounded competencies can affect the vulnerability of people at various times throughout their life span.

Accident proneness

The notion of 'accident proneness' centres around the idea that certain kinds of people are inherently more likely to experience accidents during their life by virtue of the operation of some pre-disposing personality factors which they possess. Shaw and Sichel (1971), in reviewing the theoretical and empirical literature in the area, concluded that the complexity of the issues entailed in the use of the concept accident proneness were such that the usefulness of the notion as a personality characteristic was largely bound up with the individual researcher's operational definition of the term.

Surprisingly, relatively few studies have concentrated on applying the accident proneness concept exclusively at the individual level. As is evident in the section below examining the significance of family and peer group factors, much of the clinically-based research into this area has been undertaken within the wider context of the role played by the family in fashioning the personality profile of the individual. Such research as has been undertaken at the individual level has adopted a broad 'exposure-coping' model, in which accidents are treated as normal, non-pathological aspects of behaviour, and emphasis is placed upon the capacity of the individual to cope with the incidence of 'possible accidents' he/she is likely to experience during his/her lifetime. Manheimer and Mellinger (1967), for instance, examined the accident records of 8,874 four- to eighteen-year-olds. These investigators found that children rated 'high' on a composite index of accident liability of their devising were likely to be considered daring, active, and extraverted by their mothers—all characteristics which they considered might increase the child's exposure to traffic, while leaving him/her poorly equipped to negotiate these dangers.

In a later study Mellinger and Manheimer (1967) reported that children with marked personality and behavioural maladjustments demonstrated a high level of accident liability: this they attributed to the risky decision taking which characterized such children's social reactance. While this kind of approach may appear attractive, its practical value is limited by the fact that it is difficult to see how it could improve the effectiveness of accident countermeasures. The practical utility of identifying 'high risk' individuals along the lines suggested is very much dependent upon the availability of techniques for modifying their risk taking, or selectively restricting the range of their environment so as to render it potentially less threatening. Foote (1961) has cautioned that the researcher motivated to account for individual differences in behaviour may all too readily take refuge in the concept of personality before relevant social factors have been adequately explored. The concept of accident proneness may prove yet one further instance of this tendency to 'psychologize' our subject matter.

Individual development

The value of the exposure-coping model would appear to rest on the emphasis which it places on the significance of individual development. This approach has been taken up in greater depth by cognitive-developmental psychologists, notably by Sandels (1975). Sandels suggests that young children have completely different pre-requisites from the mature adult, and act in a manner determined by their age and development. The most serious consequence of failing to take account of this developmental aspect to behaviour is that, as adult motorists, we fail to appreciate fully the circumstances of the child and fail to modify our behaviour in necessary ways.

In the area of child pedestrian accidents Sandels (1975) has documented various developmental competencies which appear to differentiate adult from child pedestrian activity. These differences may be grouped under three broad headings: (1) physical; (2) perceptual-cognitive; and (3) social-attitudinal. With respect to physical differences it is clear that the diminutive stature of the child limits his/her speed of movement and this requires that the child operates at a faster or higher rate in order to maintain margins of safety comparable to the adult. The child's height also affects his/her field of vision, and by the same token drivers find child road users difficult to detect. Their smaller size also predisposes the child pedestrian to certain forms of injury, with head, pelvic and abdominal injuries predominating (Aldman, 1963; Ryan, 1969).

With regard to perceptual limitations, and largely on the basis of her own findings, Sandels contends, first, that the child is relatively poor at judging the direction of oncoming sound and, second, that peripheral vision is of more limited assistance to children than it is to adults. There is need for caution, however, in generalizing from Sandel's laboratory-based findings to everyday pedestrian-driver encounters. Intuitively one would doubt that small developmental differences observed under laboratory conditions would generalize to the traffic environment. Sandels admits that the findings may have been due in part to the effects of experimental demands in the testing session. Tower (1976) has compared performance on a series of perceptual tasks with reported accident frequency for a group of twelve children but found zero-order correlations between these variables. Thus, while it may be the case that developmental lags in visual perceptual capacities may sometimes contribute to pedestrian accidents, it seems probable that these would have to be particularly large before one could justifiably invoke such factors as primary or even secondary causal agents.

In examining the relevance of children's cognitive abilities for an understanding of child pedestrian accidents, Sandels (1975) suggests that children appear to fixate on elements within the traffic environment as a whole, and hence tend to perceive discrete, independent events. A similar view has been expressed by Deutsch (1964) who argued that children do not always perceive the dangers in relating themselves to their environment because they find difficulty in relating antecedent events to consequences and because their relative immaturity limits their ability to cope with new experiences and situations. On a related point, Sandels (1975) provides evidence suggesting that children have difficulty in comprehending even the simplest of road signs. Cattell and Lewis (1975) reported that children as old as eleven years of age misunderstand the meaning of words such as 'danger', 'kerb', and 'pavement', a finding which may account in part for Firth's (1975) report that six- to twelve-year-old children tend to provide relatively impoverished and incomplete descriptions of road safety procedures.

Investigators of pedestrian accidents have tended to ignore another important aspect of social development, that dealing with the child's ability to adopt the perspective of other road users. The ability to assume the position of others, particularly of drivers, is a prerequisite for a proper understanding of road safety practices. Within the Piagetian perspective (e.g. Piaget and Inhelder, 1956; Shantz, 1975) there is assumed to be a gradual development away from an egocentric view of the world, to a more social viewpoint, so that only by the seventh or eighth year is the child capable of constructing the viewpoint of others with comparative ease. However, it should be noted that Piaget's analysis has not gone without criticism (cf. Borke, 1977; Hughes, 1978), partially because it has tended to ignore the possibility that the empathic ability of the adult to assume the position of the child may also be far from adequate.

The social-attitudinal differences between adults and children commented on by Sandels (1975) are somewhat loosely defined and impressionistic, but refer essentially to the relative playfulness and spontaneity of children's behaviour. Because of these characteristics children are said to be inconsistent and unpredictable pedestrians, particularly as they are inclined to use the street as a recreation site. However, to suggest nothing further than that children are overly impulsive is to oversimplify the issue. There is a danger of endorsing a romanticized image of the child's world as removed from the reality of adulthood. As becomes apparent in the following sections, children's behaviour is often determined by child-rearing practices, educational policies and social norms. Much of the theory and research conducted within the developmental perspective appears to have, unwittingly, endorsed many of the preconceptions and attitudes contained in that imperialistic view of childhood which it has sought to enlighten.

The relevance of a developmental perspective for understanding adult pedestrian accidents is valuable in at least one respect. The developmental explanation proceeds by specifying a competence-performance account of behaviour which, in theory, can be applied across the entire life-span. According to this more general theory, an imperfect correlation exists between the competence of a person and his/her performance on particular tasks, such that, on occasions, one may witness instances of apparently maladaptive or regressive behaviour on the part of an otherwise competent person. These instances of inappropriate behaviour may contribute to the occurrence of accidents (cf. Chapman, Foot, Sheehy and Wade, 1981).

The developmental approach can also provide an interesting perspective on the problem of sex differences in pedestrian accidents. There is a substantial body of empirical evidence suggesting that throughout childhood girls are developmentally more advanced than boys (cf. Maccoby and Jacklin, 1975). Consequently, one might expect girls to possess a more comprehensive repertoire of skills. The sex difference in pedestrian accidents, which has been observed to diminish in adolescence and adulthood (cf. Grayson, 1980) is also explicable in terms of a developmental progression. During late adolescence and adulthood male development accelerates and approximates that of the female.

The relevance of this broader developmental perspective for an explanation of all pedestrian accidents is clearly somewhat tenuous. In particular, it fails to take adequate account of the structure and operation of factors in the wider social environment which, as we see in the following sections, may be crucial. Furthermore, this approach faces the difficulty, which is rarely fully resolved, of explaining the reason for the competence-performance discrepancy, and one usually ends up with a somewhat unsatisfactory dualism between competence and performance. On the other hand, the developmental perspective has undoubtedly increased our awareness of the dangers of adopting a general imperialism in our treatment of the child road user.

The role of alcohol

The developmental explanation of adult pedestrian accidents, while attractive in its parsimony, is of somewhat doubtful relevance in view of the significant role which alcohol would appear to play in the occurrence of these accidents. Clayton, Booth and McCarthy (1977) examined the blood-alcohol-distribution among a sample of adult pedestrian casualties in the West Midlands Metropolitan Area from 1969 to 1975. Blood-alcohol levels were obtained from coroners' records for pedestrians who had died within twelve hours of receiving their injuries. Control data were obtained by interviewing pedestrians passing the site of the accident at the same time of day, day of week and week of year, as the occurrence of the recorded accident. Coroners' records revealed that 30 per cent of all fatally injured pedestrians had been drinking prior to their accident and 22 per cent had levels above 80 milligrams per one hundred millilitres of blood, the legal limit for drivers. Amongst the control sample 21 per cent had been drinking prior to interview and six per cent had levels in excess of 80 milligrams per one hundred millilitres of blood. There was an interesting sex difference in their results, however, in that amongst the male portion of their sample a significantly greater percentage of those involved in collisions with vehicles had been drinking, and drinking more heavily, than females. This difference is doubtless attributable to differential social drinking norms and expectancies for each sex. Surprisingly, this aspect of adult pedestrian accidents has rarely been taken into account when explaining the overall sex difference in adult pedestrian accident rates.

A further aspect to alcohol-related injuries has been identified in the Clayton *et al.* (1977) work, namely that semi-skilled and manual workers were over-represented in the sample gathered from coroners' reports. An earlier study conducted in America by Haddon, Valien, McCarroll and Umberger (1964), using a broadly comparable approach to that employed by Clayton and his colleagues, yielded an over-representation of people who were foreign born or of relatively low socio-economic status.

The part played by alcohol in contributing to adult pedestrian accidents is grossly under-researched. Its mechanism of operation is two-fold. First, it acts to impair motor, perceptual and cognitive activity generally, thereby increasing accident liability. Second, the condition of intoxication may reflect certain socially permissible drinking habits, where alcohol consumption reflects an attempt to cope with particular life stresses, for instance. On this point Clark (1971) cited research conducted in America which indicates that 47 per cent of those in his sample of fatal pedestrian injuries had prior public intoxication arrests on official police records. He points out that a certain percentage of those who were fatally injured may in fact have been alcoholic, and their drinking habits as such may have provoked a life trauma which effectively reduced their socio-economic status and dramatically altered their life-style. Most of the interpretation, therefore, has tended to emphasize the significance of consumption profiles, rather than the pharmacological effects of alcohol *per se*. There remains a fundamental interpretational problem in the research, therefore, in that, as yet there exists no feasible means of isolating the effects of alcohol consumption from the 'symptoms' which it is intended to relieve, but which may themselves impair performance.

What we require is a considerably greater understanding of social drinking customs. The dilemma for those who would seek to invent and implement social policy designed to alleviate alcohol-related problems stems from the fact that alcohol has functional and dysfunctional aspects which are largely determined by the individual consumer. Interestingly, Codling and Samson (1974) pointed out that while legislation on alcohol consumption and automobile use has been observed to generalize to vehicle passengers and pedal cyclists, its effects have stopped short of influencing the drinking patterns of pedestrians.

In comparison with other drugs, alcohol is comparatively straightforward in terms of its effects on performance, and the ease with which its presence in the human body can be detected and quantified. But the multiplicity of effects of other drugs (pharmacological, clinical and behavioural) and the attendant complexity of identification and quantification, have contributed to the discouragement of research interest in the relationship between drug taking and pedestrian accidents. Joscelyn and Donelson (1978), in reviewing the relationship between drugs and accident liability, point out that much of the limited research in this area has concentrated on the driving population, and has been primarily concerned with identifying the significance of drug abuse, particularly with regard to narcotic and hallucinogenic substances. However, Sabey (1978) points out that the more significant effects of drug consumption probably lies in the medically unsupervised use of certain medications which are freely available for the alleviation of a variety of illnesses. Assessing the impact of this form of drug taking, given that it is practised so generally, is likely to prove a formidable project.

If we are to understand the nature of the relationship between alcohol and other drug consumption for pedestrian injury, we require a broad conceptual model which considers the functional relationship, continuing interaction, and fundamental interdependence among the basic components of drinking and drug taking behaviour. Only within this broader context is it likely that we shall come to grips with the full relevance of drug-related pedestrian accidents.

Impact on the individual

While we may debate the relative significance of various factors for an understanding of pedestrian accidents, few would argue about the traumatic effects of accidentally incurred injury on the personality and life-style of the individual victim. In fact, considering the general disparities of psychological research, a remarkable concordance is found in clinical, field and experimental studies of response to the stress induced by serious life crises. The frequency of two broadly defined states appears to increase after events associated with severe shock and upset. The first of these is characterized by intrusive experience of a somatic or psychosomatic sort, and the second by denial and numbing. While these states do not occur to a prescribed pattern, they have been described as operating in a phasic mode (cf. Dohrenwend and Dohrenwend, 1974). Given the physical and psychological demands involved in coping with high levels of life style change, particularly the sort of radical change instigated by traffic-related injury, it is not surprising that many psychologists feel that such events can have a deleterious effect on the general well-being of the person.

Beyond a general appreciation of the psychological significance of accident trauma, we know little as yet. Murray-Parkes (1975) has described the emotional reactions which are usually associated with limb amputation, and notes a marked similarity between these reactions and responses usually made by bereaved individuals to the death of a loved one. He suggests that both responses may be treated as instances of grief and mourning. What is particularly characteristic about accidentally incurred injury, of course, is the unexpectedness and suddenness of the event, which leaves the individual with no time to prepare and adjust to the consequences. Thus, the analogy with bereavement following the sudden death of a near relative or friend may not be as tenuous as it might initially seem, and we might do well to treat the injured victim, and his/her family with the sympathy and support usually accorded the bereaved in shock.

It has been recognized for some time (cf. Sudnow, 1967) that the ways in which news of death and bad news is communicated to others can have a profound effect on the ability of the recipient to cope with the information. Thus, the ability of the family to cope with the news of the injury of a member, or the ability of the victim to cope with the idea of leading a life impaired or partly paralysed can be assisted or made more difficult by the ways in which that information is presented to them. Kubler-Ross (1976), considering the treatment of the dying and bereaved, has suggested that a majority of medical personnel on whose shoulders it falls to deliver 'bad news' are typically untrained in this task, and tend to proceed largely on the basis of their personal competencies in communicating such news. For those who find the task difficult and strenuous, this frequently leads to embarrassment and awkwardness. Sanson-Fisher and Poole (1979) have warned against the assumption that the ability to empathize with the news receiver is one which is normally acquired only through clinical practice, since they found no evidence to indicate that this was in fact the case with medical personnel. Pritchett and Frude (1979) have demonstrated that a minimal amount of exposure to varying styles of dealing with the communications problems associated with announcing bad news can beneficially affect subsequent performances. There is an important role for the psychologist here, not only in the training of professionals in related disciplines, but also for active engagement in assisting the accident victim and his/her family to cope with the emotional and physical difficulties likely to arise as a consequence of accident trauma.

THE FAMILY AND PEER GROUP

The family exists as the single most significant socializing institution in our society. It is the primary social group in which the child is introduced to social mores and conventions, and which actively encourages the development of skills necessary to cope in society. For the adult, the family has traditionally occupied the single largest commitment for the woman as mother and housekeeper, and for the man as breadwinner. For the elderly it provides a crucial means of social support and extended social involvement (cf. Frude, 1982). However, it is important to consider the role of the family, not in isolation from society, but in the context of its existence in the wider social order; first, because the parents, as primary socializing agents occupy not only familial roles, but other roles in society which are a necessary condition to effective functioning as parents; second, because the child is never socialized only for and into his/her family, but into wider social structures, most notably the peer group, which extend beyond the family.

The family and childhood

Despite the significance of the family throughout the life span of the individual, accident research interests have tended to concentrate on the childhood end of the developmental continuum, partly, no doubt, because of the exceptional vulnerability of children, but partly also because the formative influences of the family on the child have traditionally been viewed as containing the explanation for many behaviours in later life (cf. Mussen, Conger and Kagan, 1974).

Langford, Gilder, Wilking, Genn and Sherrill (1953) argued that social organizational features of the family environment can provide significant protective influences for its members, and they conducted pilot research in which they compared an 'accident' with a 'non-accident' control group on a variety of medical and psychometric measures. While their data were not formally reported they did suggest that their non-accident group manifested a greater degree of family cohesion to the levels evident in the families of their accident children. The authors admitted, however, that their concept of 'togetherness' was rather difficult to define, being based more upon professional impressions than objective description.

Marcus, Wilson, Kraft, Swander, Southerland and Schulhopfer (1960) have extended the Langford *et al.* approach in viewing accidents as manifestations of emotional disturbance within the family. The 'accident' group in this study comprised 23 six- to fourteen-year-old children who were recorded as having experienced one or more accidents requiring medical attention. The control groups comprised 23 'non-accident' children and 23 enuretic children. On the basis of a series of psychological measures they reported that both the accident and enuretic control group demonstrated more emotional problems than their non-accident control group of children, but there were no differences between the accident and enuretic groups. Parents of the accident group were described as being more anxious, insecure and non-assertive than the parents of children in the other two groups. This might be interpreted as providing some support for Foote's (1961) suggestion that many accidental injuries sustained during childhood can be traced to inadequacies in parental rearing practices. Krall (1964), working along similar lines, has suggested that accident-repeating children are basically less socialized and more aggressive as a consequence of frustration experienced in an authoritarian home environment. Krall studied 64 five- to eight-year-old children, 32 of whom had medical records of accidents occurring during the four-year period preceding her study. Using standardized doll-play interviews she suggested that the children with accident histories demonstrated slightly greater use of commands, threats and punishments, and more instances of affection and affection-seeking than the children with no comparable medical biography. She treated these findings as indices of greater family disorganization. Whether this interpretation is entirely justified is a moot point, since instances of affection-seeking could just as easily be taken as demonstrative of family cohesion and support.

These earlier papers by Langford *et al.*, Marcus *et al.*, Foote and Krall set a trend for much of the research work to follow in treating the concepts of frustration and aggression as crucial to an under-standing of childhood accidents generally. In Burton's (1968) work the notions of stress and attendant frustration were taken up and elaborated. She examined group of 20 five- to fifteen-year-olds officially recorded as having been involved in a pedestrian or cycling accident. A further group of children, matched on variables of age, sex, IQ, religion, social class, birth order and sibling number. On the basis of a variety of semi-projective and psychometric tests she reported that there was a greater tendency on the part of the mothers of accident prone children to recount histories of stress during pregnancy, and conflict in handling their children during infancy. Burton interpreted these results as indicative of maladaptive consequences of a failure, on the part of the mother, to cope with maternal stress and perceived rejection. These are presumed to facilitate the formation of persecution feelings in the child, usually expressed in a desire to seek sympathy and punish the parents. Thus, the child behaves impulsively, provoking hazardous encounters with the environment which the mother feels unable to control.

One of the characteristic features of the Burton, Langford *et al.* and Marcus *et al.* studies is that they have tended to concentrate on using semi-projective techniques in the quantification of both personality and group disturbances. A complimentary approach proceeds by examining more tangible aspects of family disturbance. Krall (1964), for instance, has argued that there is a strong tendency for accident-repeating children to come from broken homes, a point which has been taken up at some length by other workers. Backett and Johnston (1959) have compared 101 families in which a healthy child had survived a road accident with a matched group of families and found both a greater frequency of general illness and more serious illness among their sample of 'accident' families. Working along similar lines Ekström, Gästrin and Quist (1966) have examined the incidence of mental illness in the parents of 88 families in which one or more children had experienced an accident, and they found a greater frequency of parental mental illness in the accident sample.

Husband (1972) conducted an in-depth study of 24 children with hospital records showing that they had experienced some form of accident during the 12-month period preceding his study. He reported that in 54 per cent of the families there was a history of serious physical or psychiatric illness in at least one family member, and 29 per cent of his sample of cases lived in families where the parents were either divorced, separated, or unmarried and not cohabiting. Since no comparison figures were quoted for control purposes these data are of rather limited descriptive value.

Backett and Johnston (1959) have emphasized the importance of a factor which they have termed 'maternal preoccupation'. They reported that the mothers of their group of 'accident' children were more often preoccupied with pregnancy or employment outside the home than were the mothers of families in their control group. Read, Bradley, Morison, Lewall and Clarke (1963) studied two groups of children which they differentiated on the basis of whether or not they had been involved in a pedestrian accident and report that, among their 'accident' families, mothers were generally younger, with more commitments outside the home than families in their 'non-accident' sample. While Ekström *et al.* (1966) found no comparable trends in their data, they did find that there were more families in their accident sample who had mothers who had previously worked outside the home. Thus there would appear to be some evidence to suggest that 'maternal preoccupation' may constitute an important indicator of certain features of family organization as these affect the vulnerability of the child. Taken in conjunction with the evidence suggesting that latent feelings of aggression and hostility may significantly influence the structure of intra-family relationships, there would appear to exist a preliminary basis for suggesting that child pedestrian accidents may, in some cases, be viewed as a pathologic consequence of the increased vulnerability of the child living in such circumstances.

One needs to treat even this suggestion with a degree of caution, for much of the relevant research can be criticized on a variety of methodological and theoretical grounds. The methodological criticisms centre around the use of measurement instruments of questionable validity and reliability. Projective measures, such as the doll-play technique adopted by Krall (1953), have occupied an uneasy status in psychology by virtue of the interpretational difficulties associated with their use. All of the research papers reviewed in this section can be criticized for using assessment procedures which provide insufficient guarantees against the possibility of interpretational bias on the part of the researcher. It was common, for instance, for the interviewer to know beforehand whether a particular interviewee was a member of the experimental or control group.

The adequacy of the matching procedures for experimental and control groups can be questioned in many of the studies. Samples were poorly matched in that, with the exception of the Ekström *et al.* (1966) work, no study employed a control group consisting of children who had sustained injuries comparable to those experienced by the 'accident' children, but arising from different sources. Only Backett and Johnston (1959) employed a control sample matched for traffic exposure, despite the fact that this factor is probably a crucial determinant of the risk experienced by children (cf. Routledge, Repetto-Wright and Howarth, 1974). Some researchers (e.g. Burton, 1968) appeared to match children on a variety of variables of doubtful relevance (e.g. religion, IQ) simply with the object of meeting some mistaken notion of the purpose of matching procedures.

The use of interviewing procedures as a means of eliciting information of a biographical nature, which is presumed to have some bearing on the accident liability of the child, should be treated cautiously. Retrospective interviews, such as those employed by Burton (1968) and Marcus *et al.* (1960) promote a situation in which the mother is explicitly encouraged to seek some explanation for her child's accident in his/her history. Furthermore, since the interviews were invariably conducted some time after the accident had occurred, most of the results cannot of themselves establish that factors associated with insecurity and anxiety in the mother–child relationship precipitated the accident, since these may only have arisen as a consequence of the accident trauma.

It is undoubtedly the case that family-associated disturbances may dramatically alter the behaviour of some children in a way, and to such a degree, that it might have a significant bearing on the vulnerability of the child in the traffic environment. The nature of these disturbances, their quantification and their mechanisms of operation remain ambiguous, however. We cannot expect any radical change in this state of affairs until such time as investigators are prepared to define *a priori* the classes of relevant events which may accentuate accident liability, and indicate why these may function in a pathologic manner.

Sex stereotyping in childhood

Perhaps the least satisfactory aspect of many of the investigations considered thus far is that the majority of psychodynamically based explanations of pedestrian accidents view such phenomena as fundamentally deviant, frequently as a pathologic consequence of latent aggression within the social matrix of the family. It is difficult to see how this kind of explanation might account, for instance, for the differential representation of boys and girls in the traffic casualty statistics. An alternative to explanation based on behavioural pathology treats accidents as the psychologically meaningful outcome of engaging in certain kinds of activities. These styles of action, while not inherently pathologic, may place the child in circumstances where he/she may be poorly equipped to deal with the hazards posed. One such approach is offered by a social learning theory account of the role of the child in the family.

One of the most significant socializing influences exercised by the family centres around the differential treatment accorded to members on the basis of their gender. This differential treatment has come to be termed 'sex-typing'. One consequence of this kind of differential reinforcement of behaviours in boys and girls is that 'by the age of seven, in a whole variety of ways, the daily experience of little boys in terms of where they are allowed to go, how they spend their time and to what extent they are kept under adult supervision is already markedly different from that of little girls' (Newson and Newson, 1976, p. 100). There is evidence to suggest that this difference may extend to the pedestrian activities of boys and girls.

On the basis of interviews with 697 mothers of seven-year-old children, Newson and Newson (1976) found that 67 per cent of boys, but only 52 per cent of girls, were described as 'outdoor children'. This concurs with a finding published by Coates and Bussard (1974) and results reported by Webley (1976) that boys' mental maps of their local environment are more elaborate and extensive than those of girls. Research by Sadler (1972), in which over 2,000 mothers were interviewed, indicated that at each of seven age levels from two to eight years, more mothers of boys than of girls said that they consciously worried about the possibility of their child being involved in a traffic accident. Later evidence from the Newsons' work suggests that parental supervision is generally more stringent for girls than for boys, thus agreeing with Sadler's observation that young girls are chaperoned more often than young boys on their journeys to and from school. While there would appear to be an important exposure difference in the traffic experiences of boys and girls, it should also be noted that Routledge *et al.* (1974) failed to report any exposure differences between the sexes in school-to-home journeys. Similarly Sadler found that sex differences in chaperonage were not present on shopping errand trips. A study by Chapman, Foot and Wade (1980) however, found that streets are used as recreational sites more by boys than by girls. It would appear that while there may be only minor variations in exposure to traffic when boys and girls are engaged in purposive journeys, such as running errands, there may be substantially greater variations for less obviously goal-directed street activity.

The family and adulthood

While considerable emphasis has been placed upon the formative influences of the family during childhood, it should be emphasized that the family continues to shape the individual throughout his/her life span. Socialization does not stop in childhood, just as sex-typing is an ongoing process possessing progressively deeper repercussions for the structure and organization of affairs within the family and the wider community. Thus, Ross (1974) has pointed out that there are important sex differences associated with the levels of manifest danger evident in various occupations and leisure pursuits. The male stereotype, more than the female, incorporates an emphasis on danger, while feminine interests tend to be directed away from hazardous activities. Equally one has the impression that driving has tended to foster a chauvinistic image as a predominantly male preserve, and it may also be that styles of street movements by male and female pedestrians reflect, in some part, this image. Males may, for instance, tend to be overly assertive in negotiating vehicular traffic. It certainly seems probable that men tend to encounter traffic more in connection with their employment, and perhaps during rush-hour periods, while women tend to engage traffic more frequently on shopping journeys during periods of lower density traffic flow. Unfortunately research bearing on these issues is exceedingly sparse, although Henderson and Jenkins (1974) have found that women experience more 'traffic challenge' than men, apparently as a consequence of their greater readiness to slow down and accommodate to oncoming traffic. There are limited exposure data available to indicate the frequency and kinds of involvements which men and women have with vehicular traffic (cf. Todd and Walker, 1980), but very little by way of detailed description of adult pedestrian activity. Jennings, Burki and Onstine (1977) have suggested that looking behaviours tend to be undertaken largely by the first few pedestrians who start to cross the street, with those following on the trail of the leaders tending to look less at oncoming traffic and more at other pedestrians. Dannick (1973) has found that the presence of a law-adhering pedestrian on the pavement kerb significantly increased the probability that other pedestrians would adhere to a 'Don't walk' signal, but that a law-violating model recruited even more pedestrians. Russell, Wilson and Jenkins (1976) found that a 'high status' model pedestrian recruited a greater number of nearby pedestrians than did a 'low status' violator. Similar phenomena have been observed among children. Grayson (1975) found that children in groups are more likely to run when in the street, while Sandels (1971, 1974, 1979) cites evidence suggesting that children involved in pedestrian accidents tend to have been engaged in interaction with peers immediately prior to their collision with a vehicle.

There is evidence to suggest, therefore, that there may not only be sex differences among adult pedestrians, but significant social facilitation factors operating in pedestrian crowd movements. Grayson (1975) and Routledge *et al.* (1974), on the basis of naturalistic observational data, have found significant age differences in the crossing procedures characteristically adopted by adults and children, which complicate the issue further. Both of these pieces of research reveal a paradox in that the crossing strategies adopted by adults, which we tend to regard as successful and mature, differ in several fundamental respects from the ways in which children are taught to proceed when negotiating traffic. Specifically, adults tend to assess the situation prior to reaching the kerb, and as a consequence are more likely to enter the carriageway before oncoming traffic has passed. They tend to cross at an oblique angle, and they attempt to maximize the gap between themselves and oncoming vehicles by adroitly moving towards these vehicles and skirting immediately behind them. Children, by contrast, tend not to pay as much attention to the traffic until they reach the kerb, where they are more inclined to stop and wait for a suitable gap in the oncoming stream of traffic. They tend to cross directly and seldom adopt the technique of anticipating vehicle movements and stepping behind oncoming traffic. Clearly, the sophistication of the adult strategy makes it largely inappropriate for young children, and it emphasizes some basic contradictions in the ways we teach children to behave and the manner we choose to cross ourselves. It may be that one reason for the exceptional vulnerability of some children has to do with the ways in which they adopt the adult crossing strategy while failing to comprehend the additional judgemental skills required in using this technique. However, while there must be a clear need here to educate adults about the potentially dangerous consequences of their behaviour when this is imitated by children, instructional exercises would prove formidable to put into practice, requiring large-scale well-integrated, campaigns supported by considerable financial backing. It is likely to prove an extremely difficult exercise to change adult habits in this regard, and no less formidable a challenge to persuade children not to aspire to the adult crossing strategy.

Returning to the issue of sex differences, social learning theory can provide an important link between accidents incurred by adults and by children. It may be assumed that if the social learning theory account is to deal adequately with the sex difference evident in children's accidents (cf. Chapter 1) it will prove necessary to demonstrate, first, that there are sex differences in adult crossing style and, second, that these behavioural differences can be regarded as behavioural 'precursors' of the differences evident between boys and girls. The latter condition would have to be fulfilled if it is assumed that children align themselves more with same-sex than with opposite-sex models. With regard to the first requirement, Mackie and Older (1965) and Jacobs and Wilson (1967) have published corroborative data in that they observed that considerably more women than men used protected crossing facilities when these are available. They also found that children made still more use of these facilities, and Jacobs and Wilson also noted sex differences among children comparable to those displayed by adults. Cohen, Dearnaley and Hansel (1955) found that men tend to accept smaller inter-vehicle gaps than do women, while Salvatore (1968) found that boys made less conservative judgements of oncoming vehicle speed than did girls, although they also tended to be more accurate across a wide range of speeds examined in that study. Girls, Salvatore suggested, display greater conservativism across all traffic conditions. While Henderson and Jenkins (1974) found that women experienced more traffic conflict to that evident for men, this was due largely to the fact that men were less prepared to delay at the kerb: they crossed at the earliest possible opportunity.

We have seen that there are two interconnected pathways by which an aspect of family functioning can become part of a casual network leading to an accident. The first pathway is through the intervening variable of chronic stress arising from family relationships characterized by recurring conflict or anxiety, or arising from rapid change or crisis within the family. High levels of stress may gradually weaken a person's defences and generally lead to impaired or reduced performance thus increasing the vulnerability of the person. However, between family processes and pedestrian accidents there exists a host of intervening variables, such as constitutional predispositions, personality profiles, individual ways of coping with stress and individual attitudes, beliefs and expectations which make it unlikely that any single, easily identifiable route will be found between a specific family make-up and a particular traffic accident.

The second pathway was assumed to develop from the stabilization and repetition of a potentially dysfunctional form of behaviour. For instance, a child may be encouraged to play outside the home, thus increasing the probability of making unsupervised excursions away from the home, and generally increasing contacts with the traffic environment. Where such a pattern is particularly deep-seated (as it is assumed to be in sex-typing), further generations of adults may automatically adopt similar child-care practices, unaware of the considerably larger dangers posed for the children by the intervening growth in the traffic environment. Unlike the first pathway, which represents a psychosomatic pathologic response to family affairs, this second pathway is essentially non-pathologic in operation, and constitutes a more fundamental failure in adaptive behaviour to accommodate to continuing change in the environment. Thus, while behaviour associated with the first pathway may be expected to disappear as soon as the family disturbance disappears, behaviour arising from this second pathway is likely to prove more enduring and resistant to change.

Impact on the family

To the extent that a community has institutionalized certain forms of behaviour as 'safe' and others as 'dangerous', departures from the former may be viewed as instances of deviant behaviour. In the case of the accident victim, extended hospitalization essentially removes the person from his/her socially active role in the community. In the case of severe injury, such as mutilation, the person may face a severe personality crisis as a consequence of the somatic violation of him/herself. Such injury also poses a problem of role attribution for the family and neighbourhood in attempting a social re-definition of the significance of the person for the community. While the stigma which attaches to mental illness has received theoretical and research attention in the past (cf. Goffman, 1970), that which attaches to physical illness and impairment has received a more restricted forum of interest. There is a need for us to examine more fully the transitional crises posed in attempting to return the accident victim to his/her community. While this emphasis should not be interpreted as underplaying the magnitude of the personality disturbance associated with accidentally incurred injury, it is nonetheless the case that, as social psychologists, we have tended to undervalue the significance of those features of person-community interaction which encourage or impede the successful matching of each to the other.

A report issued by the Consumers' Association (1980), based on a survey of the consequences of pedestrian and cycling accidents for the victims and their families, has indicated that medical indices of the severity of injury, which typically rely on the length of stay in hospital in-patient treatment units, may seriously underestimate the wider impact of such injury. In particular, estimates such as these fail to take explicit account of the duration or cost of out-patient treatment, or of the wider medical and psychological impact of temporary or permanent disability. Two samples were used in this study, the first of 183 victims injured during the preceding twelve-month period, and the second a sample of 141 people who had received severe injuries during the preceding four-year period. In examining the wider social impact of accidentally incurred injury it was noted that 50 per cent of the working subjects in the first sample, and 92 per cent of those working at the time of injury in the second sample, were 'off work' for more than six weeks after their accident. Similarly, of those in full-time education, 25 per cent of those in their first sample and 50 per cent of those in their second sample missed six or more weeks of schooling. Neither medical, nor economic indicators can claim to provide adequate indices of injury impact at this level.

SOCIETY

In considering the wider social context of pedestrian accidents it is intended to address an analysis of the salient issues in terms of the attitudinal 'syndromes' which structure our interpretation and treatment of the traffic accident statistics. In so doing one can distinguish between those attitudes, opinions and beliefs which are held by the 'folk community', or society generally, and those which are endorsed by more specialized communities, particularly the research community and the administrative-bureaucratic community. While the attitudinal climate sustained within the research and bureaucratic communities has its origins in wider socio-cultural milieux, both of these organizations require some consideration in themselves because they embrace two socially powerful agencies for institutional change.

The folk community

While it has been recognized that the success of programmed interventions is crucially dependent upon the extent and accuracy of our knowledge of the target populations (Organisation for Economic Co-operation and Development, 1971), we know virtually nothing about popular conceptions of, or attitudes towards, road traffic accidents. There is a basic need for high quality research in this regard which psychology must address if it is to make an enduring contribution to road safety research.

Whatever lip service we pay to the view that accidents never 'happen' but are 'caused', society nevertheless encourages the view that accidents are the inevitable outcome of the style of life we choose to lead. One may, in fact choose between the philosophy that accidents by their very nature, happen simply because they *do* happen, or that accidents occur as a consequence of a coincidental combination of circumstances for which no one can be held entirely responsible. While these philosophies bear a superficial similarity, each reflecting a belief in the inevitability of accidents, they are quite distinct in origin (Chapman *et al.*, 1981). The first rests on a conviction that there is a hidden purpose or meaning to the major events in our lives, while the second rests on a belief that 'chance' plays a significant part in determining the outcome to our efforts. While both philosophies are, in themselves, inadequate to a comprehensive understanding of accidents, the former is probably more threatening in the degree to which it promotes an attitude of complacency in regard to traffic accidents, and in the size of the problem posed for social, education and attitude change.

While it appears to be the case that society has tended to view accidents in a somewhat fatalistic manner, the uniformity with which various attitudes are held across the community remains unclear. A survey of opinions about child pedestrian accidents held by parents, teachers, police officers and road safety officers (cf. Chapter 1) suggests a relative uniformity of belief in a fatalistic explanation for such accidents. The possibility cannot be ruled out that one reason for the historic failure of so many road safety campaigns to demonstrate any unequivocal reduction in traffic accident fatalities rests in part on their fundamentally over-simplistic assumptions about the universal acceptability of their subject matter. While people probably do hold genuine aspirations to reduce the incidence of traffic accidents, the notion should also be entertained that people possess an equally deep-rooted conviction that such enterprises are doomed to failure because of the very deterministic nature of accidents.

The manner of our formal treatment of accidents provides a further indicator of society's attitudes towards accidentally incurred injury. The formal procedure in regard to the completion of Death Certificates in Great Britain, for example, does not allow for the possibility that death may have occurred suddenly. Certificates may only be issued by the Medical Practitioner who was in attendance during the deceased's terminal illness. However, such an emphasis on fatal illness as having been protracted may be entirely inappropriate for those who die from unexpected or accidentally incurred injury. Thus, in the case of sudden, unexpected or violent death the coroner's investigations are intended to provide a quasi-judicial explanation when no causal explanation of a medical sort can be readily invoked. Clearly society regards accidental death in a manner entirely different from other 'causes' of death. Indeed it may well be the case that society is prepared to tolerate accidents by treating them as unfortunate, but necessary, costs of individual freedom. Thus, public health campaigns aimed at dealing with the regulation of traffic hazards have often been based on paternalistic principles designed to protect individuals from harms that might occur to them as a result of their own behaviour. Such campaigns are likely to be acceptable so long as people are prepared to accept, or at least not actively object to, this advice. However, where involvement is viewed as imposing unacceptable limitations on personal liberty such campaigns are likely to prove counter-productive and may even harden public opinion against the policy makers. This is not altogether surprising, for while the layperson might be prepared to admit a degree of ignorance in regard to medical, economic or political matters, for instance, s/he naturally views him/herself as something of an expert in matters relating to the conduct of his/her daily affairs and is, accordingly, less willing to tolerate constraints imposed by society in this area.

The administrative and research communities

We know little about the significance of contemporary social attitudes towards traffic accidents for policy formulation and implementation. We know even less about the commitments entertained by those groups claiming a social mandate to investigate and reduce the incidence of traffic related injury. The uses to which accident statistics are put are instructive here because they reflect an important aspect of the concerns of these specialized groups in society. One can distinguish at least two separate uses. Researchers have, for the most part, treated the accident statistics as informative indicators, descriptive of social conditions at a general level. As such their approach requires that some prior decision be made as to those aspects of accidents which need to be measured. Not surprisingly, therefore, most of the researcher's criticisms of contemporary accident reporting systems have been levelled at the tendency to concentrate on those features which are easily measurable (e.g. time-of-day, weather conditions, etc.) but which are of themselves only peripheral concerns in producing an entire picture of the actions taken by road users which lead directly to collisions.

Government agencies, by contrast, have tended to cast the accident statistics in the role of problem-oriented indices, yielding quantitative expressions of particular concentrations of problems in the traffic environment. Their use in this context can provide an important basis for identifying the requirements for policy in this area. Criticisms from within these bodies are usually motivated by a desire for greater detail in the accident reporting procedures.

Despite the common underlying dissatisfaction with the lack of detail in the accident statistics, the requirements of the researcher and policy maker have tended to remain quite distinct. The researcher's criticisms must be understood in the context of his/her desire to embrace predictive indicators, by linking his/her informative indices to a theory or model of change in the traffic environment. By doing this changes in the indicators can be assessed and interpreted as verifying or disconfirming anticipated changes in the underlying social processes modelled in the theory. The criticisms for bureaucratic administrative bodies result from their need to develop acceptable programme-evaluative indicators, designed to monitor the effectiveness of policy implementations by quantifying traffic conditions in relation to some predetermined target. The objectives of research and policy are, therefore, complimentary.

In demanding a more rationalized accident reporting system, whatever the motivation for such improvements, there is a danger of assuming that changes of this sort will help clear up many of the difficulties surrounding the explanation of traffic accidents. New methods of data compilation and analysis cannot solve our problems. The same problems will continue to re-emerge, possibly in different forms, so long as we continue to work to the old theories or models. What we require are new theories, adequate to the complexity of the phenomena of traffic accidents. The outline for one such approach is given later in this chapter.

Children and society

In considering the significance of the social order for pedestrian accidents at a more specific level, we are obliged to point to meagre descriptive evidence of a broadly demographic and sociologic sort. One of the most easily discernible features of the pedestrian accident statistics relates to the exceptionally large variations according to geographical location (cf. Chapter 8). Approximately 95 per cent of pedestrian accidents occur in built up areas, suggesting that the main problem is an urban phenomenon. Not surprisingly, therefore, most of the research has concentrated on the pedestrian in towns and cities.

Preston's (1972) analysis of child pedestrian accidents in Manchester and Salford in 1969 is instructive at this point. On the basis of extensive analyses of police documents Preston reported a significant positive correlation between the child pedestrian injury rate for various wards within the sample catchment area and an index of crowding ($r = 0.58$) and an index of social class ($r = 0.55$). This relationship Preston explained on the basis of an assumed comparability between internal and external domiciliary conditions. Thus, 'the overcrowded house is likely to be in an overcrowded street, without gardens or play spaces for children' (p. 329). Preston warned, however, that despite the apparent plausibility of this explanation, it is weakened, in her study, by the fact that those areas which exhibited overcrowding were not randomly distributed throughout the catchment area sampled, but tended to cluster around the city centre. Such areas are more likely to experience large volumes of traffic movements than the residential sites situated in the city suburbs. In such circumstances traffic density is likely to be a product of high population density, high volumes of traffic and more varied traffic movements, rather than any one of these in isolation. It seems probable that Preston's crowding and social class indicators are tapping this more complex feature of the social environment.

An interesting aspect to Preston's work is that she reported that boys in the three- to seven-year age range experienced considerably greater risk in these 'crowded' areas than did their female peers. No such differences were evident for less crowded or high social class indexed areas. Why this should be is not immediately clear, but the finding presents a challenge for the sex-typing hypothesis considered earlier.

Backett and Johnston (1959), using a clinically based procedure, had earlier reported a greater number of accident vulnerable children among more crowded families, although this difference was only significant for the younger children in their sample. Read *et al.* (1963) also found that their 'accident' group of children were likely to come from families occupying multi-dwelling houses in the more densely populated areas of the city centre. However, Backett and Johnston found no similar difference in the incidence of pedestrian accidents according to the social class of their sample of children, while Sadler (1972), using survey techniques with mothers, reported that there was no association between reported use of the street as a recreation site and social class of the father. Newson and Newson (1976) employed survey procedures comparable to Sadler's but did report a significant social class trend in the percentage of children reported as frequently engaging in street play.

Undoubtedly the most interesting feature to emerge in Preston's data was in relation to the magnitude of the differences between the correlations between injury rate and the social class and crowding indices for each sex. While the respective correlations were high for males, 0.71 and 0.63 respectively, they were negligible for the female portion of her sample, 0.01 and 0.13 respectively. This suggests that the power of her overall correlations between injury rate and low social class and overcrowding is mediated exclusively by the male portion of her sample. Why this should be is by no means clear. One might hypothesize that there are differential exposure rates for boys and girls in these areas, which essentially implies an explanation in terms of parental rearing patterns. This would require some demonstration that sex-typing is generally much stronger among 'lower' social class groups, or alternatively that the effects of sex-typing only became important in more hazardous environments. Whatever the case, it is likely to prove difficult to find supporting evidence for this type of explanation.

One must be cautious in interpreting data such as that presented by Preston. Striking though the 'between areas' differences are, they cannot provide us with any information about differences which may exist *within* areas. While studies of this sort provide a useful impetus to policy formulation, they cannot be treated as the sole basis for targeting populations, since the size of the problem is contingent upon the size of the sampling framework one chooses to adopt. Thus interventions based on 'problem area' identification can provide no guarantee of optimum utilization of resources, and may actually promote mistaken beliefs about the ecological and geographical concentration of traffic accidents within certain sections of the community.

The elderly and society

The elderly have been shown to be the most vulnerable group of adult pedestrians (Lashley, 1960; Singer, 1963). The reasons for this are not clear, but one should caution, at this stage, against speculation which may be influenced by stereotyped views of the elderly as senile and partially crippled. However, the gerontological theory of social disengagement, perhaps because it conforms with traditional views of the elderly in society, presents an interesting perspective on the elderly pedestrian which is couched in a broadly social framework.

The theory, which has several variations, commences with the observation that maturity and retirement are usually characterized by a systematic reduction in certain kinds of social interaction, coupled with partial withdrawal from the mainstream of social activity. Social pressures may often be brought to bear on the elderly, pressures to retire from the workface, for instance, and to assume a less active life. One consequence of this is that some elderly people may experience progressive marginalization of their position in the community. In attempting to maintain a high level of involvement in the community they may place exceptionally heavy demands upon themselves, which may lead to more errors, mistakes and accidents in a variety of activities. These accidents might be expected to concentrate in those environments (of which the traffic environment is one), where there are heavy demands on the use of sophisticated skills in the negotiation of potential hazards.

There is very little empirical evidence to reject or support these hypotheses, although there is a considerable amount of face validity attached to these suggestions. The theory gains some support from research published by Wiener (1968), who conducted survey and observational studies of the responses of elderly pedestrians to a road safety education campaign directed at them. Crossing behaviours were studied at two sites, two months prior to, and four months after, the campaign. Of those individuals who were reprimanded by police officers for 'jaywalking' during the period of the campaign, 62 per cent were observed to jaywalk again at the earliest possible opportunity. However, in the absence of control data indicating the general acceptability or otherwise of such reprimands for other age groups, these findings remain of limited descriptive value. An early study of accidents involving elderly pedestrians (Transport and Road Research Laboratory, 1972) and a more recent observational study of adult road-crossing practices (Wilson and Grayson, 1980) point to few overall differences in the styles adopted by young adults and the elderly. If anything they indicate the elderly pedestrian to be more cautious and safety conscious.

The literature dealing with the influence of the wider social environment is theoretically diverse, but empirically meagre in its coverage of the relevant issues. Established theories of a general sort are few, and where these are available, as in social disengagement theory, they do not approximate axiomatic systems but are largely based on rather loosely related sets of arguments for which it is difficult to construct adequate tests. Explanation at this level is made more difficult by the fact that the incidence of pedestrian accidents is characterized by complex age and sex factors, and possibly some interaction of each with the other. While a majority of child pedestrian accidents appear to be related to the child's use of the street as a recreation site, adult injuries would appear to involve a significant proportion of alcohol-related injuries. The particular vulnerability of the elderly may be due to the difficulties they experience as a consequence of a general reduction in capacities which is not coupled with a growing awareness of these limitations. Furthermore, the practical significance of some of the more general perspectives on pedestrian accidents appears highly restricted from the point of view of planned behavioural intervention. A possible point of contact between several approaches considered up to this point may centre upon the use of the family as a context for the integration of the wider community themes with the individually-based personality themes.

Impact on society

The wider impact of pedestrian accidents on society has been particularly difficult to assess in the past. Dawson (1967, 1971) has attempted to estimate the economic costs of accidents to the community in some detail, while more general estimates accompany the annual statistical reports of transportation accidents (Department of Transport, 1980). However, to use economic concepts as a method of calculating the social costs of traffic accidents is, at best, a grossly imperfect means to that end. There is, moreover, a dangerous suggestion contained in such enterprises, namely that the magnitude of social consequences can be succinctly summarized in monetary terms. The use of economic indicators is necessary and understandable. There are few comparably well developed indicators of social costing. When applied to problems of a social and psychological sort, however, the difficulties arising from the use of economic measures become not only technical, but conceptual as well. While the accident statistics constitute quite complex social indicators, they are themselves the product of a somewhat anachronistic accident reporting system, developed on an *ad hoc* basis to meet a variety of legislative and statistical interests. As a general move towards rationalizing that system serious consideration might be given to the introduction of a weighting index which would allow a more reliable and valid classification of injury severity than that permitted by current procedures. Injury impact is, of course, a multi-faceted concept, involving complex sociological, physiological and psychological factors. Physical injury is often complicated by victim characteristics associated with his/her family, personality and economic background, and with health service factors associated with the availability and application of scarce medical resources. Furthermore, the problems posed in returning the victim to the community, and their intangible effects on the victim, his/her family and society are likely to make reasonable quantification an extremely difficult task.

AN INTERACTIONAL PERSPECTIVE

Much of the research concerned with examining the social dimension to pedestrian accidents has proceeded by identifying high risk groups and then isolating factors which appear to contribute to their exceptional vulnerability. An analysis of pedestrian factors, for example, characteristically excludes any consideration of driver and environmental factors; accident promoting factors of one sort tend to be treated as uniform with respect to their effects on factors of another sort.The nature of the relationship between high-risk drivers and high-risk pedestrians, for instance, is by no means clear. It is unclear whether there is uniform risk liability of each group with respect to every other group or whether there are more complex relationships to be considered. Equally, it is difficult to determine the significance of salient environmental dimensions (cf. Chapter 8) for the important social factors discussed in this chapter. In considering Preston's (1972) work it became clear that the relationship between the physical and social environments is a complex one, rather than a simple isomorphic mapping of high risk individuals on high risk environments.

That there may be differential involvement of different groups of drivers with different groups of pedestrians has been tentatively discussed by Sandels (1979). On the basis of a detailed analysis of insurance records she noted that mothers of children appear to be over-involved in collisions with child pedestrians. Findings of this sort are difficult to interpret in the absence of base-line data regarding the relative exposure of different sub-groups of pedestrians to other sub-populations of drivers. Mothers who do drive probably find themselves negotiating child pedestrians more frequently than drivers of commercial vehicles, for instance. Brown (1980) has argued that the relative inexperience of the young driver and the child pedestrian guarantees their incompatability as road users. A strong degree of face validity attaches to the suggestion that high risk groups in the pedestrian and driver populations may be related to one another in important but enigmatic ways.

Sheehy (1979) has suggested that the road user's perception of danger and hazard is based on a complex interpretation of the actions of other road users and that accidents frequently occur as a consequence of an incorrect attribution of plans and intentions to competing co-users.

Zuercher (1977) has demonstrated that personal characteristics of pedestrians and drivers (*viz.* age, sex and attractiveness) influence the likelihood that oncoming drivers will yield to pedestrians waiting at a zebra crossing. This parallels the earlier discussed finding of Dannick (1973) and Russell *et al.* (1976) on the effects of differential model status on the strength of 'recruiting' responses on adjacent groups of pedestrians. Skelton, Bruce and Trenchard (1976) have suggested that drivers experiencing frustration may frequently 'rev' their engines in order to increase the speed of pedestrian movements on protected crossings. Ebbesen and Haney (1973) have observed that one consequence of experiencing such delay can be readily detected in the increase in the risk taking of the driver accelerating away from the site of delay. Greenbaum and Rosenfeld (1978) have found that prolonged staring at the delayed driver also has the effect of facilitating faster acceleration away from an intersection.

The perspective offered by these studies can be seen to be based on the premise that the behaviour of road users demands a broader conceptual treatment to that offered in the past. The social complexity of the traffic environment requires a research approach in which road user activity is treated as fundamentally interactive. Ordered movement is achieved as a product of jointly negotiated activity between road users, rather than in the perfunctory discharge of formal duties articulated in *The Highway Code*. If, in fact, road user behaviour could be satisfactorily explained exclusively in terms of the formal set of norms governing road user behaviour, the incidence of traffic accidents might be expected to be much higher. Thus, failure to comprehend the complex situational demands of pedestrian/driver encounters, rather than failure to understand the formal set of rules prescriptive of the conduct of such encounters, may lead to unintentional or unexpected outcomes—outcomes we traditionally term 'accidents'.

Stated another way, it can be said that the interactional position offered here emphasizes the ways in which people come to know how to do things—the ways in which they develop an understanding of traffic procedures, rather than simply what they do—or the ways in which they understand structured descriptions of the content of such procedures (cf. Sheehy, 1980). This tacit understanding of procedures occurs primarily at a more fundamental, routine level of social intercourse than that contained in the formal system of road user activity, summarized in *The Highway Code* and *Green Cross Code*. This wider normative system is difficult to describe, but is concerned with the rules of procedure and convention that structure interactions between people generally. This system involves, for instance, the obligation that each party to an interaction should avoid ambiguity and prolixity and should orient and adjust to some degree to the perspective of the other interactants. The significance of this more fundamental system of norms has not been fully elaborated in other approaches considered in this chapter, nor has the importance of the relationships between the formal and informal normative systems. Our lack of awareness of the importance of these interrelationships has probably a lot to do with the difficulties which people experience when trying to decide, or in attempting to teach others, what action to take in order to avoid collision in conflicting encounters with other road users.

THE SOCIAL ENVIRONMENT IN PERSPECTIVE

In adopting an interactional approach to pedestrian accidents we are broadening our perspective on the issue of road safety. Traditional methods of programme planning have implicitly adopted a means/end type of model as a working procedure. This essentially involves articulating the objectives of the programme in the form of a statement of goals. This done, various programmes are designed and evaluated in terms of the degree to which they meet the criteria contained in the statement of goals. The effective functioning of this method rests on an adequate coverage of the relevant goals which, in the case of road safety, is usually expressed as a reduction in the number of traffic accidents (although a target reduction is rarely specified). However, a reduction in the number of accidents is only one dimension to the complex concept of 'safety'. Pedestrian/driver interactions can be viewed along a continuum from successful, co-operative encounters, through competitive challenge, to 'near misses' and finally accidents. The quantification of goals other than a reduction in the number of accidents, such as an increase in the general co-operativeness and ease with which various pedestrian/driver manoeuvres are performed, is likely to prove one important consequence of exploiting an interactional perspective along the lines proposed here. However, because the incidence of road accidents may have proved the simplest of dimensions to quantify in the past, the goals of road safety and accident reduction have become synonymous objectives. Such a trend is potentially dangerous in failing to safeguard against the possibility that a programme which reduces the incidence of pedestrian/driver conflicts and near-misses, for example, will not be discarded because of its failure to demonstrate a reduction in pedestrian accident statistics.

In broadening our range of criteria to include behavioural indices of programme effectiveness we are doing more than simply expanding our concept of safety from a univariate to a multivariate notion. With this method the planner, once again, produces a collection of more or less detailed designs, but the process of choosing between alternatives is now placed more firmly in the hands of the population for whom the programme is intended. Both methods may, of course, lead to an identical decision in the selection of an intervention campaign, but the second method seems to be inherently more acceptable in the way in which it leaves the final decision with the 'consumer'. The traditional means/end method proceeds by attempting to incorporate all of the relevant value judgements at the beginning of the planning process, in a statement of goals. The second method proceeds along very similar lines, but is concerned with guaranteeing a more exhaustive statement of relevant goals, since the matter of final choice will be a public one. The latter method does not attempt to provide an evaluative conclusion, as is so often attempted when treating accident statistics as the sole criterion for countermeasure acceptability. It does attempt to go some way further to ensuring that the final choice about which intervention campaign to choose is as well informed as possible.

This second approach to professional intervention effectively brings the planner and public into a closer liaison than before. Problem solving is undertaken as a jointly negotiated process, rather than as the imposition of solutions of one 'informed' group on the body of another group. At this level the issues of relevance—social, environmental, legal and educational—are integrated in a coherent planning process, rather than treated in isolation from one another. For the present we lack such an approach, preferring to proceed with isolated, well-intentioned programmes of an educational, engineering or legal sort, occasionally motivated, it would seem, by the desire to prove the value of our own approach over all others. Such a parochial perspective often leads to inflated claims for the success of programmes which have been developed, implemented and evaluated in isolated circumstances, rather than in the context of a practical realization of the multiplicity of dimensions to our traffic safety problems.

While the interactionist perspective outlined here cannot purport to represent the basis for a coherent approach to the traffic accident problem along the lines envisaged, it should be interpreted as representing a formal change in willingness to move away from the discipline-bound perspective which has been demonstrated not to work in the past. In the final analysis, movement towards a coherent research and planning policy will not result solely from changes at the levels of conceptual analysis and methodological innovation, but only when the relevant issues are engaged at the more fundamental, political level of interdisciplinary contact and interaction.

REFERENCES

Aldman, B. (1963). The road accident risks for children and young people: the morbidity and mortality pattern. In *Proceedings of the Second Congress of the International Association for Accident and Traffic Medicine*. Stockholm: International Association for Accident and Traffic Medicine.

Backett, E. M., and Johnston, A. M. (1959). Social patterns of road accidents to children. *British Medical Journal*, **1**, 409–413.

Borke, H. (1977). Piaget's view of social interaction and the theoretical construct of empathy. In L. S. Siegel, and C. J. Brainerd (Eds.), *Alternatives to Piaget: Critical Essays on the Theory*. London: Academic Press.

Brown, I. D. (1980). Are pedestrians and drivers really compatible? In D. J. Oborne, and J. A. Levis (Eds.), *Human Factors in Transport Research*, Volume 2, *User Factors: Comfort, the Environment and Behaviour*. London: Academic Press.

Burton, L. (1968). *Vulnerable Children*. London: Routledge and Kegan Paul.

Cattell, R., and Lewis, G. D. (1975). Children's understanding of words used in road safety literature. *Department of the Environment, Transport and Road Research Laboratory, Supplementary Report 155UC*. Crowthorne: TRRL.

Chapman, A. J., Foot, H. C., Sheehy, N. P., and Wade, F. M. (1982). The social psychology of child pedestrian accidents. In J. R. Eiser (Ed.), *Social Psychology and Behavioral Medicine*. Chichester: Wiley.

Chapman, A. J., Foot, H. C., and Wade, F. M. (1980). Children at play. In D. J. Oborne and J. A. Levis (Eds.), *Human Factors in Transport Research*, Volume 2, *User Factors: Comfort, the Environment and Behaviour*. London: Academic Press.

Clark, B. H. (1971). Pedestrian safety and alcohol: a study of fatal pedestrian accidents in West Virginia in 1970. *Traffic Digest and Review*, **19**, 12–13.

Clayton, A. B., Booth, A. C., and McCarthy, P. E. (1977). A controlled study of alcohol in fatal adult pedestrian accidents. *Department of the Environment, Transport and Road Research Laboratory, Supplementary Report 332*. Crowthorne: TRRL.

Coates, G., and Bussard, E. (1974). Patterns of children's spatial behaviour in a moderate density housing development. In D. H. Carson (Ed.), *Man-Environment Interactions: Evaluation and Application, Part III*, 131–142. Pennsylvania: Dowden, Hutchinson and Ross.

Codling, P. H., and Samson, P. (1974). Blood alcohol in road fatalities before and after the Road Safety Act, 1967. *Department of the Environment, Transport and Road Research Laboratory, Supplementary Report 45UC*. Crowthorne: TRRL.

Cohen, J., Dearnaley, E. J., and Hansel, C. E. M. (1955). The risk taken in crossing a road. *Operational Research Quarterly*, **6**, 120–127.

Consumers' Association (1980). *Knocked Down: a Study of the Personal and Family Consequences of Road Accidents involving Pedestrians and Pedal Cyclists*. London: Consumers' Association.

Dannick, L. I. (1973). Influence of an anonymous stranger on a routine decision to act or not to act: an experiment in conformity. *Sociological Quarterly*, **14**, 127–134.

Dawson, R. F. F. (1967). Cost of road accidents in Great Britain. *Ministry of Transport, Road Research Laboratory, Laboratory Report 79*. Crowthorne: RRL.

Dawson, R. F. F. (1971). Current costs of road accidents in Great Britain. *Ministry of Transport, Road Research Laboratory, Laboratory Report 396*. Crowthorne: RRL.

Department of Transport (1980). *Road Accidents Great Britain 1978*. London: Her Majesty's Stationery Office.

Deutsch, M. (1964). On development and learning. In W. Haddon, E. A. Suchman and D. Klein (Eds.), *Accident Research: Methods and Approaches*. New York: Harper and Row.

Dohrenwend, B. S., and Dohrenwend, B. P. (1974). *Stressful Life Events; Their Nature and Effects*. Chichester: Wiley.

Ebbesen, E. E., and Haney, M. (1973). Flirting with death: variables affecting risk taking at intersections. *Journal of Applied Social Psychology*, **3**, 303–324.

Ekström, G., Gästrin, U., and Quist, O. (1966). Traffic accidents among children. In *Proceedings of the Second Congress of the International Association for Accident and Traffic Medicine*. Stockholm: International Association for Accident and Traffic Medicine.

Firth, D. E. (1975). Roads and road safety—descriptions given by four hundred children. *Department of the Environment, Transport and Road Research Laboratory, Supplementary Report 138UC*. Crowthorne: TRRL.

Foote, N. N. (1961). Sociological factors in childhood accidents. In W. Haddon, E. A. Suchman and D. Klein (Eds.), *Accident Research: Methods and Approaches*. New York: Harper and Row.

Frude, N. (1982). The Family. In A. J. Chapman, and A. Gale (Eds.), *Psychology and People*. London: British Psychological Society and Macmillan Press.

Goffman, E. (1970). *Asylums: Essays on the Social Situation of Mental Patients and Inmates*. Harmondsworth, Middlesex: Penguin.

Grayson, G. B. (1975). Observation of pedestrian behaviour at four sites. *Department of the Environment, Transport and Road Research Laboratory, Laboratory Report 670*. Crowthorne: TRRL.

Grayson, G. B. (1980). The elderly pedestrian. In D. J. Oborne and J. A. Levis (Eds.), *Human Factors in Transport Research*, Volume 2, *User Factors: Comfort, the Environment and Behaviour*. London: Academic Press.

Greenbaum, P., and Rosenfeld, H. M. (1978). Patterns of avoidance in response to interpersonal staring and proximity: effects of bystanders on drivers at a traffic intersection. *Journal of Personality and Social Psychology*, **36**, 575–587.

Haddon, W., Valien, P., McCarroll, J. R., and Umberger, C. J. (1964). A controlled investigation of the characteristics of adult pedestrians fatally injured by motor vehicles in Manhattan. In W. Haddon, E. A. Suchman and D. Klein (Eds.), *Accident Research: Methods and Approaches*. New York: Harper and Row.

Henderson, L. F., and Jenkins, D. M. (1974). Response of pedestrians to traffic challenge. *Transport Research*, **8**, 71–74.

Hughes, M. (1978). Selecting pictures of another person's view. *British Journal of Educational Psychology*, **48**, 210–219.

Husband, P. (1972). Children with increased liability to accidents. *Safety Education*, **125**, 3–4.

Jacobs, G. D., and Wilson, D. G. (1967). A study of pedestrian risk in crossing busy roads in four towns. *Ministry of Transport, Road Research Laboratory. Laboratory Report 106*. Crowthorne: RRL.

Jennings, R. D., Burki, M. A., and Onstine, B. W. (1977). Behavioural observations and the pedestrian accident. *Journal of Safety Research*, **9**, 26–33.

Joscelyn, K. B., and Donelson, A. C. (1978). Drugs and highway safety: research issues and information needs. In *Proceedings of the Twenty-Second Conference of the American Association for Automotive Medicine and the Seventh Conference of the International Association for Accident and Traffic Medicine*. Ann Arbor: International Association for Accident and Traffic Medicine.

Krall, V. (1964). Personality characteristics of accident repeating children. In W. Haddon, E. A. Suchman and D. Klein (Eds.), *Accident Research: Methods and Approaches*. New York: Harper and Row.

Kubler-Ross, E, (1976). *On Death and Dying*. London: Tavistock.

Langford, W. S., Gilder, R., Wilkin, V. N., Genn, M. M., and Sherrill, H. H. (1953). Pilot study of childhood accidents: preliminary report. *Pediatrics*, **11**, 405–415.

Lashley, G. T. (1960). The aging pedestrian. *Traffic Safety*, **57**, 10–13.

Maccoby, E. E., and Jacklin, C. N. (1975). *The Psychology of Sex Differences*. London: Oxford University Press.

Mackie, A. M., and Older, S. J. (1965). Study of pedestrian risks in crossing busy roads in inner London suburbs. *Traffic Engineering and Control*, **7**, 376–380.

Manheimer, D. I., and Mellinger, G. D. (1967). Personality characteristics of the child accident repeater. *Child Development*, **38**, 491–513.

Marcus, I. M., Wilson, W., Kraft, I., Swander, E., Southerland, F., and Schulhopfer, E. (1960). An interdisciplinary approach to accident patterns in children. In W. Haddon, E. A. Suchman and D. Klein (Eds.) (1964). *Accident Research: Methods and Approaches*. New York: Harper and Row.

Mellinger, G. D., and Manheimer, D. I. (1967). An exposure-coping model of accident liability among children. *Journal of Health and Social Behaviour*, **8**, 96–106.

Murray-Parkes, C. (1975). *Bereavement: Studies of Grief in Adult Life*. Harmondsworth, Middlesex: Penguin.

Mussen, P. H., Conger, J. J., and Kagan, J. (1974). *Child Development and Personality*. London: Harper and Row.

Newson, J., and Newson, E. (1976). *Seven Years Old in the Home Environment*. London: Allen and Unwin.

Organisation for Economic Co-operation and Development (OECD) (1971). *Road Safety*

Campaigns: Design and Evaluation. Paris: Organisation for Economic Co-operation and Development.

Preston, B. (1972). Statistical analysis of child pedestrian accidents in Manchester and Salford. *Accident Analysis and Prevention*, **4**, 323–332.

Piaget, J., and Inhelder, B. (1956). *The Child's Conception of Space.* London: Routledge and Kegan Paul.

Pritchett, D., and Frude, N. (1979). The communication of bad news—a videotape study. In D. J. Oborne, M. M. Gruneberg and J. R. Eiser (Eds.), *Research in Psychology and Medicine*, Volume 2, *Social Aspects: Attitudes, Communication, Care and Training.* London: Academic Press.

Read, J. H., Bradley, E., Morison, J. D., Lewall, D., and Clarke, D. A. (1963). The epidemiology and prevention of traffic accidents involving child pedestrians. *Canadian Medical Association Journal*, **89**, 687–701.

Ross, H. E. (1974). *Behaviour and Perception in Strange Environments.* London: Allen and Unwin.

Routledge, D. A., Repetto-Wright, R., and Howarth, C. I. (1974). The exposure of young children to accident risk as pedestrians. *Ergonomics*, **17**, 457–480.

Russell, J. C., Wilson, D. O., and Jenkins, J. F. (1976). Informational properties of jaywalking models as determinants of imitated jaywalking: an extension to model sex, race and number. *Sociometry*, **39**, 270–273.

Ryan, G. A. (1969). Children in traffic accidents. *Pediatrics Supplement*, **44**, 847–854.

Sabey, B. E. (1978). A review of drinking and drug taking in road accidents in Great Britain. In *Proceedings of the Twenty-Second Conference of the American Association for Automotive Medicine and the Seventh Conference of the International Association for Accident and Traffic Medicine.* Ann Arbor: International Association for Accident and Traffic Medicine.

Sadler, J. (1972). *Children and Road Safety: A Survey Amongst Mothers.* London: Her Majesty's Stationery Office.

Salvatore, S. (1968). The estimation of vehicular velocity as a function of visual stimulation. *Human Factors*, **10**, 27–32.

Sandels, S. (1971). A report on children in traffic. *Skandia Report I.* Skandia: Stockholm.

Sandels, S. (1974). Why are children injured in traffic? Can we prevent child accidents in traffic? *Skandia Report II.* Skandia: Stockholm.

Sandels, S. (1975). *Children in Traffic.* London: Elek.

Sandels, S. (1979). Unprotected road users. A behavioral study. *Skandia Report III.* Skandia: Stockholm.

Sanson-Fisher, R. W., and Poole, A. D. (1979). Teaching medical students communications skills: an experimental appraisal of the short and long term benefits. In D. J. Oborne, M. M. Gruneberg and J. R. Eiser (Eds.), *Research in Psychology and Medicine*, Volume 2, *Social Aspects: Attitudes, Communication, Care and Training.* London: Academic Press.

Shantz, C. U. (1975). The development of social cognition. In E. M. Hetherington (Ed.), *Review of Child Development Research*, Volume 5. Chicago: University of Chicago Press.

Shaw, L., and Sichel, A. (1971). *Accident Proneness.* Oxford: Pergamon Press.

Sheehy, N. (1979). The perception of hazard by child pedestrians. *Paper presented at the Annual Conference of the Developmental Section of the British Psychological Society*, September. Southampton.

Sheehy, N. (1980). The child pedestrian's perception of hazard. *Paper presented at the Second Annual Conference on Postgraduate Psychology.* April. Lancaster, England.

Singer, R. E. (1963). Action for pedestrian safety and control. *International Road Safety and Traffic Review.* **11**, 17–20, 22–24 and 29.

Skelton, N., Bruce, S., and Trenchard, M. (1976). Pedestrian–vehicle conflict and the operation of pedestrian light-controlled (pelican) crossings. In A. S. Hakkert (Ed.), *Proceedings of the International Conference on Pedestrian Safety*, Volume 1, 5D1–5D9. Haifa: Michlol.

Sudnow, D. (1967). *Passing On*. Englewood Cliffs, New Jersey: Prentice-Hall.

Todd, J. E., and Walker, J. (1980). *People as Pedestrians*. London: Her Majesty's Stationery Office.

Tower, D. Q. (1976). Relationships between perceptual responses and accident patterns in children: a pilot study. *American Journal of Occupational Therapy*, **30**, 498–501.

Transport and Road Research Laboratory (1972). Accidents to elderly pedestrians. *Department of the Environment, Transport and Road Research Laboratory, Leaflet 323*. Crowthorne: TRRL.

Webley, P. (1976). Children's cognitive maps. *Paper presented at the Annual Conference of the Social Section of the British Psychological Society*, September. York.

Wiener, E. L. (1968). The elderly pedestrian: response to an enforcement campaign. *Traffic Safety Research Review*, **12**, 100–110.

Wilson, D. G., and Grayson, G. B. (1980). Age related differences in the road crossing behaviour of adult pedestrians. *Department of the Environment, Transport and Road Research Laboratory, Laboratory Report 933*. Crowthorne: TRRL.

Zuercher, R. (1977). Communication at pedestrian crossings II. In A. S. Hakkert (Ed.), *Proceedings of the International Conference on Pedestrian Safety*, Volume 2, 115–118. Haifa: Michlol.

Chapter 8

Accidents and the Physical Environment

F. M. Wade, H. C. Foot and A. J. Chapman

Behavioural, educational and legal factors, in conjunction with aspects of vehicle design, are important in constructing a complete account of pedestrian accidents. But it is likewise important to appreciate how characteristics of the physical environment contribute to accidents. In this chapter we discuss environmental factors, initially by examining accident rates in relation to aspects of time and place: time factors include time-of-day, day-of-the-week and season-of-the-year; place factors include road classification, degree of urbanization and distance from home. We then focus the discussion by assessing the influence of particular environmental interventions on variables such as pedestrian behaviour and accident rates and on variables which bear a less direct relationship to pedestrian travel such as vehicle flow and driver behaviour. In these analyses the emphasis is upon measures affecting pedestrians (e.g. pedestrian precincts, footpaths and refuges), and then we discuss interventions which affect pedestrians and road users in general (e.g. culs-de-sac, Radburn estates and street narrowing). Finally, we discuss some of the chief influences on the engineers and politicians who are responsible for introducing new environmental measures into the towns and cities. Major factors influencing the way the locality as a whole is viewed include the engineers' general attitudes to transport and the role of citizen participation in political decision making.

PEDESTRIAN ACCIDENT RATES: TIME AND PLACE FACTORS

In this section the discussion centres upon surveys of pedestrian accidents indicating when and where accidents tend to occur. The relevant data for Britain are obtainable from the national road accident status survey which is compiled annually for the British Government (Department of Transport, 1980). In addition, sample surveys have been undertaken which were designed specifically to investigate particular aspects of the time and location distributions of pedestrian accidents.

Time factors

British national pedestrian casualties are analysed by *time-of-day* and *day-of-the-week*. Figure 8.1 shows the number of pedestrian casualties of all

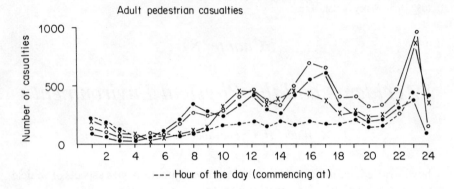

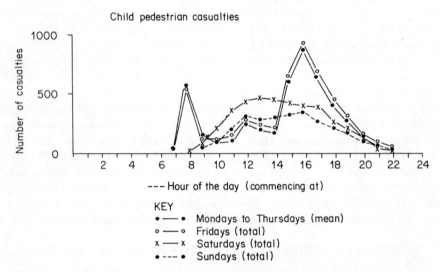

KEY
•——• Mondays to Thursdays (mean)
o——o Fridays (total)
x——x Saturdays (total)
•---• Sundays (total)

Figure 8.1 Adult and child pedestrian casualties in Britain (1978) by hour of day and
day of the week

severities for Fridays, Saturdays and Sundays, and the mean number for the
four-day period Mondays to Thursdays. Data are presented separately for child
and adult pedestrians. The main features of the within-day and within-week
variations are as follows: first, the within-day pattern for children
is different from that for adults; second, weekends show a different within-day
pattern from the weekdays for both age groups; and, third, for adults, the
pattern on Fridays can be distinguished from the pattern for the other weekdays.
During all weekdays there are three peaks in the pattern of child pedestrian

accidents: at the hours commencing 8 a.m., 12 noon (the smallest peak) and 4 p.m. (the largest peak). In contrast, the pattern for adults yields four peaks: (i) 8 a.m., (ii) 12 noon, (iii) 4 p.m. on Fridays, on 5 p.m. on Mondays to Thursdays, and (iv) at 11 p.m. In addition, adults sustain casualties during the early hours of the morning whereas children rarely do. At weekends the patterns are entirely different. Children's accidents are distributed fairly evenly through-out the day from 9 a.m. until 8 p.m., reaching a peak in the early afternoon on Saturdays and a little later on Sundays. The pattern for adults is similar except that instead of tailing away at 8 p.m., the number of casualties increases again after 9 p.m. to reach a peak at 11 p.m. It is of interest to note that for adults the late evening peak is largest on Fridays and Saturdays, and represents twice the number of casualites occurring at this time on other days of the week.

Several explanations may be advanced to account for these daily and weekly fluctuations. For example, it is possible that the large weekday, late afternoon peak for children results from the increased hazards of the home-bound journey from school relative to the early morning school-bound journey. However, the results of a survey of 474 child pedestrian accidents in Hampshire suggest that the alleged hazards of the evening school-to-home journey were not an important factor (Grayson, 1975a). In this study data were collected relating to items such as the purpose of the journey and distance from home at the time of the accident. It was found that journeys to and from school accounted for similar proportions of accidents; also, only 35 per cent of school-aged children injured between 4 p.m. and 5 p.m. were coming from school, and only half the chidren injured during this period were going home. Thus, it seems that a substantial proportion of child pedestrian accidents during the late afternoon of weekdays occur as a result of journeys other than those undertaken for the purpose of going to and from school: that is, those associated with playing, running errands and visiting.

One possible factor contributing to the late evening peak in the adult pedestrian casualty statistics is the alcohol-intoxicated state of some pedestrians at that time of day. The significance of alcohol as a factor in adult pedestrian accidents has been emphasized in several studies. For example, using data from police and coroners' records, Clayton (1973) studied the blood alcohol concentrations of a sample of adult pedestrians who died in road accidents in Birmingham (England) during the period 1970 to 1972 inclusively. Of the 30 per cent who had been drinking alcohol, two-thirds had blood alcohol concentrations (BACs) in excess of the British legal limit for drivers of 80 milligrams per 100 millilitres and one-third had BACs which exceeded 150 milligrams per 100 millilitres, the level regarded as indicative of a regular, heavy drinker. Accidents involving pedestrians with BACs above 10 milligrams per 100 millilitres occurred most frequently in the late evening and at weekends. In a controlled study of the role of alcohol, Clayton, Booth and McCarthy (1977) found that 33 per cent of fatally injured pedestrians had been drinking alcohol (BACs > 10 milligrams per 100 millilitres), 22 per cent had BACs in excess of 80 milligrams per 100 millilitres and 15 per cent had BACs above 150 milligrams per 100 millilitres. The comparable percentages for pedestrians in the control group were 21, 6 and 1 per cent respectively. Control data were obtained from roadside interviews of pedestrians (matched for sex) passing the accident site at the same time of day, day of the week and time of year as the occurrence of the accident. For both sexes the effects of alcohol on pedestrian fatal accident rates were significant for BACs above 120 milligrams per 100 millilitres; at that level the risk then increased rapidly.

Clearly the role of alcohol is significant, but it may be confounded to some extent by the effects of *darkness*. Associated with darkness hours and changes in weather, *seasonal variations* produce systematic fluctuations in casualty figures. In 1978, for example, taking pedestrians of all ages together, the British casualty rates for the autumn/fall and winter months were higher than the rates for the months from April to August. Monthly casualties were highest during November and lowest during July. Separate figures for child pedestrians are not available from British national statistical sources. However, in a study of road accidents on a sample of 257 traditional housing estates in 20 British towns, Bennett and Marland (1978) found that pedestrian accidents to children under 10 years of age were markedly more common in the summer than the winter, while pedestrian accidents incurred by adults were more prevalent in the winter. Swedish data for child pedestrians have shown a similar pattern: there are higher accident rates in the summer months, especially May and August than in winter (Sandels, 1975). Biehl, Older and Griep (1969) endorsed this age inversion in the monthly accident figures. They cited several North American and European studies which showed that during the spring and summer accident rates increase for children and decrease for adults. Interpretation is difficult, but data do suggest that children may be at greater risk through being out-of-doors more frequently during the summer than from coping with the hazards of the inclement winter weather and darkness. In contrast, adults may indeed be at greater risk during the winter because their travel patterns dictate more frequent exposure to darkness.

Smeed (1968, 1977) studied the effects of darkness on pedestrian accidents by utilizing the idiosyncrasy of 'British Summer Time'. The clocks in Britain are altered twice annually (by one hour) so that during the autumn/fall early evening clock times which are in daylight one day become dark the next, and *vice versa* during the following spring. By examining the number of pedestrian casualties in London during five weekdays before and after the change, it was found that in those hours in which light conditions were unchanged, the number of casualties was steady. However, the number was almost halved for the hours which changed from dark to light, and almost doubled in those which changed from light to dark. In addition to the darkness variable Smeed studied the effects of wet roads and found that wet weather conditions multiplied adult pedestrian casualties per hour by 1.37 in daylight and by 2.3 during the hours of darkness. No account was taken of the possible reduction in pedestrian traffic as a consequence of weather or darkness conditions. Thus Smeed suggested that the above calculated values may considerably underestimate the effects of wet and dark conditions. Singer (1963) was similarly emphatic in stressing the role of darkness; he reported that in the USA nearly six out of ten pedestrian fatalities were killed during the hours of darkness. Important contributing factors were said to be the combination of dusk/darkness and heavy pedestrian and vehicular traffic during the peak work-to-home journey hours of 4 p.m. to 8 p.m.. Swedish data from insurance company records also suggest the importance of darkness in pedestrian accidents: half the accidents to 25- to 64-year-olds took place during the hours of darkness (Sandels, 1979). The comparable British figures are less dramatic: one out of four pedestrian sustain their injuries (all severities) during hours of darkness.

Place factors

The *degree of urbanization* is an important factor in the pedestrian casualty statistics; 96.6 per cent of child casualties and 93.5 per cent of adult casualties incur their injuries in 'built-up' areas (Department of Transport, 1980). In Britain the *classification of roads* is: those of motorway status, 'A' roads, 'B' roads and minor roads. In 'built-up' areas accidents involving one vehicle and a pedestrian are concentrated on 'A' roads (44.6 per cent) and minor roads (44.5 per cent). Accidents on 'B' roads account for 10.9 per cent of the total and pedestrian accidents on roads of motorway status constitute only 0.002 per cent of the total. The proportions change in non-built-up areas; 1.6 per cent for motorways, 55.6 per cent for 'A' roads, 12.8 per cent for 'B' roads, and 30 per cent for minor roads. A study of the distribution of all road accidents in six towns of Southern England (Transport and Road Research Laboratory, 1974) showed that a main feature of the accidents on 'A' roads (arterial routes and primary distributor roads) was the high incidence of adult pedestrian casualties, particularly to those aged 60 years and over. Of the pedestrian casualties on main traffic routes, 65 per cent were adults and more than one-third of these were aged 60 years or over. On local distributor roads and residential access roads (mostly minor roads) children comprised 70 per cent of the pedestrian casualties. It is now well-documented that pedestrian accidents to young children aged up to approximately ten years occur predominantly on minor roads in residential districts and within a short distance of their homes (Grayson, 1975a; Preston, 1972; Read, Bradley, Morison, Lewall, and Clarke, 1963; Transport and Road Research Laboratory, 1977; Wade, Chapman, and Foot, 1979, 1981). Accidents to older children occur farther away from home (Grayson, 1975a; Preston, 1972) and on more major roads (Preston, 1972).

THE INFLUENCE OF ENVIRONMENTAL INTERVENTIONS: MEASURES FOR PEDESTRIANS

In this section we examine the ways in which specific environmental interventions affect pedestrian travel. The environmental interventions which are designed for almost exclusive use by the pedestrian include pedestrian road-level crossing facilities, bridges, subways, refuges and footpaths, and pedestrian-only areas. We begin this discussion with a description of research concerning road-level crossing facilities.

Pedestrian crossing facilities at road level

In Britain, road-level crossing facilities are of two main types—the zebra crossing and the pelican crossing. The *zebra crossing* is characterized by broad white stripes interspersed with roughened, low-reflectant black stripes bounded by two parallel transverse lines of slightly raised metal studs. Zebra crossings were introduced in this form in 1951 and were embellished in 1953 by the addition of flashing orange beacons, one at each end of the crossing. Within 20 metres of the crossing at each side white zigzag lines indicate the area within which drivers should not park or overtake. This crossing is not signal controlled but pedestrians have right-of-way when they step onto the crossing. *Pelican crossings*, introduced in 1969, were designed to replace zebra crossings in areas of high pedestrian flow. The distinguishing feature of the pelican crossing is the flashing amber phase visible to drivers which follows the red 'stop' light. The function of the flashing amber signal is to allow traffic to proceed if the crossing is cleared quickly but to allow slow-moving pedestrians sufficient time to cross with full priority. A steady green signal indicating that vehicles may proceed follows the flashing amber phase, and a continuous amber signal indicates that the red signal will shortly appear. The sequence of lights is pedestrian operated by means of a push button. Signals for the pedestrian have three phases: a red light to accord precedence to traffic; a steady green 'walking pedestrian' symbol accompanied by an intermittent audio signal to indicate pedestrian priority, and a flashing 'green man' to indicate continuing full priority for pedestrians already on the crossing and to instruct those not on the crossing to wait for the next steady 'green man' phase.

British national statistics for 1978 detail the extent to which crossing facilities feature in the total number of pedestrian casualties. For children, 5.9 per cent incur their injuries on pedestrian crossings and 4.9 per cent are injured within 50 metres of a crossings. For adults the figures are higher: 9.4 per cent occur on crossings and 9.2 per cent within 50 metres of a crossing. With regard to adults of retirement age and beyond, 10.7 per cent are injured on road-level crossing facilities and a further 8.9 per cent are injured within 50 metres of the crossing.

Research concerning road-level pedestrian crossing facilities is extensive and varied in both the methodology adopted and the independent variables studied. Different methodologies include development of mathematical and computer models, evaluation, study of the use of crossings, comparison of various types of crossing facilities, conversion of uncontrolled to signal-controlled crossings and the assessment of risk on and near crossings. Some studies investigate driver and/or pedestrian behaviour while others consider vehicle flow, speed or delay as the main variable.

Mathematical and computer models.   There are various mathematical and computer models whose function is to describe the mode of operation of pedestrian crossings so that predictions can be made concerning factors such as pedestrian and vehicle queues (Cresswell, 1978; Griffiths and Cresswell, 1976) and width of crossings on arterial roads (Vuchic, 1967). The construction of mathematical and computer models inevitably involves making some assumptions. Among those made in the studies by Cresswell and others are: pedestrians and vehicles arrive at the crossing independently and at random; for a given width of road, pedestrian crossing time is constant, and is a function of road width; at zebra crossings pedestrians have absolute priority and thus incur no waiting time; at pelican crossings pedestrians do not start to cross during the flashing 'green man' phase, and cross only whilst the steady 'green man' shows. Obviously these assumptions are not entirely valid.

Models concerned with developing warrants for crossings are based on similar assumptions. The development of warrants concerns establishing rules for the operation of a crossing; for example, it is necessary to determine the length of time vehicles should stop to allow pedestrians to cross, and whether traffic should always be halted immediately, or whether some minimum delay should be introduced between pedestrian priority phases. The development of warrants for crossings are based on principles concerning minimum acceptable delay. However researchers are not agreed on the criteria for such development. Thus, Pillai (1975a) and Massey (1962) suggested that warrants be based on the maximum acceptable delay to vehicles, whereas Griffiths, Hunt and Cresswell (1976) considered that a more realistic approach would be to base warrants on the minimization of the sum of pedestrian and vehicle delay costs per unit time where such costs for pedestrians are assumed to be less than those for drivers.

Some of these theoretical studies have been extended by the provision of field data for verification of some of the underlying assumptions concerning pedestrian and driver behaviour. For example, Cresswell, Griffiths and Hunt (1978) made video-tapes at three pelican crossing sites and found that, contrary to the assumption built into their computer model, pedestrians did not cross during the 'green man' phase only—they crossed whenever a suitable gap in the traffic occurred. In a similar study of zebra crossings Cresswell and Hunt

(1978) found that the computer simulation overestimated vehicle delay. This was due in part to the false nature of the assumption that pedestrians start crossing immediately on arrival, and in part because the effective pedestrian flow rate was lower than was assumed; this low rate of flow was a function of pedestrians arriving in groups of two or more at a time.

From the preceding discussion it is evident that, in addition to over-estimating vehicle delay, these models have placed a lower value on pedestrian delay relative to vehicle delay. Furthermore, from field observations Bruce and Skelton (1977) found that, in fact, pedestrians are at a considerable disadvantage relative to drivers: the main delay per pedestrian was 9 seconds and the comparable figure for drivers was 1 second. To redress the balance, Bruce and Skelton suggested that in developing computer models of crossing facilities delay should be weighted so that longer delays are considered more serious than shorter ones. The consequence of such weighting would be that pedestrian delay would be reduced and vehicle delay increased relative to the delays observed in Bruce and Skelton's field studies.

Evaluation of crossing facilities.   An early example of the evaluation of the use of a zebra crossing by adult pedestrians is a study by Older and Basden (1961) in which annual observations of a single crossing were undertaken during the period 1948 to 1959 inclusively. Pedestrian use of the crossing showed a steady increase between 1948 and 1954, with a marked increase in 1952 following the general introduction of zebra crossings. In 1954 over 80 per cent of pedestrians used the zebra on the stretch of road on which it was installed. After 1954 there was a slight decrease to 70 per cent. The proportion of drivers giving priority to pedestrians waiting to cross reached its peak of 37 per cent in 1952 and declined thereafter to a level of 25 per cent at the end of the study in 1959. Nevertheless, 25 per cent is more than twice the original observed in 1948.

The Department of Scientific and Industrial Research (1963) presented a detailed account of the investigations which were undertaken in the course of developing the zebra crossing. This account also presented an evaluation of the effects of the zebra crossing on driver and pedestrian behaviours and on casualty rates. It was found that the striping of the crossings 'resulted in an appreciable increase in the proportion of pedestrians using them and a greater improvement in the proportion of motorists giving way to pedestrians at these crossings' (p. 70). In addition, despite extraneous factors such as the reduction in the total number of pedestrian crossings and a substantial increase in the tax on petrol at that time, it was concluded that the 11 per cent decrease in pedestrian fatalities and the 7 per cent decrease in total pedestrian casualties could be attributed, in part, to the introduction of the zebra markings.

More recently, evaluation research has focused upon pelican crossing facilities. Wilson (1980) described the results of a 'before-and-after' filmed study on the effect of the audible signal which accompanies the steady 'green man' phase on adult crossing behaviour. After the audible signal was installed, the time taken to cross the road during the steady 'green man' phase decreased by nearly 5 per cent from 8.4 to 8.0 seconds; pedestrian delay after the onset of this phase decreased by about 22 per cent from 2.7 to 2.1 seconds; and, for pedestrians starting to cross during the flashing 'green man' phase, a significant reduction was observed in the proportion who failed to complete their crossing before the onset of the vehicle priority signal.

As part of a research programme to assess the overall effect of pelican crossing installations, the Transport and Road Research Laboratory (1976) reported the results of filmed observation studies undertaken at five sites in the Greater London Area. It was found that delays to pedestrians were greater than those measured at zebra crossings with comparable vehicle densities. Other findings included: longer delays for individuals aged 60 years and over relative to delays for younger adults; and longer delays for those who crossed during the steady pedestrian priority phase ('green man') than for those who crossed during other phases of the signals. At four of the five sites, between 24 and 39 per cent of pedestrians started to cross during the vehicle priority phase and at the fifth site this figure was 63 per cent. However, few pedestrians began their crossing during the flashing green phase—no more than 1.4 to 2 per cent.

Extent of crossing usage.   The extent of crossing usage has been studied by Firth (1979) who found that at two sites outside schools, one equipped with a zebra facility and one with a pelican crossing, 88 per cent of children used the zebra and 83 per cent used the pelican crossing. In the USA, Miller and Michael (1964) reported that rates of usage were dependent on the presence of an adult crossing patrol. With a patrol in attendance 98 per cent of children used the crossing in comparison with 43 per cent at an unsupervised installation. These rates are much higher than those reported in an experimental simulated study by England (1976). The simulator was an out-of-door, life-sized road, along which a single moving vehicle travelled. The road was furnished with a zebra and a pelican crossing. Children aged 7 to 11 years were instructed to cross the road, either specifically at the crossing or where they liked. Only 38 and 58 per cent of children used the zebra and pelican crossings respectively when not specifically instructed to do so. These figures were increased to 99 and 95 per cent for the group specifically told to use the crossings.

Public acceptance is another aspect of crossing usage which has received empirical attention. Pelican crossings have been criticized on the grounds that insufficient time is allowed for the pedestrian to cross and that the meaning of the flashing signals is unclear to many pedestrians and drivers. For example, the Greater London Council was reported to have been 'inundated with complaints, particularly from the aged and infirm, that crossing times are too short' (Anonymous, 1975b). Bruce and Skelton (1977) reported that if pedestrians were to complete their crossings within the steady 'green man' phase, they would have to react instantly to the onset of the signal and walk at a speed of 2.1 metres per second. These requirements were compared with findings from two observation studies which gave mean crossing speeds of 1.4 and 1.5 metres per second together with mean reaction times of 2.6 and 2.0 seconds. Thus, the observation studies showed that not only were actual walking speeds slower than was required, there was also a substantial delay before pedestrians reacted to the steady 'green man' signal. Both these factors combined gave crossing times which were far in excess of the duration of the steady 'green man' signal (between 4 and 7 seconds depending on the width of the road). However, as Bruce and Skelton pointed out, this would be quite acceptable if pedestrians and drivers used the crossings in the intended manner: pedestrians then have full priority during the 'flashing green' phase. The extent of the misunderstanding over the use of the pelican is indicated by the results of an interview and observation studies conducted by Bruce and Skelton: they reported that many interviewees had never even noticed the flashing stage of the cycle. Observations revealed considerable vehicle abuse of the crossings: it was regularly noted that vehicles started to move towards or in front of pedestrians already on the crossing when the signal was a flashing amber (and therefore flashing green to the pedestrian). It was suggested that attempts to rectify these misunderstandings via educational/propaganda efforts would prove futile. In contrast, Bruce and Skelton advocated that the rules be changed to reflect the natural inclinations of road users: in other words, both the steady and the flashing stages of the pedestrian priority phase should be lengthened and thereby occasion extra delay to vehicles—delay which would still, on average, be less than that incurred by pedestrians.

Comparisons of different types of crossing facilities.   While many of the above studies relate to both signal-controlled and uncontrolled crossings, some studies undertake direct comparisons of different types of crossing facilities. For example, Mackie and Jacobs (1965) studied 'panda' crossings (a predecessor of the pelican crossing), zebra crossings, and traffic-lights-controlled crossings. The panda was distinguished from the pelican crossing by a chevron striped road surface and a two-aspect traffic signal surmounted by a yellow globe bearing horizontal black bands. During the pedestrian priority phase a 'cross' signal showed to pedestrians and a pulsating red signal to drivers. Towards the end of the pedestrian priority phase, the 'cross' signal started to flash and a flashing amber signal was given to drivers. Mackie and Jacobs found poorer driver behaviour at panda crossings relative to traffic-lights-controlled crossings. For example, during the amber signal the proportion of drivers who stopped at the panda crossing was less than two-thirds of those who stopped at the traffic-lights-controlled crossing. Pedestrian behaviour was also examined: 57 per cent of pedestrians crossing the street on, or within, 50 metres of the panda correctly used the 'cross' phase in which to make their journeys. In comparison, more people—71 per cent—used the zebra crossing correctly.

In a more recent study the comparative safety of 51 zebras without central refuges, 33 zebras with refuges and 56 pelican crossings without refuges, has been investigated, based upon the number of personal injury accidents and pedestrian and vehicle counts for each crossing (Inwood and Grayson, 1979). (A refuge is a small central area in the carriageway around which traffic is diverted by means of bollards mounted on raised islands). For this particular sample, no evidence was found to suggest that zebras with central refuges engender better safety records than those without refuges, and no significant differences were found in pedestrian accident rates associated with zebras, zebras with refuges and pelican crossings. A reduction in accidents at pelicans relative to zebras was expected: for the same levels of vehicle and pedestrian flow, pelican crossings were expected to give rise to one-half of an injury accident per year less than zebra crossings.

Conversion of one type of crossing into another. Another area of enquiry concerns the conversion of one type of crossing into another. Rayner (1975) reported a 'before-and-after' study of personal injury accidents at 38 sites in the Greater London Area which were converted from zebra to pelican crossings. Some facilities were simply converted, others were also relocated to a new position on the street. In general, pedestrian accidents on the crossings were reduced after conversion. Rayner suggested that improved anti-skid surfacing could have had a major effect on this reduction. However pedestrian accidents within 50 metres of the crossing were dramatically increased at sites not relocated by more than 15 metres. Rayner found these results 'disappointing' and suggested that the novelty value of the new crossings could have distracted road users.

Pillai (1975b) has presented a method for calculating signal cycle times for pelican crossings which are installed as replacements for zebra facilities. Signal settings are based on field observations of local conditions and thus crossings can be adapted to a variety of locations with different road user characteristics.

Accident risk. A remaining topic discussed in the literature on pedestrian crossing facilities concerns the assessment of accident risk. The national casualty statistics cited earlier concerning the numbers of casualties on or near crossings give no clue as to their relevance in terms of pedestrian usage. Their significance can only be assessed by relating pedestrian accident figures on or near crossings to the number of pedestrians observed on the crossings or adjacent lengths of road. Relative risk (K) has been defined as a ratio where

$$K = \frac{\dfrac{\text{Accidents on crossing}}{\text{Pedestrians using crossing}}}{\dfrac{\text{Accidents within 50 yards}}{\text{Pedestrians within 50 yards}}}$$

For $K < 1$ the crossing has a lower accident rate than the road within 50 yards of the crossing, and for $K > 1$ the crossing has a higher accident rate (Mackie, 1962).

Mackie calculated the risk ratio by observing vehicle and pedestrian flows at 21 crossing sites during the summer of 1961 and obtaining relevant accident data for the period 1957 to 1960. The ratios thus derived were compared with those calculated for an earlier observation period in 1955. The mean risk ratio was 0.45 in 1955 and 0.29 in 1961 indicating the relative safety of using the crossing. The increase in relative safety from 1955 to 1961 was not statistically significant.

Risk calculations have been broadened by Garwood and Moore (1962) to include an estimate of risk at other sections of the street based on observation of seven miles of London streets. Their risk ratios in ascending order were as follows: at traffic lights, 0.17; on a zebra crossing, 0.42; 'elsewhere', 1.00; within 50 yards of a zebra crossing, 1.75; within 50 yards of traffic lights, 3.94. Hence the most dangerous portion of the street for pedestrians to cross is within 50 yards of traffic lights. A long-term assessment of risk calculated over a 10-year period from 1951 to 1961 indicated that there was no marked change in the protection provided by zebra crossings.

Spatial segregation of pedestrians and vehicles

The success of measures involving the temporal segregation of vehicles and pedestrians, reviewed in the preceding section, depends to a large extent on pedestrian and driver knowledge and observance of pedestrian priority rules. In contrast, the success of measures which accord partial or total spatial segregation involve only the usual driving skills required for adhering to the roadway.

Footpaths. The main method of partial spatial separation is the use of footpaths. Smeed (1968) had no doubt of their value. He reported that only about 5 per cent of pedestrian accidents in Britain occur on footpaths or verges, although the greater part of pedestrian travel takes place on them. The corresponding statistic for 1978 was numerically higher but was still small; 7.1 per cent of all casualties were on footpaths or verges. The percentages for children, adults of retirement age and other adults were 3.75, 7.2 and 10.2 per cent respectively. It is not known to what extent this apparent vulnerability of older pedestrians results from these individuals using footpaths more than others. In addition to these statistical studies of footpaths, empirical research has also been undertaken regarding the design criteria for pavement widths. For example, Older (1968) found that there was a linear relationship between pedestrian speed and density—except at high densities (above 3.2 persons per metre squared) where the curve flattened out representing no pedestrian movement. The maximum flow observed was 75.5 persons per metre width per minute and occurred when the density was 1.9 persons per metre squared. In these conditions the average walking speed was 0.64 metres per second. A progressive reduction was found in the speed range—from 0.9 metres per second at low densities to 0.15 metres per second at a density of 3.2 persons per metre squared or more. A considerable restriction on the observed range of speed was found for densities over 2.2 persons per metre squared. Amongst others, Barrett (1972) has also discussed pedestrian flow rate. He reported that at densities between 1.4 and 3.2 persons per metre squared slowing down occurred, and between 3.2 and 5.4 persons per metre squared shuffling was observed with complete jamming at concentrations above 5.4 persons per metre squared. Both Older and Barrett have commented on the effects of 'streaming': a phenomenon whereby pedestrians travelling in the same direction tend to follow one another in files which interweave with those coming from the opposite direction. On a two-way footpath a small counterflow reduces the capacity of a footway by approximately 15 per cent (Barrett, 1972), but when the flows are more equally balanced the capacity loss is only 4 per cent. The friction or interaction between the two flows is reduced because of the development of 'streaming'. Barrett suggested that friction is also reduced by the tendency for pedestrians to keep to the right. Stepping into the roadway is another strategy for maintaining speed. Collis (1975) noted that this strategy is adopted at densities exceeding 1 person per metre squared and he suggested that 'tolerance density' varies with pavement width; the optimum for capacity maximization is 3 metres. As one would expect the presence of shop windows and other 'distractions' also influences pedestrian speed. Older (1968) reported a reduction in flow per unit width of 15 to 20 per cent at a site with shop windows. This reduction was equivalent to a 60 centimetre reduction in pavement width.

Pedestrian refuges.   Another partial segregation measure is the provision of pedestrian refuges. A *refuge* is a small raised area in the centre of the roadway bounded by kerb stones and is usually marked by bollards warning vehicles to keep to either side of the refuge. *Centre strips* are also raised kerbed areas placed down the centre of the carriageway, but they differ from refuges in that they form a continuous strip which is broken only to allow vehicular access to side turnings on the other side of the road. Pedestrian casualties on refuges and centre strips accounted for 0.3 per cent of all casualties in Britain in 1978. Research on pedestrian refuges is sparse in comparison with investigations of other road-level crossing facilities. Sites with refuges have sometimes been incorporated into studies of unaided road crossing behaviour (e.g. Grayson, 1975b) and into investigations of crossing facilities with and without the refuge facility (Inwood and Grayson, 1979); but relatively little attention has been directed towards refuges *per se*. Smeed (1968) indicated the possible importance of refuges by suggesting that since controlled and uncontrolled pedestrian crossings delay traffic, refuges separating the traffic lanes will often be more satisfactory than pedestrian crossings with regard to pedestrian delay. They may also be important from the relative safety point of view. For example, refuges account for 0.3 per cent of pedestrian casualties whereas the corresponding figure for pedestrian crossings is 8.2 per cent. It may be that this lower rate for refuges represents either relatively little usage or low numbers of these installations. On the other hand, it may be that refuges are relatively safe crossing places. However, in a 'before-and-after' study of 101 refuges at and away from junctions, Lalani (1977) presented evidence to the contrary: the provision of refuges increased pedestrian accidents but reduced vehicle accidents. Lalani, like Smeed, concluded that refuges are provided for pedestrian convenience rather than road safety, but Lalani added that this provision may be at the expense of pedestrian safety.

Pedestrian bridges and subways. Pedestrian bridges and subways are interventions which give complete protection against road traffic through the total segregation of vehicles and pedestrians. However, this major advantage is undermined by the observation that pedestrians choose the unsafe route at road level, preferring convenience to road safety and minimizing danger of assault in subways. The Department of Scientific and Industrial Research (1963) reported the results of a UK investigation of pedestrian flow before and after the building of a subway. It was found that the main effect of the subway was to divert underground those pedestrians whose original path followed the line of the subway and whose journey times were barely increased. The amount of additional time pedestrians are prepared to occupy in using a safe route has received comment from several authors (Department of Scientific and Industrial Research, 1963; Garwood and Moore, 1962; Garwood and Tanner, 1956). Apparently 100 per cent usage of a bridge is likely to be observed when the bridge journey typically takes no more than three-quarters of the time required for the ground-level crossing. However, 100 per cent usage of a subway is likely when there is a much smaller time saving. Garwood and Moore suggested that where possible guard-rails should be installed to discourage street-level crossings or, more radically, pedestrian pavements should be raised above the ground to first-floor level and a series of bridges installed. Another factor which may discourage pedestrians from using subway crossings is the unattractive design features of stark ramps and tunnels and the consequent risk to pedestrians of being assaulted on segregated walkways especially at night (Antoniou, 1971). In this regard, streets carrying traffic are relatively safe in comparison with a deserted walkway.

Pedestrian areas. A more radical scheme than the provision of bridges and subways is the introduction of pedestrian areas. These comprise central shopping areas of towns and cities which are closed to traffic and achieve total segregation of vehicles and pedestrians on a large scale. Pedestrian areas can be either covered streets (usually purpose-built shopping centres) or existing open-air streets which have been closed to traffic or 'walk-in' office-blocks and small and large shops. We are not concerned here to provide a comprehensive overview of the many aspects of pedestrianization: this would incorporate, for example, architectural, sociological, engineering and economic factors. The reader is referred to Brambilla and Longo (1977) for a broader discussion of the planning, management and evaluation of pedestrian zones in particular North American and European cities. We seek to draw attention to just some of the ideas behind, and research into, pedestrianization of urban areas.

The function of a pedestrian precinct is to discourage or prohibit the use of private vehicles. Success, however, is dependent on solving the problems of transporting workers, shoppers and residents from the suburbs to and from the city, and making adequate provision for the delivery of goods. Moore and Older (1965) outlined two methods of achieving pedestrian and vehicle segregation: by the development of precincts in which pedestrians move at ground level and with vehicle access at the perimeter; or by elevating pedestrian travel to first-floor level and beyond as necessary (e.g. Nottingham and North American malls). Frequently the two methods are combined providing shops on two levels and more. Moore and Older traced the idea of the split-level segregated town to Leonardo da Vinci who specified that the high level roads were not to be used by vehicles but were solely for the convenience of 'gentlefolk'.

In practice the difficulties of segregating traffic can be formidable, especially in old towns and cities. For example, the creation of a pedestrian precinct may result in an undesirable increase in the amount of traffic on the surrounding streets, or it may not always be possible to provide adequate access to the pedestrian area for goods vehicles. The latter has been identified as a relatively intractable problem, particularly for establishments such as furniture stores and banks in transporting large heavy items and valuables (Brambilla and Longo, 1977). Integration of pedestrians and vehicles in pedestrian precincts can be more easily achieved in new towns or suburban areas where these facilities can be incorporated with all the other services from the beginning of the planning stage for the whole district. However, the problems of access for goods vehicles may still remain. One solution is to develop areas in which pedestrians have priority but certain vehicles are permitted to enter. These may include buses, taxis, vehicles for the disabled, goods and emergency vehicles. Some pedestrian areas allow access to some or all of these classes of vehicle, but even so access for commerical vehicles is restricted to particular times of the day (cf. Organisation for Economic Co-operation and Development, 1977).

The specific items of street furniture required in and around a pedestrian precinct have been the subject of discussion (e.g. Organisation for Economic Co-operation and Development, 1977). The OECD (1977) has pointed out that inside precincts the function of physical installations is to make areas attractive to pedestrians and to show clearly that the areas are (primarily) for *pedestrians*, especially if goods and emergency vehicles have access. The OECD suggests that these functions can be achieved by the provision of uniform, level, street surfacing (i.e. having no raised pavements), good lighting, specific directional signs for pedestrians and the inclusion of items such as seating, fountains or vegetation, for example. In precincts where limited vehicular access is permitted discontinuity in the road surface at the perimeter of the precinct would serve to alert drivers to the special nature of the street that they are about to enter. This continuity can be achieved by changing the texture of the road surface, or by installing small ramps. In addition, suitable signs prohibiting private cars and removable barriers or widely spaced blocks might be used as a deterrent to private vehicles whilst permitting the entry of emergency and goods vehicles. These and other planning ideas have been discussed more fully elsewhere (e.g. Boeminghaus, 1978; Brambilla and Longo, 1977; Ritter, 1964).

Attempts have been made to evaluate pedestrianization schemes (e.g. Brambilla and Longo, 1977; May and Westland, 1979; Organisation for Economic Co-operation and Development, 1974, 1977). The aim of a study by May and Westland was to evaluate European projects which laid emphasis on the more efficient use of existing systems through low-cost improvements. Among the projects studied were 16 which were concerned with pedestrianization of streets in various cities. One scheme, in Skövde, Sweden, involved the closure of selected streets to private vehicles by means of road signs at certain locations. The effects of these closures on retail sales were evaluated from 1970 to 1975 and compared with average Swedish data. Stores of various types showed increased sales, but food and 'heavy article' shops showed decreased sales. In general, disapproval of the scheme was reported by shopkeepers, including some of those who had experienced improved sales. A project in Mainz in the Federal Republic of Germany monitored accident rates in relation to the development of an extensive pedestrian zone which included fringe garages for parking. The closure of several streets to all vehicular traffic was undertaken between 1954 and 1974. Accidents and injuries were reported to have decreased by 15 and 25 per cent respectively between 1971 and 1975 despite an increase in car ownership of 18 per cent during the same period. Other projects reviewed by May and Westland related to combined priorities for pedestrians and buses. For example, wall-to-wall paving was installed in Trier, in the Federal Republic of Germany, and this paving was shared by pedestrians and buses. Results indicated that the number of pedestrians increased, the safety record increased and bus patronage increased slightly. A British project in London involved closure to cars of one of the main shopping streets in London: *viz.* Oxford Street. The reconstructed roadway was shared by pedestrians, buses and taxis. Not surprisingly, it was found that while the bus service, safety and environmental conditions improved, increased delays were incurred by the diverted traffic.

Whilst May and Westland were concerned only with low-cost schemes, other studies have evaluated pedestrian schemes of both low and high cost (cf.

Brambilla and Longo, 1977; Organisation for Economic Co-operation and Development, 1974). Successes included increased retail sales, increased pedestrian flow, reduced air and noise pollution levels, and merchant and citizen approval. Some schemes have been more successful than others, however. Complaints included: inadequate parking and eating facilities; poor appearance of the stores; increased vandalism; and disapproval of experimental 'street happenings'. The accident rates were sometimes studied: in some towns no change was reported, and in others overall improvements were found. In general, however, studies paid scant attention to safety factors. A full discussion of the problems encountered in evaluating schemes in terms of their accident rates is found in Grayson and Howarth (Chapter 4).

Thus far in our discussion of pedestrian zones we have considered only town and city centres. Clearly, pedestrianization is not confined to shopping areas; residential areas have also been subject to such treatment. However, our discussion of limited vehicular access to *residential* areas is postponed until the next section. Our concern in this present section has been to restrict our field of enquiry to environmental measures which affect the pedestrian more than other road users, and these include city centre pedestrian precincts.

ENVIRONMENTAL INTERVENTIONS: MEASURES AFFECTING ROAD USERS IN GENERAL

Environmental measures which affect all types of road user to varying degrees include limited vehicular access, road layout, speed control humps and types of road surfacing. We open our discussion by describing methods of limiting vehicular access to residential areas. These methods may be grouped into two broad categories: *large-scale* measures which are introduced during the planning stage; and *small-scale* interventions suitable for treating established areas.

Large-scale measures

Earlier we discussed the association between residential areas and child pedestrian accidents (See p. 241). Several measures we now describe have been designed with particular regard to the special vulnerability of the child at play in residential areas. The *cul-de-sac* and the *Radburn estate* layout are two examples of large-scale limited-access measures which are incorporated into the design of residential areas at the planning stage. A cul-de-sac is a road (system) having just one end open to vehicles and housing arranged around three sides. The idea of the Radburn estate was first adopted in Radburn, California, from which the name is derived. The chief characteristics of the system are the control of the entry and movement of motor vehicles, and the provision of an entirely separate footpath system for pedestrians. Vehicle control is achieved, for example, by a series of culs-de-sac terminating in garage courts which are surrounded on three sides by housing. Private gardens lie between

the backs of the houses and the culs-de-sac, and on the fronts of the houses
there are open spaces, grassed or planted, with footpaths giving access to the
dwellings. In these areas there is also play space for children. The culs-de-sac
are linked to peripheral distributor roads giving direct vehicular access to each
dwelling.

The relative impacts of culs-de-sac, Radburn and conventional estates have
been estimated from road user behaviour and residents' views. Miller and Cook
(1967) compared Radburn and conventional layouts on a number of dimensions,
including perceived safety, convenience and vehicle noise. The interiors of the
Radburn estates were considered by residents to be safe for pedestrian movement
and children at play, but it was observed that safety factors were sacrificed for
convenience in the actual use of amenities: adult shoppers used the most direct
route whether it was on the footpath, garage court or road; and children played
in the areas most attractive to them. In many instances the culs-de-sac were
used for play purposes, possibly because of the attraction of paved surfaces
and/or because parents could keep small children in sight from the kitchen
windows overlooking these areas. The opinion of the majority of residents was
that these courts were not suitable as children's play areas but were safer than
conventional roads.

As well as *perceived* safety, the *actual* safety of the cul-de-sac in terms of
accident rates has been studied (e.g. Bennett, 1969; Bennett and Marland, 1978).
In a study of 9 British towns Bennett found that accident rates in culs-de-sac
for all age groups were substantially less than the national average. The rate
for adults was 1.5 per cent of the national average; for children under 10 years
it was 17 per cent; and for children under 5 years it was 29 per cent of the
national average. These findings were reinforced in a later study by Bennett
and Marland. They investigated a sample of 9,003 residential streets in 257
conventional local authority estates in 20 British towns. Among the variables
studied were accident rates, vehicle density, use of the street as a bus route,
the number of streets opening onto other streets, street length and the age
structure of the population living in the study areas. Far fewer pedestrian
accidents were found to occur in culs-de-sac than in other types of residential
street. Calculated as a percentage of accidents on all residential roads, accidents
in culs-de-sac represented 7 per cent for adults, 17 per cent for all children and
33 per cent for children under 5 years of age. Both studies pointed to the relative
safety of culs-de-sac and upheld the view expressed by Radburn estate residents
that their environment is safer than the conventional street layout (i.e. streets
carrying 'through' traffic, affording frontage access to dwellings).

Small-scale measures

The protected environment of the culs-de-sac can be mimicked in already-
established areas in a variety of ways. For example, in Denmark special *play*

streets have been set up in areas where other possibilities for creating adequate play areas are insufficient. The only distinction between play streets and other streets is the legal provision that children may use the road for play purposes and that drivers are not permitted unless they have a destination in the street. However, these restrictions have been difficult to enforce and the measure has not met with popular support from local authorities (cf. Organisation for Economic Co-operation and Development, 1977). A number of cities throughout Europe, for example, have used small-scale self-enforcing devices to control vehicle intrusion into residential areas. These have included *narrowing of the carriageway*, introducing *speed control humps*, the placement of obstacles such as *bollards, chicanes* and *vegetation* (so that vehicles must drive around them slowly), and *abolishing raised pavements* (to emphasize the shared nature of the street).

Kraay (1976) has studied the effect of the combination of several small-scale measures in the *residential yards* of Delft, Holland, by investigating child pedestrian/vehicle conflicts. The 'yards' are residential streets which have been completely paved, and in which obstacles such as vegetation and bollards have been introduced. The paved areas, used by all types of road user, are for diverse activities such as walking, driving, cycling, parking and playing. In comparison with a conventional residential area, a neighbourhood incorporating residential yards was found to have more frequent and more serious child pedestrian/vehicle conflicts. Furthermore, despite the expectations of the planners, the speed of traffic in the residential yards was not reduced relative to traffic in the conventional streets. However, reporting on a visit made to this same city, Dalby and Williamson (1977) noted contradictory, but optimistic, findings: they reported that traffic had been discouraged from using 'treated' streets, and had slowed down in these streets.

On a similarly optimistic note, the success of small-scale measures has been reported in a British study undertaken by the Transport and Road Research Laboratory (1979). In this study street layouts had been modified to reduce or eliminate the extent to which traffic penetrated residential areas: the modifications included street barriers, carriageway narrowing, operation of one-way traffic, and sharp changes in the horizontal and vertical curvature and in the surface texture of the road. A consistent reduction was reported in both the road accident figures within a treated area and at the perimeter distributor roads.

One of the small-scale measures, speed control humps, has received particular research attention. Experimental speed control humps were installed for a period of one year on five public residential roads in different British towns (Sumner and Baguley, 1978, 1979a,b; Summer, Burton and Baguley, 1978). At all the sites traffic flow was reduced; the mean reduction was 37 per cent ranging from 13 to 64 per cent. Substantial speed reductions were found at all the sites. For example, at the site which showed the largest speed reduction, there was a drop of 25 kilometres per hour from 62 kilometres per hour to 37 kilometres per hour.

Residents' opinions of the installations were favourable: 84 per cent thought the humps served a useful purpose and 82 per cent were in favour of retaining the humps on their road. Of the drivers who continued to use the road during the period the humps were installed, 55 per cent favoured their retention. The effect of the measure was assessed by comparing expected and actual casualty rates for all road accidents: a significant decrease in casualty rates was noted during the period the humps were installed. The rates for the surrounding roads along which traffic was most likely to have been diverted showed a small but non-significant increase. Specific changes in pedestrian behaviour were reported; for example, kerb delays were reduced and safety gaps (the time between a pedestrian crossing the road and the next oncoming vehicle) were increased. It was noted that pedestrians often used the humps as crossing points. Overall, the speed control humps were successful in improving the pedestrian environment, specifically by reducing the flow and speed of road traffic through residential areas.

The focus of many of these small-scale interventions has not necessarily been upon safety factors. Rather, the emphasis has been upon improving the environment for pedestrians by introducing the idea that in residential districts vehicles should be seen as intruders rather than be accorded automatic priority (cf. International Federation of Pedestrians, 1973; Organisation for Economic Co-operation and Development, 1977). There are pragmatic reasons for the lack of emphasis on the safety aspects of various schemes. One explanation lies in the nature of pedestrian accidents in residential areas: within any one residential estate a pedestrian accident is a rare event. Consequently it may not be possible to evaluate in terms of accident rates the effects of measures introduced by local authorities until a period of years has elapsed. Hence the influence of various schemes has been assessed in terms of road user opinion and behaviour rather than relying solely on accident rates to establish the criteria for success. This approach contrasts with the strategy of introducing changes at particular sites which are known to be locations for accidents. This strategy, known as 'blackspot' treatment, is more appropriate on arterial roads carrying large volumes of traffic, where the benefit of interventions can be assessed over a relatively short period of time. A detailed discussion of the strategy and success of 'blackspot' remedial measures can be found in Kelly and Huddart (1977). (See also Chapter 4).

Our aim in the preceding sections of this chapter has been to outline some of the ways in which pedestrian movement is influenced by the nature of the physical environment. It must not be overlooked that features of the pedestrian's environment are shaped to a large extent by those who design, construct and modify the central and residential districts of cities and towns. We turn now to factors which influence those who make decisions concerning urban transport—an area of policy which includes bus and rail networks, road building and all public and private community transportation facilities.

FACTORS INFLUENCING THE TOWN BUILDERS

In earlier sections of this chapter we have described environmental installations which have been introduced in a number of towns and cities. The implementation of urban transport policies incorporating such facilities rests ultimately with those in control of central and local government. It is these individuals—the town builders—who most directly mould the pedestrian's environment. The aim of this section is to trace some of the factors which influence the urban transportation decision makers. This goal is pursued by (i) identifying the interested parties, (ii) determining the major locations of power within a community, and (iii) outlining some of the major influences on these individuals with special regard to their concept of 'the town'.

The identification of those interested in urban transportation is in a manner of speaking simple but controversial. People from every sphere of life have an interest in urban transport policy. Controversy arises because laypersons profess expertise on matters which professional traffic engineers feel they themselves are better placed to judge. Liebbrand (1970) claimed to speak for traffic engineers generally when he said 'especially harmful is the universally held opinion that traffic is so simple and obvious that every man knows enough about it from his own observation to enable him to pronounce a sure judgement on traffic questions' (p. 2). Liebbrand viewed the role of the traffic engineer as the specialist consultant who suggests sound urban transport policies based on scientific handling of the traffic problems. He contrasted this approach with inefficient, amateur strategies based on political expediency.

It may already be evident from this discussion that there is a degree of polarization between the professional engineer and the community politician. A similar division in the *location of power* has been identified by Grant (1977) in a British study of the politics of urban transport planning. The major sets of participants comprised the City Council, the members of which are part-time and unpaid, the salaried officers of the departments concerned with transport planning and community groups. Community groups are generally of two types: they are either protest groups or they are established bodies such as the Chamber of Commerce. In general the latter type of group favours the construction of new roads.

Grant identified two *basic approaches* to urban transportation: the 'traditional' approach which defines the major problem as vehicle movement and usually prescribes the provision of additional highway space; and the 'non-traditional' approach which advocates the improvement of public transport and stresses the inefficiency of private vehicles in their use of scarce fuel and land resources. He suggested that a major negative influence on the plans advocated by City Council engineers is their traditionally-based training: a town is viewed as a functional unit which operates in a calculable manner. It is based on estimating demand for movement rather than emphasizing aesthetic features: the emphasis is not upon creating wide green irregular-shaped spaces which might attract pedestrians; rather, the view is taken that the more built-up an area is, and the greater the utilization in terms of multi-storey buildings, the more traffic there is. Liebbrand (1973) gave a more detailed example of the functional view. He calculated the proportion of space necessary for the flow of traffic by taking into account several factors. For example, his 'pavement factor' in a main shopping area assumed 1,200 shoppers per hour per hectare which represented 2 per cent of pavement in the total area. Calculations for his 'roadway' factor were based on traffic density per hectare per hour and gave the percentage of space needed based on the number of blocks comprising an area. Town layout was another important factor: the maximum capacity of a road network is achieved with a grid-type of layout. Each deviation in shape from the regularity of the grid pattern reduces the capacity of the street network for which compensation must be made by increasing the roadway factor. These examples illustrate the functional approach to planning adopted by some 'traditional' engineers.

This approach is, of course, not the only one. In an introductory text on transportation planning, Bruton (1970) expressed the opinion that, although the use of techniques for estimating future demands for movement are necessary, it is of greater importance to address problems associated with route selection and with the establishment of community goals and objectives. Reviewing citizen participation in the transportation planning process, Hamilton (1977) noted that since the early 1960s there has been a growing trend to question decisions previously accepted as the prerogative of a few elite planners and engineers who ostensibly represented the interest of the whole community. He observed that project design staff at all levels of government are becoming increasingly frustrated by the presumably well-meant attempts of citizens to modify or defeat a growing number of projects, feelings which echo those expressed by Liebbrand (1970). On a more optimistic note, Hamilton reported that, despite the initial higher costs of planning strategies which incorporate citizen participation, the cost effectiveness of the implementation will also be much greater. Furthermore, he suggested that increased citizen involvement is likely to produce plans which are better suited to their own expressed needs. Ultimately, of course, it is the citizens who are intended to benefit most from the various plans. Hamilton concluded that citizen participation is now expected, and hence it is no longer possible for professionals simply to offer advice on a 'take it or leave it' basis, since it is likely to be 'left' as a result of pressures exerted on politicians with whom the ultimate decision rests. The practical problems of formally involving the public in the formulation of broad transportation policy have been addressed by Gregory and Robbins (1975). They reported the results of a large-scale British survey undertaken by Southampton City Council: a questionnaire, completed by 9,862 individuals, was designed to gauge public opinion on several issues including the acceptability of traffic restraint measures, the desirability of major new road construction, and the acceptability of bus priority schemes. They found little evidence of laypersons holding consistent policies: for example, about 15 per cent of those who were against major road-building went on to recommend the allocation of money to dual carriageways and motorways. A feature of the sampling method was that a proportion of questionnaires was administered to a random sample of subjects by interviewers. An extensive advertising campaign alerted the general public to the fact that copies of the questionnaire were also available for those who wished to participate. Copies could be obtained directly from the City Council or from outlets such as public libraries, shopping centres, etc. The results from the random sample were compared with a self-selected group who voluntarily returned the questionnaires by post. In contrast to the interview sample, respondents from the 'self-selected' group placed a greater emphasis on car restraint and bus priority, and less on road construction. However, taking the results of the survey as a whole, there was majority support for major new road construction, no reported nuisance value from road traffic in residential areas, and only moderate support for restricting the free use of cars in the city. Gregory and Robbins suggested that the findings of their study indicated the danger of relying on pressure groups and the more vocal sections of society for an assessment of public opinion.

In contrast to the results of the Southampton survey, the view adopted by the Environment Ministers of member countries of the Organisation for Economic Co-operation and Development (Anonymous, 1975a) takes the argument even further from the traditional approach. Their corporate opinion was that towns are 'better' with less traffic so long as adequate provision is made for the mobility of workers, residents and goods. It was urged that provision be made for those who do not have direct access to a private car (e.g. children, the elderly and the handicapped) and that measures be adopted to facilitate the safety and mobility of pedestrians and cyclists. In contrast to the traditional engineering strategy of creating more roads, the ministers advocated the introduction of measures to reduce the use of private cars and increase the use of alternative forms of transport. High on their priority list was the introduction of pedestrianization schemes to improve the environment and safety of pedestrians.

To summarize, we have seen that 'traditional' measures or urban planning have tended to favour the motorist at the expense of the pedestrian. This is because traffic engineers, many of whom have been traditionally trained, have taken a leading role in decisions affecting the style of urban construction. Increasingly the power of the engineers has been challenged and citizens' groups have exerted pressure on the politicians by voicing protest against narrow, traffic-oriented views. Their protests have been heeded to the extent that senior politicians have allied themselves to the non-traditional, environmentally-oriented approach. However, there is some evidence to suggest that these protests may not represent the view of the majority: the majority, although usually silent, supports the traditional traffic-oriented view. The degree to which local politicians can reconcile these views, remains to be seen, but it is these local politicians who most directly control the nature of the pedestrian's environment.

CONCLUSIONS

Our concern in this chapter has been to discuss the influence of the physical environment on the pedestrian. Whilst particular attention has been focused upon pedestrian accident rates, other important aspects of the physical environment have also been discussed which relate to the general quality of the pedestrian environment. These include pedestrian and driver behaviour, pedestrian and driver opinion, and vehicle speed and density. Some of the brighter prospects for reducing the accident rates have been identified. Thus, with regard to children, a major area of concern is the number of accidents which occur out of school hours in residential streets close to the child's home. The layout of residential streets is a major factor influencing child pedestrian accidents, and small-scale interventions in established areas have successfully restricted vehicle access, speed and flow: accident rates have then declined. Hence, it seems that the environmental measures most likely to affect child pedestrian accidents are those measures which force drivers to reduce their speed and acknowledge the presence of children in the child's own and neighbouring streets.

Environmental measures which might radically affect adult pedestrian accident rates are less easily discerned. Adult accidents tend to occur on major roads, and the effects of alcohol, inclement weather and darkness have also been isolated as important variables. (Of course, these are variables which are difficult to moderate through any single environmental measure). A number of installations has been found to affect the quality of the pedestrian's environment in a general sense, and some of them also have consequences for safety. The 7 per cent decrease in all pedestrian casualties which occurred when zebras were first installed has been attributed to the introduction of zebra crossings. Zebras have also been shown to be safe crossing places relative to other sections of the street. Evaluation studies of pelican crossings undertaken so far have indicated the limited success of these installations. Some savings in accidents have been reported at pelican crossings converted from zebras whereas an increase in accidents has been found along the lengths of road within 50 metres of the crossings. In addition pedestrian criticism of the crossings has been reported with regard to the meaning of the signals, the time allowed for crossing, and driver abuse of the crossings: these are factors which have consequences for safety.

Whilst the safety value of pavements along major roads is not questioned, there is doubt about the safety of pedestrian refuges. Studies have indicated that although they increase pedestrian convenience, this may be at the expense of pedestrian safety. Measures which ensure maximum pedestrian safety are bridges and subways. However, the extent of their use is determined by the degree of inconvenience to which the potential user is subject.

City centre pedestrianization schemes are intended to discourage the use of private vehicles whilst ensuring adequate access for goods and emergency vehicles. Evaluation of pedestrian areas has embraced many variables; for example, retail sales, pedestrian flow, vehicle delay, air and noise pollution, trader and citizen opinion, and safety factors. The diversity of these variables illustrates the nature of pedestrianization schemes: the emphasis has been on improving many aspects of the city environment of which safety is but one.

Ultimately, the introduction of any of these measures rests on political initiative rather than the 'proven' success or otherwise of the various installations. Even where the safety value of a measure is strongly indicated decisions concerning its implementation are based on many factors: pedestrian safety is by no means always the prime objective.

REFERENCES

Anonymous (1975a). Better towns with less traffic: Report of the Organisation for Economic Co-operation and Development Conference, Paris, April. *Traffic Engineering and Control*, **16**, 287–292.

Anonymous (1975b). GLC to press for longer crossing time at pelicans. *Traffic Engineering and Control*, **16**, 343.

Antoniou, J. (1971). Planning for pedestrians. *Traffic Quarterly*, **25**, 55–71.

Barrett, R. (1972). Moving pedestrians in a traffic-free environment. *Traffic Engineering and Control*, **14**, 235–238.

Bennett, G. T. (1969). Pedestrian accidents in culs-de-sac. *Journal of the Institute of Highway Engineers*, **16**, 23–25.

Bennett, G. T., and Marland, J. (1978). Road accidents in traditionally designed local authority estates. *Department of the Environment, Transport and Road Research Laboratory, Supplementary Report 394*. Crowthorne: TRRL.

Biehl, B. M., Older, S. J., and Griep, D. J. (1969). *Pedestrian Safety*. Paris: Organisation for Economic Co-operation and Development.

Boeminghaus, D. (1978). *Pedestrian Areas*. Stuttgart: Karl Krämer.

Brambilla, R., and Longo, G. (1977). *For Pedestrians Only*. New York: Whitney Library of Design.

Bruce, S., and Skelton, N. (1977). Pedestrian-vehicle conflict at pelican crossings. In *Proceedings of the Planning and Transport Research Computation Company, Summer Annual Meeting*, PTCR P–152, 26–34. Warwick, June.

Bruton, M. J. (1970). *Introduction to Transportation Planning*. London: Hutchinson Educational.

Clayton, A. B. (1973). Alcohol and adult pedestrian fatalities. In *Proceedings of the American Association for Automotive Medicine*. November. Oklahoma City.

Clayton, A. B., Booth, A. C., and McCarthy, P. E. (1977). A controlled study of the role of alcohol in fatal adult pedestrian accidents. *Department of the Environment, Transport and Road Research Laboratory, Supplementary Report 332*. Crowthorne: TRRL.

Collis, R. E. (1975). A possible design criterion for pavement width. *Traffic Engineering and Control*, **16**, 124–125.

Cresswell, C. (1978). Pedestrian crossing facilities. *Unpublished Doctoral Dissertation*, University College Cardiff, United Kingdom.

Cresswell, C., Griffiths, J. D., and Hunt, J. G. (1978). Site evaluation of a pelican crossing simulation model. *Traffic Engineering and Control*, **19**, 546–549.

Cresswell, C., and Hunt, J. G. (1978). Site evaluation of a zebra crossing simulation model. *Traffic Engineering and Control*, **20**, 467–470 and 474.

Dalby, E., and Williamson, A. E. (1977). Pedestrian and traffic management techniques in Delft. *Department of the Environment, Transport and Road Research Laboratory, Supplementary Report 257*. Crowthorne: TRRL.

Department of Scientific and Industrial Research (1963). *Research on Road Safety*. London: Her Majesty's Stationery Office.

Department of Transport (1980). *Road Accidents Great Britain 1978*. London: Her Majesty's Stationery Office.

England, E. (1976). Children's strategies for road crossing in an urban environment. *Unpublished Master of Science Dissertation*. Salford: University of Salford, United Kingdom.

Firth, D. E. (1979). Children's use of crossing facilities. *Traffic Education*, **4**, 18–20.

Garwood, F., and Moore, R. L. (1962). Pedestrian accidents. *Traffic Engineering and Control*, **4**, 274–276 and 279.

Garwood, F., and Tanner, J. C. (1956). Accident studies before and after road changes. In *Final Report of the Public Works Municipal Services Congress*, 329–354. London, November.

Grant, J. (1977). *The Politics of Urban Transport Planning*. London: Earth Resources Research.

Grayson, G. B. (1975a). The Hampshire child pedestrian accident study. *Department of the Environment, Transport and Road Research Laboratory, Laboratory Report 668*. Crowthorne: TRRL.

Grayson, G. B. (1975b). Observations of pedestrian behaviour at four sites. *Department of the Environment, Transport and Road Research Laboratory, Laboratory Report 670*. Crowthorne: TRRL.

Gregory, W. R., and Robbins, J. (1975). Your city—your choice: a public opinion survey for Southampton City. *Traffic Engineering and Control*, **16**, 64–67.

Griffiths, J. D., and Cresswell, C. (1976). A mathematical model of a pelican crossing. *Journal of the Institute of Mathematics Applications*, **18**, 381–394.

Griffiths, J. D., Hunt, J. G., and Cresswell, C. (1976). Warrants for zebra and pelican crossings using a minimum waiting cost criterion. *Traffic Engineering and Control*, **17**, 59–62.

Hamilton, G. D. (1977). Citizen participation in the transportation planning process: a review. *Transportation Engineering*, **47**, 32–36.

International Federation of Pedestrians (1973). Visits to Delft and Utrecht. *Third Congress of the International Federation of Pedestrians*. September. Scheveningen.

Inwood, J., and Grayson, G. B. (1979). The comparative safety of pedestrian crossings. *Department of the Environment, Transport and Road Research Laboratory, Laboratory Report 895*. Crowthorne: TRRL.

Kelly, M. S., and Huddart, K. W. (1977). The uses made of accident statistics by the Greater London Council. In *Proceedings of the Planning and Transport Research Computation Company. Summer Annual Meeting*, PTRC P-132, 208–221. June. Warwick.

Kraay, J. H. (1976). Urban planning, pedestrians and road safety. In A. S. Hakkert (Ed.), *Proceedings of the International Conference on Pedestrian Safety*, Volume 1, 3C1–3C9. Haifa: Michlol.

Lalani, N. (1977). Road safety at pedestrian refuges. *Traffic Engineering and Control*, **18**, 429–431.

Liebbrand, K. (1970). *Transportation and Town Planning*. London: Leonard Hill.

Liebbrand, K. (1973). Factors in town planning. *Traffic Engineering and Control*, **14**, 424–427.

Mackie, A. M., (1962). Accident risk to pedestrians on and within 50 yards of zebra crossings. *Traffic Engineering and Control*, **4**, 448–450.

Mackie, A. M., and Jacobs, G. D. (1965). Comparison of road user behaviour at panda, zebra and light-controlled crossings. *Traffic Engineering and Control*, **6**, 714–718 and 732.

Massey, S. A. (1962). Mathematical determination of warrants for pedestrian crossings. *Traffic Engineering*, **32**, 19–21.

May A. D., and Westland, D. (1979). Transportation system management. *Supplement to Traffic Engineering and Control*, **20**.

Miller, A., and Cook, J. A. (1967). Radburn estates revisited. Report of a user study. *The Architects' Journal*, **146**, 1075–1082.

Miller, F. D., and Michael, H. L. (1964). A study of school crossing protection. *Traffic Safety Research Review*, **8**, 51–56.

Moore, R. L., and Older, S. J. (1965). Pedestrians and motor vehicles are compatible in today's world. *Traffic Engineering*, **35**, 20–23 and 52–59.

Organisation for Economic Co-operation and Development (OECD) (1974). *Streets for People*. Paris: OECD.

Organisation for Economic Co-operation and Development (OECD) Special Research Group on Pedestrian Safety (1977). Chairman's Report and Report of Sub-Group I. The Pedestrian's Road Environment. *UK Department of the Environment, Transport and Road Research Laboratory*. Crowthorne: TRRL.

Older, S. J. (1968). Movement of pedestrians on footways in shopping streets. *Traffic Engineering and Control*, **10**, 160–163.

Older, S. J., and Basden, J. M. (1961). Road user behaviour at a pedestrian crossing. *Traffic Engineering and Control*, **3**, 94–97.

Pillai, K. S. (1975a). Pedestrian crossings. 1. Warrants for different types of pedestrian crossing based on delay to vehicles. *Traffic Engineering and Control*, **16**, 118–120.

Pillai, K. S. (1975b). Pedestrian crossings. 2. A method to design cycle time for signal-controlled pedestrian crossings. *Traffic Engineering and Control*, **16**, 120–121.

Preston, B. (1972). Statistical analysis of child pedestrian accidents in Manchester and Salford. *Accidents Analysis and Prevention*, **4**, 323–332.

Rayner, D. S. (1975). Some safety considerations in the conversion of zebra crossings to pelican crossings. *Traffic Engineering and Control*, **16**, 123–124.

Read, J. H., Bradley, E. J., Morison, J. D., Lewall, D., and Clarke, D. A. (1963). The epidemiology and prevention of traffic accidents involving child pedestrians. *Canadian Medical Association Journal*, **89**, 687–701.

Ritter, P. (1964). *Planning for Man and Motor*. Oxford: Pergamon Press.

Sandels, S. (1975). *Children in Traffic*. London: Elek.

Sandels, S. (1979). Unprotected road users. A behavioural study. *The Skandia Report III*. Stockholm: Skandia.

Singer, R. E. (1963). Action for pedestrian safety and control. *International Road Safety Traffic Review*, **11**, 17–24 and 29.

Smeed, R. J. (1968). Aspects of pedestrian safety. *Journal of Transport Economics and Policy*, **2**, 255–279.

Smeed, R. J. (1977). Pedestrian accidents. In A. S. Hakkert (Ed.), *Proceedings of the International Conference on Pedestrian Safety*, Volume 2, 7–21. Haifa: Michlol.

Sumner, R., and Baguley, C. (1978). Speed control humps in Norwich and Haringey. *Department of the Environment, Transport and Road Research Laboratory, Supplementary Report 423*. Crowthorne: TRRL.

Sumner, R., and Baguley, C. (1979a). Speed control humps in Kensington and Glasgow. *Department of the Environment, Transport and Road Research Laboratory*, Supplementary Report 456. Crowthorne: TRRL.

Sumner, R., and Baguley, C. (1979b). Speed control humps on residential roads. *Department of the Environment, Transport and Road Research Laboratory, Laboratory Report 878*. Crowthorne: TRRL.

Sumner, R., Burton, J., and Baguley, C. (1978). Speed control humps in Cuddeston Way, Cowley, Oxford. *Department of the Environment, Transport and Road Research Laboratory, Supplementary Report 350*. Crowthorne: TRRL.

Transport and Road Research Laboratory (1974). Accidents in urban areas. *Department of the Environment, Transport and Road Research Laboratory, Leaflet 388*. Crowthorne: TRRL.

Transport and Road Research Laboratory (1976). Pedestrian behaviour at pelican crossings. *Department of the Environment, Transport and Road Research Laboratory, Leaflet 629*. Crowthorne: TRRL.

Transport and Road Research Laboratory (1977). Road accidents in residential areas. *Department of the Environment, Transport and Road Research Laboratory, Leaflet 650*. Crowthorne: TRRL.

Transport and Road Research Laboratory (1979). Use of area-wide measures in urban road safety. *Department of the Environment, Transport and Road Research Laboratory, Leaflet 772*. Crowthorne: TRRL.

Vuchic, V. R. (1967). Pedestrian crossing time in determining widths of signalized traffic arterials. *Transportation Science*, **1**, 224–231.

Wade, F. M., Chapman, A. J., and Foot, H. C. (1979). Child pedestrian accidents: the influence of the physical environment. *Paper presented at the International Conference on Environmental Psychology*. July. Guildford: University of Surrey.

Wade, F. M., Chapman, A. J., and Foot, H. C. (1980). The physical environment and child pedestrian accidents in the United Kingdom: A review. *Man–Environment Systems*. In the Press.

Wilson, D. G. (1980). The effects of installing an audible signal for pedestrians at a light controlled junction. *Department of the Environment, Transport and Road Research Laboratory, Laboratory Report 917*, Crowthorne: TRRL.

Pedestrian Accidents
Edited by A. J. Chapman, F. M. Wade and H. C. Foot
© 1982, John Wiley & Sons Ltd.

Chapter 9

Pedestrian Safety and the Law

C. I. Howarth and M. J. Gunn

Attempts to reduce the number of pedestrian accidents are of three types. Ergonomic and engineering measures aim to improve the physical environment so that the opportunities for accidents to occur are reduced. Legal measures provide rules governing the interaction of pedestrians and traffic, and penalties for infringement to ensure that the rules are obeyed. Exhortatory and educational measures encourage the development of appropriate skills and attitudes, so that people can cope with an environment which remains dangerous despite the efforts of the engineers and the law-makers.

Of these three approaches, legal measures change least often, evoke the least expectation, and are least often evaluated in terms of their effect on accidents. In this chapter we develop three arguments. Firstly, education, engineering and the law are complementary approaches rather than alternatives, and that in designing road safety programmes all three must be considered and evaluated in the same way. Since legal measures are also evaluated by legal arguments which extend beyond the field of pedestrian safety, this proposition needs to be considered very carefully. Secondly, in relation to child pedestrian accidents, very little can be achieved by engineering or educational methods, and the best hope of saving the lives of children is to change the legal definition of responsibility in relation to child pedestrian accidents on residential roads. Since the concept of responsibility lies at the heart of our legal system, this proposition must be justified by legal argument as well as by empirical evidence. Finally, we present evidence that, in some cases, the law impedes the proper evaluation of safety programmes. We argue that the law can be changed so as to avoid this kind of obstruction, without having any serious effect on the consistency and power of the law in other respects.

CHILD PEDESTRIAN ACCIDENTS

First of all let us justify our pessimism about the effectiveness of educational and engineering methods in reducing child pedestrian accidents. Figure 9.1 shows that these accidents occur mainly to children between the ages of 4 and 7, and that most of them occur on minor roads (Figure 9.1 also shows that at

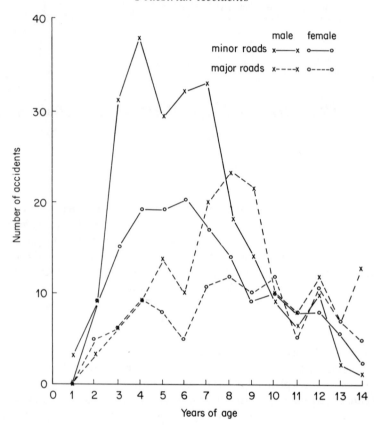

Figure 9.1   Child pedestrian accidents on major and minor roads (Nottingham, 1971–1976)

the vulnerable ages, twice as many boys as girls are involved in accidents). Grayson (1975) has found that 60 per cent of child pedestrian accidents occur within a quarter-of-a-mile of the child's home. These two pieces of information make it clear that most accidents to children occur on minor roads within a short distance of their own home. This rules out the possibility of conventional pedestrian engineering measures making any major impact on this problem. The accidents occur at widely dispersed sites, where there is a low level of both pedestrian and vehicle flow. Most accidents are isolated in that most of them occur at places where no other accidents occur. This means that the majority of the accidents occur at sites where it would be difficult to justify the use of engineering solutions, such as zebra or pelican crossings. Any attempt at an engineering solution would, in the short term, be impossibly expensive. In new housing developments a proper separation of pedestrians and traffic can be achieved at small extra cost, but in existing residential areas little can be achieved in this way.

Educational measures are equally unlikely to have much effect for quite different reasons. Studies of the behaviour of young children on the road have revealed that between the ages of five and ten their road crossing strategies change dramatically (Routledge, Repetto-Wright and Howarth, 1976). At the younger age, provided they regard the road as an obstacle at all, they adopt a very conservative strategy. They stop at the kerb, they look both ways, and cross the road only if the road is clear. In fact, they behave very much as they are taught to do by their safety education. By the age of ten, they use a very different strategy. They assess the traffic situation before they reach the kerb, and step out into the road without pausing. They do not wait for the road to be clear, but will negotiate quite small gaps in the traffic. To do this they frequently step out into the road just as a car is passing, and get as close to its rear bumper as they can manage. In fact they use the same road crossing strategy that most adults use and this is, in almost all respects, different from the one they have been taught in their safety education. It is obvious that, during their period of maximum vulnerability to road accidents, children are learning two conflicting techniques. One is taught to them in a fairly formal manner as part of their safety education. The other they learn informally from their elders, from adults and older children. It is not surprising they have so many accidents, but there is no obvious way out of the dilemma. There is no sense in which one could begin to teach adult road crossing skills to five-year-old children. It would be exceedingly dangerous to attempt it. The cautious strategies of the *Green Cross Code* and similar programmes are much more appropriate for young children, and if they are to have formal safety training it must be of this type. But there is no way in which one can prevent children learning from adults and older children, and there is no way in which one can change the way in which adults cross roads. The adult strategy is the only one which makes it possible to cross busy roads with safety. One of us (CIH) has observed children at a city centre school, who were just old enough to use the adult road crossing strategy, immediately after they had received a formal safety lesson. The children attempted to use the technique they had been taught, but this made it impossible for them to cross the road at a site which previously they had successfully negotiated every day. These formally taught techniques are appropriate for the relatively quiet roads on which, as we have seen, most of the child pedestrian accidents occur. But the pressure on children to learn adult strategies is irresistible because all children wish to be more like adults, and because the adult strategies enable them to travel farther, to go to playgrounds, visit friends, or travel independently to school.

For these reasons there is no escape from the situation in which the most vulnerable children are being taught two different and conflicting road-crossing strategies. Inevitably they interfere with each other, so that neither is practised as efficiently as it would be if children were taught only one. This puts a theoretical limit on what can be achieved by safety education, and is one of the main sources of our pessimism about educational measures. A second source of pessimism is the poor showing of educational programmes when they are empirically evaluated (see Chapter 4). No well-conducted study has ever produced a reduction in accidents of more than about 10 per cent, the best that has been claimed for the *Green Cross Code*. Some evaluations have suggested that safety education may actually increase the number of accidents, presumably by increasing exposure to traffic in the course of practising newly-acquired skills.

It is for these reasons that we see very little hope of achieving a major reduction in child pedestrian accidents by the application of either engineering or educational techniques. There is, however, one further possibility which should be considered. There is no doubt that child pedestrian accidents could be much reduced if we simply prevented children from crossing roads unattended. This measure is frequently advocated informally by the people who say 'I blame the parents', and more formally and publicly by propaganda campaigns with such slogans as 'Better under your feet than under a car'.

This approach is superficially attractive and has the advantage of shifting responsibility on to those guilt-ridden parents who have been unfortunate enough to have a child involved in a road accident. But it has no other advantages. The freedom of children to explore their environment is already so severely restricted that we tend to blame various modern ills upon it, from vandalism to the poor intellectual attainments of city-centre children, from the anomie which afflicts the residents of high-rise flats, to industrial unrest and poor economic performance. Whether we are justified in suggesting these causal connections or not, the fact that they are entertained as possibilities shows that the further restriction of children is not something which can be accepted without question, even if it would have the highly desirable result of saving their lives. Furthermore, there is reason to doubt whether purely restrictive measures would be very successful, since children in the five-year-old age-range are adept at escaping from restrictions. Simple restriction would also prevent children from coming to terms with, and learning to cope with, the motor vehicle, so that although it would save young lives it is likely that a greater number of older children would be involved in accidents. *A priori* one would expect some overall reduction in accidents as a result of simple restrictive measures, but it is unlikely to be very great.

We seem to have pushed ourselves into a very pessimistic corner, since we have argued that very little can be expected of any of the commonly proposed remedies. But the difficulty is more apparent than real, and is a result of adopting too narrow a conception of possible safety measures. In particular, there has been little consideration of the possibility of providing legal protection for child pedestrians, or of measures which use an integrated package of engineering, education and the law.

A SPECIFIC PROPOSAL

What follows is an elaboration of some ideas first developed by Howarth and Repetto-Wright (1978). Since most child pedestrian accidents occur in residential areas near to the child's home, we propose that in such areas children should be given similar rights, and similar protection, to that which all pedestrians now receive on pedestrian crossings. It is known that the statutory protection which is provided by zebra crossings does reduce the risk of accidents on those crossings (see Chapter 4), but may increase the risk of crossings of the road away from the zebra. What is being suggested is not the installation of countless zebra crossings, which would be impossibly expensive and of doubtful overall effect, but that the total area of all roads in residential areas should be given a similar legal status, at least in relation to children below some criterion age. (Nine or eleven would be suitable choices: nine is the age at which children are no longer allowed to ride bicycles on the pavement, whereas eleven is the age at which they have almost mastered the adult road crossing skills, and at which their travel patterns are extended when they go to secondary school). To be effective this change in the law would need to be accompanied by some simple engineering measures to distinguish the roads on which child pedestrians have priority, from those major roads on which it would be totally unrealistic to give priority to children. These engineering measures need involve little more than the use of a paint brush.

It would be sensible to make different rules about parking on the two categories of road, and since parked cars seem to increase the danger to child pedestrians there would be a certain natural justice in imposing those new duties on motorists in relation to those roads upon which they have the freedom to park their cars. If this were done, the same markings could be used to indicate where parking is allowed and where children must be given priority. In fact, the present yellow lines could be used almost unchanged for this purpose. The presence of yellow lines would indicate a road on which cars had priority, at least to the extent that the present law gives it to them. Children could be told to regard them as a barrier, and that they should never, under any circumstances, attempt to cross them without help.

There are some other minor engineering measures which would help. Some of these would be no more than a simple reversal of many of the changes which have been made in our residential roads over the past twenty years. Roads should be made narrower rather than wider, junctions should be made sharper rather than smoother, while corners and bends in the road should be accentuated rather than straightened. All of these changes would serve to indicate that these roads should be treated differently from major roads, and that in these areas the motorist must behave circumspectly. In areas which have not yet been reached by road improvement schemes, a policy of benign engineering neglect of residential areas might be very effective in combination with the change in the law we are suggesting. It would also be helpful to erect a new type of warning sign at the boundary between major roads and these minor residential roads.

These changes in the law, and in road layout and markings, would need to be accompanied by educational programmes designed to teach the new rules to both adults and children, and to persuade the motorist that the new rules would be just, and that it would be in his/her interest to obey them.

What is being proposed is an integrated programme of legal, engineering and educational measures. In the rest of this chapter we consider the legal implications of this proposal, and the best ways to implement it. Does it conflict with any important principles of jurisprudence? Can it be made consistent with existing laws relating to traffic behaviour?

THE CONCEPT OF RESPONSIBILITY IN LAW AND IN SAFETY RESEARCH

The relationship between these proposals and the existing state of the law is considered in detail in the next section. The concepts of 'intention' and 'responsibility' are crucial to the formulation and application of the law. Howarth and Repetto-Wright (1978) argued for a redefinition of responsibility in relation to child pedestrian accidents, and were aware that this may lead to conflict with existing conceptions, both legal and cultural, of who is responsible for these accidents. They justified their proposal by four arguments, one moral, one logical, one empirical and one pragmatic. The pragmatic argument has already been rehearsed. It can be regarded as a hypothesis that the most effective way of reducing accidents is a total package in which the proposed redefinition of responsibility plays a central role. Let us now propound and expand the other three arguments.

These other arguments are all directed against present practice in dealing with accidents when they are brought before a court of law. In both civil and criminal proceedings the usual defence of the motorist is: 'The child ran heedlessly into the path of the car, so that there was nothing I could do to prevent the accident'. It is well known that the defence is so persuasive that the police are reluctant to prosecute and that even when they do, the defence often succeeds. Moreover, the defence is usually successful in civil actions, and tends to be upheld in the appeal courts. See for example: *Knight* v. *Fellick* (1977), *Davies* v. *Journeaux* (1976), and *Moore* (*an infant*) v. *Poyner* (1975). The burden of proof in civil law requires that the case be established on 'the balance of probabilities', whereas in criminal proceedings the case must be established 'beyond reasonable doubt'. Hence, a defence which works in civil law, is even more likely to be successful in criminal law. It is therefore no surprise to find that drivers are often not prosecuted for the most serious offences when they kill or injure a child on the road.

This defence works because, in law, responsibility is something to be *apportioned*. The defence that 'the child ran heedlessly into the road' amounts to a claim that the child was mainly responsible for the accident so that the motorist was not responsible. It also works because the driver can claim s/he had no *intention* to harm the child, and that s/he was driving with *reasonable care*. It can be seen later that these concepts are central to the application of the law and it is to these that Howarth and Repetto-Wright addressed themselves when presenting their moral, logical and empirical arguments.

The simplest is the moral argument which points out that all civilized societies accept a moral responsibility for the care of children. Children are, by their very nature, less competent than adults and more likely to have accidents of many different kinds. When they interact with adults we usually expect the adult to exercise the greater degree of care, so that there are very few cases in which, when a child is harmed by an adult, the adult is not held responsible. It is accepted, for example, that a child cannot sexually seduce an adult, although a small number of children are extremely seductive and sexually precocious. Similarly, if a child and an adult get into a fight in which the child is injured, the claim that 'He started it' which might be successful if the injured party were an adult, is not usually accepted if 'he' is a child. The only common situation in which the adult's responsibility for the care of children is not the over-riding argument, is the one we are now considering. On moral grounds this is only acceptable if there is overwhelming evidence that the pedestrian vehicle accident is different in kind. The logical and empirical arguments (which now follow) suggest that it is not. If these arguments are correct, then the moral argument must be overwhelmingly in favour of the children.

The logical argument relates to the apportionment of responsibility. The claim that, when the child ran into the road, there was nothing the driver could do to stop the accident, ignores the fact that, at the moment when the accident became inevitable, there was nothing the child could do to prevent it either. Logically the situation is symmetrical so that the driver's impotence is matched by that of the child, and provides no evidence one way or the other about who is responsible. The argument only succeeds because, without making it explicit, the defence does not compare like with like. The impotence of the driver confronted with a child is not compared with the impotence of the child confronted with a car, but with the possibility, in the moments before the accident became inevitable, that the child could have done something to prevent it. If responsibility is to be determined by what happens before the accident becomes inevitable, then the driver's behaviour at that time should also be considered. It seldom is, except in so far as it may be claimed that the car was being driven within the legal speed limit, or that the driver had not been drinking. Since no law is being broken it is argued that the driver was exercising due care. This again is not comparing like with like, since a child does not break the law when he/she goes into the road. Indeed, the law is supposed to protect his/her right to do so. If we are to consider behaviour in the moments before the accident becomes inevitable, then it must be examined symetrically and in more detail. If it is found that drivers do exercise care in the moments before the accident becomes inevitable, but that children do not, then the common defence can be reworded in a more logically acceptable form, but will still succeed. If the reverse is found to be the case, there is no way in which the defence can be reworded and still remain acceptable. The logical argument therefore depends upon the empirical argument and evidence presented below.

There are two types of evidence which can be used and related to each other to assess the degree of care being taken by children and drivers in the moments before accidents become inevitable. These are the exposure measures which enable us to calculate how many potential accidents are avoided, and the observational data which make it clear who is avoiding them.

Howarth, Routledge and Repetto-Wright (1974) calculated a risk measure which they called the 'probability of an accident per potential encounter with a car'. To calculate this statistic, they counted the number of times a sample of children cross roads, and for each road crossing observed the traffic flow, and calculated the proportion of the road occupied by vehicles. If no-one, neither driver nor pedestrian, is taking any action to avoid the other, then the probability of an accident at any road crossing is the same as the proportion of the road occupied by vehicles. So the average proportion of the road occupied by vehicles at the places where children cross, should be the potential probability, per road crossing, for an accident to occur if no-one took any avoiding action. The actual probability of an accident per road crossing can be calculated by dividing the total number of accidents by the estimated total number of road crossings. The ratio of these two probabilities, the actual divided by the potential probability of an accident, is what Howarth *et al.* (1974) called the probability of an accident per potential encounter with a car. For five-year-old boys this ratio was found to be approximately 1:10,000. This means that all but one in 10,000 potential accidents is being avoided, even for five-year-old boys who, as we have seen, have the greatest number of accidents. For ten-year-old boys and girls the statistics show that all but one in 100,000 potential accidents are avoided.

This raises the question of who is avoiding them. With such a high proportion of potential accidents being avoided, it should not be difficult to observe who is taking the avoiding action. In a recent paper Howarth and Lightburn (1980) have reported the results of observing 'conflicts' between children and motor vehicles. The data were extremely clear and startling. Whereas there is a great deal of evidence of effective avoiding action being taken by child pedestrians no driver was ever seen to take avoiding action until the child was nearer than the stopping distance of the car. Drivers do not take observable action until it is almost certainly too late.

A number of observers were stationed at randomly selected sites in the city of Nottingham. Each road crossing was observed and recorded, and the behaviour of pedestrians and drivers described. The descriptions distinguished between close encounters and distant encounters. A distant encounter was defined as the situation which exists when a pedestrian arrives at the pavement at a moment when a car is more than twenty yards away, but less than one hundred yards. When this happens the pedestrian may wait to let the car pass before crossing the road, or he/she may pass in front of the car, with or without the active encouragement of the driver. In most cases the pedestrians, particularly young children, wait for the car to pass. Sometimes they pass quite safely in front of the driver. Clearly long-range anticipation of potential accidents is being shown by pedestrians, even very young pedestrians. But no long-range anticipation is shown by drivers. They vary their speed very little in the presence of children, and seldom change the position of the car on the road, for example, by moving towards the crown of the road when there are children on the pavement.

A close encounter is defined as the pedestrian and the vehicle coming within twenty yards of each other. In other contexts this has been called a 'conflict'. For these situations we recorded not only who gave way to whom, but also the extent of the avoiding action taken. Again the evidence favours the pedestrians, but by a lesser margin. By a ratio of approximately 2:1 the child pedestrians made more violent and effective avoiding actions than the drivers. This evidence is less impressive than that relating to long-range encounters, since it is more subjective. Nevertheless, it shows that, even when children have the temerity to enter a road in the proximity of a car, they are usually very well aware of the presence of the car, and take at least as active a role as the driver in avoiding the potential accident.

The picture which emerges from these studies is quite different from that which is presented in courts of law. These observations provided no evidence that drivers anticipate potential accidents with child pedestrians, whereas children clearly do. Of the 99.99 per cent of the potential accidents which are avoided most seem to be avoided because of the action of the children. If anyone is 'heedless' it is more likely to be the drivers rather than the children. There can be little doubt that the children who have accidents are more than averagely heedless on the occasion on which the accident occurs. It is also possible that some of these accidents occur to the very small number of drivers who do vary their behaviour in the presence of child pedestrians, but the probability of this occurring is exceedingly small. This evidence suggests that most child pedestrian accidents occur between a child who is uncharacteristically and exceptionally heedless, and a driver who is routinely so. If this is the case, then the logical argument previously presented must be resolved in favour of the child, and if that is done, then the moral argument is totally justified.

It is clear that a defence based on the heedlessness of the child and the inability of the driver to avoid the accident, is probably spurious. It may be helped by the feeling of juries, and indeed of all adult drivers that 'There, but for the grace of God, go I'. One is tempted to argue that we are all aware, unconsciously, of our collective potential guilt, aware that as a community of drivers we are collectively responsible for these accidents. It is an unedifying concept, and in this case casts grave doubt on the common practice of basing judgements on the behaviour and expectations of the 'reasonable man'. When the reasonable man may himself be the guilty party, how can the injured gain redress or the innocent be protected?

The arguments so far have been directed at the division of responsibility, but the evidence just presented is also relevant to the concept of 'due care'. It would seem that the behaviour of drivers in residential areas is neither 'careful' nor that which is 'due' to other road users in those areas.

We can also address ourselves to the question of 'intent'. It is certainly true that most drivers do not intend, consciously, to harm children. But this is another aspect of the collective incompetence of drivers in this respect. Most drivers do not *know* that their manner of driving takes so little account of the safety of children; so that when accidents occur there is clearly no intent involved. But would this continue to be the case if the implications of their behaviour were presented to them? Would it continue to be so if the *Highway Code* were to incorporate a clear injunction to vary speed and position of the car on the road when there is a possibility that a child may be around? We suspect that in no individual case would it ever be possible to establish intent, so that the proposed rules or sanctions could not usefully be related to those offences which assume intent. However, this issue is left open until we have considered the existing structure of the law into which any new laws must be fitted.

THE LAW IN RELATION TO PEDESTRIAN ACCIDENTS

In this very brief survey existing offences are considered only so far as is necessary for the purpose of our argument. If further information is required then specialist books on criminal law and road traffic offences should be consulted (e.g. Halnan and Spencer, 1980; Smith and Hogan, 1978; Williams, 1978).

The first group of offences to be considered are those serious offences which the driver commits either in an intentional or a reckless manner. These consist of *murder* (which requires the proof of intent), *manslaughter* (which requires proof of intent or of grossly negligent behaviour), *causing death by reckless driving* (Section 1, Road Traffic Act 1972), *reckless driving* (Section 2, Road Traffic Act 1972), and *non-fatal offences against the person* (within the Offences Against the Person Act, 1861).

Offences requiring intention or reckless

Murder consists of the unlawful killing of a person by someone who intends to kill, or to cause grievous bodily harm to that other person and that other person dies of the attack within a year and a day. The necessary proof of intent has been considerably discussed both in the courts and by academic writers. It is generally agreed that the offence of murder means that a person can intend to kill or cause grievous bodily harm when he or she does the act knowing that it is at least highly probable (or possibly probable), that death or grievous bodily harm will result. This concept of the mental element of murder follow the decision in the House of Lords in *Hyam* v. *Director of Public Prosecutions* (1975). To give an idea of how this might operate in relation to road traffic offences we must consider a situation in which D drives his or her car at P whom D desires to kill and does so. This would be murder, as it would if D's intention were to cause grievous bodily harm. It would also be murder for D to drive his or her car at a bus stop knowing that it was highly probable that the people in the queue would be killed or suffer grievous bodily harm, even if he or she did not desire that result. This offence is rarely prosecuted, for the obvious reason that it rarely occurs. It does, however, fix one end of the continuum of offences involving death or injury caused by motor vehicles.

Manslaughter is a less heinous offence which can be committed it any of three ways. Again the victim must die within a year and a day, and the act leading to death must be perpetrated in the course of an *unlawful act*, or the act must be committed *recklessly*, or in a *grossly negligent* manner.

Unlawful act The House of Lords in *Director of Public Prosecutions* v. *Newbury and Jones* (1976) makes it clear that a person is guilty of manslaughter when he or she is intentionally involved in a criminal act, which is unlawful and dangerous and that act inadvertently causes death. Whether the act is dangerous depends on whether all sober and reasonable people would recognize its danger, and legally this is regarded as an objective decision.

Recklessness has recently received detailed consideration by the Court of Appeal in the case of *Regina* v. *Stephenson* (1979). The Court defined the concept as follows:

> A man is reckless when he carries out the deliberate act appreciating that there is a risk that (a certain occurrence) will result from his act. It is however not the taking of every risk which could properly be classed as

reckless. The risk must be one which is in all the circumstances unreasonable for him to take. (p. 1203) See Addendum.

What needs to be proved therefore is that D did something, recognizing that there was a risk of killing someone, but nevertheless takes that risk and death results.

Gross Negligence is the committing of an act which the reasonable man would not have done. The reasonable man is a creation of the courts. It is generally accepted that the normal person would not be capable of fulfilling all the attributes of the reasonable man at the same time and in every situation. The concept exists to ensure the raising of standards of behaviour in circumstances in which the results are felt to be so serious that this is a valid method of raising them. In the context of manslaughter the negligence needs to be *gross*, which would appear to mean a more reprehensible failure to achieve the standard of the reasonable man than is necessary to demonstrate in less heinous offences. The most commonly used test is unfortunately circular in that it says the degree of negligence should be 'criminal', that is:

> The negligence of the accused went beyond a mere matter of compensation between subjects and showed such disregard for the life and safety of others as to amount to a crime against the state and conduct deserving of punishment. (per Lord Hewart in *Rex* v. *Bateman*, 1925, p. 11)

As in the case of murder, there are very few prosecutions for manslaughter by motor vehicle. But its rarity has a different explanation, and follows from the discovery that juries are reluctant to find any driver guilty of the offence of manslaughter. The reason for this may again be the feeling summarized by the expression 'There, but for the grace of God, go I'. This situation led to the introduction of the offence of *motor manslaughter* in 1930. This has now been replaced by the offence of *causing death recklessly* under Section 1. Road Traffic Act 1972 as substituted by Section 50(1) Criminal Law Act 1977:

> A person who causes the death of another person by driving a motor vehicle on the road recklessly shall be guilty of an . . . offence'.

Causing death recklessly The constituent elements of this are obvious in that it consists of death resulting from somebody's reckless act. We have already referred to the definition of recklessness as expressed by the Court of Appeal in *Regina* v. *Stephenson* (1979). In the context of road accidents the courts have been considering whether recklessness should be considered subjectively or objectively. The Court of Appeal in *Regina* v. *Davis* (1979) assumed that the offence must be considered in a subjective light. Hence recklessness on the road would appear to have the same meaning as that quoted from *Regina* v. *Stephenson* in relation to criminal damage under the Criminal Damage Act 1971 (see above). However the Court of Appeal has at last considered the issue of recklessness in relation to the offence of causing death by reckless driving in *Regina* v. *Murphy* (1980). This decision appears to retain the requirement of a subjective test, but in a slightly different form. Thus, as Lord Justice Eveleigh explained:

> A driver is guilty of driving recklessly if he deliberately disregards the obligation to drive with due care and attention or is indifferent as to whether or not he does so and thereby creates a risk of an accident which a driver driving with due care and attention would not create. (p. 151)

The court is here attempting to avoid the 'requirement that the driver should have appreciated and consciously rejected a risk'. It is necessary to do this because the essence of the offence lies in the reckless driving which is what the driver *does*, not in the result of the driving, which in the offence being considered is death. The relevance of the death is only that the possible punishment for driving recklessly is increased from two years for the ordinary offence of driving recklessly (see below) to five years. So the court is saying that the standard of careful driving is that as established by Section 3 Road Traffic Act (see below), and if a person falls below that standard either by deliberate choice or because of indifference, then he or she will be driving recklessly, and hence guilty of the offence. If, as a result of the reckless driving he or she kills somebody then he or she will be liable for the more serious punishment. Thus the test for recklessness with relation to the two offences is a combination of a subjective and an objective one. Readers should be aware that the Scottish courts have taken a different approach, and that this conflict will be resolved by the House of Lords during 1981. (See Addendum)

The three offences of murder, manslaughter and causing death recklessly are all concerned with the situation in which death results. There are, in addition, a number of offences which are committed in an intentional or reckless manner, which do not result in death.

The first of these is the specific offence, *Reckless Driving* in the Road Traffic Act, 1972 Section 2, substituted by Section 50(1), Criminal Law Act 1977:

> A person who drives a motor vehicle on a road recklessly shall be guilty of an offence.

This offence needs no further consideration, since it is the same as the offence of causing death by reckless driving except that it does not result in death.

Secondly there is a group of offences usually referred to as the *non-fatal offences against the person*. The first of these is defined by Section 18 Offences Against the Person Act, 1861 which states that a person who:

> unlawfully or maliciously by any means whatsoever wounds or causes grievous bodily harm to any person ... with ... intent ... to do ... grievous bodily harm

shall be guilty of an offence.

This offence also requires the demonstration of intent which, in this case, according to *Regina* v. *Belfon* (1976) in the Court of Appeal, means a desire to produce the result or to intend to do an act, knowing that it is certain that grievous bodily harm will result. This contrasts directly with the meaning of intention in murder cases, where probability rather than certainty is all that is required. The lesser offences ensure that the causing of lesser harm will also be an offence (See also Sections 20 and 47, Offences Against the Person Act, 1861 and common law assault and battery).

The common denominator in all these offences is the requirement that they be committed *intentionally* or *recklessly*. These concepts require some form of subjective realization of risk on the part of the perpetrator. It is this which makes these offences difficult to relate to Howarth and Repetto-Wright's (1978) arguments about responsibility, or to Howarth and Lightburn's (1980) evidence about the care which drivers show towards child pedestrians. This is because the research does not *prove* that the drivers realize the risk they are taking with the lives of others, although it does show that, looked at objectively, many of the accidents could be avoided if the drivers took more care. It is possible that there are more reckless drivers around than had been previously realized, but the research does not prove this, nor does it suggest any new way of identifying which of the drivers involved in accidents were in fact reckless.

What the research does point to however, is a consideration of the offence of careless driving, since this is an offence defined by an objective standard as to whether a driver has managed to attain a particular standard of care. Therefore we need to consider in some detail the offence of careless driving, which is provided for in Section 3 Road Traffic Act 1972 as amended.

Offences which do not involve intention or recklessness

Careless driving   The standard of driving which is required of the driver is that he/she should drive with due care and attention. Academic writers have discussed whether the absence of either is enough, or whether the offence requires the absence of both. It is now generally agreed that the absence of either due care *or* attention is sufficient to amount to the commission of the offence.

Driving without due care and attention implies *negligence*, and in relation to negligence it has been judicially stated that the obligation imposed on the driver by the civil law and the criminal law are the same (Lord Chief Justice Widgery in *Scott* v. *Warren*, 1974). Consequently, in order to be found guilty of this offence, it must be shown by the prosecution, beyond reasonable doubt, that the defendant drove in a manner that, on an objective standard, is unacceptable. The definition of 'unacceptable' is that the manner of driving should fall short of the way the reasonable man would have driven if he found himself in the same circumstances. It follows from this that in deciding the standard the driver must achieve we can refer to civil cases in which the victim of the accident has sued the driver, claiming damages for personal injuries caused to him or her as a result of the accident. However, in the case of *Hume* v. *Ingleby* (1975) the court felt that although the defendant might have been found liable in negligence were this a civil case, nevertheless he was not found guilty of a criminal offence.

This case requires some consideration. It appears to conflict with the earlier decision of the same court in the case of *Scott* v. *Warren* (1974). It also flies in the face of two earlier decisions which also seem to equate the standard of care required in both the civil and the criminal law. They are *Regina* v. *Evans* (1963) and *Regina* v. *Gosney* (1971). The explanation would appear to be that, although the standard of care which has to be attained by drivers is the same in both the criminal and the civil law, the burden of proof on the prosecutor (usually the police who instigate criminal proceedings) is that he/she should prove the case beyond reasonable doubt, whereas the plaintiff (the person bringing the case for damages in the civil law) needs only establish his/her case on the balance of probabilities. It is therefore easier for a plaintiff to prove his/her case than it is for a prosecutor. In *Hume* v. *Ingleby* it appears that what is being said is that the prosecution may have proved its case on the balance of probabilities, but that this is not sufficient to prove that the person is guilty of a criminal offence. So the original proposition, that the standard of care demanded by the civil law is the same, still stands.

We must next consider the nature of the required standard of care. That is, what must be done to constitute the offence of careless driving? The standard would appear to have been laid down by Lord Chief Justice Goddard in *Simpson* v. *Peat* (1952). He stated that:

> the question for the justices is: was the defendant exercising that degree of care and attention that a reasonable and prudent driver would exercise in the circumstances? (p. 27)

In legal terminology, the standard is an objective one. Consequently the courts have decided that the inexperienced driver has no excuse for failing to attain the standard of the reasonable, prudent driver, merely because of his inexperience (*McCrone* v. *Riding*, 1938). The civil law takes a similar view (*Nettleship*

v. *Weston*, 1971). Also in *Simpson* v. *Peat* (1952) it was pointed out that it was no excuse to say that the driver made an error of judgement. This indicates the difficulty of attaining the objective standard. The last part of the quotation from Lord Goddard refers to the circumstances of the incident. This indicates that, although the standard of care to be expected from the driver is an objective one, the circumstances in which it occurs are to be taken as the driver thought them to be; that is, they are established subjectively.

To say that the standard is the objective one which the reasonable, prudent driver would achieve, does not give concrete guidance as to the way in which a driver is expected to drive. The only guidance available comes from an examination of those decided cases which have reached the law reports, and a careful reading of the *Highway Code*. This is perhaps the major problem with this offence, indeed with any offence of negligence, and is referred to later when we consider whether any alterations in the definition of this offence can be of use in improving the standard of driving. The decisions of the courts can only give limited guidance, since they arise from specific ('particular fact') situations, and the decision as to whether or not care has been exercised is necessarily decided *ex post facto*. However, some guidance about the standard of care can be gleaned from the reports, and this is particularly important to our argument, since the evidence presented earlier in this chapter (second section) is most readily applied to the definition of the standard of care.

At this point it is helpful to look more carefully at the relevant civil cases already quoted as examples of the willingness of the courts to accept the plea of a driver that the pedestrian, usually a child, ran out in front of the car, and that there was nothing the driver could do about it. In considering these cases we do not wish to argue that the decision in any case should have been different. Rather, we are suggesting that the underlying assumptions of the decisions are incorrect, and that if this is recognized a different result might be achieved in similar cases in the future. And if findings of the research are to be believed, fairer solutions would follow.

When the courts accept the argument that the accident was the responsibility of the pedestrian, it follows that the driver is not liable for the injury caused. A good example of this is *Davies* v. *Journeaux* (1976) decided by the Court of Appeal. In this case the driver saw an 11-year-old child standing at the edge of the pavement, but nevertheless an accident occurred when the child ran out into the road. According to the evidence of Howarth and Lightburn (1980) and the arguments already presented, the starting assumption should have been that the driver was responsible for this accident, but the Court of Appeal (reversing the first instance judgement of Arnold J.) held that the driver was not negligent since, although he had seen the child, he had to keep a constant all-round watch. Failure to pay due attention to the child was not established, since the driver could not be expected to keep his eyes on the child all the time. Nor had he been negligent in failing to warn the child by sounding his horn, since a driver cannot be expected to be under a duty to do so. We do not wish to suggest that in this case the driver was negligent, and that the court therefore reached an incorrect decision on the facts. Instead we wish to question the underlying assumptions that permeate this sort of decision. At present the underlying assumption is that the driver is not to blame, whereas our evidence suggests that this supposition may be wrong, and that in the vast majority of cases, it may be the motorist who is to blame for these accidents. Further examples of the current underlying assumption will be found in *Knight* v. *Fellick* (1977) and *Moore* (*an infant*) v. *Poyner* (1975). In these and other cases we are not saying that the driver is always responsible, but that the starting presumption should be that he/she is responsible, and then place the onus on him/her to disprove his/her responsibility.

The other source of concrete information about the standard of care which should be expected of drivers is the *Highway Code*. Section 38(5) of the Road Traffic Act 1972 states:

A failure on the part of a person to observe a provision of the Highway Code shall not itself render that person liable to criminal proceedings of any kind, but any such failure may in any proceedings (whether civil or criminal...) be relied upon by any party in the proceedings as tending to establish or to negative any liability which is in question in these proceedings.

This indicates that the *Highway Code* is a helpful guide in establishing what is to be expected of a driver in achieving the standard of driving with due care and attention. But it is only a guide: breach of the Code is not conclusive. In both *Kerley* v. *Downes* (1973) and *Powell* v. *Phillips* (1973) it was stated by the Court of Appeal that breach of the *Highway Code* is only one of the circumstances to be taken into account in deciding whether or not a driver has exercised due care and attention. In any case, failure to obey the *Highway Code* does not mean that a driver will be guilty of the offence of careless driving, since he or she will fall short of the required standard only in the circumstances as he/she believes them to be. Nevertheless the *Highway Code* is a useful guide in the sense that a driver who drives in accordance with the Code is unlikely to be considered guilty of an offence, and more importantly, driving in accord with the *Highway Code* should produce fewer accidents. However, compliance with the Code does not totally exclude the possibility of negligence, as was pointed out in *Goke* v. *Willett* (1973) which was a civil case.

THE LEGAL IMPLEMENTATION OF OUR PROPOSALS

From this survey of the law as it relates to pedestrian accidents it appears that the most appropriate implementation of our proposals could be achieved by revising our conception of what constitutes due care and attention. It would seem that the most obvious way to achieve this would be by introducing something akin to the concept of *res ipsa loquitur* (literally, things speak for themselves) into the consideration of this offence. This is a civil law concept that is used in the law of tort. What it amounts to is that the plaintiff (the person bringing the action, the victim of the accident) establishes the facts of what happened and then claims, without having to establish anything further, that those facts, *prima facie* establish negligence on the part of the defendant. It is then up to the defendant to disprove that he/she is negligent.

This proposal probably requires the imposition on the defendant of a *legal* burden to disprove negligence. The weight of authority seems to be in favour of this proposition although an alternative to it must be mentioned. This alternative would be to place only an *evidential* burden on the defendant.

Imposing an evidential burden means that the defendant does not have to disprove that s/he was negligent, rather it merely requires that s/he should adduce some evidence to show that the accident could have happened without negligence on his/her part, provided that that is a reasonable explanation of what happened. It would appear, however, that a legal burden is imposed upon the defendant, and it is on this assumption that we continue. The imposition of a legal burden means that, once the plaintiff has shown facts which suggest that the accident must have occurred as a result of negligence, the defendant then has the burden of establishing that the accident occurred without negligence on his or her part. In order to establish this, the defendant has to show that it was more likely than not (in legal parlance, on a balance of probabilities) that the accident occurred without negligence. This is in comparison with the burden placed upon the prosecution on a criminal case, such as a prosecution under the Road Traffic Acts, which requires that the prosecution adduce evidence upon which the jury can be 'sure' that the defendant is guilty, that is, beyond a reasonable doubt.

Before going on to consider the applicability of the doctrine of *res ipsa loquitur* in this sphere we need to explain why we reject the doctrine of strict liability as a possible means of reducing the number of child pedestrian accidents in urban areas. There seem to be two general reasons and one specific reason why strict liability would be inapplicable. Of the general reasons the first is that strict liability imposes criminal liability regardless of the state of knowledge of the defendant, which flies in the face of the usual requirement that a person should be guilty of an offence only if he or she is in some way aware of, or knows of, what he/she is doing or omitting to do. So strict liability is, therefore, felt to be unjust, particularly as it can impose liability in a situation where a person cannot know of a state of affairs for which he/she is liable. This argument has in the past been countered by the argument that it is in the public interest to impose strict liability in certain circumstances in order to prevent harm, or to ensure that so-called criminals should not go free. However, the weight of these arguments is diminishing, as has been recognized by the Law Commission in its *Report on the Mental Element in Crime* (1978). In this Report the Law Commission has a strong preference for restricting criminal offences to those which require some sort of intention, recklessness or knowledge. Nevertheless, they do recognize that in certain very exceptional circumstances, the weight of argument might be so great as to permit an offence of strict liability, provided Parliament makes it quite clear that this is what is intended. It would seem that in most of the cases in which public interest is argued as requiring the imposition of strict liability, the point could be well satisfied by the introduction of negligence rather than strict liability. This point ties in with the second general objection to the doctrine of strict liability, which is that it is unnecessary. It should be borne in mind that there is a halfway-house between intention and recklessness on the one hand and innocence on the other, a factor which the judges often seem to miss. This halfway-house is negligence which would seem to satisfy most of the arguments put forward for imposing strict liability on the grounds of public interest. If indeed there are cases which are felt to be of very great harm and of frequent occurrence which are as a result of negligence, then the burden upon the defendant could be increased by something akin to the doctrine of *res ipsa loquitur* as used in the civil law, and it is that which we are proposing here.

In connection with the study there would also appear to be a specific reason for not making use of the doctrine of strict liability. This is the fact that there is a marked distinction between the areas in which strict liability is made use of at present, such as in pollution control, the possession of dangerous drugs and the Motor Vehicles (Construction and Use) Regulations. In these cases the only people concerned are the defendant and his/her employees or contractors. In the area that we are considering, however, there is an independent, volitional human being involved as well as the driver, that is the child. However extensive the responsibility of the driver is, and however careful the child might be, it may be regarded as unreasonable to hold the driver strictly liable when the behaviour of this independent human being cannot be accurately predicted. If strict liability were introduced in this area then the driver could be held liable for an accident which was in fact the sole responsibility of the child, and we do recognize that on very rare occasions accidents may occur. Therefore, we have come to the conclusion that the introduction of something akin to the civil law doctrine of *res ipsa loquitur* is more acceptable.

It would seem that there may be some academic support for this sort of approach. This comes from *Cross on Evidence* by Professor Sir Rupert Cross (1979). However, it must be pointed out that it is unlikely that he would approve of the introduction of *res ipsa loquitur* into the criminal law in the way that we are suggesting. However, he does say:

... there may well be a limited number of situations in which it is sociologically desirable to hold the defendant liable for an unexplained accident. Everything depends on the answer to the question whether such accidents are, more often than not, the outcome of negligence. If the answer is in the affirmative, less injustice will be occasioned by placing the legal burden of disproving negligence upon the defendant than by leaving negligence to be proved by the plaintiff. (p. 151)

We have made this suggestion despite the fact that the nearest precedent to what we are suggesting is the special status of the pedestrian which already exists on zebra crossings. Here the doctrine of strict liability applies, and continues to be considered appropriate, despite the fact that some accidents on zebra crossings are entirely due to the unpredictable, and indeed foolhardy, behaviour of pedestrians on them. There are two reasons why we think it unlikely that this precedent is likely to be followed in any possible legislation about the status of child pedestrians in residential areas. The first is that the status of zebra crossings was first established many years ago. Lawyers are now less willing to recommend the use of strict liability. The second is that the zebra crossing is of limited extent and very clearly marked. This makes its special status easier to accept. If strict liability were to apply to all residential roads then this would change the way the law works in a very large proportion of our road systems. Most importantly it would reduce the possibilities open to the defence because there are few ways in which to avoid liability for a crime of strict liability: a form of liability which is now generally assumed to be unacceptable.

It is commonly stated that the doctrine of *res ipsa loquitur* has no role to play in the criminal law. This is strictly true as the law stands today, but is there any good reason why this should continue to be so in the future? The objections to it are related to the assumption that the accused should be presumed innocent until the prosecution can prove his/her guilt, to the satisfaction of the court, beyond reasonable doubt. This is a fundamental presumption of the criminal law which should only be derogated from in exceptional circumstances. However, when policy considerations have been of sufficient import, this principle has already been derogated from in particular circumstances. The most obvious examples of this are the areas of strict liability, to which we have already referred, which have been introduced in relation to food and drugs regulations. These ensure that the purveyor of food or the possessor of drugs is liable for an offence if the food is not of the required quality, or if the drug is a controlled drug, whatever the state of his/her knowledge. In these cases the legislature has felt that the dangers of allowing this sort of behaviour are so great that it cannot be permitted even if it means being very harsh on some individuals. It would seem that, if the danger is sufficiently great, one may derogate from the principle of the presumption of innocence in the criminal law. The evidence presented in this chapter establishes the nature of the danger. Approximately 500 deaths per year and 10,000 serious injuries to children under the age of sixteen, are a clear indication of the size of the danger.

In comparing our proposal to the law about possession of drugs we do not wish to imply that the doctrine of *res ipsa loquitur* operates in the sphere of drug offences. It does not, but the make-up of the offence leads to something akin to the doctrine. This can be seen by an examination of Section 5(2) Misuse of Drugs Act 1971 which makes the possession of a controlled drug an offence of strict liability. That is, the person is liable whether or not he/she knows the substance to be a drug. However, in the cases of *Warner* v. *Metropolitan Police Commissioner* (1969) with regard to the possession of drugs in containers and *Regina* v. *Carver* (1978) with regard to the possession of minute quantities of drugs, allowance was made for lack of knowledge on the part of the possessor who thus avoided the strictures of strict liability. But these cases do not affect the general position with regard to the offence under Section 5(2) Misuse of Drugs Act. The prosecution has to establish that the possession of a controlled drug is an offence of strict liability, then the statute provides that the defendant can avoid liability by establishing, in exceptional circumstances, that he/she was neither deliberate nor negligent in his/her possession of the drug (Section 28 Misuse of Drugs Act). This is much the same as our approach, although our proposal has a less stringent starting point, in that the assumption we are proposing is that the driver drove in a negligent manner, not that he/she is guilty of the offence. These are precursors of our approach, albeit not directly in point.

The judiciary may not be opposed to the idea of introducing the concept of *res ipsa loquitur* into the area of traffic law. The most obvious indication of this is in the judgement of Lord Chief Justice Parker in *Wright* v. *Wenlock* (1971) where he was denying the general application of the doctrine of *res ipsa loquitur,* but went to say:

> At the same time, the facts of a particular case may be such that, in the absence of some explanation, the only proper inference is careless driving. (p. 231)

He reiterated this sentiment in *Rabjohns* v. *Burgar* (1971). It would seem that if the argument is conclusively put, then the judiciary would not be totally against the introduction of the doctrine of *res ipsa loquitur* in this field.

The doctrine of *res ipsa loquitur* would need to be backed up by specific guidance in the *Highway Code*, which could be suitably modified. It would also be necessary to mark very clearly those roads on which the doctrine would apply since we are not suggesting that it should apply to child pedestrian accidents on busy main roads. It would also be necessary to give adequate publicity to the changes in the law and their implications. The need for an integrated package of this kind has already been described.

The changes we are proposing would clearly require legislation. How therefore should they be put to the legislature? Because of the nature of the legislature in the UK, the support of the House of Commons is essential, and the best method of obtaining that support may be through the operation of pressure groups. These are accepted as having a place in the constitutional arrangements of this country, since they represent the views of certain groups of people on particular topics. The Trades Union Congress, the Police Federation, and the National Union of Mineworkers are all examples of successful and effective pressure groups. So too is the National Association for the Welfare of Children in Hospital. It may be that the best way to achieve the implementation of our proposal would be via the creation of a pressure group to obtain the ear of a small group of Members of Parliament to set the legislative process in motion.

WOULD IT WORK?

In the first section we argued that no other remedy is likely to make much impact on the incidence of child pedestrian accidents. So our proposal is *faut de mieux*.

But our proposal may not work either. The pragmatic arguments presented in the first section were incomplete, since we had not yet formulated our specific ideas. Let us now consider what evidence there is to suggest that the presumption of *res ipsa loquitur* in relation to child pedestrian accidents in residential areas, combined with the engineering and educational measures we suggested (third section) will be any more effective than the other remedies which have been tried.

There is, of course, no direct evidence that these measures would save the lives of children. But there is some indirect evidence. The nearest comparable case is the zebra crossing. On these the doctrine of strict liability applies, in much the same way as it does in the sphere of drug offences. There is no doubt that it is safer for a pedestrian to cross at a zebra crossing than on an unprotected section of the road (see Chapter 4), although there is some doubt about the overall effect of the zebra on pedestrian safety, since there is some evidence that the presence of a zebra may make road crossings on adjacent segments of road more dangerous. Since our proposal is to make the new law apply to the whole area of residential roads, this adverse effect of zebra crossings would not apply. But it could be argued that the zebra crossing has its effect because it is clearly marked and of limited extent, and that the deterrent effect of the law would be weakened by applying it to a more general area of the road. Against this is the possibility that it may be easier for motorists to adopt a more cautious strategy consistently in well-marked residential areas than to change their strategies abruptly as they negotiate different types of crossing.

There is indeed some evidence that the existence of the offences of dangerous and careless driving has a deterrent effect on drivers (Giora Shoham, 1974). Unfortunately this study was conducted in Israel where conditions and the laws are rather different from those in the UK; but the results are of some interest. Giora Shoham compared the effects of light and severe punishment on recidivism. He found that severe punishment slightly increases the interval before an offence is repeated, but that the probability of recidivism was least if the drivers were simply given a warning after their first offence.

Ben-David, Lewin, Haliva and Tel-Nir (1972), also in Israel, investigated the effect of writing letters to drivers, warning them of inadequacies in their driving on particular roads. It was found by observation that these letters approximately halved the incidence of inadequate behaviour for a period of up to six month after the letters were sent.

None of this evidence is precisely to the point, but all of it is encouraging. Nevertheless there is no way in which we can be completely sure, beforehand, that the measures we are suggesting will achieve their primary purpose of saving lives. In such a circumstance every scientist knows what should be done. There should be a pilot study to test the efficacy of the measure before it is applied universally. But this piece of conventional wisdom is not at all conventional for lawyers and legislators. It would be difficult enough to persuade Parliament to change the law as we suggest. It may be impossible to get them to accept the possibility that the laws they pass should not, during a trial period, apply universally to the whole country (see Chapter 4), or that they should be abandoned, in short order, if the trial is a failure.

Moreover, many lawyers would claim that to apply a law to people in some parts of the country but not in others, conflicts with the concept of equity. There are two counter-arguments to this.

The first depends on the presumption that an experiment or trial is necessary because there is uncertainty about the best course of action. Until that uncertainty is resolved the principle of equity cannot be applied since there is no way of knowing who is deprived by the unequal treatment.

The second argument is by precedent. There are very many instances in which different people are treated differently, and where different laws are considered appropriate to different places. The most extreme example of this is the existence of different laws in England and Wales compared with those in Scotland or in Northern Ireland. More frequent examples are the byelaws enacted by local authorities using powers delegated to them by Parliament. These byelaws suggest a mechanism by which we may be able to get the law changed, but delay its universal adoption until it has been properly evaluated. It may be possible to get Parliament to pass the law as an enabling legislation, giving local authorities the power to implement it if they so wish. If the local authorities would then cooperate with the Transport and Road Research Laboratory and the Ministry of Transport to implement it according to some

sensible experimental design and to evaluate the results, then we might achieve
the best of all possible worlds. It is unlikely that, simply by taking thought, we
have been able to design the best possible combination of measures. But if our
suggestions are monitored and evaluated, there is every reason to expect that we
shall discover ways to improve them. Grayson and Howarth (Chapter 4) have
proposed that evaluation and the improvement of safety programmes should be
a continuous process. With a little ingenuity some aspects of traffic law could be
evaluated and continuously improved in the same way. There is no inevitable
conflict between this scientific approach and the dialectical manner in which the
law is usually evaluated.

ADDENDUM

Since the chapter was written the concept of 'recklessness' has been considered
by the House of Lords in two cases. The first of these is *Regina* v. *Caldwell* (1981)
which overrules *Regina* v. *Stephenson* (1979). The definition put forward by the
House of Lords is that a person is reckless when, if s/he does an act which in fact
creates an obvious risk of a particular consequence, s/he either realizes the risk
but nevertheless does the act or does not give any thought to the possibility of
there being such a risk. The last part of the definition has introduced an objective
element into the concept of recklessness which had until this decision been
thought to be a purely subjective concept as defined by the Court of Appeal in
Regina v. *Stephenson* (p. 275–276).

The second case is *Regina* v. *Lawrence* (1981). This case is the decision
predicted in the text on p. 277. As a result of the House of Lords decision in this
case an offence under Sections 1 and 2 Road Traffic Act 1972, as substituted by
Section 50(1) Criminal Law Act 1977, is committed where a person drives in a
manner that creates an obvious and serious risk of causing physical injury to any
other road user, accompanied by the mental element of the offence which is that
the person either recognizes the risk but nevertheless takes it or does not give any
thought to the risk. So the test for recklessness in relation to these two offences
would appear to be tinged with objectivity and is therefore similar in approach to
Regina v. *Caldwell*.

These cases do not weaken the argument put forward in the text since the
senior judges are saying that the concept of recklessness requires either some
form of subjective realization of risk or blatant failure to see the risk on the part
of the perpetrator and as such is still difficult to relate to the evidence about the
responsibility of drivers as indicated in the evidence mentioned in page 278.
Indeed, if anything, these two cases lend support to the supposition that the
judiciary would not be totally against the introduction of the doctrine of *res ipsa
loquitur* in this field as they are an indication of the attitude of senior judges in not
allowing people to avoid the obvious consequences of their behaviour.

ACKNOWLEDGEMENT

We wish to thank Professor J. C. Smith for reading a draft of this chapter and commenting helpfully upon it, although we suspect he is not totally in sympathy with our approach.

GENERAL REFERENCES

Ben-David, G., Lewin, I., Haliva, Y., and Tel-Nir, N. (1972). The influence of personal communication on the driving behaviour of private motorists in Israel. *Accident Analysis and Prevention,* **4**, 269–301.

Cross, R. (1979). *Cross on Evidence.* London: Lutterworth.

Giora Shoham, S. (1974). Punishment and traffic offences. *Traffic Quarterly,* **28**, 61–72.

Grayson, G. B. (1975). The Hampshire child pedestrian accident study. *Department of the Environment, Transport and Road Research Laboratory, Laboratory Report 668.* Crowthorne: TRRL.

Halnan, P. J., and Spencer, J. (1980). *Wilkinson's Road Traffic Offences.* London: Oyez Publications.

Howarth, C. I., and Lightburn, A. (1980). How drivers respond to pedestrians and vice versa—or close encounters of the fourth kind. In D. J. Oborne and J. A. Levis (Eds.), *Human Factors in Transport Research.* Volume 2. *User Factors: Comfort, the Environment and Behaviour.* London: Academic Press.

Howarth, C. I., and Repetto-Wright, R. (1978). The measurement of risk and the attribution of responsibility for child pedestrian accidents. *Safety Education,* **144**, 10–13.

Howarth, C. I., Routledge, D. A., and Repetto-Wright, R. (1974). An analysis of road accidents involving child pedestrians. *Ergonomics,* **17**, 319–330.

Law Commission (1978). *Report on the Mental Element in Crime. Law Commission Report Number 89.* London: Her Majesty's Stationery Office.

Routledge, D. A., Repetto-Wright, R., and Howarth, C. I. (1976). The development of road crossing skill by child pedestrians. In A. S. Hakkert (Ed.), *Proceedings of the International Conference on Pedestrian Safety,* Volume I, 7CI–7C9. Haifa: Michlol.

Smith, J. C., and Hogan, B. (1978). *Criminal Law.* London: Butterworths.

Williams, G. (1978). *Textbook of Criminal Law.* London: Stevens.

REFERENCES TO CASES

Since legal references are usually given in abbreviated form we have used the conventional abbreviations for them. For the benefit of non-lawyers these abbreviations refer to the following law reports:

A. C.	Law Reports Appeal Cases
Q. B.	Law Reports Queen's Bench Division
All E. R.	All England Law Reports
Crim. App. Rep.	Criminal Appeal Reports
Crim. L. R.	Criminal Law Review
R. T. R.	Road Traffic Reports

The reader will notice below that most of the dates are in square brackets and one in round brackets. This also is a convention in legal references. Square brackets refer to the date of publication; the volume number following refers to the volumes produced in that year, e.g. 1971 2 Q. B. 674 refers to page 674 of the second volume of the Law Reports Queen's Bench Division which were published in 1971. If there is no number after the square bracket, then only one volume appeared in that year. Round brackets refer to the year in which the case was decided and may not be the year of publication. These volumes are numbered consecutively from first publication, so that the case can be found unambiguously from the volume and page numbers alone.

CASES MENTIONED IN TEXT

Davies *v*. Journeaux [1976] R. T. R. 111
Director of Public Prosecutions *v*. Newbury and Jones [1976] 2 All E. R. 365
Goke *v*. Willett [1973] R. T. R. 422
Hume *v*. Ingleby [1975] Crim. L. R. 396
Hyam *v*. Director of Public Prosecutions [1975] A. C. 55
Kerley *v*. Downes [1973] R. T. R. 188
Knight *v*. Fellick [1977] R. T. R. 316
McCrone *v*. Riding [1938] 1 All E. R. 157
Moore (an infant) *v*. Poyner [1975] R. T. R. 127
Nettleship *v*. Weston [1971] 3 All E. R. 581
Powell *v*. Phillips [1973] R. T. R. 19
Rabjohns *v*. Burgar [1971] R. T. R. 234
Regina *v*. Belfon [1976] 3 All E. R. 46
Regina *v*. Caldwell [1931] 1 All E. R. 961
Regina *v*. Carver [1978] Q. B. 472
Regina *v*. Davis [1979] R. T. R. 316
Regina *v*. Evans [1963] 1 Q. B. 412
Regina *v*. Gosney [1971] 2 Q. B. 674
Regina *v*. Lawrence [1981] 1 All E. R. 974
Regina *v*. Murphy [1980] R. T. R. 145
Regina *v*. Stephenson [1979] 2 All E. R. 1198
Rex *v*. Bateman (1925) 19 Crim. App. Rep. 8
Scott *v*. Warren [1974] R. T. R. 104
Simpson *v*. Peat [1952] 2 Q. B. 24
Warner *v*. Metropolitan Police Commissioner [1969] 2 A. C. 256
Wright *v*. Wenlock [1971] R. T. R. 228

Part IV

Pedestrian Accidents: An Annotated Bibliography

Pedestrian Accidents:
An Annotated Bibliography

N. P. Sheehy, F. M. Wade, A. J. Chapman and H. C. Foot

This bibliography lists published and unpublished papers relating to pedestrian accidents, behaviour and education, the majority of which are written in the English language. Papers on alcohol and driving have been included only if they refer directly to pedestrian activities. Also included are reports on driving which have been cited by chapter authors to illustrate aspects of pedestrian accidents. References obtained from secondary sources (which were not otherwise obtainable) are not annotated. The annotation is as listed below.

Type of Accident

a   (Prefix) A study prefixed by 'a' deals in some way with accidents of various kinds including pedestrian accidents.

r   (Prefix) The prefix 'r' indicates that the study relates to all road users and/or road accidents, including pedestrians and/or pedestrian accidents.

Primary Classification

D   Publication contains original data.

s   Data are of a descriptive nature.

c   Data are correlational. Also included are non-experimental frequency and proportion data.

x   Data are experimental. A *D*x classification indicates that at least one variable in the study was experimentally manipulated.

R   Publication is of a general review nature.

T   Publication presents a theoretical perspective on pedestrian accidents.

M   The emphasis in the publication is on methodological issues.

G   Discussion papers, including articles of general interest.

Ge   Publications classified as *Ge* present a report or discussion of general road safety education practices and recommendations.

Secondary Classification

P   Publication deals with some aspect of the pedestrian.

ch   Publication deals in some way with pedestrian accidents to children.

ad   Adults are the focus of attention.
el   The publication is concerned with pedestrian accidents to the elderly.
hc   The paper concerns handicapped people.
Dr   Publication is concerned with some aspect of the driver.
V   The focus of interest is on aspects of the vehicle and its capacity to injure.
En   Publication concerns aspects of the pedestrian's physical environment.
Ens Publication focuses on the pedestrian's social environment.
Enl Aspects of the legal environment are discussed.

Additional Information
B   Some aspect of behaviour or personality is studied.
Ed   A study classified as *Ed* relates to the evaluation of educational measures.
N   The study is based on observation of naturally occurring events.

Prefixes appear before the primary classification and relate to all subsequent symbols for a particular paper. Recommendations for prophylactic measures are contained in most *D* and *T* papers: they have not been classified separately.

Adamsson, B. (1971). Co-operation between teachers, parents and others concerned with road safety. In *Proceedings of the Second Conference of Governmental Experts on Road Safety Education in Schools.* Vienna: Council of Europe.
r*G Ed*
Alderson, M., and Whitehead, F. (1974). *Reviews of UK Statistical Sources*, Volume 2, *Mortality Statistics.* London: Heinemann.
R Ds
Aldman, N. (1966). The road accident risks for children and young people: the morbidity and mortality pattern. In *Proceedings of the Second Congress of the International Association for Accident and Traffic Medicine.* Stockholm: International Association for Accident and Traffic Medicine.
r*Ds P*ch
Aldman, N., Lundell, B., and Thorngren, L. (1979). Physical simulation of human leg–bumper impacts. In *Proceedings of the Fourth International Conference on the Biomechanics of Trauma.* Lyon: International Research Committee on the Biokinetics of Impact.
Alexander, F., and Flagg, G. W. (1965). The psychosomatic approach. In B. B. Wolman (Ed.), *Handbook of Clinical Psychology.* New York: McGraw-Hill.
a*T*
Allen, B. L. (1963). Pandas versus zebras—comparative study of control at a pedestrian crossing. *Traffic Engineering and Control*, **4**, 616–619.
Ds En
American Automobile Association (1964). *Manual on Pedestrian Safety.* Washington: American Automobile Association.
American Automobile Association (1965). Pedestrian control through legislation and enforcement. *Pedestrian Safety Program Series No. 2.* Washington: American Automobile Association.
Anonymous (1967). Giving precedence to pedestrians round the corner: the law. *The Motor, August*, 44.
G Enl
Anonymous (1967). Male pedestrians' high accident toll. *Road Safety New Zealand*, **4**, 22.

Anonymous (1969). How child accidents happen. *Federation International des Pietons Bulletin, December*, 27–28.

Anonymous (1975). Better towns with less traffic. Report of Organisation for Economic Co-operation and Development Conference, Paris, April. *Traffic Engineering and Control*, **16**, 287–292.
G En

Anonymous (1975). GLC to press for longer crossing time at pelicans. *Traffic Engineering and Control*, **16**, 343.
G En

Anonymous (1975). Road users. *New Behaviour*, **1**, 32.
R G

Anonymous (1976). How safe are pelican crossings? *New Scientist*, June, 702.
G En

Anonymous (1978). Road accidents: the unnecessary epidemic? *British Medical Journal*, October, 1178.
rT

Antoniou, J. (1971). Planning for pedestrians. *Traffic Quarterly*, **25**, 55–71.
R En

Appel, H., Kühnel, A., Stürtz, G., and Glöckner, H. (1978). Pedestrian safety vehicle-design elements—results of in-depth accident analyses and simulation. In *Proceedings of the Twenty-Second Conference of the American Association for Automotive Medicine*. Morton Grove, Illinois: American Association for Automotive Medicine.
Dx V

Appel, H., Stürtz, G., and Behrens, S. (1976). Influence of front end design of passenger cars on injuries of pedestrians in car to pedestrian collisions. In *Proceedings of the Conference on the Biomechanics of Injury to Pedestrians, Cyclists and Motor Cyclists*. Lyon: International Research Committee on the Biokinetics of Impact.
Dc V

Appel, H., Stürtz, G., and Gotzen, L. (1975). Influence of impact speed and vehicle parameter on injuries to children and adults in pedestrian accidents. In *Proceedings of the Second International Conference on the Biomechanics of Serious Trauma*. Lyon: International Research Committee on the Biokinetics of Impact.

Appleyard, D., and Lintell, M. (1975). Streets: dead or alive. *New Society*, **33**, 9–11.
rDc En

Arbous, A. G., and Kerrich, J. E. (1953). The phenomenon of accident proneness. *Industrial Medicine and Surgery*, **22**, 141–148. Reprinted in Haddon *et al.* (1964).
aT

Ashford, N. J. (1979). The provision of transport for the handicapped. *Ergonomics*, **22**, 189–197.
rG Phc

Ashton, S. J. (1975). The cause and nature of head injuries sustained by pedestrians. In *Proceedings of the Second International Conference on the Biomechanics of Serious Trauma*. Lyon: International Research Committee on the Biokinetics of Impact.
Dc V

Ashton, S. J. (1978). Pedestrian injuries and the car exterior. *Unpublished Doctoral Dissertation*. United Kingdom: University of Birmingham,
Dc V

Ashton, S. J. (1979). Some factors influencing the injuries sustained by child pedestrians struck by the fronts of cars. In *Proceedings of the Twenty-Third Stapp Car Crash Conference*. Warrendale: Society of Automotive Engineers.

Ashton, S. J. (1980). A preliminary assessment of the potential for pedestrian injury reduction through vehicle design. In *Proceedings of the Twenty-Fourth Stapp Car Crash Conference*. Warrendale: Society of Automotive Engineers.

Ashton, S. J. (1981). Pedestrian injuries: the influence of vehicle design. In H. C. Foot, A. J. Chapman and F. M. Wade (Eds.), *Road Safety: Research and Practice.* Eastbourne: Praeger.
R V

Ashton, S. J., Bimson, S., and Driscoll, C. (1979). Patterns of injury in pedestrian accidents. In *Proceedings of the Twenty-Third Conference of the American Association for Automotive Medicine.* Morton Grove, Illinois: American Association for Automotive Medicine.

Ashton, S. J., Hayes, H. R. M., and Mackay, G. M. (1974). Child pedestrian injuries. In *Proceedings of the First Meeting on the Biomechanics of Serious Trauma in Children.* Lyon: International Research Committee on the Biokinetics of Impact.

Ashton, S. J., and Mackay, G. M. (1979). A review of real world studies of pedestrian injury. In *Unfall-und-Sicherheitsforschung Strassenverkehr.* Cologne: Heft 21.
R V

Ashton, S. J., and Mackay, G. M. (1979). Some characteristics of the population who suffer trauma as pedestrians when hit by cars and some resulting implications. In *Proceedings of the Fourth International Conference on the Biomechanics of Trauma.* Lyon: International Research Committee on the Biokinetics of Impact.

Ashton, S. J., Pedder, J. B., and Mackay, G. M. (1977). Pedestrian injuries and the car exterior. In *Society of Automotive Engineers Transactions*, Paper 770092. Warrendale: Society of Automotive Engineers.

Ashton, S. J., Pedder, J. B., and Mackay, G. M. (1977). Pedestrian leg injuries, the bumper and other front structures. In *Proceedings of the Third International Conference on the Biokinetics of Impact.* Lyon: International Research Committee on the Biokinetics of Impact.
Dc V

Ashton, S. J., Pedder, J. B., and Mackay, G. M. (1978). Influence of vehicle design on pedestrian leg injuries. In *Proceedings of the Twenty-Second Conference of the American Association for Automotive Medicine.* Morton Grove, Illinois: American Association for Automotive Medicine.
Dc V

Ashton, S. J., Pedder, J. B., and Mackay, G. M. (1978). Pedestrian head injuries. In *Proceedings of the Twenty-Second Conference of the American Association for Automotive Medicine.* Morton Grove, Illinois: American Association for Automotive Medicine.
Dc V

Ashworth, R. (1971). Delays to pedestrians crossing the road. *Traffic Engineering and Control*, **13**, 114–115.
Ds En N

Avery, G. C. (1974). *The Capacity of Young Children to Cope with the Traffic System: A Review. Traffic Accident Research Unit.* New South Wales, Australia: Department of Motor Transport.
R Pch B

Backett, E. M., and Johnston, A. M. (1959). Social patterns of road accidents to children: some characteristics of vulnerable families. *British Medical Journal*, **1**, 409–413. Reprinted in Haddon *et al.* (1964).
Dc Pch Ens

Bacon, D. G. C., and Wilson, M. R. (1976). Bumper characteristics for improved pedestrian safety. In *Proceedings of the Twentieth Stapp Car Crash Conference.* Warrendale: Society of Automotive Engineers.

Bäckström, K. (1973). Children's traffic club: an interview study of the club made in the home. Stockholm: National Road Research Institute.

Bäckström, K. (1976). The child in traffic. *Paper presented at the Conference of the International Federation of Pedestrian Associations* June. Geilo, Norway: University of Geilo.
Ge

Baird, J. D., and Jones, G. P. (1974). Relationship between vehicle frontal geometry and pedestrian accident severity. In *Proceedings of the Third International Congress on Automotive Safety*. San Francisco: International Congress on Automotive Safety.
Dc V

Baker, S. P. (1972). Injury control, accident prevention and other approaches to reduction of injury. In P. E. Sartwell (Ed.), *Preventive Medicine and Public Health*. New York: Appleton Century Crofts.
aT

Baker, S. P. (1977). International differences in pedestrian fatalities. In A. S. Hakkert (Ed.), *Proceedings of the International Conference on Pedestrian Safety*, Volume 2, 1–5. Haifa: Michlol.
Dc P

Baker, S. P., Robertson, L. S., and O'Neill, B. (1972). Drivers involved in fatal pedestrian collisions. In *Proceedings of the Sixteenth Conference of the American Association for Automotive Medicine*. Chapel Hill: American Association for Automotive Medicine.
Dc Dr B

Barrett, G. V., Kobayashi, M., and Fox, B. H. (1969). Feasibility of studying drivers' reaction to sudden pedestrian emergencies in an automobile simulator. *Human Factors*, **10**, 19–26.
Dx Dr B

Barrett, R. (1972). Moving pedestrians in a traffic-free environment. *Traffic Engineering and Control*, **14**, 235–238.
R En

Bartholomew, W. M. (1967). Pedestrian accidents in service areas of selected recreation facilities. *Traffic Safety Research Review*, **11**, 117–120.
Dx En

Bartz, J. A. (1972). Development and validation of a computer simulation of the crash criteria in three dimensions. In *Proceedings of the Sixteenth Stapp Car Crash Conference*. New York: Society of Automotive Engineers.

Bein, D. (1976). The criminal liability of the pedestrian. In A. S. Hakkert (Ed.), *Proceedings of the International Conference on Pedestrian Safety*, Volume 1, 6B1–6B8. Haifa: Michlol.
T Enl

Ben-David, G., Haliva, Y., Friedman, P., Snyder, M., and Tel-Nir, N. (1973). The influence of personal communication on urban driving behaviours. *Paper presented at the First International Conference on Driver Behaviour*. Zurich, October.

Ben-David, G., Lewin, I., and Haliva, Y. (1970). The influence of advisory letters in changing the driving behaviour of private motorists in Israel. *Accident Analysis and Prevention*, **2**, 189–206.
Dx Dr N

Ben-David, G., Lewin, I., Haliva, Y., and Tel-Nir, N. (1972). The influence of personal communication on the driving behaviour of private motorists in Israel. *Accident Analysis and Prevention*, **4**, 269–301.
Dx Dr N

Bennett, G. T. (1969). Pedestrian accidents in culs-de-sac. *Journal of the Institute of Highway Engineers*, **16**, 23–25.
Dc En

Bennett, G. T., and Marland, J. (1978). Road accidents in traditionally designed local

authority estates. *Department of the Environment, Transport and Road Research Laboratory, Supplementary Report 394.* Crowthorne: TRRL.
Dc En

Berfenstam, R. (1966). Children and young people in road traffic. In *Proceedings of the Second Congress of the International Association for Accident and Traffic Medicine.* Stockholm: International Association for Accident and Traffic Medicine.
G

Bergman, S. E. (1976). Pedestrian and bicycle facilities and traffic controls: programs of the US Federal Highway Administration. In A. S. Hakkert (Ed.), *Proceedings of the International Conference on Pedestrian Safety*, Volume 1, 2C1–2C3. Haifa: Michlol.
G En

Bez, U., Hoefs, R., and Stahl, H. W. (1979). The V-shaped front—its influence on injury severity in pedestrian accidents and side impacts. In *Proceedings of the Seventh International Technical Conference on Experimental Safety Vehicles.* Washington DC: United States Department of Transportation.

Biehl, B. (1977). Pedestrian safety and behaviour. In A. S. Hakkert (Ed.), *Proceedings of the International Conference on Pedestrian Safety*, Volume 2, 123–126. Haifa: Michlol.
G P

Biehl, B. M., Older, S. J., and Griep, D. J. (1969). *Pedestrian Safety.* Paris: Organisation for Economic Co-operation and Development.
R G

Blikra, G., and Ringkjøb, R. (1966). Traffic injuries in children. In *Proceedings of the Second Congress of the International Association for Accident and Traffic Medicine*, Stockholm: International Association for Accident and Traffic Medicine.
rDs V

Blomberg, R. G., and Preusser, D. (1975). Identification and test of pedestrian safety messages for public education programmes. *Report Number DOT-HS-099-3-705.* Washington, DC: United States Department of Transportation.

Blomgreen, G. W., Scheuneman, T. W., and Wilkins, J. L. (1963). Effect of exposure to a safety poster on the frequency of turn signalling. *Traffic Safety Research Review*, 7, 15–22.

Bø, O. (1972). *Road Casualties—An Epidemiological Investigation.* Scandinavian University Books.

Böcher, W., and Geiler, M. (1981). Handicapped people in traffic. In H. C. Foot, A. J. Chapman and F. M. Wade (Eds.), *Road Safety: Research and Practice.* Eastbourne: Praeger.
R Phc

Boeminghaus, D. (1978). *Pedestrian Areas.* Stuttgart: Karl Kramer.
G En

Bongard, E. V., and Winterfeld, V. C. (1977). Children's traffic knowledge and their comprehension of the dangers involved (children aged 5–9). In A. S. Hakkert (Ed.), *Proceedings of the International Conference on Pedestrian Safety*, Volume 2, 131–135. Haifa: Michlol.
Dc Pch Ed

Brambilla, R., and Longo, G. (1977). *For Pedestrians Only.* New York: Whitney Library of Design.
G En

Brown, I. D. (1961). Measuring the spare 'mental capacity' of drivers by a subsidiary task. *Ergonomics*, 4, 35–40.
rDx Dr B

Brown, I. D. (1965). A comparison of two subsidiary tasks used to measure fatigue in car drivers. *Ergonomics*, 8, 467–473.

r*Dx Dr B*
Brown, I. D. (1965). Effects of a car radio on driving in traffic. *Ergonomics*, **8**, 475–479.
r*Dx Dr B*
Brown, I. D. (1966). Subjective and objective comparisons of successful and unsuccessful drivers. *Ergonomics*, **9**, 49–56.
r*Dx Dr B*
Brown, I. D. (1979). Can ergonomics improve primary safety in road transport systems? *Ergonomics*, **22**, 109–116.
r*Dx Dr B*
Brown, I. D. (1980). The traffic offence as a rational decision: exposure of a problem and suggested countermeasures. In S. M. Lloyd-Bostock (Ed.), *Psychology in Legal Contexts: Applications and Limitations*. London: Macmillan.
Brown, I. D. (1980). Experience and exposure are a confounded nuisance in research on driver behaviour. *Paper presented at The International Driver Behaviour Research Association, Symposium on Risk-Exposure Measurement in Road Traffic Safety Research*, June. Aarhus, Denmark.
Brown, I. D. (1980). Error-correction probability as a determinant of drivers' subjective risk. In D. J. Oborne and J. A. Levis (Eds.), *Human Factors in Transport Research*, Volume 2, *User Factors: Comfort, the Environment and Behaviour*. London: Academic Press.
Brown, I. D. (1980). Are pedestrians and drivers really compatible? In D. J. Oborne and J. A. Levis (Eds.), *Human Factors in Transport Research*, Volume 2, *User Factors: Comfort, the Environment and Behaviour*. London: Academic Press.
r*Dr P*
Brown, I. D., Kane, J., MacEachern, L., and Petrachuk, D. (1973). The effect of two appeals upon turn signalling behavior. *Unpublished Report*. Kingston, Ontario: Queen's University.
Brown, I. D., and Poulten, E. C. (1961). Measuring the spare 'mental capacity' of car drivers by a subsidiary task analysis. *Ergonomics*, **4**, 35–40.
r*Dx Dr B*
Brown, I. D., Tichener, A. H., and Simmonds, D. C. V. (1969). Interferences between concurrent tasks of driving and telephoning. *Journal of Applied Psychology*, **53**, 419–424.
r*Dx Dr B*
Bruce, S., and Skelton, N. (1977). Pedestrian-vehicle conflict at pelican crossings. In *Proceedings of the Planning and Transport Research Computation Company. Summer Annual Meeting*, PTCR P-152, 26–34. Warwick, June.
R Pad Pch En
Brun, F., Lestrelin, D., Castan, F., Fayon, A., and Tarrière, C. (1979). A synthesis of available data for improvement of pedestrian protection. In *Proceedings of the Seventh International Technical Conference on Experimental Safety Vehicles*. Washington DC: United States Department of Tansportation.
Bruton, M. J. (1970). *Introduction to Transportation Planning*. London: Hutchinson Educational.
G
Buchanan, C. (1963). *Traffic in Towns. A Study of the Long Term Problems of Traffic in Urban Areas*. London: Her Majesty's Stationery Office.
G En
Bull, J. P., and Roberts, B. J. (1973). Road accident statistics—a comparison of police and hospital information. *Accident Analysis and Prevention*, **5**, 45–55.
r*Dc*
Burow, K. H. (1971). Injuries of the thorax and lower extremities to forces applied by

blunt objects. In *Proceedings of the Fifteenth Stapp Car Crash Conference*. New York: Society of Automotive Engineers.

Burton, L. (1968). *Vulnerable Children*. London: Routledge and Kegan Paul.
rDc Pch Ens B

Buschschluter, S. (1975). Child accidents. *New Society*, **32**, 655–656.
aG Pch

Cain, D. (1978). A child's safety is our responsibility. *Traffic Education*, **3**, 14–18.

Cameron, M. H., Stanton, H. G., and Milne, P. W. (1976). Pedestrian accidents and exposure in Australia. In A. S. Hakkert (Ed.), *Proceedings of the International Conference on Pedestrian Safety*, Volume 1, 1B1–1B10. Haifa: Michlol.
Dc P B N

Cantilli, E. J. (1981). Highway safety: past and future. In H. C. Foot, A. J. Chapman and F. M. Wade (Eds.), *Road Safety: Research and Practice*. Eastbourne: Praeger.
rG

Carr, B. R., Goldberg, H., and Farbar, C. M. L. (1974). The Canadian breathalizer legislation: an inferential evaluation. In *Proceedings of the Sixth International Conference on Alcohol, Drugs and Traffic Safety*. Toronto.

Cattell, R., and Lewis, G. D. (1975). Children's understanding of words used in road safety literature. *Department of the Environment, Transport and Road Research Laboratory, Supplementary Report 155UC*. Crowthorne: TRRL.
Ds Pch Ed

Cawkell, E. W. (1971). Driver education and the use of driving simulators in schools. In *Proceedings of the Second Conference of Governmental Experts on Road Safety Education in Schools*. Vienna: Council of Europe.
rR Dr Ed

Cawkell, E. M. (1971).The Green Cross Code. *Traffic Engineering and Control*, **13**, 116.
Ge

Ceder, A. (1976). Pedestrian/traffic interactions: Part 1: an algorithm to assign pedestrian groups dispersing at public gatherings. In A. S. Hakkert (Ed.), *Proceedings of the International Conference on Pedestrian Safety*, Volume 1, 5E1–5E8. Haifa: Michlol.
M

Ceder, A. (1976). Pedestrian/traffic interactions: Part 2: pedestrians and traffic models—a case study. In A. S. Hakkert (Ed.), *Proceedings of the International Conference on Pedestrian Safety*, Volume 1. 5F1–5F4. Haifa: Michlol.
Dx P B N

Cesari, D., Heger, A., Friedel, B., Mackay, G. M., Tarrière, C., and Weissner, R. (1979). A preliminary report about the work of the joint biomechanic research project (KOB). In *Proceedings of the Seventh International Technical Conference on Experimental Safety Vehicles*. Washington DC: United States Department of Transportation.
Dx V

Chambers, F., and Nuttall, G. H. (1976). How to plan a primary school project. *Safety Education*, **138**, 23–24.
Ge

Chapman, A. J., Foot, H. C., Sheehy, N. P., and Wade, F. M. (1982). The social psychology of pedestrian accidents. In J. R. Eiser (Ed.), *Social Psychology and Behavioral Medicine*. Chichester: Wiley.
R T

Chapman, A. J., Foot, H. C., and Wade, F. M. (1980). Children at play. In D. J. Oborne and J. A. Levis (Eds.), *Human Factors in Transport Research*, Volume 2, *User Factors: Comfort, the Environment and Behaviour*. London: Academic Press.

Dc Pch *B N*

Chapman, A. J., Sheehy, N. P., Foot, H. C., and Wade, F. M. (1981). Child pedestrian behaviour. In H. C. Foot, A. J. Chapman and F. M. Wade (Eds.), *Road Safety: Research and Practice.* Eastbourne: Praeger.

R T

Chapman, D. P., and James, F. J. (1973). The Stats 19 road accident data procedure and its research applications. *Department of the Environment, Transport and Road Research Laboratory, Supplementary Report 11UC.* Crowthorne: TRRL.

R M

Chapman, R. (1973). The concept of exposure. *Accident Analysis and Prevention,* **5,** 95–110.

r*R M*

Chapman, R. A. (1976). Perception of shortest gaps by pedestrians. *Zeitschrift für Verkehrssicherheit,* **22,** 55–58.

Dc Pad *B N*

Chapman, R. G. (1978). Accidents on urban arterial roads. *Department of the Environment, Transport and Road Research Laboratory, Laboratory Report 838.* Crowthorne: TRRL.

r*D*s

Churchman, A. (1976). Children's street play: can it be accommodated? In A. S. Hakkert (Ed.), *Proceedings of the International Conference on Pedestrian Safety,* Volume 1, 3G1–3G7. Haifa: Michlol.

R Pch *B*

Churchman, A., and Tazmir, Y. (1976). Pedestrian behaviour patterns and experiences in a shopping center combining two design alternatives for traffic segregation. In A. S. Hakkert (Ed.), *Proceedings of the International Conference on Pedestrian Safety,* Volume 1, 3E1–3E4. Haifa: Michlol.

Dc *P En B N*

Clark, B. H. (1971). Pedestrian safety and alcohol: a study of fatal pedestrian accidents in West Virginia in 1970. *Traffic Digest and Review,* **19,** 12–13.

Dc Pad *B*

Clark, D. E. (1978). Under fives—the Birmingham approach. *Traffic Education,* **3,** 24–25.

Clayton, A. B. (1973). Alcohol and adult pedestrian fatalities. In *Proceedings of the American Association for Automotive Medicine.* Oklahoma City, November.

Dc Pad *B*

Clayton, A. (1975). Road accidents: how can psychology help? *New Behaviour, July,* 20–22.

r*G M*

Clayton, A. B., Booth, A. C., and McCarthy, P. E. (1977). A controlled study of the role of alcohol in fatal adult pedestrian accidents. *Department of the Environment, Transport and Road Research Laboratory, Supplementary Report 332.* Crowthorne: TRRL.

Dc Pad *B*

Codling, P. J., and Samson, P. (1974). Blood-alcohol in road fatalities before and after the Road Safety Act, 1967. *Department of the Environment, Transport and Road Research Laboratory, Supplementary Report 45 UC.* Crowthorne: TRRL.

r*Dc* Pad *Dr*

Cohen, J. (1966). Patterns of accidents and possibilities of prevention. In *Proceedings of the Second Congress of the International Association for Accident and Traffic Medicine.* Stockholm: International Association for Accident and Traffic Medicine.

r*T*
Cohen, J., Dearnaley, A. J., and Hansel, C. E. M (1955). The risk taken in crossing a road. *Operational Research Quarterly*, **6**, 120–127.

Dc Pad B
Cohen, J., and Preston, B. (1968). *Causes and Prevention of Road Accidents*. London: Faber and Faber.

r*T*
Colborne, H. V. (1971). Road safety and pre-school children. *Safety Education*, **121**, 11–12.

Ge
Colborne, H. V. (1971). Two experiments on methods of training children in road safety. *Ministry of Transport, Road Research Laboratory, Laboratory Report 404.* Crowthorne: RRL.

Dx Pch Ed
Colborne, H. V. (1972). Factors affecting the safety of young children as pedestrians. *Unpublished Master of Science Dissertation*, Salford, United Kingdom, *University of Salford*.

G Pch
Colborne, H. V., and Sargent, K. J. A. (1971). A survey of road safety in schools: education and other factors. *Ministry of Transport, Road Research Laboratory, Laboratory Report 388.* Crowthorne: RRL.

Dc Pch Ed
Colborne, H. V., and Sheppard, D. (1966). Testing a poster for infants. *Safety Education*, **107**, 8–10.

Dc Pch Ed
Collis, R. E. (1975). A possible design criterion for pavement width. *Traffic Engineering and Control*, **16**, 124–125.

Dc En B N
Connolly, D. (1979). Audisafe: a general accident preventive device. *Ergonomics*, **22**, 199–210.

r*G En*
Consumers' Association (1980). *Knocked Down: a Study of the Personal and Family Consequences of Road Accidents involving Pedestrians and Pedal Cyclists*. London: Consumers' Association.

r*Ds Enl Ens*
Council of Ministers of Transport (1971). *Second Conference of Governmental Experts on Road Safety Education in Schools*. Vienna: Council of Europe.

R Ed
Cowley, J. E., and Solomon, K. T. (1976). An overview of the pedestrian accident situation in Australia. In A. S. Hakkert (Ed.), *Proceedings of the International Conference on Pedestrian Safety*, Volume 1, 1D1–1D9. Haifa: Michlol.

R Ds
Cresswell, C. (1978). Pedestrian crossing facilities. *Unpublished Doctoral Dissertation*. University College Cardiff, United Kingdom.

Dc En B N
Cresswell, C., Griffiths, J. D., and Hunt, J. G. (1978). Site evaluation of a pelican crossing simulation model. *Traffic Engineering and Control*, **19**, 546–549.

Dc En B N
Cresswell, C., and Hunt, J. G. (1978). Site evaluation of a zebra crossing simulation model. *Traffic Engineering and Control*, **20**, 467–470 and 474.

Dc *En B N*
Cryer, A. J. (1973). Footbridge, subways—a variety of needs—the comprehensive view. *Civil Engineering and Public Works Review*, **68**, 247–252.

G En
Culkowski, P. E., Keryeski, J. M., Mason, R. P., Schotz, W. C., and Segal, R. J. (1971). Research into impact protection for pedestrians and cyclists. *Report Number VJ-2672-V2*. Buffalo, New York: Cornell Aeronautical Laboratory.

Cyster, R. (1980). The use of video recording in traffic education in primary schools. *Traffic Education*, **5**, 5–6.

Ge
Daecher, C. W. (1976). The interaction of pedestrian movement with traffic movement in relation to anticipated roadway and sidewalk changes. In A. S. Hakkert (Ed.), *Proceedings of the International Conference on Pedestrian Safety*, Volume 1, 5B1–5B6. Haifa: Michlol.

Dc En N
Dalby, E. (1977). Space-sharing by pedestrians and vehicles. In A. S. Hakkert (Ed.), *Proceedings of the International Conference on Pedestrian Safety*, Volume 2, 107–113. Haifa: Michlol.

Dc P En N
Dalby, E. (1979). Area-wide measures in urban road safety. *Department of the Environment, Transport and Road Research Laboratory, Supplementary Report 517.* Crowthorne: TRRL.

Dalby, E., and Williamson, A. E. (1971). Pedestrian and traffic management techniques in Delft. *Department of the Environment, Transport and Road Research Laboratory, Supplementary Report 257.* Crowthorne: TRRL.

G En
Daniel, S., Eppinger, R. H., and Cohen, D. (1979). Considerations in the development of a pedestrian safety standard. In *Proceedings of the Seventh International Technical Conference on Experimental Safety Vehicles*. Washington DC: United States Department of Transportation.

Danner, M., and Langweider, K. (1979). Collision characteristics and injuries to pedestrians in real accidents. In *Proceedings of the Seventh International Technical Conference on Experimental Safety Vehicles*. Washington DC: United States Department of Transportation.

Dannick, L. I. (1973). Influence of an anonymous stranger on routine decisions to act or not to act: an experiment in conformity. *Sociological Quarterly*, **14**, 127–134.

Dx Pad B
Darlington, J. O. (1976). Education in road safety in the county of Hereford and Worcester. *Safety Education*, **136**, 20–21.

Ge
Darlington, J. O. (1977). Teach the teachers and they will teach the child. *Traffic Education*, **2**, 12–13.

Davies, R. F. (1979). The Green Cross Man Wallchart: distribution, acceptance and use amongst teachers. *Department of the Environment, Transport and Road Research Laboratory, Supplementary Report 518.* Crowthorne: TRRL.

Ds Pch Ed
Davis, D. I., and Pavlinski, L. A. (1978). Improving prospects for pedestrian safety. *Traffic Quarterly*, **32**, 349–362.

G
Dawson, R. F. F. (1967). Cost of road accidents in Great Britian. *Ministry of Transport, Road Research Laboratory, Laboratory Report 79*. Crowthorne: RRL.

r*G*

Dawson, R. F. F. (1971). Current costs of road accidents in Great Britain. *Ministry of Transport, Road Research Laboratory, Laboratory Report 396.* Crowthorne: RRL.

r*G*

Dean, C. (1981). The organization of road safety in Great Britain. In H. C. Foot, A. J. Chapman and F. M. Wade (Eds.), *Road Safety: Research and Practice.* Eastbourne: Praeger.

r*G*

Denby, M. (1979). Road Safety education 'roundabout'. Getting R.S.E. alive, active and virile! *Safety Education, Summer,* 38–39.

Ge

Denham, P. M. (1957). Miami's pedestrian control program. *Traffic Digest and Review,* **5,** 1–3.

Denton, G. G. (1976). Pedestrian behaviour—a cross-cultural study of speed perception. In A. S. Hakkert (Ed.), *Proceedings of the International Conference on Pedestrian Safety,* Volume 1, 7D1–7D8. Haifa: Michlol.

Dx Pad B

Denton, G. G. (1971). The influence of visual pattern on perceived speed. *Department of the Environment, Transport and Road Research Laboratory, Laboratory Report 409.* Crowthorne: TRRL.

r*Dx Dr B*

Department of Education and Science (1972). *The Health of the School Child 1969–1970.* London: Her Majesty's Stationery Office.

G Ds

Department of Education and Science (1974). *The Health of the School Child 1971–1972.* London: Her Majesty's Stationery Office.

G Ds

Department of Education and Science (1977). *Health Education in Schools.* London: Her Majesty's Stationery Office.

G

Department of the Environment (1973). *Children at Play.* Design Bulletin 27. London: Her Majesty's Stationery Office.

Dc Pch B N

Department of the Environment (1973). *Pedestrian Safety.* London: Her Majesty's Stationery Office.

G En

Department of the Environment, Scottish Development Department, Welsh Office and Central Office of Information (1976). *Green Cross Man Wallchart. Notes for teachers.* London: Her Majesty's Stationery Office.

Ge

Department of Scientific and Industrial Research (1963). *Research on Road Safety.* London: Her Majesty's Stationery Office.

R En

Department of Transport (1979). *Road Accidents Great Britain 1977.* London: Her Majesty's Stationery Office.

r*Ds*

Department of Transport (1980). *Road Accidents Great Britain 1978.* London: Her Majesty's Stationery Office.

r*Ds*

Department of Transport and Central Office of Information (1978). *Driving.* London: Her Majesty's Stationery Office.

r*Ge*
Department of Transport and Central Office of Information (1978). *The Highway Code.* London: Her Majesty's Stationery Office.
r*G*
Department of Transport, Road and Motor Vehicle Traffic Safety (1970). *Report on Publicity Effects concerning Certain Items in the Highway Code.* Ottawa: Department of Transport.

Department of Transportation (1979). *Proceedings of the Seventh International Technical Conference on Experimental Safety Vehicles.* Washington DC: United States Department of Transportation.

Dier, R. D. (1952). A study of a school crossing hazard. *Traffic Quarterly*, **6**, 102–115.
Dc En
Dipietro, C. M., and King, L. E. (1970). Pedestrian gap acceptance. *Highway Research Record*, **308**, 80–91.
Dc Pad B N
van der Does, V. I. (1976). Changing structure of the community. In A. S. Hakkert (Ed.), *Proceedings of the International Conference on Pedestrian Safety*, Volume 1, 2A1–2A6. Haifa: Michlol.
G
van der Does, V. (1981). Discrimination against minority groups: the elderly and the handicapped. In H. C. Foot, A. J. Chapman and F. M. Wade (Eds.), *Road Safety: Research and Practice.* Eastbourne: Praeger.
G
Dolphin, J., Kennedy, L., O'Donnell, S., and Wilde, G. J. S. (1970). *Factors influencing Pedestrian Traffic Violations.* Ontario: Department of Psychology, Queen's University.

Downing, C. S. (1980). Pre-school children and their parents. *Unpublished Report, Department of Environment and Department of Transport, Transport and Road Research Laboratory.* Crowthorne: TRRL.

Downing, C. S. (1981). Improving parental road safety practice and education with respect to pre-school children. In H. C. Foot, A. J. Chapman and F. M. Wade (Eds.), *Road Safety: Research and Practice.* Eastbourne: Praeger.
Ge
Drew, G. C. (1963). The study of accidents. *Bulletin of the British Psychological Society*, **16**, 1–10.
G
Ducker, R. (1975). *Threat Detection Training Programmes for Child Pedestrian Safety.* Volume I and II. Washington: National Highway Traffic Safety Administration.

Duff, J. T. (1967). Road accidents in urban areas. *Journal of the Institution of Highway Engineers, May*, 61–73.

Duffall, J. R., and Hopper, R. (1975). Sleeping policemen—their effectiveness in regulating vehicle speeds. *Chartered Municipal Engineers*, **8**, 151–159.
Ds En
Ebbesen, E. E., and Haney, M. (1973). Flirting with death: variables affecting risk taking at intersections. *Journal of Applied Psychology*, **3**, 303–324.
Dc Dr N
Echavidre, J. P., and Gratador, J. (1979). Peugeot VLS 104 and pedestrian protection. In *Proceedings of the Seventh International Technical Conference on Experimental Safety Vehicles.* Washington DC: United States Department of Transportation.

Economic Commission for Europe (1970). *Statistics of Road Traffic Accidents in Europe, 1969.* New York: United Nations.

rDs
Ekström, G., Gästrin, U., and Quist, O. (1966). Traffic accidents among children. In *Proceedings of the Second Congress of the International Association for Accident and Traffic Medicine*. Stockholm: International Association for Accident and Traffic Medicine.

rDs Pch Ens
Ekström, G., Gästrin, U., and Quist, O. (1966). Traffic injuries and accident proneness in childhood. In *Proceedings of the Second Congress of the International Association for Accident and Traffic Medicine*. Stockholm: International Association for Accident and Traffic Medicine.

rDc Pch B Ens
Elkington, J. E., McGlynn, R., and Roberts, J. (1976). *The Pedestrian. Planning and Research*. London: Transport and Environment Studies.

R En
Ellingstad, V. S., and Westra, D. P. (1976). Evaluation methodologies for traffic safety programs. *Human Factors*, **18**, 313–326.

M
Elswood, D. (1970). A road safety project for 8–12's. *Safety Education*, **119**, 8–9.

Ge
England, E. S. (1976). Children's strategies for road crossing in an urban environment. *Unpublished Master of Science Dissertation*, University of Salford, United Kingdom.

R Dx Pch B En
Eppinger, R. H., and Pritz, H. B. (1979). Development of simplified vehicle performance requirement for pedestrian injury mitigation. In *Proceedings of the Seventh International Technical Conference on Experimental Safety Vehicles*. Washington DC: United States Department of Transportation.

Eysenck, H. J. (1962). The personality of drivers and pedestrians. *Medicine, Science and the Law*, **3**, 416–423.

T
Faulkner, C. R. (1975). Distribution of accidents in urban areas of Great Britain. *Department of the Environment, Transport and Road Research Laboratory, Supplementary Report 159 UC*. Crowthorne: TRRL.

rDs
Fiala, E., Fabricus, B., and Niklas, J. (1968). Pedestrian accident tests with catapult. *Report Number 40*, Berlin: Motor Vechile Institute, Berlin Technical University.

Finlayson, H. M. (1971). Motivation, skill and children's road behaviour. *Safety Education, Autumn*, 20–21.

G Pch B
Finlayson, H. M. (1972). Children's road behaviour and personality. *British Journal of Educational Psychology*, **42**, 225–232.

Dc Pch B
Firth, D. E. (1973). The road safety aspects of the Tufty Club. *Department of the Environment, Transport and Road Research Laboratory, Laboratory Report 604*. Crowthorne: TRRL.

Dc Pch Ed
Firth, D. E. (1974). The Tufty Club. Some comments on the major criticisms. *Safety Education, Summer*.

Dc Pch Ed
Firth, D. E. (1975). Roads and road safety—descriptions given by four hundred children. *Department of the Environment, Transport and Road Research Laboratory*, Supplementary Report 138 UC. Crowthorne: TRRL.

Dc Pch *B Ed*
Firth, D. E. (1978). The child pedestrian in the road environment. Present trends and implications. *International Symposium on The Child in the World of Tomorrow.* July. Athens: Institute of Child Health.
G *Pch*
Firth, D. E. (1979). Children's use of crossing facilities. *Traffic Education,* **4**, 18–20.
Dc Pch *B N*
Firth, D. E. (1980). Methodological problems in pedestrian research. In D. J. Oborne, and J. A. Levis (Eds.), *Human Factors in Transport Research,* Volume 2, *User Factors: Comfort, the Environment and Behaviour.* London: Academic Press.
M
Fisher, A. J., and Hall, R. R. (1972). The influence of car frontal design on pedestrian accident trauma. *Accident Analysis and Prevention,* **4**, 47–58.
Dc *V*
Fisk, A. (1974). Suggestions for a syllabus of road safety education in nursery and primary schools. *Safety Education,* **132**, 14–15.
Ge
Fisk, A., and Cliffe, H. (1975). The effects of teaching the Green Cross Code to young children. *Department of the Environment, Transport and Road Research Laboratory, Supplementary Report 168 UC.* Crowthorne: TRRL.
Dc Pch *Ed*
Foot, H. C., Chapman, A. J., and Wade, F. M. (Eds.) (1981). *Road Safety: a Review of Research and Practice.* Eastbourne: Praeger.
r*R*
Foote, N. N. (1961). Sociological factors in childhood accidents. In *Behavioral Approaches to Accident Research.* New York: Association for the Aid of Crippled Children. Reprinted in Haddon *et al.* (1964).
a*T*
Fleck, J. T., Butler, F. E., and Vogel, S. (1974). *An Improved Three-Dimensional Computer Simulation of Motor Vehicle Crash Victims.* Buffalo: Calspan Corporation.
Fleig, P. H., and Duffy, D. J. (1967). A study of pedestrian safety behaviour using activity sampling. *Traffic Safety Research Review,* **11**, 106–112.
Fonseka, C. P. (1969). Causes and effects of traffic accidents. *Volume 4, Report Number 33.* Birmingham, United Kingdom: Department of Transportation and Environmental Planning, University of Birmingham.
Fowler, J. E., Axford, R. K., and Butterfield, K. R. (1976). Computer simulation of the pedestrian impact—development of the contact model. In *Proceedings of the Sixth International Technical Conference on Experimental Safety Vehicles.* Washington DC: United States Department of Transportation.
Fowler, J. E., and Newman, D. P. (1980). The use of computer simulation for the design of safer vehicles. In *Proceedings of the Conference on Progress Towards Safer Passenger Cars in the United Kingdom.* London: Institute of Mechanical Engineers.
Garbrecht, D. (1977). Pedestrian factors and considerations in the design or rebuilding of town centres and suburbs. In A. S. Hakkert (Ed.), *Proceedings of the International Conference on Pedestrian Safety,* Volume 2, 51–67. Haifa: Michlol.
G *En*
Garwood, F., and Moore, R. L. (1962). Pedestrian accidents. *Traffic Engineering and Control,* **4**, 274–276 and 279.
Dc *En*
Garwood, F., and Tanner, J. C. (1956). Accident studies before and after road changes. In *Final Report of the Public Works Municipal Services Congress,* 329–354. London, November.

r*D*x *En*
Gerber, D., Huber, O., and Limbourg, M. (1977). *Verkehrserziehung in Vorschulalter.* Berlin: Bundesanstalt für Strassenwesen.

Gill, L. L., Mercer, S. W., and Ward, S. (1974). The effect of two appeals upon turn signalling behaviour: a cross validation. *Unpublished Report*, Queen's University, Ontario.

Gissane, W., and Bull, J. P. (1961). A study of 183 road deaths in and around Birmingham in 1960. *British Medical Journal*, **1**, 1716.

r*D*s
Gissane, W., and Bull, J. (1964). A study of motorway (M1) fatalities. *British Medical Journal*, **1**, 75–80.

r*D*s
Gissane, W., Bull, J., and Roberts, B. (1970). Sequelae of road injuries—a review of one year's admissions to an accident hospital. *Injury*, **I**, 195–203.

r*D*c
Glover, E. M. (1976). Mind that child! *Safety Education*, **136**, 15.

Gögler, E. (1962). *Road Accidents*. Series Chirugica Geigy Number 5.

Goldschmidt, J. (1977). Pedestrian delay and traffic management. *Department of the Environment, Transport and Road Research Laboratory, Supplementary Report 356.* Crowthorne: TRRL

*D*c *En*
Goodenough, D. R. (1976). A review of individual differences in field dependence as a factor in auto safety. *Human Factors*, **18**, 53–62.

r*R*
Gordon, J. E. (1948). The epidemiology of accidents. *American Journal of Public Health*, **39**, 504–515. Reprinted in Haddon *et al.* (1964).

r*T*
Gorges, R., Bauerfeld, F., and Schlägel, T. (1976). Examination of traffic behaviour of children at the age of 5 and 7. *Zeitschrift für Verkehrserziehung*, March.

Götzen, L., Suren, E. G., Behrens, S., Richter, D., and Stürtz, G. (1976). Injuries of older persons in pedestrian accidents. In *Proceedings of the Conference on Biomechanics of Injury to Pedestrians, Cyclists and Motorcyclists.* Lyon: International Research Committee on the Biokinetics of Impact.

Grant, J. (1977). *The Politics of Urban Transport Planning*. London: Earth Resources Research.

G En
Gratten, E., Hobbs, J. A., and Keigan, M. E. (1976). Anatomical sites and severities of injury in unprotected road users. In *Proceedings of the Conference on Biomechanics of Injury to Pedestrians, Cyclists and Motorcyclists.* Lyon: International Research Committee on the Biokinetics of Impact.

Grayson, G. B. (1975). The Hampshire child pedestrian accident study. *Department of the Environment, Transport and Road Research Laboratory, Laboratory Report 668.* Crowthorne: TRRL.

*D*c *Pch B En*
Grayson, G. B. (1975). Observations of pedestrian behaviour at four sites. *Department of the Environment, Transport and Road Research Laboratory, Laboratory Report 670.* Crowthorne: TRRL.

*D*c *P B N*
Grayson, G. B. (1976). Children as pedestrians. *Safety Education*, Summer, 132.

Grayson, G. B. (1979). Methodological issues in the study of pedestrian behaviour. *Unpublished Doctoral Dissertation.* Nottingham, United Kingdom: University of Nottingham.

M

Grayson, G. B. (1980). The elderly pedestrian. In D. J. Oborne and J. A. Levis (Eds.), *Human Factors in Transport Research*, Volume 2, *User Factors: Comfort, the Environment and Behaviour*. London: Academic Press.

G Pel

Grayson, G. B. (1981). The identification of training objectives: what shall we tell the children? *Accident Analysis and Prevention*, **13**, 169–173.

Grayson, G. B., and Firth, D. E. (1972). A conceptual framework for child pedestrian research. *Department of the Environment, Transport and Road Research Laboratory, Unpublished Technical Note 748*. Crowthorne: TRRL.

Greenbaum, P., and Rosenfeld, H. M. (1978). Patterns of avoidance in response to interpersonal staring and proximity: effects of bystanders on drivers at traffic intersection. *Journal of Personality and Social Psychology*, **36**, 575–587.

Dc Pad Dr B

Greenwood, M., and Woods, H. M. (1919). The incidence of industrial accidents upon individuals with special reference to multiple accidents. *Industrial Fatigue Research Board, Report Number 4*. London: Her Majesty's Stationery Office. Reprinted in Haddon *et al.* (1964).

aT

Gregory, W. R., and Robbins, J. (1975). Your city—your choice: a public opinion survey for Southampton City. *Traffic Engineering and Control*, **16**, 64–67.

G Dc En

Griffiths, J. D., and Cresswell, C. (1976). A mathematical model of a pelican crossing. *Journal of the Institute of Mathematics Applications*, **18**, 381–394.

Dc En

Griffiths, J. D., Hunt, J. G., and Cresswell, C. (1976). Warrants for zebra and pelican crossings using a minimum waiting cost criterion. *Traffic Engineering and Control*, **17**, 59–62.

Ds En N

Guilford, J. S. (1973). Prediction of accidents in a standardized home environment. *Journal of Applied Psychology*, **57**, 306–313.

aG Dx B

Guttinger, V. A. (1976). *Velligheid van kin deren in woonwijken, ded 2: toepassing van de konflictmethode in een veldonderzoek*. Leiden: Nederlands Instituut voor Praeventieve Geneeskunde TNO.

Guttinger, V. A. (1979). The validation of a conflict observation technique for child pedestrians in residential areas. *Proceedings of the Second International Traffic Conflicts Technique Workshop*, May. Paris.

M

Haar, R., Luccini, E., and Weissner, R. (1976). Automobile and pedestrian—the accident situation. In A. S. Hakkert (Ed.), *Proceedings of the International Conference on Pedestrian Safety*, Volume 1, 4A1–4A6. Haifa: Michlol.

Dx V

Hacker, H. M., and Suchman, E. A. (1963). A sociological approach to accident research. *Social Problems*, **10**, 383–389.

aT

Haddon, W. (1966). The prevention of accidents. In D. W. Clark and B. MacMahon (Eds.), *Textbook of Preventive Medicine*. New York: Little, Brown and Co.

aT

Haddon, W., Suchman, E. A., and Klein, D. (Eds.) (1964). *Accident Research: Methods and Approaches*. New York: Harper and Row.

a*G*

Haddon, W., Valien, P., McCarroll, J. R., and Umberger, C. J. (1961). A controlled investigation of the characteristics of adult pedestrians fatally injured by motor vehicles in Manhattan. *Journal of Chronic Diseases*, **14**, 655–678. Reprinted in Haddon *et al.* (1964).

D*c P*ad

Haight, F. (1972). Recent publications. Accident Proneness, Shaw, L. and Sichel, H., Book Review. *Accident Analysis and Prevention*, **4**, 353–355.

a*T*

Hakkert, A. S. (1976). A study of fatal pedestrian accidents. In A. S. Hakkert (Ed.), *Proceedings of the International Conference on Pedestrian Safety*, Volume 1, 4C1–4C4. Haifa: Michlol.

D*c P*

Hakkert, A. S. (Ed.) (1976). *Proceedings of the International Conference on Pedestrian Safety*. Volume 1, *Session Reports*. Haifa: Michlol.

G P

Hakkert, A. S. (Ed.). (1977). *Proceedings of the International Conference on Pedestrian Safety*. Volume 2, *Guest Lectures, General Reports, Comments, Statements and Closing Reports*. Haifa: Michlol.

G P

Hakkert, A. S., Mahalel, D., and Livneh, M. (1976). Trends and patterns of pedestrian accidents in Israel. In A. S. Hakkert (Ed.), *Proceedings of the International Conference on Pedestrian Safety*, Volume 1, 1F1–1F10. Haifa: Michlol.

*R D*s

Hakkert, A. S., and Mahalel, D. (1978). The effect of traffic signals on road accidents—with special reference to the introduction of a blinking green phase. *Traffic Engineering and Control*, **19**, 212–215.

D*c En N*

Hale, A. R., and Hale, M. (1970). Accidents in perspective. *Occupational Psychology*, **44**, 115–121.

a*G*

Hall, R. R., and Fisher, A. J. (1972). Some factors affecting the trauma of pedestrians involved in road accidents. *Medical Journal of Australia*, **1**, 313–317.

D*c V*

Halnan, P. J. (1979). *Wilkinson's Road Traffic Offences*. London: Oyez Publications.

Hamilton, G. D. (1977). Citizen participation in the transportation planning process: a review. *Transportation Engineering*, **47**, 32–36.

R En

Harris, D. E. (1979). Stop! Look! Listen! *Safety Education*, **4**, 21–23.

Ge

Harries, A. J., and Christie, A. W. (1954). Research on two aspects of street lighting: accident statistics and road surface characteristics. *Public Lighting*, **19**, 553–563 and 563–569.

D*c En*

Harris, J. (1976). Research and development towards protection for pedestrians struck by cars. In *Proceedings of the Sixth International Technical Conference on Experimental Safety Vehicles*. Washington DC: United States Department of Transportation.

Harris, J. (1977). Research and development towards improved protection for pedestrians struck by cars. *Department of the Environment, Transport and Road Research Laboratory, Supplementary Report 238*. Crowthorne: TRRL.

D*x V*

Harris, J., and Radley, C. P. (1979). Safer cars for pedestrians. In *Proceedings of the*

Seventh International Technical Conference on Experimental Safety Vehicles. Washington DC: United States Department of Transportation.
Dx V

Harrison, S. L. (1969). Childhood injury control: who will take what action? Suggestions for national priorities. *Pediatrics Supplement*, **44**, 891–892.
aG

Hauer, E. (1978). Traffic conflict surveys: some study design considerations. *Department of the Environment, Transport and Road Research Laboratory, Supplementary Report 352*. Crowthorne: TRRL.
rM

Havard, J. D. J. (1973). Child pedestrians casualties as a public health problem. In *Proceedings of the Third Congress of the International Federation of Pedestrians.* September. Scheveningen.
T

Heimstra, N. W., Nichols, J., and Martin, G. (1969). An experimental methodology for analysis of child pedestrian behaviour. *Pediatrics Supplement*, **44**, 832–838.
Dc Pch B N

Heinrich, H. C. (1979). Behavioural counter-measures—education. *Symposium on Safety of Pedestrians and Cyclists. Road Research.* Paris: Organisation for Economic Co-operation and Development.

Heinrich, H. C., and Langosch, I. (1976). Effects of different methods of traffic education on children in their first year of school. In A. S. Hakkert (Ed.), *Proceedings of the International Conference on Pedestrian Safety*, Volume 1, 8B1–8B7. Haifa: Michlol.
Dc Pch Ed

Henderson, L. F. (1971). The statistics of crowd fluids. *Nature*, **229**, 381–383.
Ds Pad B N

Henderson, L. F., and Jenkins, D. M. (1974). Response of pedestrians to traffic challenge. *Transport Research*, **8**, 71–74.
Ds Pad B N

Hendriks, J. P. M. (1974). Address to open the Third Congress of the International Federation of Pedestrians. In *Proceedings of the Third Congress of the International Federation of Pedestrians.* Scheveningen, September.
G

Herridge, J. T., and Pritz, H. B. (1973). A study of the dynamics of pedestrians and generally unsupported transit occupants in selected accident modes. In *Proceedings of the Seventeenth Conference of the American Association for Automotive Medicine.* Lake Bluff, Illinois: American Association for Automotive Medicine.
Dx V

Higgs, M. H. (1972). Opinions on the design and measurements of the effect of a road safety leaflet. *Department of the Environment, Transport and Road Research Laboratory, Laboratory Report 483*. Crowthorne: TRRL.
Dc Pch Ed

Hobbs, J. A. (1967). The work of the road accident injury group. *Department of the Environment, Transport and Road Research Laboratory, Laboratory Report 108*. Crowthorne: TRRL.
rM

Hoffman, E. R., Payne, A., and Prescott, S. (1980). Children's estimates of vehicles' approach times. *Human Factors*, **22**, 235–240.
Dx Pch

Hogg, R. (1977). A study of male motorists' attitudes to speed restrictions. *Department of the Environment, Transport and Road Research Laboratory, Laboratory Report 276*. Crowthorne: TRRL.

r*Dc Dr B*
Horn, B. E. (1975). Combatting road accidents. *Accident Analysis and Prevention*, **7**, 113–119.

r*G*
Howarth, C. I. (1980). The need for regular government sponsored studies of the exposure of pedestrians and cyclists. Paper presented at the Conference of the International Driver Behaviour Research Association. Aarhus, Denmark, June.

Howarth, C. I. (1980). Pedestrian behaviour—some comments. In D. J. Oborne and J. A. Levis (Eds.), *Human Factors in Transport Research*, Volume 2, *User Factors: Comfort, the Environment and Behaviour*. London: Academic Press.

G
Howarth, C. I., and Lightburn, A. (1980). How drivers respond to pedestrians and vice versa—or close encounters of the fourth kind. In D. J. Oborne and J. A. Levis (Eds.), *Human Factors in Transport Research*, Volume 2, *User Factors: Comfort, the Environment and Behaviour*. London: Academic Press.

Dc Pch Dr B N
Howarth, C. I., and Lightburn, A. (1981). A strategic approach to child pedestrian safety. In H. C. Foot, A. J. Chapman and F. M. Wade (Eds.), *Road Safety: Research and Practice*. Eastbourne: Praeger.

G Pch En Enl
Howarth, C. I., and Repetto-Wright, R. (1978). The measurement of risk and the attribution of responsibility for child pedestrian accidents. *Safety Education*, **144**, 10–13.

T Dc Pch B
Howarth, C. I., Routledge, D. A., and Repetto-Wright, R. (1974). An analysis of road accidents involving child pedestrians. *Ergonomics*, **17**, 319–330.

Dc Pch B
Hubbard, D. (1979). Parental responsibility with regard to road safety. Paper presented at the National Road Safety Congress. The Royal Society for the Prevention of Accidents. Blackpool, October.

G
Huddart, K. W., and Dean, J. D. (1981). Engineering programmes for accident reduction. In H. C. Foot, A. J. Chapman and F. M. Wade (Eds.), *Road Safety: Research and Practice*. Eastbourne: Praeger.

r*G En*
Huelke, D. R., and Davies, R. A. (1969). A study of pedestrian fatalities in Wayne County, Michigan. Highway Safety Research Institute Report Number Bio9, University of Michigan.

r*Dc P B*
Husband, P. (1972). Children with increased liability to accidents. *Safety Education*, **125**, 3–4.

a*R Pch B Ens*
Husband, P., and Hinton, P. E. (1969). The child with repeated accidents. *Midwife and Health Visitor*, **5**, 279.

a*Dc Pch B Ens*
Hyden, C. (1976). A traffic-conflicts technique and its practical use in pedestrian safety research. In A. S. Hakkert (Ed.), *Proceedings of the International Conference on Pedestrian Safety*, Volume 1, 1C1–1C8. Haifa: Michlol.

M
Illingworth, C. M. (1977). Paediatric accident and emergency: medical and surgical. *Public Health, London*, **91**, 147–149.

aDc Pch
Ingram, V. (1978). Road safety and moral education. *Traffic Education*, **4**, 29–30.
Ge
International Association for Accident and Traffic Medicine (1966). *Proceedings of the Second Congress of the International Association for Accident and Traffic Medicine*. Stockholm: International Association for Accident and Traffic Medicine.
G
International Federation of Pedestrians (1973). Visits to Delft and Utrecht. *Third Congress of the International Federation of Pedestrians*. Scheveningen, September.
G En
Inwood, J., and Grayson, G. B. (1979). The comparative safety of pedestrian crossings. *Department of the Environment, Transport and Road Research Laboratory, Laboratory Report 895*. Crowthorne: TRRL.
Dc En
Jackson, R. H. (1978). Hazards to children in traffic: a paediatrician looks at road accidents. *Archives of Disease in Childhood*, **53**, 807–813.
R Pch
Jackson, R. H. (1978). *Children, the Environment and Accidents*. London: Pitman Medical.
aR G
Jackson, R. H., and Wilkinson, A. W. (1976). Why don't we prevent childhood accidents? *British Medical Journal*, **1**, 1258–1262.
G R
Jacobs, G. D. (1966). Pedestrian behaviour on a length of road containing guardrails. *Traffic Engineering and Control*, **7**, 556–561.
Ds En
Jacobs, G. D. (1968). A comparison of shopping times in high street and precinct types of shopping area. *Department of the Environment, Transport and Road Research Laboratory, Laboratory Report 150*. Crowthorne: TRRL.
Dc Pad En Ens
Jacobs, G. D. (1968). The effects of vehicle lighting on pedestrian movement in well lighted streets. *Department of the Environment, Transport and Road Research Laboratory, Laboratory Report 214*. Crowthorne: TRRL.
Dx Pad B N
Jacobs, G. D. (1976). A study of accident rates on rural roads in developing countries. *Department of the Environment, Transport and Road Research Laboratory, Laboratory Report 732*. Crowthorne: TRRL.
Jacobs, G. D., Older, S. J., and Wilson, D. G. (1968). A comparison of X-way and other pedestrian crossings. *Ministry of Transport, Road Research Laboratory, Laboratory Report 145*. Crowthorne: RRL.
Dc En
Jacobs, G. D., and Sayer, I. A. (1977). A study of road accidents in selected urban areas in developing countries. *Department of the Environment, Transport and Road Research Laboratory, Laboratory Report 775*. Crowthorne: TRRL.
Jacobs, G. D., and Wilson, D. G. (1967). A study of pedestrian risk in crossing busy roads in four towns. *Ministry of Transport, Road Research Laboratory, Laboratory Report 106*. Crowthorne: RRL.
Dc P B En N
Jacobs, H. H. (1961). Research problems in accident prevention. *Social Problems, Spring*, 329–341.

a*M*

James, W. J. (1978). Road safety education in school for partially sighted children. *Safety Education*, **143**, 31–32.

Ge

Jamieson, D. G., Duggan, A. W., Tweddell, J., Pope, L. I., and Zvribulis, V. W. (1971). Traffic collisions in Brisbane. *Special Report Number 2*. Canberra, Australia: Australian Road Research Board.

Jamieson, D. G., and Tait, I. A. (1966). Traffic injury in Brisbane report of a general survey. *National Health and Medical Research, Special Report Series Number 13*. Canberra, Australia: National Health and Medical Research.

Japanese Automobile Manufacturers Association (1968). Experiments on the behaviour of a pedestrian in a collision with a motor vehicle—summarized report. Japanese Automobile Manufacturers Association.

Jefatura Central De Trafico (Madrid) (1964). The pedestrian walk. *International Police Chronicle*, **12**, 13–56.

Jehu, V. J., and Pearson, L. C. (1976). The trajectories of pedestrian dummies struck by cars of conventional and modified frontal design. *Department of the Environment, Transport and Road Research Laboratory, Laboratory Report 718*. Crowthorne: TRRL.

Dx V

Jennings, R. D., Burki, M. A., and Onstine, B. W. (1977). Behavioral observations and the pedestrian accident. *Journal of Safety Research*, **9**, 26–33.

Dc Pad B N

Johansson, G., and Rumar, K. (1966). Drivers and road signs: a preliminary investigation of the ability of car drivers to get information from road signs. *Ergonomics*, **9**, 57–62.

rDx Dr B

Johnson, R. T. (1965). Freeway pedestrian accidents: 1958–1962. *Highway Research Record*, **99**, 274–280.

Ds Pad

Jolly, K. W. (1977). *Children and Traffic, Book 1—On The Pavement*. London: Macmillan Education.

Ge

Jolly, K. W. (1977). *Children and Traffic, Book 2—The Young Traveller*. London: Macmillan Education.

Ge

Jolly, K. W. (1977). *Children and Traffic, Book 3—Preparing for the Road*. London: Macmillan Education.

Ge

Jolly, K. W. (1977). Don't let them die on the roads—teach them. *Traffic Education*, **2**, 16–18.

Ge

Jolly, K. W. (1977). Teaching the 4Rs. Trends in curriculum reform and their implications for the future of road safety education in schools. *Safety Education*, **140**, 3–5.

Ge

Jones, M. H. (1976). Faulting the driver in pedestrian-motor vehicle collisions. In A. S. Hakkert (Ed.), *Proceedings of the International Conference on Pedestrian Safety*, Volume 1, 6E1–6E2. Haifa: Michlol.

R Dr B

Jones, T. O., Repa, B. S., and Potgiesser, J. L. (1974). A general overview of pedestrian accidents and protection countermeasures. In *Proceedings of the Third International Congress on Automotive Safety*. San Francisco, July.

R G

Jones, T. S. M. (1977). Young children and their school journey. *Department of the Environment, Transport and Road Research Laboratory, Supplementary Report 342.* Crowthorne: TRRL.

rDs Pch B

Joscelyn, K. B., and Donelson, A. C. (1978). Drugs and highway safety: research issues and information needs. In *Proceedings of the Twenty-Second Conference of the American Association for Automotive Medicine and the Seventh Conference of the International Association for Accident and Traffic Medicine.* Ann Arbor: International Association for Accident and Traffic Medicine.

R M

Kahneman, D., Ben Ishai, R., and Lotan, M. (1973). Relation of a test of attention to road accidents. *Journal of Applied Psychology*, **58**, 113–115.

rDc Dr B

Karsten, A., Jeuk, U., Schmidt, V., and Trilling, A. (1977). The present situation of traffic information and education for old people in the Federal Republic of Germany. In A. S. Hakkert (Ed.), *Proceedings of the International Conference on Pedestrian Safety*, Volume 2, 119–121. Haifa: Michlol.

Ge Pel

Katz, A., Zaidel, D., and Elgrishi, A. (1975). An experimental study of driver and pedestrian interaction during the crossing conflict. *Human Factors*, **17**, 514–527.

Dx P Dr B

Kelly, M. S., and Huddart, K. W. (1977). The use made of accident statistics by the Greater London Council. In *Proceedings of the Planning and Transport Research Computation Company. Summer Annual Meeting* PTRC. P-132, 208–221. Warwick, June.

rG En

Kemp, A. (1979). Traffic and safety education in middle schools. *Traffic Education*, **4**, 13–14.

Ge

Kenchington, M. J., Alderson, G. J. K., and Whiting, H. T. A. (1977). An assessment of the role of motion prediction in child pedestrian accidents. *Department of the Environment, Transport and Road Research Laboratory, Supplementary Report 320.* Crowthorne: TRRL.

Dc Pch B

Kerr, S. (1980). Traffic education means life. *Traffic Education*, **5**, 27–29.

Kerr, W. (1957). Complementary theories of safety psychology. *Journal of Social Psychology*, **45**, 3–9. Reprinted in Haddon *et al.* (1964).

T

Kipnis, B., and Balasha, D. (1976). The effects of a bypass on vehicle-pedestrian safety and business activity along a town's major arterial: the case of Ramia, Israel. In A. S. Hakkert (Ed.), *Proceedings of the International Conference on Pedestrian Safety*, Volume 1, 3F1–3F7. Haifa: Michlol.

Dx P En

Klein, D. (1969). Some applications of delinquency theory to childhood accidents. *Pediatrics Supplement*, **44**, 805–810.

aT

Klein, D. (1979). Social barriers to traffic safety. In I. R. Johnston (Ed.), *Proceedings of the Seventh International Conference on Alcohol, Drugs and Traffic Safety.* Canberra: Australian Government Publishing Service.

G
Knoblauch, R. L. (1976). The rural/suburban pedestrian accident problem. In A. S. Hakkert (Ed.), *Proceedings of the International Conference on Pedestrian Safety*, Volume 1, 1E1–1E5. Haifa: Michlol.

Dc P
Kraay, J. H. (1976). Urban planning, pedestrians and road safety. In A. S. Hakkert (Ed.), *Proceedings of the International Conference on Pedestrian Safety*, Volume 1, 3C1–3C9. Haifa: Michlol.

R En
Kraay, J. H., and Noordzij, P. C. (1976). Road traffic regulations, law enforcement and the pedestrian. In A. S. Hakkert (Ed.), *Proceedings of the International Conference on Pedestrian Safety*, Volume 1, 6A1–6A5. Haifa: Michlol.

R Enl
Krall, V. (1953). Personality characteristics of accident repeating children. *Journal of Abnormal and Social Psychology*, **48**, 99–107. Reprinted in Haddon *et al.* (1964).

Dc Pch B Ens
Kramer, M. (1974). A new test device for pedestrian-vehicle accident simulation and evaluation of leg injury criteria. In *Proceedings of the Eighteenth American Association for Automotive Medicine*. Lake Bluff, Illinois: American Association for Automotive Medicine.

Dx V
Kramer, M. (1975). Pedestrian vehicle accident simulation through dummy tests. In *Proceedings of the Nineteenth Stapp Car Crash Conference*. Warrendale: Society for Automotive Engineers.

Dx V
Kramer, M. (1979). Improved pedestrian protection by reducing the severity of head impact onto bonnet. In *Proceedings of the Seventh International Technical Conference on Experimental Safety Vehicles*. Washington DC: United States Department of Transportation.

Dx V
Kramer, M., Burow, K., and Heger, A. (1973). Fracture mechanism of lower legs under impact loads. In *Proceedings of the Seventeenth Stapp Car Crash Conference*. New York: Society for Automotive Engineers.

Dx V
Krieger, K. W., Padgaonkar, A. J., and King, A. J. (1976). Full scale experimental simulation of pedestrian vehicle impacts. In *Proceedings of the Twentieth Stapp Car Crash Conference*. Warrendale: Society for Automotive Engineers.

Dx V
Kroj, G. (1974). Dangers for children in the Street. *Symposium on Working Place Safety*. July. Bad Grund, Germany: Ergonomics Information Analysis Centre.

R Ds Pch
Kroj, G., and Pfafferott, I. (1975). Empirische Grundlegung der Verkehrserziehung. *Zeitschrift für Verkehrserziehung, September*, 5–15.

Kruse, W. L. (1976). Calspan/Chrysler research safety vehicle—front end design for property and pedestrian protection. In *Proceedings of the Sixth International Technical Conference on Experimental Safety Vehicles*. Washington DC: United States Department of Transportation.

Kubler-Ross, E. (1976). *On Death and Dying*. London: Tavistock.

G
Kühnel, A. (1974). Vehicle pedestrian collision experiments with the use of a moving dummy. In *Proceedings of the Eighteenth Conference of the American Association for Automotive Medicine*. Lake Bluff, Illinois: American Association for Automotive Medicine.

Kühnel, A., and Appel, H. (1978). First step to a pedestrian safety car. In *Proceedings of the Twenty-Second Stapp Car Crash Conference*. Warrendale: Society of Automotive Engineers.

Kühnel, A.,Wanderer, U., and Otte, D. (1975). Ein Vergleich von realen mit nachgefahren Fussgangerunfallen. In *Proceedings of the Second International Conference on the Biomechanics of Serious Trauma*. Lyon: International Research Committee on the Biokinetics of Impact.

Lalani, N. (1977). Road safety at pedestrian refuges. *Traffic Engineering and Control*, **18**, 429–431.

Dx En

Langford, W. S., Gilder, R., Wilkin, V. N., Genn, M. M., and Sherrill, H. H. (1953). Pilot study of childhood accidents: preliminary report. *Pediatrics*, **11**, 405–415.

aDc Pch B Ens

Larder, D. (1977). Children, the environment and accidents. *Safety Education, Spring*, 8–11.

aG

Larder, D. (1978). World Health Organization Conference on childhood accident prevention. *Safety Education, Summer*, 21–28.

aG En

Lashley, G. T. (1960). The aging pedestrian. *Traffic Safety*, **57**, 10–13.

Lawton, H. A., and Azar, J. G. (1964). Some observations of the behaviour of older pedestrians. *Medical Times*, **92**, 69–74.

Lea, N. D. (1978). A study of means to improve pedestrian and bicycle safety. Report TP 1004. Ottawa: Transport Canada.

Lefkowitz, M., Blake, R. R., and Moulton, S. J. (1955). Status factors in pedestrian violation of traffic signals. *Journal of Abnormal and Social Psychology*, **51**, 704–710.

Dx Pad B N Ens

Leisch, J. P., and Wiedelman, W. J. (1976). Pedestrian safety at interchanges and intersections in conjunction with bus transport operations. In A. S. Hakkert (Ed.), *Proceedings of the International Conference on Pedestrian Safety*, Volume 1, 5A1–5A7. Haifa: Michlol.

R En

Levin, P. H., and Bruce, A. J. (1968). The location of primary schools. Building Research Station Current Papers. Current Paper 39/68.

Dc Pch B En

Lewis, D. (1965). *The Pedestrian in the City*. London: Elek.

G En

Lewis, G. D. (1970). The impact of some road safety posters and pictorial aids to teaching upon children of a primary school. *Safety Education, Spring*, 12–15.

Dc Pch Ed

Lewis, G. D. (1973). Children's use of aids to conspicuity. *Department of the Environment, Transport and Road Research Laboratory, Laboratory Report 534*. Crowthorne: TRRL.

Dc Pch B

Lewis, G. D. (1979). The Tamworth child pedestrian proficiency scheme. *Traffic Education*, **4**, 16–17.

Lewis, P. A. (1979). System failures on road traffic networks: can ergonomics help? *Ergonomics*, **22**, 117–127.

Liebbrand, K. (1970). *Transportation and Town Planning*. London: Leonard Hill.

G En

Liebbrand, K. (1973). Factors in town planning. *Traffic Engineering and Control*, **14**, 424–427.

G En
Lightburn, A., and Howarth, C. I. (1979). A study of observer variability and reliability in the detection and grading of traffic conflicts. *The Second International Traffic Conflicts Technique Workshop*. Nottingham, May.
r*M*
Limbourg, M. (1976). Street crossing behaviour of children aged 4–9. *Zeitschrift für Experimentelle und Angewandte Psychologie*, **23**, 666–677.
Dc Pch B N
Limbourg, M., and Gerber, D. (1978). Das Tubingen Eltern Trainingsprogramm für die Verkehrserziehung von Kindern im Vorschulalter. *Unpublished Report*, Bundesanstalt für Strassenwesen, Cologne.
Limbourg, M., and Gerber, D. (1978) Das Verhalten von 3—bis 7 jähringen Kindernbei der Strassenüberquerung unter Ablenkungsbedingungen. *Zeitschrift für Verkehrserziehung*, **2**, 10–13.
Dx Pch B N
Limbourg, M., and Günther, R. (1975). Dimensions of children's traffic environments. *Zeitschrift für Verkehrssicherheit*, **21**, 11–18.
Limbourg, M., and Günther, R. (1975). Erleben und Verhalten von 4 bis 9 jährigen Kindern im Strassenverkehr. *Zeitschrift für Verkehrserziehung*, **1**, 3–9.
Limbourg, M., Höpfner, S., and Niebling, C. (1977). Die Stabilität des Verhaltens von 4 bis 9 jährigen Kindern bei der Strassenüberquerung. *Zeitschrift für Verkehrserziehung*, **3**, 3–8.
Dc Pch B N
Limbourg, M., and Senkel, B. (1977). Behaviour of children as pedestrians–state of the art, 1976. In A. S. Hakkert (Ed.), *Proceedings of the International Conference on Pedestrian Safety*, Volume 2, 127–129. Haifa: Michlol.
G Pch B
Lindström S. (1966). How can town planning contribute towards creating a safe environment for children in respect to road accidents. In *Proceedings of the Second Congress of the International Association for Accident and Traffic Medicine*. Stockholm: International Association for Accident and Traffic Medicine.
G En
Lomax, D. E., and Downes, J. D. (1977). Patterns of travel to school and work in Reading in 1971. *Department of the Environment, Transport and Road Research Laboratory, Laboratory Report 808*. Crowthorne: TRRL.
r*Ds P B*
Lovemark, O. (1969). Method for the planning of pedestrian traffic systems in mixed street. *Planfor Report Number 16*, Helsingborg, Sweden: University of Helsingborg.
Low, M. (1969). Welcoming remarks. *Pediatrics Supplement*, **44**, 791–792.
a*T*
Lucchini, E., and Weissner, R. (1978). Influence of bumper adjustment on the kinematics of an impacted pedestrian. In *Proceedings of the Third International Meeting on Simulation and Reconstruction of Impacts*. Lyon: International Research Committee on the Biokinetics of Impact.
Lund, K., and Nordentoft, E. L. (1977). Traffic injuries to elderly pedestrians. In *Proceedings of the Third International Conference on Impact Trauma*. Berlin: International Research Committee on the Biokinetics of Impact.
Ds Pel
Mackay, G. M. (1965). Automobile design and pedestrian safety. *International Road Safety and Traffic Review*, *Summer*, 29–31.

G V
Mackay, G. M. (1969). Some features of traffic accidents. *British Medical Journal,* **4,** 799–801.
r*Ds V*
Mackay, G. M. (1972). Safer cars by 1977. *New Scientist,* **27,** 210–214.
G V
Mackay, G. M. (1972). Traffic accidents: a modern epidemic. *International Journal of Environmental Studies,* **3,** 223–227.
r*T*
Mackay, G. M. (1973). The epidemiology of injury—a review. In *Proceedings of the International Conference on the Biokinetics of Impact.* June. Amsterdam.
r*R T*
Mackay, G. M. (1973). Vehicle design and the pedestrian. In *Proceedings of the Third Congress of the International Federation of Pedestrians.* September. Scheveningen: University of Scheveningen.
R V
Mackay, G. M., and Fonseka, C. P. (1967). Some aspects of traffic injury in urban road accidents. In *Proceedings of the Eleventh Stapp Car Crash Conference.* New York: Society of Automotive Engineers.
Mackie, A. M. (1962). Accident risk to pedestrians on and within 50 yards of zebra crossings. *Traffic Engineering and Control,* **4,** 448–450.
Dc En
Mackie, A. M. (1967). Progress in learning the meanings of symbolic traffic signs. *Ministry of Transport, Road Research Laboratory, Laboratory Report 91.* Crowthorne: RRL.
Mackie, A. M., and Jacobs, G. D. (1965). Comparison of road user behaviour at panda, zebra and light-controlled crossings. *Traffic Engineering and Control,* **6,** 714–718 and 732.
Dx Dr Pad B N
Mackie, A. M., and Older, S. J. (1965). Study of pedestrian risk in crossing busy roads in London inner suburbs. *Traffic Engineering and Control,* **7,** 376–380.
Dc P B
Maddocks, G. B:, Sibert, J. R., and Brown, B. M. (1978). A four week study of accidents to children in South Glamorgan. *Public Health,* **92,** 171–176.
a*Dc Pch*
Magnusson, G. (1966). Traffic accidents among children. A critical survey and bibliography of articles reported in the Index Medicus from 1957 to 1965. In *Proceedings of the Second Congress of the International Association for Accident and Traffic Medicine.* Stockholm: International Association for Accident and Traffic Medicine.
R G
Mahalel, D., and Hakkert, A. S. (1976). Time series analysis of pedestrian accidents. In A. S. Hakkert (Ed.), *Proceedings of the International Conference on Pedestrian Safety,* Volume 1, 1H1–1H6. Haifa: Michlol.
M
Malamuth, N. M., Shayne, E., and Pogue, B. (1978). Infant cues and stopping at crosswalks. *Personality and Social Psychology Bulletin,* **4,** 334–336.
Dc Dr B
Manheimer, D. I., and Mellinger, G. D. (1967). Personality characteristics of the child accident repeater. *Child Development,* **38,** 491–513.
a*Dc Pch B*
Marcus, I. M., Wilson, W., Kraft, I., Swander, D., Southerland, F., and Schulhopfer, E.

(1960). An interdisciplinary approach to accident patterns in children. *Monographs of the Society for Research in Child Development*, **25**, 17–19 and 39–54. Reprinted in Haddon *et al.* (1964).
aDc Pch B Ens

Maring, G. E. (1972). Pedestrian travel characteristics. *Highway Research Record*, **406**, 14–20.
Ds Pad B

Marks, H. (1957). Child pedestrian safety: a realistic approach. *Traffic Engineering*, **28**, 13–19 and 25.
Ds Pch

Marland, R. E., and Burg, F. D. (1969). The injury control program of the United States Public Health Service. *Pediatrics Supplement*, **44**, 888–890.
aG

Martin, G. L., and Heimstra, N. W. (1973). The perception of hazard by children. *Journal of Safety Research*, **5**, 238–246.
aDc Pch B

Martland, W. D. (1974). Road accident prevention. *Safety Education, Spring*, 10–12.
Ge

Marvin, W. L. (1951). Driver observance of crosswalk and stop lines. *Traffic Engineering*, **21**, 157–159.
Dx Dr En B

Massey, S. A. (1962). Mathematical determination of warrants for pedestrian crossings. *Traffic Engineering*, **32**, 19–21.
Ds En

May, A. D., and Westland, D. (1979). Transportation system management. *Traffic Engineering and Control Supplement*, **20**.
G En

Mayne, A. J. (1954). Some further results in the theory of pedestrians and road traffic. *Biometrica*, **41**, 375–389.
Ds

Mayne, A. J. (1963). The problem of the careless pedestrian. In *Proceedings of the Second International Symposium of the Theory of Traffic Flow*. Paris: Organisation for Economic Co-operation and Development.
T Pad

Mayyasi, A. M., Pulley, P. E., Pooch, U. W., and Harvey, A. E. (1974). Pedestrian injury model. In *Proceedings of the Third Congress on Automotive Safety*. San Francisco, July.
T

McCarroll, J. R., Braunstein, D. W., Cooper, W., Helpern, M., Seremetis, M., Wade, P. A., and Weinberg, S. B. (1962). Fatal pedestrian accidents. *Journal of the American Medical Association*, **180**, 127.

McDowell, M. R. C., Darzentas, J., and Wennell, J. (1981). Driver gap acceptance as a measure of accident risk. In H. C. Foot, A. J. Chapman and F. M. Wade (Eds.), *Road Safety: Research and Practice*. Eastbourne: Praeger.
rM

McGarvie, A., Davies, R. F., and Sheppard, E. J. (1980). A study of a road safety film for children. *Department of the Environment, Transport and Road Research Laboratory, Supplementary Report 578*. Crowthorne: TRRL.
Dc Pch Ed

McGivern, D. (1975). A student road safety project. *Safety Education*, **135**, 7–8.

McGuire, F. L. (1976). Personality factors in highway accidents. *Human Factors*, **18**, 433–442.

r*R Dr B*
McInerney, T. J. (1959). The pedestrian safety campaign in New York city. *Traffic Quarterly*, **13**, 283–293.

McLean, A. J. (1972). Car shape and pedestrian injury. In *Proceedings of the Symposium on Road Safety*. Canberra: Australian Department of Transport.

Dc V
McLean, A. J., and Mackay, G. M. (1970). The exterior collision. In *Automobile Safety Conference Compendium*. Publication Number P30. New York: Society of Automotive Engineers.

McLean, J. R., and Hoffman, E. R. (1971). Analysis of drivers' control movements. *Human Factors*, **13**, 407–418.

r*Dx Dr B*
McLean, J. R., and Hoffman, E. R. (1972). The effects of lane width on driver steering control and performance. In *Proceedings of the Sixth Conference of the Australian Road Research Board*, **6**, 418–440.

McLean, J. R., and Hoffman, E. R. (1973). The effects of restricted preview on driver steering control and performance. *Human Factors*, **15**, 421–430.

r*Dx Dr B*
McLean, J. R., and Hoffman, E. R. (1975). Steering reversals as a measure of driver performance and steering task difficulty. *Human Factors*, **17**, 248–256.

R M
McManagle, J. C. (1952). The effects of roadside features on traffic accidents. *Traffic Quarterly*, **6**, 228–243.

r*Dc En*
McMillen, A. (1976). Pedestrian movement in a local plan. *The Planner*, **62**, 20–22.

Ds P B N
McNicol-Smith, J., and Letheren, B. F. (1961). *Alfred Hospital Accident Survey, 1960–1961*. Melbourne, Australia: University of Melbourne.

Meadows, A. (1976). Traffic education in schools. *Safety Education, Spring*, 23–25.

Ge
Meadows, A. (1977). Traffic education in Kent schools. *Safety Education*, **140**, 24–25.

Ge
Mellinger, G. D., and Manheimer, D. I. (1967). An exposure-coping model of accident liability among children. *Journal of Health and Social Behaviour*, **8**, 96–106.

a*T*
Meredith, P. (1973). Dyslexia and road accidents. *Where*, **77**, 46–47.

Dc Pch B
Meyer, R. J. (1969). The horizon of childhood injury. *Pediatrics Supplement*, **44**, 793.

a*T*
Michon, J. A., van der Molen, H. H., Rothengatter, T. A., Vinjé, M. P., and Welvaart, A. M. P. (1979). Research on child traffic education. *Information Leaflet Number 7A*. Groningen: University of Groningen, Traffic Research Centre.

Michon, J. A., and Wertheim, A. H. (1978). Drowsiness in driving. In Commission of the European Communities *Driver Fatigue in Road Traffic Accidents*, EUR 6065EN. Luxembourg: CEC.

Mihal, W. L., and Barrett, G. V. (1976). Individual differences in perceptual information processing and their relation to automobile accident involvement. *Journal of Applied Psychology*, **61**, 229–233.

r*Dc Dr B*
Miller, A., and Cook, J. A. (1967). Radburn estates revisited. Report of a user study. *The Architects' Journal*, **146**, 1075–1082.

G En
Miller, F. D., and Michael, H. L. (1964). A study of school crossing protection. *Traffic Safety Research Review*, **8**, 51–56.
Dc Pch En
Ministry of Transport (1967). Road safety—a fresh approach. *Command 3339*. London: Her Majesty's Stationery Office.
rG
Mitchell, C. G. B., and Town, S. W. (1979). Access to recreational activity. *Department of the Environment, Transport and Road Research Laboratory, Supplementary Report 468*. Crowthorne: TRRL.
rDs P B
van der Molen, H. H. (1975). Charakterisierung und Auswertung von Verkehrsunterrichtsexperimenten mit Kindern. *Workgroep Verkeerskunde Report. VK–75–09*. University of Groningen, Holland.
van der Molen, H. H. (1977). Observational studies of children's road crossing behaviour: a review of the literature. In A. S. Hakkert (Ed.), *Proceedings of the International Conference on Pedestrian Safety*, Volume 2, 77–98. Haifa: Michlol.
R Pch B
Montanari, V. (1974). Fiat technical presentation. In *Proceedings of the Fifth International Technical Conference on Experimental Safety Vehicles*. Washington DC: United States Department of Transportation.
Moore, R. L. (1956). Psychological factors of importance in traffic engineering. *Paper presented at the World Touring and Automobile Association (OTA) International Study Week in Traffic Engineering*. London, October.
Moore, R. L., and Older, S. J. (1965). Pedestrians and motor vehicles are compatible in today's world. *Traffic Engineering*, **35**, 20–23 and 52–59.
R P B En
Morris, J. P. (1972). *Road Safety Publicity: Quantifying the Effect of Public Service Advertising*. London: the Advertising Association.
rDx Dr P Ed
Mourant, R. R., and Rockwell, T. H. (1972). Strategies of visual search by novice and experienced drivers. *Human Factors*, **14**, 325–335.
rDc Dr B
Mourant, R. R., Rockwell, T. H., and Rackoff, N. J. (1969). Drivers' eye movements and visual workload. *Highway Research Record*, **292**, 1–10.
Muhlrad, N. (1976). Introduction of the pedestrian and two-wheeler safety factor in the planning process. Case study in a French new town: Le Vaudreuil. In A. S. Hakkert (Ed.), *Proceedings of the International Conference on Pedestrian Safety*, Volume 1, 3B1–3B10 Haifa: Michlol.
G En
Munsch, G. (1973). Wege zur Bildung des Verkehrssinnes. Allegmeiner, Deutscher Automobil Club, In *Der Schriftenreihe Jugendverkehrserziehung*, Heft.
Murray-Parkes, C. (1975). *Bereavement: Studies of Grief in Adult Life*. Harmondsworth, Middlesex: Penguin.
G
Näätänen, R., and Summala, H. (1976). *Road User Behaviour and Traffic Accidents*. Oxford: North Holland Publishing Company.
Nagayma, Y., Morita, T., Miura, T., Watanabem, J., and Murakami, N. (1979). Motorcyclists' visual scanning patterns in comparison with automobile drivers. *Society of Automotive Engineers Technical Paper Series, Number 790262*.
Naisbitt, J. (1961). The great holiday massacre: a study of impact. *Traffic Safety*, **58**, 12–15, 36 and 48–49.

National Safety Council. (1969). Needs and objectives for a national programme on child safety. *Pediatrics Supplement*, **44**, 876–880.
aG
National Safety Council. (1976). *Accident Facts*. Chicago: National Safety Council.
Nel, P. W. (1981). Traffic signs for pedestrians. In H. C. Foot, A. J. Chapman and F. M. Wade (Eds.), *Road Safety: Research and Practice*. Eastbourne: Praeger.
R P
Nelson, P. G. (1974). Pattern of injury survey of automobile accidents, Victoria, Australia, June 1971–June 1973. Royal Australian College of Surgeons, Melbourne.
Newson, J., and Newson, E. (1968). *Four Years Old in an Urban Community*. London: Allen and Unwin.
G
Newson, J., and Newson, E. (1976). *Seven Years Old in the Home Environment*. London: Allen and Unwin.
G
Nicholl, J. P. (1981). The usefulness of hospital in-patient data in road safety studies. In H. C. Foot, A. J. Chapman and F. M. Wade (Eds.), *Road Safety: Research and Practice*. Eastbourne: Praeger.
rR M
Northern, N. M. (1975). Road safety education for younger pupils. *Safety Education*, **135**, 5–6.
Nummenmaa, T. (1970). Development of structured descriptions of events in childhood. Unpublished Research Report 44, Department of Psychology, University of Tampere. Finland.
Nummenmaa, T., Ruuhilehto, K., and Syvänen, M. (1975). Traffic education programme for preschool aged children and children starting school. Central Organisation for Traffic Safety, Helsinki, Finland. Report Number 17.
Nummenmaa, T., and Syvänen, M. (1970). Film as a means of traffic instruction for children: an experiment. *Unpublished Research Report* 49. Tampere, Finland: Department of Psychology, University of Tampere.
Nummenmaa, T., and Syvänen, M. (1974). Teaching road safety to children in the age range 5–7 years. *Paedogogica Europaea*, **9**, 151–161.
R Dx Pch Ed
Nussenblatt, Z. (1976). The pedestrian—the judicial aspect. In A. S. Hakkert (Ed.), *Proceedings of the International Conference on Pedestrian Safety*, Volume 1, 6D1–6D12. Haifa: Michlol.
R P Enl
Odendaal, J. R. (1976). Traffic law enforcement and the pedestrian. In A. S. Hakkert (Ed.), *Proceedings of the International Conference on Pedestrian Safety*, Volume 1, 6C1–6C5. Haifa: Michlol.
R Enl
Odendaal, J. R., and Nel, P. W. (1976). Pedestrian behaviour in a heterogeneous society. In A. S. Hakkert (Ed.), *Proceedings of the International Conference on Pedestrian Safety*. Volume 1, 2E1–2E7. Haifa: Michlol.
R P B
Older, S. J. (1968). Movement of pedestrians on footways in shopping streets. *Traffic Engineering and Control*, **10**, 160–163.
Dc P B N
Older, S. J., and Basden, J. M. (1961). Road user behaviour at a pedestrian crossing. *Traffic Engineering and Control*, **3**, 94–97.
Dc Pad B N
Older, S. J., and Grayson, G. B. (1974). Perception and decision in the pedestrian task.

Department of the Environment, Transport and Road Research Laboratory, Supplementary Report 49 UC. Crowthorne: TRRL.
T
Older, S. J., and Grayson, G. B. (1976). An international comparison of risk in four cities. In A. S. Hakkert (Ed.), *Proceedings of the International Conference on Pedestrian Safety*, Volume 1, 1A1–1A7. Haifa: Michlol.
Dc *P B N*
Older, S. J., and Spicer, B. R. (1976). Traffic conflicts—a development in accident research. *Human Factors*, **18**, 334–350.
r*M*
Organisation for Economic Co-operation and Development (1971). *Road Safety Campaigns: Design and Evaluation.* Paris: Organisation for Economic Co-operation and Development.
R M
Organisation for Economic Co-operation and Development (1971). *Lighting, Visibility and Accidents.* Paris: Organisation for Economic Co-operation and Development.
r*G En*
Organisation for Economic Co-operation and Development (1974). *Streets for People.* Paris: Organisation for Economic Co-operation and Development.
r*G En*
Organisation for Economic Co-operation and Development (1976). *Adverse Weather, Reduced Visibility and Road Safety.* Paris: Organisation for Economic Co-operation and Development.
r*G En*
Organisation for Economic Co-operation and Development Special Research Group on Pedestrian Safety (1977). Chairman's Report and Report of Sub-Group I: The Pedestrian's Road Environment. *UK Department of the Environment, Transport and Road Research Laboratory.* Crowthorne: TRRL.
R En
Organisation for Economic Co-operation and Development Special Research Group on Pedestrian Safety (1978). *Chairman's Report and Report of Sub-Group II: Road Safety Education. Department of the Environment, Transport and Road Research Laboratory.* Crowthorne: TRRL.
R Pch B Ed
Organisation for Economic Co-operation and Development Special Research Group on Pedestrian Safety (1978). *Chairman's Report and Report of Sub-Group III: Mass Media Communications for Pedestrian Safety. Department of the Environment, Transport and Road Research Laboratory.* Crowthorne: TRRL.
R Dr P Ed
Organisation for Economic Co-operation and Development (1981). *Methods for Evaluating Road Safety Measures.* Paris: Organisation for Economic Co-operation and Development.
Osborne E. A. (1975). Road safety. Sharing the responsibility. *Safety Education, Spring*, 6–7.
Ge
Owens, D. A., and Leibowitz, H. W., and Norman, J. (1976). Pedestrian night accidents and night myopia. In A. S. Hakkert (Ed.), *Proceedings of the International Conference on Pedestrian Safety*, Volume 1, 4B1–4B5. Haifa: Michlol.
R G
Padgaonkar, A. J., Krieger, K. W., and King, A. J. (1976). A three-dimensional mathematical simulation of pedestrian-vehicle impact with experimental verification. *Paper 76–WA/Bio-1.* American Society of Mechanical Engineers.

Page, T. J., Iwata, B. A., and Neef, N. A. (1976). Teaching pedestrian skills to retarded persons: generalization from the classroom to the natural environment. *Journal of Applied Behavioural Analysis*, **9**, 433–444.
Dx Phc *Ed*

Pease, K., and Preston, B. (1967). Road safety education for young children. *British Journal of Educational Psychology*, **33**, 305–312.
Dx Pch *Ed*

Pelz, D. C., and Schuman, S. H. (1971). Are young drivers really more dangerous after controlling for age and experience? *Journal of Safety Research*, **3**, 68–79.

Pfefer, R. C., Hutter, J. A., and Sorton, A. (1976). Some considerations in planning for safe and efficient pedestrian facilities. In A. S. Hakkert (Ed.), *Proceedings of the International Conference on Pedestrian Safety*, Volume 1, 3A1–3A13. Haifa: Michlol.
Dc *En*

Piccolino, E. B. (1968). Depicted threat, realism and specificity: variables governing safety poster effectiveness. *Dissertation Abstracts International*, **28B**, 4330.

Pillai, K. S. (1975). Pedestrian crossings. 1. Warrants for different types of pedestrian crossing based on delay to vehicles. *Traffic Engineering and Control*, **16**, 118–120.
G *Ds*

Pillai, K. S. (1975). Pedestrian crossings. 2. A method to design cycle time for signal-controlled pedestrian crossings. *Traffic Engineering and Control*, **16**, 120–121.
G *Ds*

Preston, B. (1972). Statistical analysis of child pedestrian accidents in Manchester and Salford. *Accident Analysis and Prevention*, **4**, 323–332.
Dc Pch B *En Ens*

Preston, B. (1980). The effectiveness of children's road safety education. In D. J. Oborne and J. A. Levis (Eds.), *Human Factors in Transport Research*, Volume 2, *User Factors: Comfort, the Environment and Behaviour*. London: Academic Press.
G Pch *Ed*

Preston, B. (1980). Teaching the Green Cross Code. *Traffic Education*, **5**, 3–4.

Price, R. (1966). Knowledge as the basis for prevention of child and young people road traffic accidents. In *Proceedings of the Second Congress of the International Association for Accidents and Traffic Medicine*. Stockholm: International Association for Accident and Traffic Medicine.
r*G*

Prigogine, Y., Roche, M., Sheppard, D., and Wind, G. H. (1975). *Manual on Road Safety Campaigns*. Paris: Organisation for Economic Co-operation and Development.
G P Dr *Ed*

Pritz, H. B. (1976). A preliminary assessment of the pedestrian injury reduction performance of the Calspan Research Safety Vehicle. In *Proceedings of the Sixth International Technical Conference on Experimental Safety Vehicles*. Washington DC: United States Department of Transportation.

Pritz, H. B. (1977). Experimental investigation of pedestrian injury minimization through vehicle design. *Paper 770095*. Warrendale: Society of Automotive Engineers.

Pritz, H. B. (1979). Vehicle design for pedestrian protection. In *Proceedings of the Seventh International Technical Conference on Experimental Safety Vehicles*. Washington DC: United States Department of Transportation.

Pritz, H. B., Hassler, C. R., Herridge, J. T., and Weis, E. B. (1975). Experimental study of pedestrian injury minimization through vehicle design. In *Proceedings of the Nineteenth Stapp Car Crash Conference*. Warrendale: Society of Automotive Engineers.

Pritz, H. B., Weis, E. B., and Herridge, J. T. (1975). Body-vehicle interaction: experimental study. Volume 1. *Summary Report Number DOT-HS-801-473*. Washington DC: United States Department of Transportation.

Pritz, H. B., Weis, E. B., and Herridge, J. T. (1975). Body-vehicle interaction: experimental study. Volume 2. *Summary Report Number DOT-HS-801-474*. Washington DC: United States Department of Transportation.

Psychologie (1977). Psychology and traffic. *Psychologie*, **36**, Part 4, Whole Issue.

Quenault, S. W. (1967). Driver behaviour—safe and unsafe drivers. *Ministry of Transport, Road Research Laboratory, Laboratory Report 70*. Crowthorne: RRL.
r*Dc Dr B*

Quenault, S. W. (1967). The driving behaviour of certain professional drivers. *Ministry of Transport, Road Research Laboratory, Laboratory Report 93*. Crowthorne: RRL.
r*Dc Dr B*

Quenault, S. W. (1968). Development of the method of systematic observation of driver behaviour. *Department of the Environment, Road Research Laboratory, Laboratory Report 213*. Crowthorne: RRL.
r*M N*

Quenault, S. W. (1968). Dissociation and driver behaviour. *Ministry of Transport, Road Research Laboratory, Laboratory Report 212*. Crowthorne: RRL.
r*T Dr*

Quenault, S. W. (1968). Driver behaviour—safe and unsafe drivers II. *Ministry of Transport, Road Research Laboratory, Laboratory Report 146*. Crowthorne: RRL.
r*Dc Dr B*

Quenault, S. W., and Parker, P. M. (1973). Driver behaviour—newly qualified drivers. *Department of the Environment, Transport and Road Research Laboratory, Laboratory Report 567*. Crowthorne: TRRL.
r*Dx Dr B*

Ramet, M., and Cesari, D. (1976). Bilateral study—100 injured pedestrians connection with the vehicle. In *Proceedings of the Conference on Biomechanics of Injury to Pedestrian, Cyclists and Motorcyclists*. Lyon: International Research Committee on the Biokinetics of Impact.
Dc V

Rapoport, A. (1961). Some comments on accident research. In *Behavioral Approaches to Accident Research*. New York: Association for the Aid of Crippled Children. Reprinted in Haddon *et al.* (1964).
a*G*

Rapoport, A. (1981). On the perceptual separation of pedestrians and motorists. In H. C. Foot, A. J. Chapman and F. M. Wade (Eds.), *Road Safety: Research and Practice*. Eastbourne: Praeger.
R En

Rayner, D. S. (1975). Some safety considerations in the conversion of zebra crossings to pelican crossings. *Traffic Engineering and Control*, **16**, 123–124.
Dx P B N

Read, J. H. (1969). Traffic accidents involving child pedestrians: a program for their prevention. *Pediatrics Supplement*, **44**, 838–847.
R G

Read, J. H., Bradley, E. J., Morison, J. D., Lewall, D., and Clarke, D. A. (1963). The epidemiology and prevention of traffic accidents involving child pedestrians. *Canadian Medical Association Journal*, **89**, 687–701.
Ds Pch Dr En Ens

Reading, J. B. (1973). Pedestrian protection through behaviour modification. *Traffic Engineering*, **43**, 14–16 and 19–23.

Dx Pch *B*

Reichman, S. (1977). Pedestrian culture *vis-à-vis* motorized culture, some policy reflections on urban transportation. In A. S. Hakkert (Ed.), *Proceedings of the International Conference on Pedestrian Safety*, Volume 2, 69–76. Haifa: Michlol.

Dc *P B N*

Reiss, M. L. (1976). Young pedestrian behaviour (as derived from structured classroom surveys). In A. S. Hakkert (Ed.), *Proceedings of the International Conference on Pedestrian Safety*, Volume 1, 8A1–8A8. Haifa: Michlol.

Dc Pch *B*

Rennie, A. M., and Wilson, J. R. (1980). How drivers respond to pedestrians and vice versa. In D. J. Oborne and J. A. Levis (Eds.), *Human Factors in Transport Research*, Volume 2, *User Factors: Comfort, the Environment and Behaviour*. London: Academic Press.

Richard, H. (1977). Safety of children on their way to and from school. In A. S. Hakkert (Ed.), *Proceedings of the International Conference on Pedestrian Safety*, Volume 2, 137–139. Haifa: Michlol.

G *Pch*

Rigby, J. P. (1979). A review of research on school travel patterns and problems. *Department of the Environment, Transport and Road Research Laboratory, Supplementary Report 460*. Crowthorne: TRRL.

rDs Pch *B*

Rigby, J. P., and Hyde, P. J. (1977). Journeys to school: a survey of secondary schools in Berkshire and Surrey. *Department of the Environment, Transport and Road Research Laboratory, Laboratory Report 776*. Crowthorne: TRRL.

rDs Pch *B*

Riggins, R. S., Kraus, J. F., Tranti, C. E., and Bormani, N. O. (1976). Epidemiological and clinical features of spinal cord injured pedestrians. In *Proceedings of the Meeting on the Biomechanics of Injury to Pedestrians, Cyclists and Motorcyclists*. Lyon: International Research Committee on the Biokinetics of Impact.

Ritter, P. (1964). *Planning for Man and Motor*. Oxford: Pergamon Press.

G *En*

Robbins, D. H., Bennett, R. O., and Bowman, B. M. (1973). *MVMA Two-Dimensional Crash Victim Simulation*. Highway Safety Research Institute. Michigan: University of Michigan, USA.

Roberts, I. G. (1973). Road safety in Hertfordshire schools. *Safety Education*, **128**, 16–18.

Roberts, I. G. (1977). Road safety in middle schools in Hertfordshire. *Traffic Education*, **2**, 24–26.

Robertson, H. D. (1976). Intersection improvements for pedestrians. In A. S. Hakkert (Ed.), *Proceedings of the International Conference on Pedestrian Safety*, Volume 1, 5C1–5C6. Haifa: Michlol.

R *En*

Robertson, J. S., McLean, A. J., and Ryan, G. A. (1966). Traffic accidents in Adelaide, South Australia. *Special Report Number 1*. Canberra: Australian Road Research Board.

Robertson, L. A., and Baker, S. P. (1976). Motor vehicle sizes in 1440 fatal crashes. *Accident Analysis and Prevention*, **8**, 167–175.

rDc

Robinson, C. C. (1951). Pedestrian interval acceptance. *1951 Proceedings of the Institute of Traffic Engineers*, 144–150.

Ds *Pad B N*
Rockwell, T. H. (1972). Skills, judgements, and information acquisition in driving. In
T. W. Forbes (Ed.), *Human Factors in Highway Traffic Safety Research*. New York:
Wiley.
Rosellen, H. P. (1979). Zebra crossings painted out as statistics show up dangers. *The
German Tribune*, **913**, 8.
Dc *En*
Ross, H. E., White, M. C., and Young, R. D. (1974). Drop tests of dummies on a mock
vehicle exterior. In *Proceedings of the Third International Congress on Automobile
Safety*. Washington DC: United States Department of Transportation.
Ross, S. P., and Seefeldt, C. (1978). Young children in traffic: how can they cope? *Young
Children*, **33**, 68–73.
Ge
Rothengatter, T. A. (1978). Learning foundations of traffic education. *Report VK-77-01*,
Traffic Research Centre, Rijksuniversiteit Groningen, Groningen.
Rothengatter, T. (1981). Traffic education for young children. In H. C. Foot, A. J.
Chapman and F. M. Wade (Eds.), *Road Safety: Research and Practice*. Eastbourne:
Praeger.
R *Pch Ed*
Rothengatter, T. A., (1981). *Traffic Safety Education for Young: Children—An Empirical
Approach*. Swets and Zeitlinger.
R D *Pch Ed*
Rothengatter, T. A., and Brakenhoff-Splinter, J. (1979). Training road crossing be-
haviour for children. *Report VK 79-02, Traffic Research Centre*. Groningen:
Rijksuniversiteit Groningen.
Routledge, D. A. (1975). The behaviour of child pedestrians: an approach to the
problem of the child pedestrian accidents. *Unpublished Doctoral Dissertation*,
Nottingham: University of Nottingham, United Kingdom.
R Dc *Pch B N*
Routledge, D. A., Repetto-Wright, R., and Howarth, C. I. (1974). A comparison of
interviews and observation to obtain measures of children's exposure to risk as
pedestrians. *Ergonomics*, **17**, 623–638.
M Dc *Pch B N*
Routledge, D. A., Repetto-Wright, R., and Howarth, C. I. (1974). The exposure of
young children to accident risk as pedestrians. *Ergonomics*, **17**, 457–480.
Dc *Pch B N*
Routledge, D. A., Repetto-Wright, R., and Howarth, C. I. (1976). The development of
road crossing skill by child pedestrians. In A. S. Hakkert (Ed.), *Proceedings of the
International Conference on Pedestrian Safety*, Volume 1, 7C1–7C9. Haifa: Michlol.
Dc *P B N*
Routledge, D. A., Repetto-Wright, R., and Howarth, C. I. (1976). Four techniques for
measuring the exposure of young children to accident risk as pedestrians. In A. S.
Hakkert (Ed.), *Proceedings of the International Conference on Pedestrian Safety*,
Volume 1, 7B1–7B7. Haifa: Michlol.
M Dc *Pch B N*
Royal Society for the Prevention of Accidents. (1971). The Green Cross Code. *Safety
Education, Autumn*, 3–4.
Ge
Royal Society for the Prevention of Accidents. (1971). A road safety fortnight. *Safety
Education, Autumn*, 22–23.
Ge
Royal Society for the Prevention of Accidents. (1973). *Suggestions for Road Safety*

Teaching for the Middle Years (8–13 years of age). Birmingham: Royal Society for the Prevention of Accidents.
Ge

Royal Society for the Prevention of Accidents (1973). *Suggestions for Teaching Safety to Children of 3 to 7*. Birmingham: Royal Society for the Prevention of Accidents.
Ge

Royal Society for the Prevention of Accidents. (1975). *Suggestions for Teaching Road Safety*. Birmingham: Royal Society for the Prevention of Accidents.
Ge

Royal Society for the Prevention of Accidents (1976). Why young children dash into the road. *Safety Education, Autumn* 25.
Ds Pch B

Rumar, K. (1966). Night driving: visibility of pedestrians. *Paper presented at the Seventh International Road Safety Congress of the World Touring and Automobile Organisation (OTA)*. London, September.

Rumar, K. (1976). Pedestrian safety in night driving. In A. S. Hakkert (Ed.), *Proceedings of the International Conference on Pedestrian Safety*, Volume 1, 7A1–7A5. Haifa: Michlol.
R Dr B

Russam, K. (1975). Road safety of children in the United Kingdom. *Department of the Environment, Transport and Road Research Laboratory, Laboratory Report 678*. Crowthorne: TRRL.
R G

Russam, K. (1977). The psychology of children in traffic. In A. S. Hakkert (Ed.), *Proceedings of the International Conference on Pedestrian Safety*, Volume 2, 99–106. Haifa: Michlol.
R G

Russam, K. (1977). The psychology of children in traffic. In R. H. Jackson (Ed.), *Children, the Environment and Accidents*. London: Pitman.
R G

Russam, K. (1977). The psychology of children in traffic. *Department of the Environment, Transport and Road Research Laboratory, Supplementary Report 295*. Crowthorne: TRRL.
R G

Russell, J. C., Wilson, D. O., and Jenkins, J. F. (1976). Informational properties of jaywalking models as determinants of imitated jaywalking: an extension to model, sex, race and number. *Sociometry*, **39**, 270–273.
Dc P B

Ryan, G. A. (1969). Children in traffic accidents. *Pediatrics Supplement*, **44**, 847–854.
rT

Sabey, B. E. (1973). Accidents in urban areas. In *Report of the Conference on Traffic Engineering and Road Safety*. October. Brighton.
rDs En

Sabey, B. E. (1979). A review of drinking and drug-taking in road accidents in Great Britain. *Department of the Environment, Transport and Road Research Laboratory, Supplementary Report 441*. Crowthorne: TRRL.
rR Dr B

Sabey, B. E. (1980). Road safety and value for money. *Department of the Environment, Transport and Road Research Laboratory, Supplementary Report 581*. Crowthorne: TRRL.
G

Sabey, B. E., and Staughton, G. C. (1975). Interacting roles of road environment, vehicle and road user in accidents. *Paper presented at the Fifth International Conference of the International Association for Accident and Traffic Medicine.* September. London: University of London.

Sabey, B. E., and Staughton, G. C. (1980). The drinking driver in Great Britain. *Paper presented at the Eighth International Conference on Alcohol, Drugs and Traffic Safety.* June. Stockholm, Sweden: University of Stockholm.

Sabey, B. E., and Staughton, G. C. (1980). The drinking road user in Great Britain. *Department of the Environment, Transport and Road Research Laboratory, Supplementary Report 616.* Crowthorne: TRRL.
R Dc P B

Sadler, J. (1972). *Children and Road Safety: A Survey Amongst Mothers.* London: Her Majesty's Stationery Office.
Dc Pch B Ens

Salvatore, S. (1974). The ability of elementary and secondary school children to sense oncoming car velocity. *Journal of Safety Research*, **6**, 118–123.
Dc Pch B

Salwen, L. H. (1967). Personality factors in the accident repeating boy. *Dissertation Abstracts*, **28 (5-B)**, 2149–2150.
aDc Pch B

Sandels, S. (1966). Young children's ability to understand traffic education. In *Proceedings of the Second Congress of the International Association for Accident and Traffic Medicine.* Stockholm: International Association for Accident and Traffic Medicine.
R Pch B Ed

Sandels, S. (1970). Young children in traffic. *British Journal of Educational Psychology*, **40**, 111–116.
Dx Pch B Ed

Sandels, S. (1971). A report on children in traffic. *Skandia Report I.* Stockholm: Skandia.
G Pch B

Sandels, S. (1974). Road accidents to children: what makes them happen? In *Proceedings of the Third Congress of the International Federation of Pedestrians.* Scheveningen, September.
R Pch Dr En

Sandels, S. (1974). Why are children injured in traffic? Can we prevent child accidents in traffic? *Skandia Report II.* Stockholm: Skandia.
G Pch Dr

Sandels, S. (1975). *Children in Traffic.* London: Elek.
Dc Pch B Ed

Sandels, S. (1979). Unprotected road users. A behavioral study. *Skandia Report III.* Stockholm: Skandia.
Ds Pch Dr B

Sargent, K. J. A., and Sheppard, D. (1974). The development of the Green Cross Code. *Department of the Environment, Transport and Road Research Laboratory, Laboratory Report 605.* Crowthorne: TRRL.
Dc Pch Ed

Sattler, K. O. (1979). Children's traffic training 'inadequate'. *The German Tribune*, **913**, 8.
Dc Pch Ed

Schenirer, T., and Tchelet, M. (1976). Facilities for pedestrians on interurban roads in Israel. In A. S. Hakkert (Ed.), *Proceedings of the International Conference on Pedestrian Safety*, Volume 1, 5H1–5H11. Haifa: Michlol.
G En

Schioldborg, P. (1974). Children, traffic and traffic training: an analysis of the children traffic club. *Unpublished Report, Psychological Institute* Oslo, Norway: University of Oslo.

Schioldborg, P. (1976). Children, traffic and traffic training. *Paper presented at the Fifth Congress of the International Federation of Pedestrians.* June. Geilo, Norway: University of Geilo.

Dc Pch Ed

Schools Council Project. (1977). *Health Education 5–13.* London: Nelson.

Schreiber, J., and Berry, C. (1978). *Communicating Road Safety to the Young Pedestrian—Evaluation of Road Safety Resource Material for Infants Schools.* Rosebery, New South Wales, Australia: Traffic Accident Research Unit, Department of Motor Transport.

Schreiber, J., and Lukin, J. (1978). *Communicating Road Safety to the Young Pedestrian: an Exploratory Research Programme.* Rosebery, New South Wales, Australia. Traffic Accident Research Unit, Department of Motor Transport.

Schuster, D. H. (1970). Attitudes toward driving safely and their modification. *Human Factors,* **12**, 89–94.

G R Dr

Shaoul, J. E. (1976). The use of intermediate criteria for evaluating the effectiveness of accident countermeasures. *Human Factors,* **18**, 575–586.

M

Shapiro, H. A. (1977). The mechanism of head injuries and their prevention. In A. S. Hakkert (Ed.), *Proceedings of the International Conference on Pedestrian Safety,* Volume 2, 23–50. Haifa: Michlol.

G

Shapiro, L., and Mortimer, R. G. (1969). A literature review and bibliography on research and practice in pedestrian safety. *Highway Safety Research Institute, Report HUF-3.* Ann Arbor: University of Michigan.

Sharon, E. (1977). Pedestrian safety and the children. In A. S. Hakkert (Ed.), *Proceedings of the International Conference on Pedestrian Safety,* Volume 2, 141–142. Haifa: Michlol.

G

Shaw, J. I., and McMartin, J. A. (1973). Effect of who suffers in an automobile accident on judgemental strictness. In *Proceedings of the Eighty-First Annual Convention of the American Psychological Association.* Washington DC: American Psychological Association.

rDx Dr

Shaw, J. I., and McMartin, J. A. (1977). Personal and situational determinants of attribution of responsibility for an accident. *Human Relations,* **30**, 95–107.

Dx B

Shaw, L., and Sichel, H. (1971). *Accident Proneness.* Oxford: Pergamon Press.

aR T

Sheehy, N. (1979). The perception of hazard by child pedestrians. *Paper presented at the Annual Conference of the British Psychological Society, Developmental Section.* September. Southampton.

T R

Sheehy, N. (1980). The child pedestrian's perception of hazard. *Paper presented at the Second Annual Conference on Postgraduate Psychology.* Lancaster, England, April.

T Dx Pch

Sheppard, D. (1975). The driving situation which worry motorists. *Department of the Environment, Transport and Road Research Laboratory, Supplementary Report 129 UC.* Crowthorne: TRRL.

r*Dc Dr B*
Sheppard, D. (1975). Teaching pedestrian skills. A graded structure. *Safety Education*,
135, 13–17.
Ge
Sheppard, D. (1975). To learn or not to learn the Green Cross Code. *Safety Education*, **133**
5–7.
Ge
Sheppard, D. (1976). Teachers' views about teaching road safety. *Department of the
Environment, Transport and Road Research Laboratory, Supplementary Report 185 UC.*
Crowthorne: TRRL.
Ds Pch Ed
Sheppard, D. (1977). Ways in which school crossing patrols instruct children about
crossing roads. *Department of the Environment, Transport and Road Research
Laboratory, Laboratory Report 779.* Crowthorne: TRRL.
Ds Pch Ed
Sheppard, D. (1980). The development of methods for teaching pedestrian skills to
children. In D. J. Oborne and J. A. Levis (Eds.), *Human Factors in Transport Research*,
Volume 2, *User Factors: Comfort, the Environment and Behaviour.* London: Academic
Press.
R Ed
Sheppard, D. (1981). Designing road safety teaching and publicity materials for children.
In H. C. Foot, A. J. Chapman and F. M. Wade (Eds.), *Road Safety: Research and
Practice.* Eastbourne: Praeger
R Pch Ed
Sheppard, D., and Colborne, H. V. (1968). Understanding of road safety propaganda.
Safety Education, Autumn, 12–13.
Dc Pch Ed
Sheppard, E. J. (1969). A study of two road safety films. *Safety Education*, **115**, 19–20.
Sheppard, E. J. (1975). Comprehension by children of aerial views in road safety teaching
aids. *Department of the Environment, Transport and Road Research Laboratory,
Supplementary Report 152 UC.* Crowthorne: TRRL.
Ds Pch Ed
Shinar, D. (1978). *Psychology on the Road: The Human Factor in Traffic Safety.* New
York: Wiley.
r*R*
Shinar, D., McDowell, E. D., Rackoff, N. J., and Rockwell T. H. (1978). Field
dependence and driver visual search behaviour. *Human Factors*, **20**, 553–559.
r*Dc Dr B*
Singer, R. E. (1963). Action for pedestrian safety and control. *International Road Safety
Traffic Review*, **11**, 17–20, 22–24 and 29.
G P Ed En
Singh, A. (1976). Road safety education in primary and middle schools. *Department of the
Environment, Transport and Road Research Laboratory, Supplementary Report 207 UC.*
Crowthorne: TRRL.
Ds Pch Ed
Singh, A. (1979). Children and traffic: evaluation of the effects of traffic education on the
knowledge and attitudes of children aged 5–13. *Traffic Education*, **4**, 8–12
Singh, A. (1980). Evaluation of the final draft of the 'children and traffic' series of teachers'
guides. *Department of the Environment, Transport and Road Research Laboratory,
Supplementary Report 556.* Crowthorne: TRRL.
Dx Pad Pch Ed
Skelton, N., Bruce, S., and Trenchard, M. (1976). Pedestrian vehicle conflict and the

operation of pedestrian light-controlled (pelican) crossings. In A. S. Hakkert (Ed.), *Proceedings of the International Conference on Pedestrian Safety*, Volume 1, 5D1–5D9. Haifa: Michlol.
Dc *P B N*

Slop, M. (1976). Application of pedestrian crossings. In A. S. Hakkert (Ed.), *Proceedings of the International Conference on Pedestrian Safety*, Volume 1, 1G1–1G9. Haifa: Michlol.
R En

Smeed, R. J. (1968). Aspects of pedestrian safety. *Journal of Transport Economics and Policy*, **2**, 255–279.
R P Enl En B

Smeed. R. J. (1977). Pedestrian accidents. In A. S. Hakkert (Ed.), *Proceedings of the International Conference on Pedestrian Safety*, Volume 2, 7–21. Haifa: Michlol.
Dc *P En*

Snyder, M. G., and Knoblauch, R. L. (1971). Pedestrian safety: the identification of precipitating factors and possible countermeasures. *Operations Research Report Number FH. 11-7312*. Washington DC: United States Department of Transportation.

Solheim, K. (1964). Pedestrian deaths in Oslo traffic accidents. *British Medical Journal*, **1**, 81.
Ds *P*

Soliday, S. M. (1975). Development and preliminary testing of a driver hazard questionnaire. *Perceptual and Motor Skills*, **41**, 763–770.
Dc *Dr*

Staughton, G. C., and Storie, V. J. (1977). Methodology of an in-depth accident investigation survey. *Department of the Environment, Transport and Road Research Laboratory, Laboratory Report 762*. Crowthorne: TRRL.
r*M*

Stcherbatcheff, G., Tarrière, C., Duclos, P., Fayon, A., Got, C., and Patel, A. (1975). Reconstructions experimentales d'impacts tête-vehicle de pietons accidente. In *Proceedings of the Second International Conference on the Biomechanics of Serious Trauma*. Lyon: International Research Committee on the Biokinetics of Impact.

Stcherbatcheff, G., Tarrière, C., Duclos, P., Fayon, A., Got, C., and Patel, A. (1975). Simulation of collisions between pedestrians and vehicles using adult and child dummies. In *Proceedings of the Nineteenth Stapp Car Crash Conference*. Warrendale: Society of Automotive Engineers.

Stephens, M. (1978). Health and traffic education 5–13 and 13–18. *Traffic Education*, **3**, 18–20.

Stokes, J. (1976). Safety—a school project. *Safety Education*, **138**, 8–9.

Storey, L. H. (1965). New street marking system controls pedestrian traffic. *Traffic Engineering*, **25**, 32 and 34.
G En

Storie, V. J. (1977). Male and female driver: differences observed in accidents. *Department of the Environment, Transport and Road Research Laboratory, Laboratory Report 761*. Crowthorne: TRRL.
r*Dc Dr B*

Stürtz, G., and Suren, E. G. (1976). Kinematics of real pedestrian and two-wheel rider accidents and special aspects of pedestrian accidents. In *Proceedings of the Conference on Biomechanics of Injury to Pedestrians, Cyclists and Motorcyclists*. Lyon: International Research Committee on the Biokinetics of Impact.

Suchman, E. A., and Schertyer, A. L. (1960). Accident proneness. In *Current Research in Childhood Accidents*. New York: Association for the Aid of Crippled Children. Reprinted in Haddon *et al.* (1964).

a*T*

Suchman, E. A. (1961). A conceptual analysis of the accident phenomenon. *Social Problems*, **8**, 241–253. Reprinted in Haddon *et al.* (1964).

a*T*

Sumner, R., and Baguley, C. (1978). Speed control humps in Norwich and Haringey. *Department of the Environment, Transport and Road Research Laboratory, Supplementary Report 423*. Crowthorne: TRRL.

r*Dx En*

Sumner, R., and Baguley, C. (1979). Speed control humps in Kensington and Glasgow. *Department of the Environment, Transport and Road Research Laboratory, Supplementary Report 456*. Crowthorne: TRRL.

r*Dx En*

Sumner, R., and Baguley, C. (1979). Speed control humps on residential roads. *Department of the Environment, Transport and Road Research Laboratory, Laboratory Report 878*. Crowthorne: TRRL.

r*Dx En*

Sumner, R., Burton, J., and Baguley, C. (1978). Speed control humps in Cuddeston Way, Cowley, Oxford. *Department of the Environment, Transport and Road Research Laboratory, Supplementary Report 350*. Crowthorne: TRRL.

r*Dx En*

Sumner, R., and Shippey, J. (1977). The use of rumble areas to alert drivers. *Department of the Environment, Transport and Road Research Laboratory, Laboratory Report 800*. Crowthorne: TRRL.

Svenson, O. (1976). Experience of mean speed related to speed over parts of a trip. *Ergonomics*, **19**, 11–20.

r*Dx Dr B*

Swedish National Board of Planning (SCAFT) (1968). *The SCAFT Guidelines: Principles for Urban Planning with Respect to Road Safety*. Stockholm: University of Stockholm.

Swinney, S. (1974). Automatic time-lapse 16 mm cine camera for street scene photography. *Traffic Engineering and Control*, **15**, 450–451.

M N

SWOV (1976). Drinking and driving. *Institute for Road Safety Research. Publication 1976—4E*. Voorburg: SWOV.

r*G Dr*

SWOV (1976). Pedestrians, two wheelers and road safety. *Institute for Road Safety Research. Publication 1976—3E*. Voorburg: SWOV.

*D*c

SWOV (1977). Drinking by motorists. *Institute for Road Safety Research. Publication 1977—2E*. Voorburg: SWOV.

*D*c *Dr*

SWOV (1977). The pedestrian as a road user. *Institute for Road Safety Research Publication 1977—1E*. Voorburg: SWOV.

r*D*c *P*

SWOV (1978). Ten years of road safety in the Netherlands. *Institute for Road Safety Research. Publication 1978—1E*. Voorburg: SWOV.

r*G D*c

Taneda, K., Kondo, M., and Higuchi, K. (1973). Experiments in passenger car and pedestrian dummy collisions. In *Proceedings of the First International Conference on the Biokinetics of Impact*. Lyon: International Research Committee on Biokinetics of Impact.

Tanner, J. C. (1951). The delay to pedestrians crossing a road. *Biometrika*, **38**, 383–392.

Ds En

Tarrants, W. E., and Veigel, C. H. (1978). The evaluation of highway traffic safety programs. *Report Number DOT-HS-802-525.* Washington DC: United States Department of Transportation.

Taylor, H. (1977). Pedestrian safety: the role of research. *Department of the Environment, Transport and Road Research Laboratory, Supplementary Report 319.* Crowthorne: TRRL.

R P Ed En

Tepley, S. (1972). Pedestrian zone in Munich—maturation for pedestrian movement. *Traffic Engineering,* **43**, 18–24.

Dc P B En

Tharp, K. J. (1974). Multidisciplinary accident investigation pedestrian involvement. *Report Number DOT-HS-801-165.* Washington DC: United States Department of Transportation.

Tharp, K.J., and Tsongos, H.S. (1976). Injury factors traffic in pedestrian collisions. In *Proceedings of the Conference of the Biomechanics of Injury to Pedestrians, Cyclists and Motorcyclists.* Lyon: International Research Committee on the Biokinetics of Impact.

Thomas, C., Stcherbatcheff, G., Duclos, P., Tarrière, C., Foret-Bruno, J. Y., Got, C., and Patel, A. (1976). A synthesis of data from a multi-disciplinary survey on pedestrian accidents. In *Proceedings of the Conference on the Biomechanics of Injury to Pedestrians, Cyclists and Motorcyclists.* Lyon: International Research Committee on the Biokinetics of Impact.

Thomson, G. A. (1978). A model for determining the effectiveness of intersection priority rules. *Accident Analysis and Prevention,* **10**, 313–333.

rM

Tillman, W. A., and Hobb, G. E. (1949). The accident prone automobile driver. *American Journal of Psychiatry,* **106**, 321–331. Reprinted in Haddon *et al.* (1964).

rDc Dr B

Todd, J. E., and Walker, A. (1980). *People as Pedestrians.* London: Her Majesty's Stationery Office.

Dc Pad B N

Tonge, J. I., O'Reilly, M. J. J., and Davison, A. (1964). Fatal traffic accidents in Brisbane from 1935–1964. *Medical Journal of Australia,* **2**, 811.

Tonge, J. I., O'Reilly, M. J. J., Davison. A., and Johnson, N. G. (1972). Traffic crash fatalities, injury patterns and other factors. *Medical Journal of Australia,* **2**, 5.

Tower, D. Q. (1976). Relationships between perceptual responses and accident patterns in children: a pilot study. *American Journal of Occupational Therapy,* **30**, 498–501.

Dx Pch B

Transport and Road Research Laboratory. (1972). Accidents to elderly pedestrians. *Department of the Environment, Transport and Road Research Laboratory, Leaflet 323.* Crowthorne: TRRL.

Ds Pel

Transport and Road Research Laboratory. (1974). Accidents in urban areas. *Department of the Environment, Transport and Road Research Laboratory, Leaflet 388.* Crowthorne: TRRL.

rDs En

Transport and Road Research Laboratory. (1974). Pedestrian injuries. *Department of the Environment, Transport and Road Research Laboratory, Leaflet 317.* Crowthorne: TRRL.

Transport and Road Research Laboratory. (1976). Pedestrian behaviour at pelican crossings. *Department of the Environment, Transport and Road Research Laboratory, Leaflet 629.* Crowthorne: TRRL.

Ds En
Transport and Road Research Laboratory. (1977). Motion prediction and accident prevention. *Department of the Environment, Transport and Road Research Laboratory, Leaflet 644.* Crowthorne: TRRL.

Dx Pch B
Transport and Road Research Laboratory. (1977). Road accidents in residential areas. *Department of the Environment, Transport and Road Research Laboratory, Leaflet 650.* Crowthorne: TRRL.

rDs En
Transport and Road Research Laboratory. (1978). A new rapid test of visual contrast sensitivity function for drivers. *Department of the Environment, Transport and Road Research Laboratory, Leaflet 696.* Crowthorne: TRRL.

rG Dr B
Transport and Road Research Laboratory. (1978). Progress in road safety education. *Department of the Environment, Transport and Road Research Laboratory, Leaflet 695.* Crowthorne: TRRL.

G Ed
Transport and Road Research Laboratory. (1979). Cost of road accidents in Great Britain in 1977. *Department of the Environment, Transport and Road Research Laboratory, Leaflet 776.* Crowthorne: TRRL.

rG
Transport and Road Research Laboratory. (1979). Injuries to unprotected road users. *Department of the Environment, Transport and Road Research Laboratory, Leaflet 792.* Crowthorne: TRRL.

rDs
Transport and Road Research Laboratory. (1979). Pedestrian injuries related to car accidents. *Department of the Environment, Transport and Road Research Laboratory, Leaflet 872.* Crowthorne: TRRL.

Ds V
Transport and Road Research Laboratory. (1979). Potential for accident and injury reduction in road accidents. *Department of the Environment, Transport and Road Research Laboratory, Leaflet 684.* Crowthorne: TRRL.

rDs Ed En Enl
Transport and Road Research Laboratory. (1979). The use of area-wide measures in urban road safety. *Department of the Environment, Transport and Road Research Laboratory, Leaflet 772.* Crowthorne: TRRL.

rDx En
Transport and Road Research Laboratory. (1979). The use of video-recording in road safety teaching in primary school. *Department of the Environment, Transport and Road Research Laboratory, Leaflet 843.* Crowthorne: TRRL.

Ds Pch Ed
Turgel, J. (1976). The OECD road research programme. In A. S. Hakkert (Ed.), *Proceedings of the International Conference on Pedestrian Safety*, Volume 1, 2B1–2B4. Haifa: Michlol.

R
Turton, M. (1977). Road safety for infants. *Traffic Education*, **2**, 24–26.

Twigg, D. W., Tocher, J. L., and Eppinger, R. H. Optimal design of automobiles for pedestrian protection. *Paper 770094.* Warrendale: Society of Automotive Engineers.

Uken, E. A. (1976). Pedestrian training programmes for developing nations. In A. S. Hakkert (Ed.), *Proceedings of the International Conference on Pedestrian Safety*, Volume 1, 8D1–8D6. Haifa: Michlol.

R Pad *Ed*
Vidolovits, L. (1976). Pedestrians in public places—urban design. In A. S. Hakkert (Ed.), *Proceedings of the International Conference on Pedestrian Safety*, Volume 1, 3D1–3D8. Haifa: Michlol.
G En
Vuchic, V. R. (1967). Pedestrian crossing time in determining widths of signalized traffic arterials. *Transportation Science*, **1**, 224–231.
Dc En
Wade, F. M., Chapman, A. J., and Foot, H. C. (1979). Child pedestrian accidents: a medical perspective. In D. J. Oborne, M. M. Gruneberg, and J. R. Eiser (Eds.) *Research in Psychology and Medicine*, Volume II, *Social Aspects, Attitudes, Communication, Care and Training*. London: Academic Press.
R T
Wade, F. M., Chapman, A. J., and Foot H. C. (1979). Child pedestrian accidents: the influence of the physical environment. *Paper presented at the International Conference on Environmental Psychology*. July. Guildford: University of Surrey.
R Pch En
Wade, F. M., Chapman, A. J., and Foot, H. C. (1981). The physical environment and child pedestrian accidents in the United Kingdom: a review. *Man-Environment Systems*. In the press.
R Pch En
Wade, F. M., Foot, H. C., and Chapman, A. J. (1978). Child pedestrian accidents: the influence of the social environment. *Paper presented at the British Psychological Society Conference*. London, December.
R Pch Ens
Wade, F. M., Foot, H. C., and Chapman, A. J. (1979). Child pedestrian accidents: the behaviour of the child pedestrian. *Paper presented at the British Psychological Society Annual Conference*. Nottingham, April.
R Pch B
Wade, F. M., Foot, H. C., and Chapman, A. J. (1979). The child's recreational use of the street. *Paper presented at the British Psychological Society Conference*. December. London.
Dc Pch B
Wade, F. M., Foot, H. C., and Chapman, A. J. (1979). The social environment and child pedestrian accidents. *Learning*, **1**, 39–40 and 48.
R Pch Ens
Wakeland, H. H. (1962). Systematic automobile design for pedestrian injury protection. In *Proceedings of the Fifth Stapp Car Crash Conference*. Minneapolis: University of Minnesota.
Walesa, C. (1977). Development of risk perception in children and adults. *Polish Psychological Bulletin*, **8**, 171–176.
Dx Pch B
Waller, J. A. (1966). High accident risk among middle-aged drivers and pedestrians. *Geriatrics*, **21**, 125–137.
rDs Pad Dr
Walsh, L. B., and Nickson, F. (1972). *Pedestrian Safety for Urban Streets*. Volumes I, II and III, San Jose, California: City of San Jose Pedestrian Safety Project.
Wanderer, U. N., and Weber, H. M. (1974). Field results of exact accident data acquisition on scene. *Paper 740568*. Warrendale: Society of Automotive Engineers.
Wass, C. (1977). Traffic accident exposure and liability. *Institute of Road, Traffic and Town Planning Report*. Lyngby, Denmark: Technical University of Denmark.

Watson, W. (1969). Childhood injuries: a challenge to society. *Pediatrics Supplement*, **44**, 794–798.
aT

Watts, G. R. (1973). Road humps for the control of vehicle speeds. *Department of the Environment, Transport and Road Research Laboratory, Laboratory Report 597.* Crowthorne: TRRL.
rDx En

Watts, G. R., and Quimby, A. R. (1980). Aspects of road layout that affect drivers' perception of risk taking. *Department of the Environment, Transport and Road Research Laboratory, Laboratory Report 920.* Crowthorne: TRRL.

Weldon, E. (1971). Towards a theory of driving behaviour. *Accident Analysis and Prevention*, **3**, 113–119.
rT Dr

Wiener, E. L. (1968). The elderly pedestrian: response to an enforcement campaign. *Traffic Safety Research Review*, **12**, 100–110.
Dc Pel Ed

Wilde, G. J. S. (1973). A general survey of efficiency and effectiveness of road safety campaigns, achievements and challenges. In *Proceedings of the International Congress on Road Safety Campaigns.* October. The Hague.

Wilde, G. J. S. (1973). Social psychological factors and use of mass publicity. *Canadian Psychologist*, **14**, 1–7.
R T

Wilde, G. J. S., Cake, L. J., and Le Brasseur, R. (1974). Mass media safety campaigns: an annotated bibliography of recent developments, 1970–1973. *National Highway Traffic Safety Administration Report Number NHTSA-4-7304A.* Washington DC: United States Department of Transportation.

Wilde, G. J. S., and Curry, C. A. (1970). Psychological aspects of road research: a study of the literature, 1959–1968. Canadian Ministry of Transport, Road and Motor Vehicle Traffic Safety, Ottawa.

Wilde, G. J. S., L'Hoste, J., Sheppard, D., and Wind, C. (1971). *Road Safety Campaigns: Design and Evaluation.* Paris: Organisation for Economic Co-operation and Development.
R P Dr Ed

Wilde, G. J. S., O'Neill, B., and Cannon, D. (1975). A psychometric investigation of driver's concern for road safety and their opinions of various measures for accident prevention. *Studies of Safety in Transport.* Kingston, Ontario: Queen's University.

Wilson, D. G. (1980). The effects of installing an audible signal for pedestrians at a light controlled junction. *Department of the Environment, Transport and Road Research Laboratory, Laboratory Report 917.* Crowthorne: TRRL.
Dx Pad B N

Wilson, D. G., and Grayson, G. B. (1980). Age-related differences in the road crossing behaviour of adult pedestrians. *Department of the Environment, Transport and Road Research Laboratory, Laboratory Report 933.* Crowthorne: TRRL.
Dc Pad B N

Wilson, D. G., and Older, S. J. (1970). The effects of installing new zebra crossings in Rugby and Chelmsford. *Ministry of Transport, Road Research Laboratory, Laboratory Report 358.* Crowthorne: RRL.

Wilson, J., and Rennie, A. (1981). Elderly pedestrians and road safety. In H. C. Foot, A. J. Chapman and F. M. Wade (Eds.), *Road Safety: Research and Practice.* Eastbourne: Praeger.
R Pel B

Woods, G. R. (1975). A pedestrian origin-destination survey for the siting of a pelican crossing. *Traffic Education and Control*, **16**, 328.

Ds B En
Wooler, J. (1968). Road traffic accidents in Adelaide and Brisbane, Australia. In *Proceedings of the Fourth Conference of the Australian Road Research Board*. Canberra: Australian Road Research Board.
World Health Organization (1976). The epidemiology of road traffic accidents. *World Health Organization Regional Publications European Series Number 2*. Copenhagen: World Health Organization.
G Dc M
Yaksich, S. (1965). The new image of the older pedestrian. *Traffic Safety*, **65**, 22–24 and 35–36.
Yeaton, W. H., and Bailey, J. S. (1978). Teaching pedestrian skills to young children: An analysis and one-year follow up. *Journal of Applied Behavioral Analysis*, **11**, 315–329.
Dx Pch Ed
Yu, J. C. (1971). Pedestrian accident prevention. *Traffic Quarterly*, **25**, 391–401.
G P Ed En Enl
Yule, M. (1973). The road safety of young children. *Australian Family Safety*, **7**, 6–7.
Zaidel, D., Algarishi, A., and Katz, A. (1976). Factors affecting the use of pedestrian overpasses. In A. S. Hakkert (Ed.), *Proceedings of the International Conference on Pedestrian Safety*, Volume 1, 7F1–7F16, Haifa: Michlol.
Dc P En B N
Zimolong, R. (1981). Traffic conflicts: a measure of road safety. In H. C. Foot, A. J. Chapman, and F. M. Wade (Eds.), *Road Safety: Research and Practice*. Eastbourne: Praeger.
rR M
Zuercher, R. (1976). Communication at pedestrian crossings. In A. S. Hakkert (Ed.), *Proceedings of the International Conference on Pedestrian Safety*, Volume 1, 7E1–7E7. Haifa: Michlol.
Dx Pad Pel Dr B N
Zuercher, R. (1977). Communication at pedestrian crossings II. In A. S. Hakkert (Ed.), *Proceedings of the International Conference on Pedestrian Safety*, Volume 2, 115–118. Haifa: Michlol.
Dx Pad Pel Dr B N
Zwalen, H. T. (1974). Distance judgement capabilities of children and adults in a pedestrian situation. In *Proceedings of the Third International Congress on Automotive Safety*, Volume II. July. San Francisco.

Author Index

Subject Index